2nd Edition

Xero®

FOR

DUMMIES®

A Wiley Brand

by Heather Smith

FOR

DUMMIES®

A Wiley Brand

Xero® For Dummies®

2nd Edition published by
Wiley Publishing Australia Pty Ltd
42 McDougall Street
Milton, Qld 4064
www.dummies.com

National Library of Australia
Cataloguing-in-Publication data:

Creator:	Smith, Heather Nicolette
Title:	Xero For Dummies / Heather Smith
ISBN:	9780730319375 (pbk.)
	9780730319382 (ebook)
Edition:	2nd edition.
Series:	For Dummies.
Notes:	Includes index.
Subjects:	Xero (Computer program)
	Accounting — Computer Programs —
	Handbooks, manuals, etc.
Dewey Number:	657.02855369

Cover image: © Xero Limited and affiliates, 2015. Xero® and the Xero logo are registered trademarks of Xero Limited.

Typeset by diacriTech, Chennai, India

Printed in Singapore by
C.O.S. Printers Pte Ltd

10 9 8 7 6 5 4 3 2 1

Contents at a Glance

Table of Contents

Part II: Daily Activities 107

Foreword

. . . .

*W*e're thrilled to have seen the success of the first edition of *Xero For Dummies*. We created Xero to help small businesses to be more productive. We figured that helping small business increase in scale is purposeful and worthwhile.

Business can be fun. For most small business owners, it's certainly all-consuming. In our previous roles we liked building businesses; we didn't like the drudgery of administrative jobs and working late into the night to meet a looming tax return deadline. As we talked to other business owners it became clear that we weren't alone — for most, doing the books was the number one pain of running a small business. It's great to hear that the number of business owners is growing, but also that they're capturing a better lifestyle, free to work anywhere at any time.

It's also been great to see a thriving community of accountants, bookkeepers and add-on partners all working together to make life easier for small business owners. Many bookkeepers are creating their own new businesses, helping others, in turn, grow. As the nature of work changes, small business ownership is becoming a way of working for many people around the world.

The move to the cloud is in full swing and is driving productivity across economies. We're seeing an exciting focus on small business as a sector that creates jobs and can deal with some of the big issues, like youth employment.

The move to mobile in business has been a revelation, but it feels as if we're still just at the beginning of an exciting journey as business software gets smarter and does much more for you.

This book is a great way for you to learn to work in the cloud, and we're sure that as you go through it, or dip into it to take what you need, you'll see that doing your accounts can be easy and rewarding. And hopefully your work will become just a bit more fun.

We love our community of customers and partners. And we love to hear what we can do better. Thank you for learning more about Xero and what we're doing, and feel free to send me or the team a note on Twitter at any time. You can contact us via @roddrury or @xero.

Rod Drury
CEO, Xero

Introduction

· ·

*P*eople frequently ask me how I manage to do so much. I tell them the answer is pretty simple: I'm organised, I use Xero and a suite of Xero add-ons, and you should too! In your hands you have the essential guide to complement your journey with Xero. Taking your business to the cloud, and leveraging the power of Xero and its ecosystem, streamlines administration, and frees up time to grow the business or enjoy some work–life balance.

I just can't believe the effect I am seeing Xero have on the small business community! Small-business owners have had a mind shift, and no longer see their accounting solution as a burdensome tax requirement. Rather, they realise they now have access to real-time informative dashboards that they can confidently use in business decisions.

Bookkeepers are reducing their travel time by remotely supporting clients, and minimising time spent on data entry through utilisation of bank feeds and data-extraction solutions. Furthermore, contemporary bookkeepers are expanding their services and offering management accounting advice and other value-add services.

Accountants are able to utilise the single ledger, working with clients on their own financial data. No longer do they communicate with clients once a year. Instead, accountants are working with small business on a regular basis, assisting with high-end CFO support like modelling or budgeting.

Complementary businesses are also thriving around Xero, including add-on solution providers, cloud integrators and a few writers (like me!).

Whether you've just started your journey with Xero, or you've been around for a while and are ready for some more expert tips or help with the more advanced options, you are sure to find this book useful.

Xero For Dummies, 2nd Edition, covers all you need to know to sign up and use this cloud-based accounting software solution — from the basic set-up to implementing daily routines and end of period procedures, and generating useful reporting information. Understanding what you can do with Xero — how you can use its many features — can enhance the productivity of your business, centralising data and giving you a clearer idea of exactly what is going on within it.

About This Book

Xero For Dummies, 2nd Edition, provides a comprehensive outline of how to use the Xero accounting cloud solution. The main focus throughout the book is how you can use Xero's cloud and integrated business management solutions to turbo boost the way your business runs.

The book steps you through everything you need to know about Xero, taking you through the whole process. You're never left hanging, wondering what you're supposed to do next. I'm with you every step of the way. But the book sticks to the practicalities — I know you don't need to be slowed down with unnecessary background information and theories.

Note: One of the great features of Xero being a cloud-based accounting solution is that Xero can make upgrades or updates to its pages or processes at any time — and the next time you access your file, the upgrades have been implemented. No more waiting for the next software release! But this may mean a page or process you're looking at online isn't exactly the same as that shown in this book. Don't worry — the process should still be similar enough that you can use this book to guide you through.

Some really interesting information is provided in the sidebars through the book (those grey boxes with text inside); however, these are self-contained. So you can skip over them while working through the more meaty areas if you choose.

I've also used the following conventions throughout the book:

- ✔ I've included information for users with Adviser status, and provided information about features only users with this access may be able to see. In Xero, your user role defines what you have access to. This book outlines all the features someone with full access, or Adviser status, may have in their Xero business solution. If you don't have full access, this book still provides heaps of information on the features you can access. Check with your accountant or Xero adviser if unsure about anything.

  Note: For US users, this user status is spelt *Advisor*. Rest assured that the information in this book that relates to this user status is the same — however it's spelt.

- ✔ I've used *consumer tax* to cover GST, VAT, sales tax or any other tax your government has created for your business! Because this book has been written for an international audience, I've used this term as an all-encompassing reference for any sort of tax that could be added to a purchase — hope that makes cents! (Sorry — accounting humour.)

✔ I generally use the term *bank accounts* to keep things simple; however, this term actually includes bank accounts and credit card accounts, and online payment facilities like PayPal.

Foolish Assumptions

It's never nice to assume anything about people without walking a mile in their shoes. But to write this book I had to assume a few things ... Firstly, I assumed you buckle down to work with a nice cup of tea, and when things get really hard you grab the chocolate. (Or is that just me?)

Here are some other assumptions I've made:

✔ You can navigate your way around a computer or a mobile device and understand the basic steps required to access the internet.

✔ You don't have a background in bookkeeping or accounting. Through my work I've been exposed to literally thousands of people who have no accounting or bookkeeping background and I've trained them in the essentials and got them up and running. So I've used this experience to write this book in a way that highlights what's important, and breaks it down appropriately.

✔ You probably don't have access to Hermione's Time Turner or the TARDIS from *Doctor Who*, and your time is important to you. You want to work as efficiently and effectively as possible — so I've included lots of productivity enhancers.

Icons Used in This Book

Throughout the book I've used different icons, which appear on the left side of the page. These highlight handy pieces of information that enhance your understanding and ability to use Xero. The following outlines what they stand for.

Xero is used internationally, and while the main skeleton of the software is identical for all users, some elements are specific to a particular jurisdiction. I've used this icon to highlight information that only relates to a specific country or jurisdiction — if the information doesn't relate to your country's version of Xero, skip over it.

This icon highlights pearls of wisdom you should make a mental note about — or even write down for yourself in an actual notebook!

This icon flags tricky procedures or in-depth detail. Depending on your level of skill, you may want to ask your accountant for further advice on topics marked with this icon.

These show handy strategies and shortcuts to speed up your productivity or just generally make life easier — gained through my own experience.

This icon outlines something you should be aware of and highlights any issues so you're prepared and empowered. If you're reviewing a section that contains a warning — make sure you take the time to read it.

Beyond the Book

In addition to the material in the print or ebook you're reading right now, *Xero For Dummies*, 2nd Edition, also comes with some access-anywhere goodies on the Net. Check out the free Cheat Sheet at www.dummies.com/ cheatsheet/xero for some quick, helpful tips, and for the latest updates on companion material for this book, visit www.dummies.com/go/xerofd2e. Here you'll find four online-only Appendixes for free download. Three of these talk you through converting to Xero from MYOB, Sage and QuickBooks, and the fourth gives you all the info you need to master your pay run. Also check out www.dummies.com/extras/xero for some (free!) articles about Xero.

Where to Go from Here

This book is written in *modular* style (and, no, that doesn't relate to a new lounge suite). It means you can pick up the book, open it at any page, select a heading that takes your fancy, and read the information under that heading.

It also means *Xero For Dummies*, 2nd Edition, is not a story book — you don't need to read it from cover to cover. Review the Table of Contents or the Index, locate what you're looking for and jump straight into the section.

If you're totally new to Xero, or need more of an idea of what it's all about, you should take a quick read of Chapter 1. Or, if you're a people person, Chapter 5 is all about setting up contacts in Xero.

If you need to set up your Xero file, start at Part I. If you're already set up and you simply need to enter data, start in Part II, which covers contacts, sales, purchases and reconciling your accounts. If you need to do routine tasks in Xero, including preparing for period end, start in Part III.

Just make sure you keep this edition of *Xero For Dummies* handy and, whenever you need to enhance your understanding of a feature, grab the book, open up the relevant section and enjoy!

One last thing — with all the free time you'll be enjoying once you're up and running with Xero, feel free to drop by and say Hi! to me on Twitter at @HeatherSmithAU. You could even share with me a photo of you enjoying this book.

Part I
Getting Started with Xero

In this part ...

- ✔ Discover the many advantages of Xero, including — but not limited to — collaborative working with bookkeepers and accountants, live bank feeds, remote invoicing, single ledger and Xero's ability to seamlessly integrate with other solutions.

- ✔ Find out the pros and cons of working in the cloud and answers to any questions you may have about the online environment.

- ✔ Get the scoop on who should be in your Xero advisory team and how they can assist your business.

- ✔ Delve into the nitty-gritty of setting up Xero from scratch, or find out how to convert from another accounting software solution.

- ✔ Become familiar with the way Xero sets up tax rates and understand how the system uses these to produce useful information for tax time.

Chapter 1

Getting to Know Xero

*A*s a fresh-faced graduate, I arrived in Cheltenham, England, to start my first real job at an aerospace manufacturing business. Using a pencil, I worked with a team of account clerks, processing journals on huge A2-size (420 × 594) sheets of paper. Towards the end of the day, we all handed our paper to a tiny grey-haired lady. She gathered the paper and, using a huge noisy mechanical calculator, added up our journal entries and updated the trial balance. When all the work was entered and the debits equalled the credits, she rang her bell, signalling we could go home.

One day a magical grey box arrived on my desk, and inside its screen were rows and columns. 'What is this sorcery you have brought to our office?' my fellow workers cried. I explained the magical box was a computer and what was inside was a spreadsheet. I could enter numbers and formulas and the computer would process the results. (Yes, I'm a dinosaur and worked in offices pre-computers!) Pretty soon after that, we said goodbye to the mechanical calculator and shipped it off to the local museum.

In the last 20 years, desktop accounting software has replaced a team of accounts assistants and grey-haired ladies ringing bells. And, with the emergence of the internet, the practice of accounting is again undergoing revolutionary changes. Using Xero as your accounting system, you have the ability to access and process accounts online from anywhere you can access the internet. Furthermore, this accounting software has the capability to seamlessly communicate with other software solutions, reducing the need for mundane data entry.

In this chapter, I give you a rundown of Xero, covering what it is and what it can do for you. I help you explore the different editions available, based on the needs of your business, take you through the home page and Xero's main dashboard, and outline the different user roles available — again, the user role you choose depends on the needs of your business and how much involvement you want to have in its accounts. Finally, I give you an overview of how Xero's tools and reports can help you with your strategic planning.

Understanding the Advantages of Xero

Xero is a subscription-based online small business accounting software. It does everything you would expect business accounting software to do; however, what is unexpected and quite revolutionary is the following:

- ✔ Users who've been given permission to access the Xero data file can access Xero over the internet and do accounting anywhere, anytime. Furthermore, users can access the same file simultaneously.

- ✔ You can authorise transactions that occur on your bank, credit card and online payment gateway statements to directly feed into the Xero system. Just like receiving email into your inbox, transactions feed into your accounts, ready for you to process. See Chapter 4 for more on bank feeds.

- ✔ You can create and send invoices, and do your bank reconciliation via mobile devices, issuing clients invoices while on-site with them.

- ✔ Through the concept of a single ledger, both you, as the business owner, and your accountant can access the same data, reducing the need to transfer data and improving efficiencies. Your tax accountant can finalise end of year accounts directly into the business data file. See Chapter 11 for more on this.

- ✔ The software can be enabled to communicate with other Xero users, or other online software programs. For example, Xero users can invite other Xero users to connect with them. This unlocks a portal between the two users' data files — so, for example, when an *invoice* is created in one file, it appears to the other file as a *draft bill*. This opening up of data files minimises data entry, improves accuracy and hopefully helps with cash flow! More complex communication connections can include CRMs, inventory management, e-commerce and other add-on business solutions. See Chapter 16 for more on this.

Xero has been described as those vitamins disguised as gummy candies — users enjoy the software so much they forget they are actually doing accounting.

Pros and cons of working in the cloud

Do you recall the first time the internet really worked for you? From my apartment in Toronto I co-ordinated a reunion with friends from Singapore, New York and Texas via email. We were to meet beside the Snuffleupagus at Sesame Place in Pennsylvania. I was so impressed: I arrived at 10 am and everyone was there! We hugged and shrieked in excitement. Using email had saved us a small fortune in telephone charges and it was a breeze to use — all of us from the moguls to the mums understood how to do it. These days, imagining a time before email is hard.

One day, imagining a time when everyone didn't conduct all their business in the cloud will be hard!

Working *in the cloud*, means working via the internet — the files you're accessing and working on aren't stored on your computer. As with everything, benefits and concerns of working online exist. But, indisputably, working across the internet is the way of the future. Governments across the world are funding infrastructure that enables access to high-speed internet connections, ensuring their citizens remain competitive.

Without realising it you may already be using cloud services. If you're using a smart phone, email, internet banking, Skype, Google Apps, or storage services like Dropbox or Evernote, you're embracing the internet — and some of these devices or services make use of the cloud.

If you're not already convinced, here are some of the benefits of cloud computing:

- **Reduced costs:** Working in the cloud means you have no requirement for in-house servers to host other computers on the network. This reduces your ownership, maintenance and insurance costs.

- **Real-time data:** You can access accurate and timely reports, which can assist with informed decision-making.

- **Productivity gains:** The time taken to respond to issues is minimised because data can be accessed wherever you can access the internet. Integration features mean you don't need to re-key data, because fields are matched and flow from one area to another. You also don't need to install or upgrade anything on your computer.

- **No platform issues:** Mac or PC? You no longer have any need to worry what platform you are working on as you access the internet via an internet browser.

- **Collaboration:** Multiple users from around the globe can simultaneously log in and view the same information, depending on their access levels. Yes, you can review business reports while cruising the Nile!

- **Flexibility:** Applications can evolve to suit business needs.

- **Reasonable pricing:** Many applications have reasonably priced packages available, and offer options to suit different business requirements, from the micro through to the enterprise business. You can start with a low-cost package and, as you grow your business, move to a bigger package.

- **Reliable data backups:** Data is stored in the cloud. If your computer crashes, or the business floods or is affected by fire, you can still access your data via the internet.

(continued)

(continued)

Note: Backups of your own important data should still be made — just think of the cloud backups as a trapeze you can grab. In a way (and with slightly mixed metaphors!), it's a double safety net! In the case of Xero, you can manually download the complete General Ledger from Xero (see Chapter 9) or use an automated back-up solution like LedgerBackUp (`http://www.ledgerbackup.com` — see Chapter 16 for more on add-ons).

✔ **Cool factor:** Getting out your iPhone after enjoying a coffee meeting with a client, taking a photo of a receipt and uploading it straight to your accounting package as an expense claim is pretty darn cool!

As with everything, you should be aware of some aspects of cloud computing. Here are some of the concerns of cloud computing:

✔ **Availability of internet access:** Access to the cloud is dependent on internet access. No, or slow, internet access may affect your decision to work in the cloud.

✔ **Data storage questions:** Because data can be stored anywhere in the world, you need clear information on its actual location. What country, under what jurisdiction, is the data stored in? *Note:* Xero data is stored with Rackspace in the United States, a leading hosting provider. The United States has sensible laws governing the protection and confidentiality of data.

✔ **Longevity:** Will the software provider be around to look after your data forever (well, as long as you need it to be, at least)?

✔ **Security:** What security is being maintained over business data? *Note:* The security encryption of Xero is equivalent to that used by online banking. If you're happy to use online banking, you should be happy to use Xero. All users require unique passwords to access the application and Xero logs users out after 60 minutes of inactivity.

✔ **Ownership:** Who has ownership of your data in the clouds? *Note:* With Xero, the direct subscriber to Xero owns the data.

Everything we do in business incurs some risk, including the way we operate. If you consider the risks of your own computer crashing, or being susceptible to a virus, floods, theft or fires, you may be far better off putting your faith in an organisation that has the infrastructure and systems in place to better protect and store your data.

Exploring Xero's Different Editions

Xero offers a number of different editions. As your business grows, you can upgrade packages, or, if you decide you no longer need a larger package, after 30 days you can downgrade.

The editions come in starter, standard and premium packages. The uses and features of each package are as follows:

✔ **Starter:** The starter package is suited to the micro or start-up business, with limited transactions. This package allows you to send and receive

5 invoices per month and reconcile 20 bank statement lines per month. The Australian version of this package also enables the processing of one employee through payroll.

✔ **Standard:** The standard package is suited to the typical small business. Using this package, you can send and receive hundreds of invoices per month, and reconcile hundreds of bank statement lines per week. The Australian and US versions of this package enables the processing of up to five employees through payroll.

✔ **Premium:** The premium packages are for larger businesses processing more than five employees through payroll. The package size grows in relation to the number of employees to be processed through the system. As well as being able to send and receive hundreds of invoices per month and reconcile hundreds of bank statement lines per week, using the premium package you also have multi-currency capabilities, payroll direct deposit in the US version, and auto-superannuation in the Australian version.

All editions allow you to access your files anywhere online, invite unlimited users, use live bank feeds and to cancel online at any time.

All editions also include the following features:

✔ Automatic backups

✔ Demo company files so you can explore options

✔ Free trial version before you sign up (only available if you sign up to Xero directly, rather than through an accountant or bookkeeper)

✔ No set-up fees, upgrade requirements or contracts

✔ Unlimited customer support

Depending on the regional option you select, you may have access to additional features in Xero. For example:

✔ The Australian version includes a robust in-built payroll (see www.dummies.com/go/xerofd2e for more), Activity statements (Chapters 6 and 10) and the premium version allows for the automated superannuation payments.

✔ The US version includes 1099 and GAAP compliance, as well as integration with the Track1099 e-filing and preparation tools (Chapter 10), and the ability to produce checks (Chapter 7).

✔ The New Zealand version includes GST Return.

✔ The UK version includes VAT Returns, VAT Audit Returns and online filing facilities with HMRC (see Chapter 10).

Checking the company history pages

New Zealand is not only famous for rugby, spectacular scenery and hobbits scurrying around Middle-earth. Somewhere along the way, it has also become the incubator and launch pad for many digital enterprises, including Xero. Founders Hamish Edwards and Rod Drury first met in 2003, when Hamish was virtual CFO of Rod's software company. In April 2006 co-founder Craig Walker joined the team. (His offer from Drury went something along the lines of 'I'm doing my next big thing — you in? You start on Monday'.) Frustrated by clunky desktop-based accounting packages, technology evangelist Drury wanted more. On 1 May 2006, Walker started writing code on what would become the first version of the yet to be named Xero. The fourth co-founder, Philip Fierlinger, joined in July 2006. By this time, accounting expertise plus technological ingenuity plus business acumen equalled Xero, revolutionising and simplifying how business owners run a business.

Discarding existing models, Edwards, Drury, Walker and Fierlinger started clean and built a single ledger online accounting system that enabled integration with bank feeds.

Xero has attracted an impressive board line-up, including Craig Winkler, co-founder of MYOB accounting software, and Peter Theil, co-founder of PayPal. The company has also hired a skilled in-house team and attracted a symphony of passionate ambassadors to rally around their product. Jump on social media and you're likely to find suggestions and discussions, as many people offer ideas about what features they love and what they would like to see made available in Xero.

Due to the online nature of the software, no longer do users need to wait for annual updates. Online updates are implemented by head office in the wee hours of the morning. Businesses don't need to waste time installing updates and upgrading files — they simply start their day accessing new features.

Xero is listed on the New Zealand Stock Exchange and Australian Securities Exchange. It is available globally and has local teams in Australia, New Zealand, the United States and Europe.

Homepage: Checking Out the Dashboard

Once you have set up your Xero account (see Chapters 2 and 3), you just have to log into your account, using your password to access the MyXero homepage — what Xero calls the main dashboard. Across the top of the dashboard is the menu bar for quick access to all areas of Xero.

Here's a quick overview of the different parts of the main dashboard's menu bar:

- **Dashboard:** Provides an overview of bank, credit card and online payment gateway accounts, key accounts, money coming in, money going out and expense claims

- **Accounts:** Shows bank account details, sales (Chapter 6), purchases, pay run (except Australia), expense claims (Chapter 7) and fixed assets (Chapter 14)

- **Payroll:** Only Australian and US users can access advanced payroll features; Australian users see the ebook *Mastering Australian Payroll with Xero In A Day For Dummies*, available at www.dummies.com, for more information. NZ, UK and global users can download the free online Appendix 'Mastering Your Pay Run' — just go to www.dummies.com/go/xerofd2e.

- **Reports:** Access reports and the Budget Manager feature (Chapter 12)

- **Adviser:** Can only be seen by users with Adviser access (see Chapter 4 for more on setting access for users)

- **Contacts:** Shows customers, suppliers and employees added as Contacts (Chapter 5) and a list building feature called Smart Lists

- **Settings:** Outlines general settings (Chapter 2)

Understanding Your Team Needs

'Avast belay, yo ho, heave to, A-pirating we go, And if we're parted by a shot, We're sure to meet below!' . . . and that was my one line in the Singaporean pantomime production of *Peter Pan*. In the theatre, everyone in the crew has a defined role, yet each role is interdependent on the other players. If the lighting guy had missed his cue, we would have been in darkness; if the sound guy flicked the wrong switch, we might not have been able to hear; and if I had forgotten my one line — well, the audience may well have wanted their money back! We supported each other, we improvised and we covered each other backs, for the greater good of the production and the audience's enjoyment.

Xero is an innovative and time-saving product – but it doesn't work on its own. The Xero file needs to be processed on a regular basis, with reports prepared, taxes submitted, and data extracted to help with business decisions. If you set up and activate all your business bank accounts and maybe set up a few coding rules (see Chapter 4), you can save yourself a lot of time. But don't think you can then ignore Xero and return in 12 months' time to find everything done for you! If you try this approach, what you're likely to have is lots and lots of pieces of a puzzle, waiting to be reviewed, coded and reconciled.

The Xero file needs to be processed on a regular basis, with reports prepared, taxes submitted, and data extracted to help with business decisions. Ideally, you need to establish a supportive Xero advisory team focused on helping your business achieve its goals. The collaborative and transparent nature of Xero lends itself to working with this team of specialists, who in their own way support each other and your business. Your team might include:

- **Accountants.** Your accountant works from the top of your business down, looking at the overall business. Just like you can go to different types of doctors, you can also access different types of accountants for the health of your business:

  - *Tax accountants* assist businesses in meeting compliance obligations, preparing financial statements and minimising taxation. Tax accountants can review reports and provide rolling tax advice during the year. They can maintain the Fixed Asset Register and prepare depreciation schedules from within the accounts. Tax accountants can enter the end of financial year journals directly into Xero's single ledger and confirm your financial reports from Xero match the prepared financial reports.

  - *Management accountants* assist businesses with strategic planning, business growth, cash flow budgeting and financial analysis. Management accountants assist in developing a useful chart of accounts, customising report layouts so information is presented in an informative manner and issue monthly management reports. Using graphs, words and numbers, a management accountant can help you understand how the business is tracking and what can be done to improve it.

- **Bookkeepers.** They work from the bottom of businesses up, entrenched in the detail, assisting with data entry, reconciling reports, and following up with accounts payable and accounts receivable. Bookkeepers can identify complicated transactions, such as a fixed asset purchases, and flag them for the tax accountant to review and approve.

  Your bookkeeper may assist with the preparation of consumer tax reporting where relevant.

✔ **Xero advisers or implementation specialists.** Xero's implementation specialists can gather your business data and assist in efficiently and effectively setting up your Xero data file. They can train you in using Xero within your business environment, and provide ongoing technical support as you need it. Obviously, you only need to set up Xero once, so investing in some useful up-front support is wise because it gets you started faster and ensures you're heading in the correct direction. Your Xero adviser or 'cloud integrator' specialist may also be able to suggest and install various add-on solutions that can benefit your business.

You and your team need to clearly communicate with each other, maintain open relationships and respect each other, and you each need to understand the interdependent nature of each other's role. Avoid having people on your team who are always ready to lay the blame on other parties — it's unproductive and drains resources. Working at the coal face of small business, I'm sometimes concerned by the animosity and disrespect some people show one another.

Here's how each member on your team could use Xero to get along:

✔ The management accountant asks the bookkeeper to code all transactions in Xero related to a particular project to a specified tracking option (see Chapter 12 for more on tracking).

✔ The bookkeeper uses the Xero Discuss feature to ask the tax accountant for advice on how to code the purchase of computers (see Chapter 8 for more on the Discuss tab and Chapter 14 for more on fixed assets).

✔ The tax accountant advises all users of your Xero file to code any cost relating to entertainment to the entertainment expense code — clearly detailing what it was for and who was in attendance — so she can review expenses at the end of the period (see Chapter 11).

✔ The Xero specialist provides training to all users to show them how to effectively and efficiently use Xero!

For many start-ups and micro businesses the 'team' could mainly be one person wearing several hats — that is, the business owner may play many of the roles mentioned in the preceding paragraphs. Or you may need a number of people in your team to suit the nature of your business. Working with a team of specialists provides you with leverage and a depth of knowledge in the business that can facilitate business growth.

Finding, and keeping, a great accountant

I hate group assignments. I'm sure it's just a technique teachers use to minimise marking. I always seem to end up with someone utterly incompetent on my team who slows everything down, and I end up carrying this person through the assignment. I first experienced this while at university when, for one of my subjects, I was the leader of our computer programming group assignment. Our group met, decided on a plan of attack, divided up the work and arranged to meet up again so everyone could pass their work to me. I would then just have to compile it.

When the day came for everyone to submit their work, one of the team members — I'll call her the *stunned mullet*, because her total lack of interest was all she contributed to group discussions — handed me her computer programming submission. It was a print out with someone else's name on it. I asked around and eventually found the actual author. I approached him and a great friendship formed. And now (not so many years later), he has the great honour of doing my taxes!

The benefits of having a great relationship with an accountant who knows and understands your business are many. Accountants provide advice over myriad topics and can assist with:

✔ Developing tax-minimisation strategies

✔ Formulating business goals

✔ Identifying suitable key performance indicators (KPIs)

✔ Keeping you abreast of changes to financial legislation that affect your business

✔ Preparing budgets and cash flow forecasts

✔ Providing specialist advice to suit your business circumstances

Once you've found a good one, your accountant can form an integral part of your business advisory board. Developing a consultative, positive, practical and effective working relationship with a modern tax accountant is critical for your business's ongoing success.

So how do you find a modern, savvy, actively involved accountant? Most are in high demand and many have closed books, so ask around your business networks for recommendations and introductions. A list of Xero Certified accountants can be found on the Xero website (www.xero.com/advisors). If you have a couple of options, take a look at the accountant's website — if you're using Xero cloud software, you want the accountant to be technically sophisticated and a decent website is a basic requirement.

Once you think you're ready to meet with a possible accountant for your business, here are some aspects you can find out more about:

✔ Does the accountant have experience in the industry your business is within? Some businesses are a little complicated; for example, e-commerce, import, export, gambling and wine businesses have specific idiosyncrasies. Is the accountant aware of them, or will it be a steep learning curve that you end up paying for?

✔ How long has the accountant been established?

✔ How many existing clients does the accountant have using Xero?

✔ How well does the accountant know Xero?

✔ How will you communicate with each other and how often? Will the accountant monitor your business and offer timely insights on a regular basis or as and when you need them? What suits your requirements?

✔ What are the fees?

✔ What services does the accountant offer?

✔ What qualifications does the accountant hold?

Above all, make sure you feel comfortable with your accountant. And once you've found one you can work with, keep that accountant close to your business.

Integrating Xero into Your Strategic Planning

Strategic planning is the exercise of defining the vision for your business and developing goals to move forward and bridge the gap from where you currently are to where you want to be. As a small business owner, you may see undertaking strategic planning as daunting, overwhelming, time-consuming and unnecessary. But wait there! By utilising Xero and inviting your team to view transparent data, and ensuring the data entered into Xero is accurate, you're in a better position to understand where your business is at and what it can achieve.

Generating accurate, complete and timely data entry

I have a client who went on a cruise around the Greek Islands. While he lay on a deck chair eating dolmades and drinking ouzo, he reflected on one of his many businesses that imported electronics and sold them in Australia: Why was the business not making money? The cheap electronics had a significant profit margin applied to them, so why was the business running up losses? He considered winding up the business, but before he pulled the plug he called me in to review the records. I examined and corrected the custom invoices. I delved further and realised the bookkeeper had overwritten the purchase price and entered the exact same purchase and sales price. (Bizarre but true.) The reworked accounts improved the bottom line by quarter of a million dollars!

Running a successful business involves continually making correct decisions. While no magical formula exists for always making the correct decisions, I do know the process needs guts, foresight and intuition — and correct, timely data. So you bring the guts, foresight and intuition and this book shows you how to generate accurate, complete and timely data in Xero!

Introducing Management Reporting and analysis capabilities of Xero

An older accountant told me a story. He worked for a large organisation producing and distributing monthly management reports. A cheeky upstart joined the company, took his reports, added colour to them, turned them into graphs and everyone loved them. Imagine that! Well, Xero is that cheeky upstart. Colour and graphs guide you around your business reports. Teeny red and green indicators scattered across many reports alert you to be pleased or concerned with comparative movements. Management Reports highlight cash movements, profitability, performance and position of the business. (See Chapter 12 for more on Xero's Management Reports and Budget Manager tool.)

Taking Advantage of Support Options

If you have any questions about Xero, hopefully the following chapters in the book can provide all the answers. But, if your problem is perhaps beyond the scope of this book, you do have other support options available. Xero offers an amazing amount of support material on its website, including training videos — go to www.xero.com/training, xero.com/tv and community.xero.com to check them out.

Once signed up to Xero, you're sent regular e-newsletters updating you with all the relevant news. When you're logged onto Xero, a small envelope also appears at the very top of the screen. Clicking on the envelope displays messages from Xero — informing you, for example, about feature updates and any bank feed issues. If you have an issue when reconciling your accounts, you can also make use of the Discuss tab to leave a message for your Xero adviser (see Chapter 8 for more).

Access any support you need to help your business. For example, an IT specialist can ensure you're accessing a high-speed internet connection. This may involve reviewing your existing network and your internet provider's plan. Technology is rapidly advancing, so reviewing this set-up on a regular basis can improve productivity.

Accessing Xero on your iPhone

You can download the Xero Touch app from the App Store and use it on Apple and android mobile devices. If you're using another mobile device, you can access Xero via your browser at m.xero.com. Limited features that can be accessed via the mobile version include the following:

✔ Dashboard view of bank account balances

✔ Bank reconciliation

✔ Ability to create new invoices, and view draft, unpaid and overdue invoices (see Chapter 6 for more)

✔ Ability to view contact details — and call them from your phone (Chapter 5)

✔ Access to expense claims functions (Chapter 7)

It is ubercool that Xero can be accessed on your phone!

Using Xero in a Training Environment

Xero For Dummies is a comprehensive resource for any Xero training environment. At the time of writing, no Xero training platform is available, so if you want to organise a training session you need to establish your own live Xero training file — which is easy to do.

I recommend taking the following steps as you prepare for your training sessions:

1. **Set up as many generic email addresses as you'll need for your training group.**

   It's a bit of a gamble to assume that all the students in your group can access their email remotely, so if you set generic addresses up yourself you guarantee email access for everyone in your training group. You can use Gmail or a similar free email service, and even re-use these email addresses if they're purely for training purposes (you may want to set up something memorable such as student1@gmail. com, student2@gmail.com, and so on, or create email addresses containing your company name).

2. **Set up a single Xero file.**

   See Chapter 2 for more on setting up a Xero file. This file can also be re-used for different training groups — though you may prefer to start with a fresh file each time.

3. **Invite your students, via their generic student email addresses, to have full access to the live Xero training file.**

   See Chapter 4 for inviting Users to access Xero. Inviting students as users enables them to work simultaneously on the same training file.

Be aware all users see what you're entering in the training file, so don't enter private information.

You can access sample data and lesson plans at www.heathersmithsmallbusiness.com/XeroTM; the password to access these files is 'Charlie'.

Chapter 2

Getting Organised: Setting Up Xero from Scratch

Customers of mine, a husband and wife partnership who run an electrical importing business out of their small apartment, recently confided to me that prior to investing in their business accounting system they were close to divorce. Signing up to Xero was such a relief. They now know who owes them money and who they owe money to. They understand how different areas in the business are tracking and are more informed when making decisions. They no longer lie in bed awake at night worrying or having protracted discussions about the business. They are in control. Who knew investing in an accounting system could buy you a peaceful night's sleep and save your relationships?!

So what are you waiting for? This chapter provides everything you need to know to set yourself up on Xero and start organising your accounts. I cover assessing your system requirements and making sure you have all the necessary information at your fingertips before you start. I help you work through the basic steps required when signing up and take you through the Chart of Accounts. I provide some help on adding options in that all-important matter — getting paid — and give a quick run-through of your consumer tax options.

The instructions for the Xero set-up process covered in this chapter and the appearance of Xero's set-up wizard shown in the figures were correct at the time of writing. Because of the cloud-based nature of Xero, processes and screen designs can change at any time, but don't worry. Even if you're looking at something slightly different to the screenshots shown in this chapter, the basic principles behind the set-up process, and the information required to complete it, will be the same. If in any doubt, check out the Xero help centre for information on the latest updates.

How do you eat an elephant? One chunk at a time. If you need to take a break during the Xero set-up process, the file stays in place, so you can return to it later on. Sometimes it can be easier to tackle one section of the set-up process, understand this area fully, sleep on it, and then move onto the next area.

Preparing for Set-Up

Before jumping straight in to signing up to Xero, getting yourself organised and checking you have everything you need is worthwhile.

Checking your browser and system requirements

Xero is accessed on the internet, so you don't need to worry about how working on a mac, a PC or a mobile device may change performance, or whether you have enough memory or space to install software. You simply need access to the internet! However, to ensure efficient and effective access to Xero online, including viewing graphical charts, you may need to install or update to the latest versions of certain products or tools, or change settings to support requirements.

At a bare minimum, here's what you need to use or set up (in the order you need to look at them):

- **Supported internet browser:** Options include Internet Explorer 10 and above, Mozilla Firefox, Safari 7.0 and above, Google Chrome and, if accessing via a mobile device, Opera Mini or the device's default browser.

- **Javascript:** You can activate this in your browser (further help can be found at www.activatejavascript.org).

✔ **Cookies:** Set your browser to enable cookies from `www.xero.com`. This allows the website to work properly on your browser, and can typically be activated through your internet browser preferences or settings options.

For optimal performance, consider the following:

✔ Install Adobe Flash player (available at `get.adobe.com/flashplayer`).

✔ On a regular basis, refresh the browser by clearing the cache and cookies. You can do this by deleting browsing history or clearing website data through the browser settings.

✔ Install Skype, so contacts can be called via Xero (this is optional but allows you to make free or cheap phone calls — see Chapter 5 for more).

✔ If using the Firefox browser, turn off Firebug because it can slow access.

If you've checked your requirements and set your browser up correctly and Xero is still not loading properly, check that you can access the internet! Xero does require access to the internet to work, and no offline option is available.

Snappy tips to master your browser

To optimise your Xero work time, I offer here a few tips I've gathered along the way in regards to working with monitors and browsers.

Firstly, I recommend working with two desktop monitors side by side, with one monitor in landscape and one in portrait position. (That is, the whole monitor turned on its side, not just the page shown in portrait view.) Some pages in Xero are long, and having the whole screen in portrait position allows an extended view.

Secondly, because you're accessing Xero via a web browser, you can also make use of the pretty nifty shortcuts your browser offers. Each browser type may use slightly different names, but here are some of the more useful features you're likely to have available:

✔ **Duplicate.** Click on the address bar of a web page you already have open, press Alt-Enter, and the same page opens in a different window or tab. This option, available on Firefox, Internet Explorer and Google Chrome, allows you to open a single Xero file and access different pages within it via many tabs across the browser — useful if you want to work in one area, such as reconciling, and you want to see how your work affects another area, such as the reports.

✔ **Paste and Go.** Once you've copied a hyperlink, open a new browser window or tab, right-click in the address field, and choose the option Paste and Go.

(continued)

(continued)

You're taken to the address without having to paste and then press enter — saving you one key stroke. This option is available on Firefox and Chrome, and labelled 'Go to copied address' in Internet Explorer.

✔ **Refresh/Reload.** To view updated Xero data if you or someone else is working in Xero on another screen, simply click the Refresh/Reload symbol. All browsers should offer the refresh option, usually around the end of the address bar.

Finally, if you want to guide someone to look at a particular area of Xero, you can copy the hyperlink from the address bar in the browser and email the hyperlink to the person. If they click on it while logged into the same Xero file, and as long as they have the appropriate user access, they will go directly to the particular area you referenced.

Collecting your business data

You're probably champing at the bit to start setting up your Xero file. Before you jump in, gather some data so you can easily access everything you need as you need it.

If you don't know where to find any of the data required by Xero at set-up (or don't know what it is), your accountant, lawyer or business adviser may be able to assist. If your business is new, you may not yet have all the required data, which is fine.

Collect all you can of the following:

✔ Bank account details

✔ Business logo

✔ Business type

✔ Chart of accounts

✔ Conversion date and balances — the date the accounting records start from and balances at that date

✔ Details of accounts payable and accounts receivable

✔ Display name (this is usually just the name people use to refer to your business — see the section 'Organisation Settings', later in this chapter, for more)

✔ Financial year end date

✔ Last invoice number

✔ Legal or trading name

✔ Organisation type

✔ Terms and conditions for payment

✔ Time zone details

Table 2-1 shows the additional information you may need to gather, based on the region your business is based in.

Table 2-1	Additional Data Required for Set-Up by Region		
Australia	*New Zealand*	*United Kingdom*	*United States & Global*
Australian Business Number (ABN)	GST basis	VAT scheme	Tax basis
	GST period	VAT period	Tax ID number
Branch details (optional)*	GST number	VAT registration number	Tax ID display name
Activity statement settings			
GST accounting method		BAC number	Tax period
Tax File Number			
GST calculation			
PAYG withheld period			
PAYG income tax method			
Fringe Benefits Tax details			
Fuel tax credits details			
Wine Equalisation Tax details			

* Branch details only required if you operate your business from more than one location; for example, you operate a group of shops across multiple locations.

Working through the Set-Up Guide

Once you've checked your system and gathered your required information (refer to the preceding section), you're ready to jump right in and sign up for a Xero account.

Getting started

Follow these steps to get started:

1. **Go to the Xero homepage** (www.xero.com) **and click the Try Xero for Free button.**

The Sign Up window appears (shown in Figure 2-1).

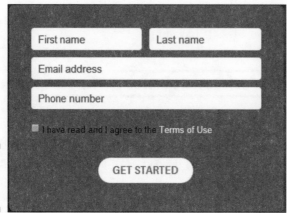

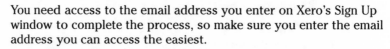

Figure 2-1:
The Sign
Up window.

2. **Fill in your contact details and other required fields.**

   All contact details must be complete before proceeding.

   You need access to the email address you enter on Xero's Sign Up window to complete the process, so make sure you enter the email address you can access the easiest.

   At the time of writing, Xero has customised solutions available for Australia, New Zealand, the United States, the United Kingdom and a global edition. Selecting the country where your business is registered to pay taxes in the Business Location field means Xero can customise your package to suit your needs. If you're based outside of these countries, Xero may still be able to customise what you're provided, so take a look!

3. **Read the Terms of Use and, if you're satisfied with them, check the box to indicate you accept them.**

   You can access the Terms of Use by clicking the link on the Sign Up window or at www.xero.com/about/terms. You must agree to the Terms of Use before proceeding.

4. **Click the Get Started button.**

   This submits your sign-up details. Once you've completed the Sign Up page, you should receive an email from Xero with the subject heading 'Activate your account', with a hyperlink to enable you to activate your account.

Here's how to activate your account:

1. **Click the hyperlink in the email from Xero.**

   You're taken to the Activate Your Account window (shown in Figure 2-2).

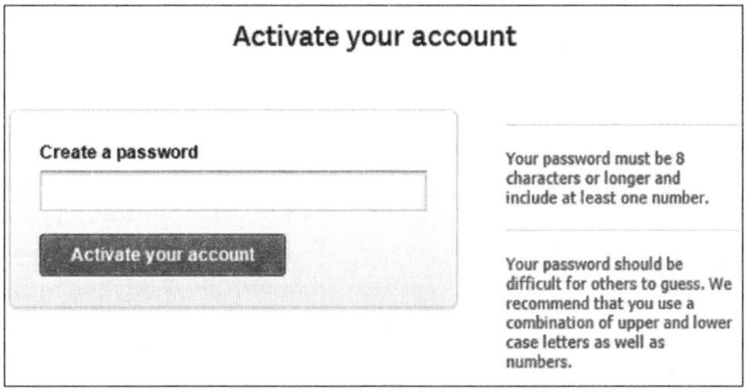

   ## Activate your account

   Create a password

   [   ]   Your password must be 8 characters or longer and include at least one number.

   Activate your account

   Your password should be difficult for others to guess. We recommend that you use a combination of upper and lower case letters as well as numbers.

   Figure 2-2: The Activate Your Account window.

2. **Create your password.**

   Remember to use the typical security protocols, such as combining upper and lower case letters and numbers. The password needs to be at least eight characters long and include a number.

3. **Click the green Activate Your Account button.**

   You're taken through to the Xero dashboard.

4. **Click the green Add Your Business button to add your details to Xero.**

   Enter the commonly used name of your business and select the country where the business pays taxes.

   When adding your business details, you can access the Xero Demo Company. This is always available and is an opportunity to explore and test a working file.

   Once you've selected a country, the base currency is defined as that of the country selected and can't be changed. If down the track you realise you want an alternative base currency, you'll need to redo your set-up. Additional currency can be added to Xero if using multi-currency options in the Xero Premium edition (see Chapter 15).

5. **Choose to start a free limited trial or jump right in and commit to purchasing a subscription with Xero now.**

   What you choose is up to you! Grab your credit card and work through the Purchase Now option, or test the waters first and click Start Trial. You can commit to purchasing a Xero subscription during the trial period.

Choosing your trial or subscription option opens the Xero Set-Up window. Across the top of the window is a guide to the steps about to be taken during the set-up process.

6. **Click the green Next button.**

Clicking this button brings you to the Organisation Settings dashboard, covered in the following section.

Organisation Settings

Business organisation details, including organisation name, type of business, contact details and contact links can be entered in the Organisation Settings dashboard (Figure 2-3). In this section, I go through how to complete most of the elements on this dashboard.

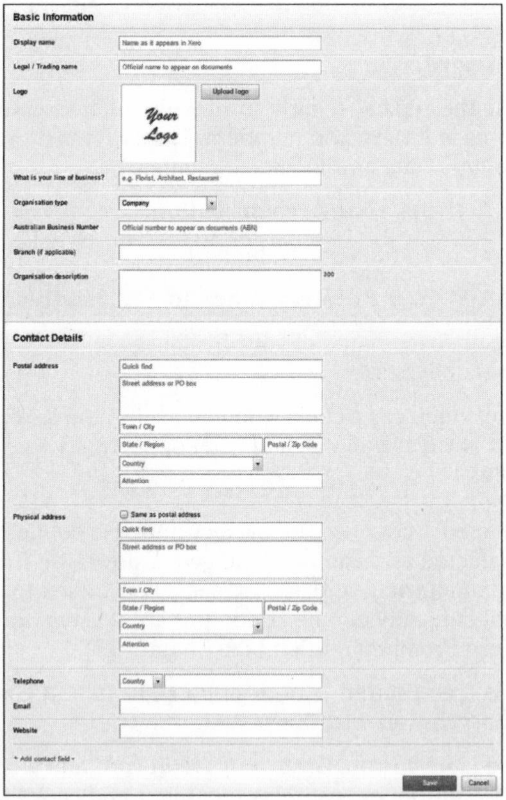

Figure 2-3:
The Organisation Settings dashboard.

The first part of the Organisation Settings dashboard is the Organisation Name & Type area. Here's how to complete this section:

1. **Click the Display Name field and enter the business name.**

   Your business name is typically the name Joe Public would use to refer to your business, and this name is what appears within Xero.

2. **Enter the legal/trading name of the business in the Legal/Trading Name field.**

   This is the name that appears on documents produced by Xero. It may be a long and clumsy name and may include terms like *atf* (as trustee for) or *trading as*. If you're a sole trader, your legal or trading name may be the same as your display name. If you're uncertain, check with the adviser who set up your business structure.

3. **Select the Organisation Type from the drop-down list of options.**

   The Organisation Type field is optional, and is for information purposes only. The selection makes no difference to the file set-up, and can be changed at any time. A plethora of choices is available, so if you're uncertain, leave this field and check with your adviser.

4. **Enter the sort of business you're operating in the What is Your Line of Business? field.**

   Completing this field is also optional. As you start to enter your business genre, the field suggests options, which can be overridden if required.

5. **Enter your Australian Business Number and Branch details and/or VAT details, as required.**

   Australian users need to enter their ABN and branch details (if they operate from more than one location). UK users need to enter their VAT Registration Number.

The next part of the Organisation Settings dashboard is the Contact Details area and this is quite straightforward — simply enter the postal and physical addresses of your business.

Enter your postal address information in the Contact Details area of the Organisation Settings dashboard and click Copy Postal to copy the details to the Physical Address/Registered Address column. You can then amend as necessary.

Capitalising the Town and/or City entries in your postal and physical addresses ensures correspondence is properly delivered — making this another efficient business practice.

The final block of the Organisation Settings dashboard is the Social Links area. This enables you to connect with your customers via the online invoices that you send them — they can 'like' you on Facebook, tweet you on twitter, connect with you on LinkedIn and/or join your circle on GooglePlus.

Before adding links within Xero to all the social networking sites you're active on, you may want to consider your business's social media strategy. For instance, you may opt to only add links to a Facebook business page rather than share your personal details by adding a link to your personal Facebook page.

After adding social links, check that the links work — see Chapter 6, where you can explore online invoicing, for more details. (I did this recently and realised my links weren't working and I had to correct them. Practising what I preach!)

Once you've entered your details in the Organisation Settings dashboard, click the green button on the bottom right labelled Next and the Financial Settings dashboard customised to your region appears (see the following section).

You can still access (and edit) the Organisation Settings dashboard after you first fill it out — simply select Settings on the menu bar and then General Settings. Under the Organisation heading, click Organisation Settings.

Financial Settings

Financial information about the business that may affect reporting parameters can be defined in the Financial Settings dashboard. At the sign-up stage you indicated where the business is registered to pay taxes (refer to the section 'Getting started', earlier in this chapter, for more).

Where your business is registered to pay tax affects the options available through the Financial Settings dashboard in Xero. If at all unsure, seek specialist advice for your own particular circumstances.

The first field to complete in the Financial Settings window is the Financial Year End. This date is the annual date that your business financial reports are prepared to. In many businesses, the financial year end aligns with the income tax year end for the country the business pays tax in. Enter your business's financial year end date in the first field and tab to the next field to enter the month.

Xero next asks you to choose the consumer tax options for your region (refer to Table 2-1 for the options that may apply). If in any doubt about how to complete this section, however, check with your accountant or Xero adviser.

To complete the Financial Settings window, you just need to enter the time zone you are working in. Selecting a time zone in Xero customises the date stamps, which is useful for maintaining an audit trail. Click on the drop-down menu and select the closest location to where the business is registered to pay tax. One setting governs all users, no matter where they are located.

Once you're happy with the details you've entered, click the green Next button and the Invoice Settings dashboard appears (covered in the following section).

If you need to access the Financial Settings after your initial set-up, select Settings on the menu bar and then select General Settings. Under the Organisation heading, click Financial Settings.

Invoice Settings

The Invoice Settings dashboard allows you to customise various features of the invoice template your company sends out. The options available are extensive, and deciding on the look and feel of your invoice, as well as ensuring it clearly conveys all the information it should, can take a little while. So rather than customise the invoice template now, you can click the grey No, Skip This Step button to skip the Invoice Settings dashboard at this stage and continue setting up the shell of the data file. If you know how you'd like your invoices to look and/or want to work through the Invoice Settings dashboard now, click the green Yes button and hop ahead to Chapter 6, which covers this topic in detail.

The green Next button appears. Clicking it gives you the option to invite other users to access your Xero file (covered in the following section).

Invite users

Adding users to Xero means people other than you can access your accounts, such as other staff members or your accountant. (Refer to Chapter 1 for help with identifying your support team and their different user roles, as well as your team needs.) To invite additional users to access your file, follow these steps:

1. **Within the User dashboard, click the Invite a User button.**

   Enter the additional user details, select the user role and indicate whether the user can manage other users and/or have access to payroll. (See Chapter 4 for more detail on the different user levels available in Xero and the sort of people each level can be used for.)

2. **Customise the user invite by clicking the blue Continue button.**

   A customisable invitation for the additional user appears. Add further information explaining why you are inviting them to access Xero.

3. **Send the invite by clicking the green Send Invite button.**

4. **Continue through the set-up process by clicking the green Next button.**

If you need to access the Users dashboard after inviting users during set-up, click on Settings on the menu bar and select General Settings. Under the Organisation heading, select Users.

See Chapter 4 for more on adding new users after the set-up stage.

Once you've invited users (and perhaps added currency), click the green Next button. You are now at the stage of setting up a chart of accounts for the business (covered in the following sections).

Understanding Bookkeeping Basics

The single most important part of setting up any accounting system is the chart of accounts — think of it as the backbone of the accounting system, because all transactions are coded through these general ledger accounts. Don't get confused — a bank account is a type of general ledger account, but not all 'accounts' are bank accounts. Getting your head around some bookkeeping basics before you set up your Chart of Accounts in Xero — so you can get them set up correctly from the start — is a good idea. Of course, if you feel you already have a good grasp of these bookkeeping basics, feel free to skip ahead to 'Setting Up Your Chart of Accounts', later in the chapter.

Setting up your chart of accounts to reflect business operations allows you to easily identify the performance of all areas. Let me give you an example. A customer asked me to review their profit and loss statement. On this statement, they had one single line for income: Consultancy, $2 million. Nice! Underneath the lonely income line were many lines of expenses — and expenses had been broken down to such detail I knew they had spent $300 on office flowers that year. Fortunately, the customer's invoices were very detailed, so it was an easy exercise of defining different types of income accounts, re-allocating them to invoices and — *ta da* — the owners now had details of the different income streams generated by the business.

Knowing the different ways the business was making money highlighted which streams were the strongest — for example, the owners could now identify a steady stream of income was being generated from a support contract with a customer who was guaranteed a 48-hour response time. They promoted this support-style contract to other customers and — you guessed it — a few took them up. This generated additional regular income for the business, with minimal extra effort on their behalf.

Working out how account types affect your reports

Each element of the chart of accounts, known as a *general ledger account*, is allocated an account type, and the account type that's allocated affects how the information is grouped on financial reports. Figure 2-4 shows where the different account types are grouped on two popular reports: the Profit and Loss Statement and the Balance Sheet.

Depending on how you set up your accounts, not a lot of difference may exist between some of the account types. Fixed Assets and Non-Current Assets, for example, could be deemed the same. Or you could have Fixed Assets defined as representing an asset with a medium life span and Non-Current Assets as an asset with a long life span.

The following sections provide a guide to the different account types. Grab a pad and pencil and, as you read through the lists, jot down how they apply to your own business, decide your interpretation and stay consistent.

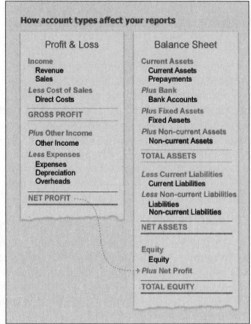

Figure 2-4:
How account types are grouped on your reports.

Assets

Assets cover the following:

- **Current Assets:** Owned by the business for less than 12 months — for example, accounts receivable, inventory
- **Prepayments:** Payments made in advance — for example, rent paid in advance
- **Bank Accounts:** Accounts held at financial institutions
- **Fixed Assets:** Owned by the business for between one and five years — for example, computer equipment
- **Non-Current Assets:** Owned by the business for over a year — for example, motor vehicles, office equipment, furniture and fittings

Liabilities

Liabilities cover the following:

- **Current Liabilities:** Monies owed by the business, to be paid back within 12 months — for example, accounts payable or credit cards

- ✔ **Liabilities:** Monies owed by the business, to be paid back within one to five years — for example, car loans

- ✔ **Non-Current Liabilities:** Monies owed by the business, to be paid back after a year — for example, a mortgage on the building premises

Equity

Equity covers the net worth of the business to the owner. As seen on the Balance Sheet, this is the assets minus the liabilities.

Revenue

Revenue covers the following:

- ✔ **Revenue:** Income other than sales

- ✔ **Sales:** Monies earned from business operations

- ✔ **Other Income:** Income not related to the operations of the income — for example, bank interest

See the section 'Developing your own chart of accounts', later in this chapter, for more on how different income streams can be reflected in revenue accounts within your Chart of Accounts in Xero.

Expenses

Expenses covers the following:

- ✔ **Direct costs:** Costs incurred in providing goods or services, inclusive of freight — for example, purchase of stock

- ✔ **Expenses:** Costs associated with running the business — for example, telephone charges

- ✔ **Depreciation:** The allocation of the value of capital assets to expenses, over the life of the assets — for example, depreciation on cars owned by the business

- ✔ **Overheads:** Fixed costs associated with running the business — for example, rent

See the following section for more on how direct costs relating to specific income streams can be reflected in expense accounts within your Chart of Accounts in Xero.

Creating a chart of accounts that works for you

By taking the time to define what you want to know, useful information can be easily generated. Account types, excluding bank, credit card and online payment methods, can be altered at any time. So if you have been working with a file and realise you should make some changes, you can!

This section covers some points you can take into consideration when developing a suitable chart of accounts for your business.

Measure what matters

Think about the kind of information you need to help you understand how the business is performing and so improve your decision-making process. Can you easily identify specific income streams and the direct costs of products or services you provide relating to these separate income streams? This information allows you to identify gross profit per product or service on the fly. Understanding what area of your business is more profitable (and perhaps what area isn't bringing in the cash) makes it easier to decide where energies and such costs as advertising budgets should be focused.

Keep it simple

The primary purpose of management reports is to help managers and business owners manage the business. Use language and terminology you understand. Override technical accounting speak and replace it with lingo that helps internal staff quickly understand and digest information. If you don't like the term *accounts receivable*, for example, change it to *dudes who owe us money*. I promise the accounting secret police won't come knocking at your door.

If business reports are required for outside bodies, you can extract the reports from Xero and easily reword any of the more individual terms you've used to suit the required accounting lingo. You, and any of your internal staff, being able to quickly view reports and understand what they mean on a day-to-day basis is more important for your business success.

Less is more

If, somewhere during the process, account lines have been generated that you are unlikely to use in the next couple of years, remove them. Adding new accounts is quick and easy — so, for example, don't hang on to the Building Premises account line in hope that one day you may own your building. Live for today and develop a streamlined chart of accounts that suits your business now. Ask yourself whether the way you've split income or expense streams is really useful. Will this help you make efficient and effective decisions in your business?

Developing your own chart of accounts

When it comes to developing a chart of accounts, I like to start with a blank canvas, work out the essentials, and allow the chart to organically grow with the business. Adding new accounts as you're developing the business is easy — so don't feel compelled to do it all now!

Speak with your accountant and ask if she has a preferred chart of accounts. I encourage all my clients to speak with their own tax accountant before developing a customised chart of accounts with them.

In this section, I share a few simple methods I use when I work with customers on developing a useful chart of accounts. *Note:* If your business is relatively straightforward, the insight you need about different income streams and the direct costs associated with these may be generated by simply using Xero's Tracking features. (See Chapter 12 for more on Tracking in Xero.)

Looking at income and direct costs

Say I had a customer who needed to define a suitable chart of accounts for his catering business. I ask to look at his business card and work out the business involves the following services (in order of income generated):

- ✔ Full-service caterer
- ✔ Dinnerware and linens
- ✔ Chef and wait staff
- ✔ DJ

Of course, if he didn't have a business card, I could ask to look at his website or other advertising material, but typically the back of a business card sums up the business — and, if it doesn't, the conversation probably becomes about designing business cards to promote what the business does! Back on track, in this example the caterer clearly has four main streams of sales income, each with associated direct costs. These four income streams, and the direct costs associated with each stream, need to be reflected in the account types created within Xero (and so also reflected on Xero's Chart of Accounts).

If, for example, the caterer wanted to understand the gross profit generated by offering the services of a DJ, in his chart of accounts he would allocate an account showing *DJ sale income* to account type Sale, and an account showing *DJ direct cost* to account type Direct Cost. To identify the gross profit, he can then deduct the direct cost of employing the DJ from the sales income generated through hiring the DJ.

Setting up a meaningful chart of accounts and ensuring data is allocated correctly means useful reports can be produced and analysed. Take the time to understand what your business does, and how allocating account types can affect your reports.

Understanding other expenses

Along with direct costs (refer to preceding section), three other expense account types are possible: Expense, Depreciation and Overhead. These represent the overall operating expenses for the business and I like to break them up over four groups:

- ✔ **Promotion:** This relates to any advertising, marketing or promotional spend incurred by the business and is allocated to account type Expense. A catering business, for example, may include Facebook advertising and website design here.

- ✔ **People:** This relates to staff expenditure, including wages, amenities, and training advertising. Expenditure for full-time staff could be allocated to Overhead while expenditure on casual is allocated to account type Expense. Continuing to use the catering business example, people expenses for this type of business may include wages, workers' insurance and kitchen amenities.

- ✔ **Place:** This relates to all expenses associated with the location the business occupies and is allocated to account type Overhead. A catering business may include rent, electricity and rates here.

- ✔ **Provisions:** This relates to all the general expenses of the business and may be allocated to account type Expense, Depreciation or Overhead. For example, a catering business may include telephone expenses, petrol expenses, depreciation, and subscriptions here.

Do not create *promotion*, *people*, *place* and *provisions* as account types. How these terms can be used is covered in Chapter 9, which discusses customising report templates.

Refer to the section 'Working out how account types affect your reports', earlier in this chapter, for details of what to include in the Equity, Assets and Liabilities section of your Chart of Accounts within Xero. See Chapter 9 for more on reporting outcomes.

Setting Up Your Chart of Accounts

In the following sections I take you through the two main ways of setting up your Chart of Accounts in Xero — using Xero's default set-up, or customising it to meet your needs.

If in any doubt during this foundational step of setting up your Chart of Accounts, speak with some experts. A management accountant can help you ascertain what useful information can be generated from your business accounts, which in turn can assist in making business decisions. However, you should also speak with your tax accountant as she may have a default chart of accounts she prefers you to use. The fees you pay to your tax accountant may be significantly reduced if you use her suggested chart of accounts because your accountant will undertake less work during the annual tax preparation process.

Using Xero's default Chart of Accounts

As you work through the Xero set-up process, when you come to the Chart of Accounts stage, you have the option of selecting the default Chart of Accounts provided by Xero or importing an existing Chart of Accounts file from another Xero file. Each of the options still allows you to edit the Chart of Accounts afterwards (see the sections 'Adding a new account' and 'Deleting an account', later in this chapter).

Australian and New Zealand users have the option of importing an existing chart of accounts file from Xero, MYOB or BankLink.

Choose the Xero default Chart of Accounts by selecting the Use the Default Chart of Accounts Provided by Xero option. To confirm the option, click the green button labelled Next. Xero's default Chart of Accounts is perfectly suitable for simple straightforward businesses.

Interestingly reports list accounts in alphabetical order, grouped by the account type. (See the section 'Adding a new account', later in this chapter, for more on this.)

Reporting within Xero isn't driven by the account code structure. Selecting the appropriate account type and utilising reporting options is more important (see Chapter 9 for more).

Note: If you choose not to use the default Chart of Accounts provided by Xero, you can import your own chart of accounts. Detailed information about converting from another system, including dealing with discrepancies, can be found in Chapter 3.

Customising your Chart of Accounts

Here I take you through some ways you can customise either Xero's default Chart of Accounts, or a chart of accounts you've imported.

Adding a new account

Your boss has just walked in and shared a brilliant way to monitor expenses in the business. He wants you to set up 30 individual accounts for all employees to monitor their taxi expenditure, another 30 accounts to monitor their telephone expenditure and so on. Frighteningly, this is a true story — but this is not how you want to monitor expenditure in the business! Your accounts list would become huge, unruly and unusable, and better ways are available to monitor that sort of expenditure (for example, a single expense account to track all taxi fare expenditure — see Chapter 12 for more on Xero's Tracking feature).

If you're comfortable that it improves your reporting capabilities, here is how to add a new account:

1. **From the dashboard, click on Settings on the menu bar, then General Settings. Under Organisation click on Chart of Accounts.**

   The Chart of Accounts dashboard appears. If you scroll to the very bottom, you will notice this page defaults to show 200 items per page.

   Note: If you're using the set-up wizard and have moved to this step after inviting users, you simply start at the next step. (For more on the set-up wizard, refer to 'Working through the Set-Up Guide', earlier in this chapter.)

2. **Click on the Add Account button on the top left side.**

   The Add New Account window opens (see Figure 2-5).

3. **Click in the Account Type field.**

   Refer to the section 'Working out how account types affect your reports', earlier in this chapter, for guidance on the appropriate account type to select. Adding a bank, credit card and online payment option account is covered in the section 'Adding Ways to Get Paid', later in this chapter.

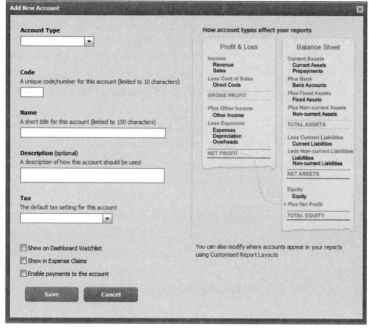

Figure 2-5:
The Add
New
Account
window.

4. Click the Code field and enter the identifying Code you wish to associate with the account.

The unique code can be alpha-numeric, up to ten characters long, and can include decimals and symbols if required. Once you start using Xero, however, you tend to rely on the account name rather than the number because Xero easily recognises these names and can suggest matching account names as soon as you start typing in the field.

5. Click the Name field and enter the account name.

This is your business, so don't worry about using fancy accounting terminology — use words you know. For example, a customer of mine once asked why her accountant listed her office pot plants on the balance sheet. The accountant had used the term *plant*, referring to the building premises. Office pot plants, the garden variety, are unlikely to be listed on your balance sheet, but if the term (or any other) confuses you, use another.

6. Click the Description field and enter any relevant information.

This field is useful for additional explanatory notes about the account, such as what should be coded here — an example could be a note that the account should include all overseas travel expenses, including flights. This field is optional.

7. **Review the suggested Tax setting.**

   Xero autofills a default tax setting when you select the Account Type. This setting can be overridden, so make sure it suits the account you're creating. (See the section 'Tax Rates', later in this chapter, for help with selecting the correct tax rate.)

8. **Check the box beside Show on Dashboard Watchlist (if desired).**

   The Account Watchlist is on the top right corner of the home dashboard. Select accounts you want to closely monitor to appear here, like Sales, Office Expenses and clearing accounts.

   Only select about five accounts to appear on your Accounts Watchlist — otherwise, information overload occurs and the area loses its benefit.

9. **Check the box beside Show in Expense Claims (if desired).**

   Checking this box allows the account to be selected when processing expense claims. This can be utilised to restrict what staff can allocate to an expense claim. (See Chapter 7 for more on expense claims.)

10. **Check the box beside Enable Payments to This Account (if desired).**

    Checking this box enables payments to be receipted into the account. Bank, credit card and online payment option accounts are automatically available as accounts into which you can receive money, but this option enables additional accounts to be available.

11. **Click the green Save button.**

    This saves the settings you have entered, but the account can be edited afterwards if necessary.

Deleting an account

Maybe you've realised that you have some accounts you never use. Streamline and simplify your Chart of Accounts, and permanently delete the ones you never use!

Here is how to delete an account:

1. **From the menu bar, click on Settings ⇨ General Settings, then under Organisation click on Chart of Accounts.**

   The Chart of Accounts dashboard appears.

2. **Check the box on the left of the account you want to delete and click the red Delete button at the top of the list of accounts.**

A confirmation window appears asking you to confirm you really want to delete this account. Once confirmed this process can't be undone, so make sure this is the correct account.

Some accounts can't be deleted. If you're trying to delete such an account, Xero automatically switches the process to the archive option (see following section).

3. **Click the green OK button.**

   This removes the account from your active accounts list.

Archiving an account

If you're feeling nervous about permanently deleting an account, archiving an account so it's stored in a retrievable format is the option for you! To archive an account, follow these steps:

1. **From the menu bar, click on Settings ⇨ General Settings, then under Organisation click on Chart of Accounts.**

   The Chart of Accounts dashboard appears.

2. **Check the box on the left side of the account you want to archive and click the blue Archive button.**

   A confirmation window appears asking you to confirm that you want the selected account to be archived.

3. **Click the green OK button.**

   This removes the account from your active 1accounts list.

Once you've customised your Chart of Accounts, click the green Next button to access Account Balances and choose your conversion date.

Handling your cash

Ideally, all business transactions should go through business bank accounts; however, the reality is sometimes that doesn't happen. To monitor personal spending on behalf of the business, or through the business, set up an owner's loan account or a petty cash account.

Select the Enable Payments option to enable recognition of business cash transactions. Also, show these accounts on the Dashboard Watchlist to monitor spending. (Refer to the earlier section 'Adding a new account' for more on how to select these options or settings.)

The Archive option is not available during the set-up process.

Putting Your Accounts into Practice

The following sections take you through some practical aspects you may need to go through once you have the main aspects of your accounts set up — conversion balances and historical invoices.

Checking your conversion balances

Conversion balances are the account balances as at the conversion date, when you start using Xero. Conversion balances follow basic accounting principles in that the debits need to equal the credits. A simple conversion balance of a new start-up business recognises company shares and the value of those shares as follows:

Cash   DR $2

Shares in Company   CR $2

This entry is reflected in Figure 2-6, which shows the Conversion Balances dashboard. If the business has been operational, the conversion balances are more detailed. If accounts haven't been locked, users with Standard or Adviser status can save conversion balances — but if you're

Account	Debit	Credit	
090 - Business Bank Account	2.00		
970 - Owner A Share Capital		2.00	

Add Comparative Balances   **Conversion Date**

1 Jul ▓▓ - 30 Jun ▓▓

Confirm your 30 Jun ▓▓ account balances

Add a new line   Show all accounts   Remove zero balances

Total Debits	2.00	Total Credits	2.00

Adjustments   0.00
This accounts for the difference between debits and credits and for FX gains and losses

☐ Lock balances at 30 Jun 2014
Locking ensures no accidental edits to balances or transactions are made before this date. Only users with Adviser roles will be able to make any changes. Read more

Save   Cancel

Figure 2-6:
The Conversion Balances dashboard.

at all unsure, engage an expert on your Xero support team to enter the conversion balance. Even if you don't have all this information, you can start entering some now — any amount that doesn't balance appears as an adjustment. Ask your accountant for the conversion balances or obtain a copy of your trial balance as at the date of conversion. The trial balance provides details of the balances of all the general ledger accounts.

Note: If you're using the set-up wizard, Account Balances, which includes Conversion Balances, is the window you'll be taken to after you've set up your Chart of Accounts. However, entering and correcting Conversion Balances is likely something you'll prefer to come back to after setting up the main aspects of your accounts, so the following steps also outline how to access the Conversion Balances dashboard after set-up.

To access the Conversion Balances dashboard, follow these steps:

1. **Click Settings on the menu bar, select General Settings and under the heading Organisation and select Conversion Balances**.

   The Conversion Balances dashboard appears.

   If you're a brave soul and are still working through the set-up wizard, you'll be taken to the next step.

2. **Click the Conversion Date button and enter the relevant date.**

   If you're working in the set-up wizard, click the green Next button.

   If you were starting as at 1 July, the conversion month would be July, and select the relevant Year.

   Make sure you're really comfortable with the conversion date you select. It can be changed, but doing so is a bit of a hassle and you may need a consultant to assist you.

   Note: An added incentive of setting the conversion date for the start of the financial year is you have the opportunity to include comparative balances, because the balances are typically easy to access from financial reports prepared by you or your accountant. (See 'Adding Comparative Balances', later in this chapter, for more.)

3. **Click on the blue Show All Accounts hyperlink and carefully enter the balances.**

   Show all accounts is written in very tiny letters beside the button Add a New Line.

   Make sure you have a list of what all the account balances are and only enter positive balances. For example, a bank account's ledger balance is typically debit in nature; however, if the balance is overdrawn, enter the balance in the credit column. Once all balances have been entered the

Adjusting conversion balances further down the track

If you've entered conversion balances and then realise a big hairy mistake was made in an earlier financial year, don't stress — you can go back and change the conversion balances. First, however, you need to check with your tax accountant on how the error should be dealt with, and whether amended records need to be submitted to the tax office or allowed for in the current period.

Once you and your tax accountant have agreed on a course of action, you can go ahead and change the conversion balances. Sound scary? It's easy-peasy — simply follow the steps outlined in the section 'Checking your conversion balances', earlier in this chapter.

Note: When making changes to existing conversion balances in Xero, you need to uncheck the box beside Lock Balances At . . .' before you begin (refer to Step 4 in 'Checking your conversion balances').

debit and credit columns should equal, with the difference (if any) left over in the adjustments column. Keep in mind that your accountant can come back and update these balances at a later date if you don't have the complete information at hand.

4. **Check the box beside Lock Balances At . . .**

   This ensures no-one accidentally changes balances; however, an Adviser can change them if necessary.

5. **Click the green Save button.**

   If you're working through the set-up wizard, click the green Next button.

   If conversion balances contain a balance for either the accounts payable or accounts receivable account, the detail behind the balances needs to be entered (see the section 'Entering historical invoices, bills and credit notes', later in this chapter). If you've no accounts payable or accounts receivable balance, congratulations! The set-up is complete.

Adding Comparative Balances

If your business was in operation prior to moving to Xero, the previous full-year balances for all or selected lines of the chart of accounts can be entered into your Xero file through the Comparative Balances function. In other words, you can add in the balances for accounts within your chart of accounts from before you started in Xero, as at the end of the previous financial year. If the detailed history of your business isn't already in Xero, utilising Comparative Balances is an opportunity to incorporate summary level historical data into your reporting.

Historical insights assist with understanding trends in data over time, which aids your future decision-making processes in your business.

Note: Adding in Comparative Balances is different from adding in historical invoices (covered in the following section). Comparative Balances show the overall balance of a specific account as at the end of the financial year. Invoices show a specific transaction within an account.

Before attempting to add Comparative Balances, ensure a Conversion Date has been set in Xero — refer to the earlier section on 'Checking your conversion balances'.

To enter the Comparative Balances of your accounts as they were before moving to Xero, follow these steps:

1. **Click Settings on the menu bar, select General Settings, go to the Organisation heading and select Conversion Balances.**

2. **Click the +Add Comparative Balances button.**

   The Comparative Balances window appears, where the dates of the previous financial year appear in a new tab (see Figure 2-7).

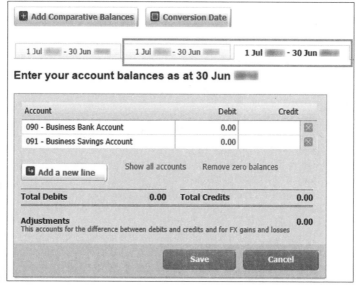

Figure 2-7: The Comparative Balances window.

3. **Click on the blue Show All Accounts hyperlink and carefully enter the relevant historical balances for each account.**

   You can access these balances in the final Chart of Accounts you or your accountant would have prepared at the end of the previous financial year.

4. **Click the green Save button.**

Entering historical invoices, bills and credit notes

If an Accounts Receivable conversion balance was entered, after saving the conversion balances, the Conversion Balances Sales Invoices dashboard appears. At the bottom right of the screen the red text reads Balance out by #; the amount is the Accounts Receivable conversion balance entered. The object here is to enter the historical invoice and credit note details, reducing the balance to zero.

Grab the details for the outstanding sales and enter them using the Add Invoice button and Add Credit Note button. (See Chapter 6 for guidance on entering Sales Invoices and Credit Notes.) Any details you add can be edited by clicking on the relevant row, or deleted by clicking the cross at the far right. The transactions entered here can also be entered via the normal Sales dashboard (see Chapter 6), and you can receive payment against them just as you would a normal invoice.

Once total Sales Invoices match total Accounts Receivable, green text at the bottom of the balance reads Matched and the balance is zero. The opportunity to proceed to the next step is now available via the highlighted green Next button. Your balance must be zero before you're able to proceed.

If an Accounts Payable conversion balance was entered, after matching the total Sales Invoices and the total Accounts Receivable balance, you've the opportunity to enter supplier bills and supplier credit notes, via the Add Bill and Add Credit Note buttons. It's the mirror image of the Conversion Balances Sales Invoices dashboard and the goal is to match the total accounts payable balance. Once matched, click the green Next button and Hurrah! The conversion balances should now be saved and you can click the green Finish button.

In Australia, the term *credit note* was replaced with *adjustment note* in 2000 with the introduction of GST, but I think people generally understand what's meant when the term credit note is used.

Adding Ways to Get Paid

Whatever sort of business you run, money transactions are likely to be a critical element of running the business. Bank accounts, credit cards and online payment facilities can be set up in Xero — the following sections show you how.

Setting up bank accounts

To access the area to add a bank account, follow these steps:

1. **Click on Settings on the dashboard menu bar, then General Settings. Then under Organisation click on Chart of Accounts.**

   The Chart of Accounts dashboard appears.

2. **Click on the Add Bank Account button on the top left side and select Bank Account.**

   The Add Bank Account window opens.

3. **Enter your business bank name in the Your Bank field.**

   The field suggests bank accounts that it recognises. Carefully select the matching bank. If your bank is there, hurrah! You should have access to automatic bank feeds. If, however, the bank isn't recognised, try alternative names or abbreviations. If that still doesn't work, transactions need to be manually imported. Manually importing bank statements is covered in Chapter 4.

4. **Click the Account Name field and enter the business bank account name.**

   When naming a bank account, suffix it with the last four digits of the bank account number for easy identification — for example, ABC Business x1234. When you refer to source documents like shopping receipts or bank statements, they may include the last four digits of the account you paid from. This crosscheck allows for easy identification.

   If you're using the add-on solution Receipt Bank, which scans and extracts transactional data, adding an account number–specific suffix becomes even more useful, because the financial document you're scanning frequently includes the payment reference on it. For example, say you pay for something with a card number that ends in 1234, so the shopping docket includes the x 1234 reference. When you scan the shopping docket, Receipt Bank extracts the data, including the payment details information, and can then easily link the payment shown in the shopping docket with the account in Xero ending in *x* 1234.

5. **Click in the Code field and enter an account code.**

   Refer to the section 'Adding a new account', earlier in this chapter, for insights into selecting an appropriate account code.

   The remaining fields, while similar, are customised to the country the Xero file was set up for, as shown in Table 2-2. Currency options are available in all Xero Premium packages, irrespective of their region. The Code field does not appear if you set up the bank account from the Bank Accounts screen.

Table 2-2	Xero Bank Account Settings Fields by Region			
Australia	*New Zealand*	*United Kingdom*	*United States*	*Global*
BSB	Bank Account Number	Sort Code	Bank Account Number	Bank Account Number
Account Number		Account Number		
DE User ID				
Include Self-balancing Transaction in the ABA File				

6. **Select the currency that you're working with in the Currency field (if required).**

   You only need to select the currency if you're working in multiple currencies.

   Multi-currency options are only available in the Premium version of Xero. Further information on this is in Chapter 15.

7. **Select the Bank Account Number fields and enter the required details.**

   Some Australian banks utilise direct entry user identification when the business makes batch payments. If you're in Australia and your bank uses these, Xero allows you to enter the Direct Entry User ID in the DE User ID field. When processing a payroll batch payment, a DE User ID field is a requirement. Enter the information and then check the self-balancing transaction option underneath. If you intend to make batch payments but you're unsure whether your bank has a Direct Entry User ID associated with the account, just ask your account manager at your bank. Also check whether you need to include a self-balancing transaction in the ABA file. This field is optional — if unsure, leave it blank. (Batch payments are covered in Chapter 7.)

8. Click the green Save button.

Once saved, the account appears on the home dashboard. (Make sure you also set up bank feeds for your bank accounts — see Chapter 4 for more.)

Including credit cards

Credit cards enable short-term loans for your business. To set up a credit card account in Xero, follow these steps:

1. Follow Steps 1 to 6, skipping Step 5, from the 'Setting up bank accounts' section.

2. Enter the last four digits of your credit card in the Credit Card Number field

Figure 2-8 shows the full Add Credit Card Account window. The credit card number details are added near the bottom.

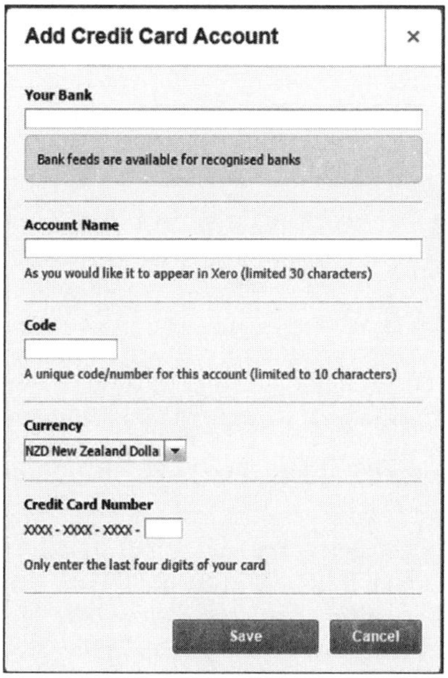

Figure 2-8: The Add Credit Card Account window.

3. Click the green Save button.

Once saved the account appears on the home dashboard. (The next step in setting up credit card accounts is setting up your bank account feeds — see Chapter 4.)

Online payment options

Xero enables feeds from online payment gateways like PayPal, and other online payment gateways soon! To set up a PayPal account in Xero, you need to have a business or Premier PayPal account. If you do, follow these steps:

1. **Click on Settings on the dashboard menu bar, then General Settings. Under Organisation, click on Chart of Accounts.**

   The Chart of Accounts dashboard appears.

2. **Click in the Account Name field and enter the relevant information.**

3. **If you're working within multi-currency, select the currency that you're working with in the Currency field.**

   Multi-currency options are only available in the Premium version of Xero. Further information can be found in Chapter 15.

4. **Check the box to the left of the Set Up Automatic PayPal Import option.**

   The Add PayPal Account window expands to reveal further fields (shown in Figure 2-9).

Figure 2-9: The Add PayPal Account window.

Add PayPal Account ✕

Account Name

As you would like it to appear in Xero (limited 30 characters)

Code

A unique code/number for this account (limited to 10 characters)

Currency
NZD New Zealand Dolla ▼

☑ Set up automatic PayPal import
View help

PayPal email

The email you use to login to PayPal

Import data from PayPal starting from

● All available transactions
Import up to 30 days of transaction history.

○ Specify a start date 19 Nov ▼

Save   Cancel

5. **Enter your PayPal email address in the PayPal Email field.**

   The PayPal email address is the address you use to log into your PayPal account.

6. **Enter your conversion date in the date field next to the Specify a Start Date option.**

   Refer to the section 'Checking your conversion balances', earlier in this chapter, for more on conversion dates. Up to 30 days of transactions can be imported.

7. **Click the green Save button.**

   Note: Once you've added PayPal as a payment option, you're sent an 'Activate your PayPal account in Xero' email. Keep this on file, because you need it when setting up live bank feeds for PayPal within Xero (see Chapter 4 for more on this).

   If when you use PayPal the money automatically sweeps into or out of your bank account, your PayPal account is likely directly linked with your bank account. (This means your PayPal account operates like a debit card. If you receive statements from your PayPal account, you've set it up so it operates more like a credit card.) If money automatically goes into and out of your account from PayPal, you probably don't need to add your PayPal account to Xero — doing so means you'll just be doubling up on entries.

Tax Rates

Unfortunately, complying with the relevant consumer tax reporting requirements for the country your business is based in can be a burden that takes your focus away from the importance of utilising management reports. But the reporting element is a necessary evil for many businesses. One of the big benefits of using an accounting system is that it can easily assist in allocating and calculating consumer tax — so you can focus on the bigger picture.

Globally, consumer tax has many guises: Good and Services Tax (GST), Value Added Tax (VAT) and Sales Tax. The overriding principles are generally the same — if you're required to collect consumer tax, it's added to the goods and services that you sell and procure — but different treatments and applications exist between jurisdictions. The preset tax rates available in Xero by country are outlined in Table 2-3.

If necessary, additional tax rates can be added via the New Tax Rate button.

You need to check that the available tax rates suit your business. You're ultimately responsible for what you report to the tax office in the country your business is based in. Seek specific advice for your circumstances. Although you can't alter the tax rates of your bank, credit card or online payment accounts set up through Xero, you need to check that the other accounts in the Chart of Accounts are associated with the correct default tax rates. Again, seek specific advice for your circumstances.

Table 2-3	Xero Tax Rate Settings by Region			
Australia	*New Zealand*	*United Kingdom*	*United States**	*Global**
GST Free Expenses	15% GST on Expenses (15%)	20% (VAT on Expenses)	Sales Tax on Imports (0%)	Sales Tax on Imports (0%)
GST Free Exports	15% GST on Income (15%)	20% (VAT on Income)	Tax Exempt (0%)	Tax Exempt (0%)
GST on Capital	GST on Imports	5% (VAT on Expenses)	Tax on Purchases (0%)	Tax on Purchases (0%)
GST Free Capital	No GST	5% (VAT on Income)	Tax on Sales (0%)	Tax on Sales (0%)
GST on Capital Import	Zero Rated	No VAT		
GST on Expenses		Exempt Expenses		
GST on Imports		Zero Rated Expenses		
GST on Income		Zero Rated Income		
Input Taxed		Zero Rated EC Income		
BAS Excluded		Zero Rated EC Expenses		
		VAT on Imports		
		Exempt Income		

* The default setting for these tax rates is 0 per cent, which can be overridden.

You don't need to create an extra tax rate for tax treatments that you're unsure of. When processing the transaction, simply leave the transaction unreconciled, click on the Discuss tab and enter your query — for example, *I purchased this overseas and am not sure how to code it* — and ask your Xero advisory team to assist.

If necessary, additional tax rates can be added via the New Tax Rate button. If you opt to use Xero's Global version, you may need to set up additional Tax Rates to comply with the tax laws of the country your business is based in. For example, consumer tax is different in each Canadian province, so if your business were based in Canada and selling to different Canadian provinces you would need to add multiple tax rates for each province.

To add a new tax rate follow these steps:

1. **From the main dashboard, click on Settings ⇨ General Settings ⇨ Tax Rates, and then click the New Tax Rate button.**

   The Add New Tax Rate window opens (see Figure 2-10).

2. **Click in the Tax Rate Display Name field and enter the relevant information.**

   For example, you could enter 'Tax on Sales — Quebec'.

3. **In the Tax Components fields enter the Tax, select Compound (if relevant), and then enter the actual tax rate as a percentage.**

   If an additional tax component is required — if, for example, the area is governed by both a federal and a state tax, repeat Step 3 and add another Tax Component.

4. **Click the Save button.**

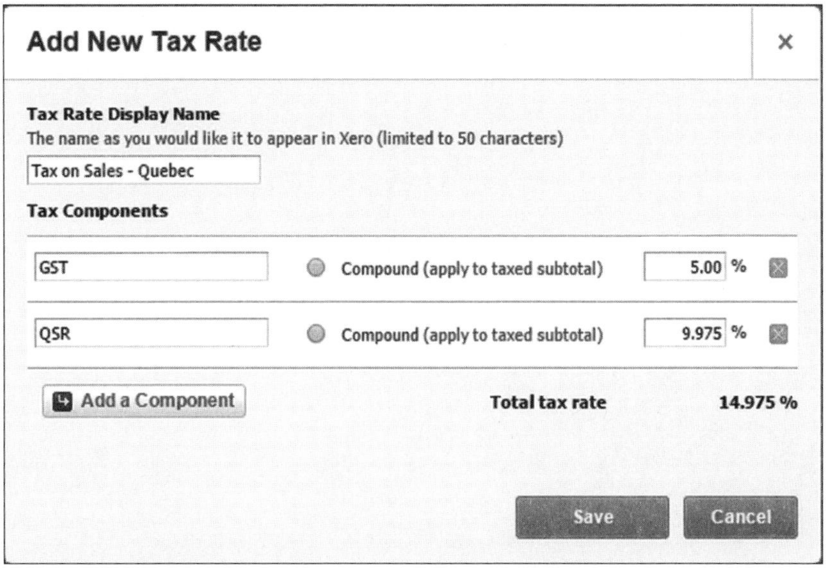

Add New Tax Rate   ×

Tax Rate Display Name
The name as you would like it to appear in Xero (limited to 50 characters)

Tax on Sales - Quebec

Tax Components

| GST | ○ Compound (apply to taxed subtotal) | 5.00 % | ⊠ |
| QSR | ○ Compound (apply to taxed subtotal) | 9.975 % | ⊠ |

⊞ Add a Component   **Total tax rate**   **14.975 %**

Save   Cancel

Figure 2-10: The Add New Tax Rate window.

Chapter 3

Converting to Xero from Another System

In This Chapter

▶ Converting data from a paper-based or spreadsheet accounting system

▶ Moving data from a computerised accounting solution

▶ Importing prepared data into Xero

▶ Working through any issues involved with turning off your old system

*I*f you've been maintaining business records in a non-computerised system (okay, I mean a shoebox) or a computerised format, you can move your data across to Xero. Changing accountants or changing accounting systems is a significant business decision — but don't let this stop you! Empower yourself and take responsibility for the project. This chapter outlines what is involved in converting to Xero from another system. You can simply bring opening balances into Xero or you can go through a more complex and involved conversion process, where you import historical transactions into Xero. Converting to Xero is an opportunity to detox your data — cleaning and streamlining it — and customise your data to generate useful business information. Have a specialist on call and give the conversion a go!

In this chapter, I take you through some tips for converting to Xero from a non-computerised system and from a computerised system, including some general guidance on working with CSV files and preparing your data for importing. I then take you through the specific processes for importing data into Xero, and cover some common issues that arise when turning off your old system.

Note: The process for exporting data from accounting systems is different for each system. I cover the specific processes relating to exporting and preparing data from MYOB, Sage and QuickBooks in Appendixes A, B and C, respectively. Jump online to www.dummies.com/go/xerofd2e to download each of these Appendixes for free.

Preparing to Import Data from a Non-Accounting Program

If you've been in business a while but don't have an existing computerised accounting system, the next few sections are for you. I discuss how you can utilise your paper- and/or spreadsheet-based records to assist in moving to Xero.

Converting paper-based records

If your existing records are paper-based — and I mean anything from a shoebox through to comprehensive documentation — gather the records and identify what needs to be entered into Xero. Use the last confirmed trial balance, which may be the last time an accountant prepared financial records, as a basis for your chart of accounts (see the section 'Confirming the switchover date', later in this chapter, for more). It is like piecing together a jigsaw puzzle — once you start entering data into Xero, records should fall into place easily.

Moving from paper records to a computerised system is labour-intensive. All that data entry! Only enter what needs to be entered — if you've a historical list of clients, for example, don't feel like they all need to be entered; simply enter them on an as-needed basis.

An alternative to entering data yourself is an extracting solution like Receipt Bank, where scanned receipts are uploaded and analysed, data is extracted and pushed into Xero. (Refer to Chapter 2 for more information on manually entering data into Xero, and see Chapter 16 for more on extracting solutions.)

Working with spreadsheets

If you maintain accounting records using spreadsheets, and are considering converting to Xero, the process you undertake is dependent on your spreadsheet layout. Assess what accounting information can be extracted from it. If the information is in a database format — for example, customers are listed in rows, with their details stretched out across columns — you may be able to easily manipulate data so it can be imported into Xero using templates available through Xero (see the sections 'Downloading Xero templates' and 'Preparing data for import', later in this chapter, for more information).

If, however, your spreadsheets have been maintained in a random fashion, transforming them to a suitable layout for importing data into Xero may be time-consuming.

It may be that you need to manually enter data, following guidelines provided in Chapter 2. Alternatively, you may be able to adopt a hybrid approach, importing some data and manually entering the remaining data.

Getting Ready to Convert from an Accounting Program

At Christmas, our extended family gather to celebrate the festive season, and one of the highlights is the Ray Cresswell jigsaw marathon. The first jigsaw puzzle comes out on Christmas Eve — this is a 200-piece puzzle with large pieces, which suits the beginners and the kids. The family gathers, the kids get involved, pieces of the puzzle are turned over, the corners are found, the border is formed, scenes are created, and the puzzle is completed. The next puzzle commences on Christmas Day (in that space after the presents have been opened and the bucks fizz drunk, and before Christmas dinner is served). This puzzle has a few more pieces, and these pieces are a bit smaller, but our approach is exactly the same. This scene repeats over the next few days, until the biggest, toughest and meanest puzzle, with 2,000 teeny-tiny pieces, is unboxed. We gather, eager and well-prepared for the marathon challenge. Applying our well-practised approach, we tackle and conquer the puzzle. Success is ours!

Essentially all accounting systems are the same as jigsaw puzzles — you just need to work out where all the pieces are supposed to go. Accounting systems are simply databases, or lists (or pieces) of data in different tables. To convert between solutions, you just need to export the data lists from the original system, review the format of the data, and import the data into the new system — in this case, Xero. With a systematic approach, you can work through each stage of the process.

The first part of the conversion is setting up your file framework for the imported data. Once you've done this, the conversion process moves through the following stages, regardless of the system you're converting from:

✓ **Export data:** Export available data from your previous accounting system and save it to your computer (see the section 'Setting up file directories', later in this chapter, for information on how to set up your files).

✔ **Prepare data for importing:** Use the conversion as an opportunity to tidy up your data lists and trim dead wood. Delete unused accounts and contacts that are no longer around. If historical data is imported, associated records, like contacts, can't be edited or deleted — otherwise, the records won't match. Save updated files in CSV text file format (see the section 'Understanding the CSV file format', later in this chapter, for more).

✔ **Import/update data into Xero:** The Xero file needs to be created before data can be imported into it. Work through Chapter 2 before embarking on this section. As some of the data you need to import is reliant on or linked to other data, you should also import/update data in the following order:

   • Tax Rates (review and manually update existing rates if necessary — the tax rates cannot be imported)

   • Chart of Accounts

   • Contacts

   • Inventory

   • Sales

   • Purchases

   • Bank Transactions

   • Manual Journals

   • Fixed Assets

✔ **Review and manually clean up imported data where necessary:** If erroneous data is imported in error, select it to be archived. (And then review the process to identify what went wrong.)

✔ **Repeat until finished.**

You can't save a back-up of your Xero file prior to import. While this might seem a bit scary, in most processes you have the opportunity to review data before finally importing it.

Table 3-1 provides a conversion checklist, and includes example file names for exported and imported data.

The conversion from your existing computerised accounting system to Xero is an exciting and immensely satisfying challenge. In the following sections, I provide information about the conversion process that can be applied to all conversions, regardless of what system you're converting from.

Table 3-1	Conversion Checklist — Summary				
Data	**Export** ✓	**File Name**	**Prepare & Review** ✓	**Sign Off** ✓	**File Name**	**Import** ✓
Chart of Accounts		AccountsExport			AccountsImport	
Contacts		ContactsExport			ContactsImport	
Inventory		InventoryExport			InventoryImport	
Sales		SalesExport			SalesImport	
Purchases		PurchasesExport			PurchasesImport	
Bank Transaction		<BankName> Export			<BankName> Import	
Manual Journals		JournalsExport			JournalsImport	
Fixed Assets		FixedAssets Export			FixedAssets Import	

For step-by-step information relating to exporting and preparing data specific to the accounting system you're converting from, jump online and visit www.dummies.com/go/xerofd2e to download Appendix A for MYOB, Appendix B for Sage and Appendix C for QuickBooks. Once data has been exported and prepared from your old accounting system, the process for importing that data into Xero is the same — see the section 'Importing Data into Xero', later in this chapter, for more.

If you know Xero will be connected to another business solution, research how the add-on syncs with Xero and establish if you need to be aware of any peculiarities. For example, when the commercial property management solution Re-Leased syncs with Xero, the Contact information is pushed into Xero, so the optimal Xero–Re-Leased set-up involves entering Contact details into Re-Leased first, and not entering them into Xero, and so avoiding duplication of work. For more information on add-ons, see Chapter 16.

Periodically Xero offers free conversion services. Your existing accounting data file is converted into an active Xero file. So before you start manually converting your data, you might like to check xero.com for any special offers on conversions to Xero, or you can contact your Xero Advisory Team to see if they have any suitable current conversion deals.

Getting ready to convert

Before starting a conversion, you need to prepare yourself to ensure the process runs smoothly and you stay organised. The areas you need to understand initially are how to set up your file directories and how to access Xero templates. The following sections take you through these areas.

Before starting your data conversion, work through Chapter 2 and create a Xero file the data can be imported into. When you get to the point where you're ready to import your own chart of accounts, you can jump back to this chapter.

Setting up file directories

Lots of files are created and used during the conversion process. Keep track of them by creating a simple file directory system that works for you. For example, you could create a high-level file directory called 'CONVERSION-BusinessName' and three sub-folders called 'DataReadyForImporting' 'ExportedData' 'XeroTemplates'. You can then save all files used during the conversion to the relevant subdirectory.

When working with virtual teams, using an online storage solution makes it easy for all members of the team to access the conversion files. Simply set up a specific online storage folder and save a link to the folder in the 'CONVERSION-BusinessName' file. Online storage options include Dropbox, Google Drive and Sugar Sync.

I tend not to add spaces to folder names because sometimes the spaces mean the folder names don't work across platforms, and these procedures are to be applied universally. If you prefer to add spaces or use different names, feel free to; however, I have used these examples throughout this chapter and the associated appendix, which you can find online at www.dummies.com/go/xerofd2e for free download.

Keeping a copy of the original and converted data files can be useful if you need to review data at a later date.

Downloading Xero templates

Xero has a number of downloadable templates to assist with converting your files. By entering data from the old accounting system into these templates, and matching unaltered column headings, you can organise your data in a format easily imported into Xero.

Access the Xero downloadable templates by following these steps:

1. **From the Xero dashboard, click on the relevant directions for the data you need to download, as provided in Table 3-2.**

For example, to access the Xero Contacts template from the Xero dashboard, click on Contacts⇨AllContacts.

2. **Click the blue Import button for the required template and then on the Download Template File link.**

3. **Save the template to your file directory.**

For example, you could save the template within your 'XeroTemplates' folder within the 'CONVERSION-BusinessName' folder.

4. **Repeat the three preceding steps until you've downloaded all required templates.**

Table 3-2	Downloadable Template Information	
Data	*Directions*	*CSV File Name*
Chart of Accounts	Settings⇨Chart of Accounts⇨Import⇨Chart of Accounts CSV file	ChartOfAcounts
Contacts	Contacts⇨All Contacts⇨ Import⇨Template file	Contacts
Bank Statements	Manage Account⇨Import a statement⇨CSV template	BankStatements
Inventory	Settings⇨General Settings⇨Inventory Items⇨Import⇨Template file	InventoryItems
Sales	Accounts⇨Sales⇨Import ⇨Template file	AccountsReceivableTemplate
Purchases	Accounts⇨Purchases⇨Import ⇨Template file	AccountsPayableTemplate
Manual Journals	Adviser⇨Manual Journals⇨Import ⇨Template file	ManualJournal
Fixed Assets	Accounts⇨Fixed Assets⇨Import⇨Template file	FixedAssets

As well as using the downloadable template for bank statements, you can create your own Excel template for importing bank statement information. Before doing this, however, see Chapter 4, which covers exporting bank statement information from your actual bank account. To create a bank statement template, list the following bank statement fields at the top of an Excel spreadsheet as column headers: Transaction Date, Transaction Amount, Payee, Description, Reference, Transaction Type, Cheque No., Account Code, Tax Type, Analysis Code and Region. Populate the Excel spreadsheet with the relevant data and save the file as a CSV (comma delimited for PC users) format.

On the CSV downloaded templates, the asterisks (*) at the left of the column header name indicate the field is mandatory.

When preparing the data for importing, sit your two excel files side by side and carefully copy the data from the original file into the Xero template file, to ensure you're copying data across to the correct fields.

Don't ever change the header row of the template file — it must remain unchanged for fields to align correctly during importing.

Converting exported CSV files into Excel

When working with data from different software solutions such as accounting programs, understanding and being able to navigate and manipulate CSV file formats is useful, because this is a common file format. You can then import the CSV file into a spreadsheet program such as Excel, making data manipulation easier.

Note: In Appendixes A, B and C, I cover converting to Xero from MYOB, Sage and QuickBooks (respectively). Jump online to www.dummies.com/go/xerofd2e to download each of these Appendixes for free. All these accounting solutions allow you to export data as a CSV file.

Understanding the CSV file format

CSV is an initialism for *comma-separated values*. CSV is a simple file format where data values are separated by commas — similar to in a spreadsheet, where data is separated into columns. Most programs (such as MYOB, Sage and QuickBooks) allow you to import and export files in CSV format. The CSV files can then be easily edited and, if fields are correctly matched, can be imported into Xero.

CSV files are deceptive! They look like Excel files. Check as you save them that you're saving to .csv format, not .xls format.

Using the Excel Import Wizard to convert text files to CSV files

When extracting data from an existing system, extracting it in Excel or CSV format is desirable. If that's not an option, you may be able to opt to extract files in text file format. When a text file is then opened in Microsoft Excel, the Excel Import Wizard automatically activates and takes you through an extraction process to show data in Excel.

To view the text files in spreadsheet format, follow these steps:

1. **Open Microsoft Excel and go to File⇨Open to search in your file directory of saved files.**

   The file directory is shown in Figure 3-1. As shown at the bottom right of Figure 3-1, select the Text Files option from the drop-down menu to access the text files. (If the Text Files option isn't selected, the files don't display, even if they are in the folder.)

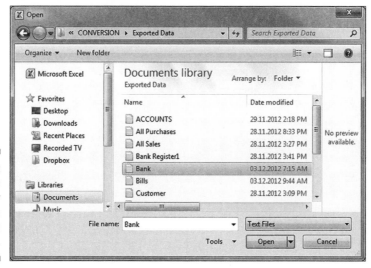

Figure 3-1: Using the file directory to open a text file in Excel.

2. **Select the required file and click Open.**

   The Text Import Wizard window (Step 1 of 3) appears (shown in Figure 3-2).

   Did your heart just skip a beat?! Don't be terrified! The Text Import Wizard looks a lot scarier than it really is.

3. **Click Next.**

   The Text Import Wizard window (Step 2 of 3) appears (shown in Figure 3-3).

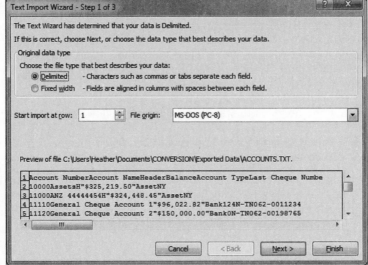

Figure 3-2: Text Import Wizard window (Step 1 of 3).

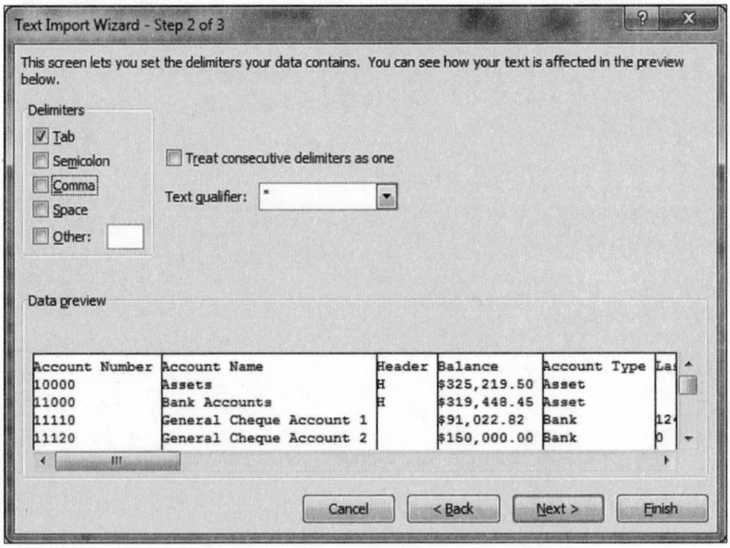

Figure 3-3: Text Import Wizard window (Step 2 of 3).

4. **Check the Comma box.**

5. **Click Next and then Finish.**

Voila! Your Excel spreadsheet is populated with data that hopefully makes some sense to you!

Once you have the data in Excel, you can manipulate the way it's presented so you can see everything more clearly. Simply select all the data in the spreadsheet by hovering over the top left corner block and clicking it. With the data range still highlighted, resize the columns by hovering over the column border and double clicking the double-sided arrow (see Figure 3-4). The columns and rows resize to fit the data contained within them. Now you can easily see and edit your data.

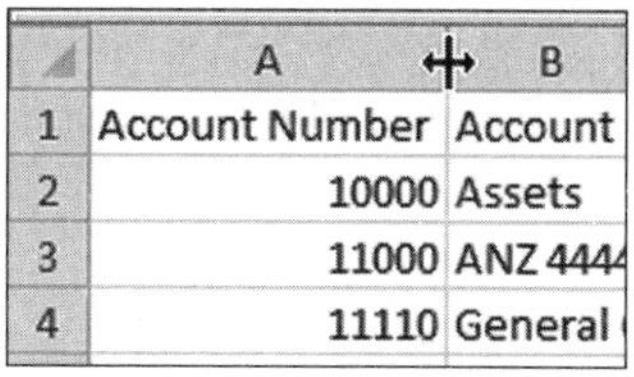

Figure 3-4:
Resize Excel
spreadsheet
columns.

	A	B
1	Account Number	Account
2	10000	Assets
3	11000	ANZ 4444
4	11110	General

Once satisfied with your data, save the file by selecting Save As. Clearly identify the file — for example, by renaming it <FILE>Import.csv. Ensure the Save As type is CSV (comma delimited) and save the file into the appropriate folder — for example, you could use a 'CONVERSION/ DataReadyForImporting' folder. (Refer to the section 'Setting up file directories', earlier in this chapter, for more.) Microsoft Excel pops up with an alert box to make sure you really want to save the file as a text file. Click Yes to confirm.

Microsoft Excel is perhaps a little overzealous about making sure you've saved your changes before you close the file, and asks if you want to save the file before closing. If you're positive you've saved it, and haven't made any further changes, you can simply click Don't Save!

Preparing data for import

Once you've exported your data, and if necessary converted it to a CSV file (see the preceding section for some general information on these processes), you're ready to prepare your data for importing.

Here are some useful techniques for preparing data in Excel for importing into Xero:

✔ Convert dollar values to numbers — dollars values aren't recognised.

✔ Enter dates in day/month/year format.

✔ Users of the US version of Xero enter dates in month/day/year format.

✔ Import amounts as a single column — when data is split between deposits and withdrawals, for example, the columns need to be merged and the withdrawals recognised as a negative number, by prefixing them with a negative symbol.

✔ Remove consumer tax from values (if required) — imported data must be exclusive of consumer tax, so this tax must be removed from data before it can be imported. Most information extracted doesn't include consumer tax — so this hopefully won't be an issue for you — but may be required if you're converting from MYOB.

Here's how you can convert amounts to a single column, using the example of combining deposit and withdrawal columns:

1. **Insert an additional column in the Excel spreadsheet, beside the Withdrawal column, and label it** Amount.

   The new column is shown in Figure 3-5.

2. **Combine the Deposit and Withdrawal column by entering a formula in the Amount column to subtract Withdrawals from Deposits.**

   For example, using the spreadsheet shown in Figure 3-5, you could enter the formula '=+C2-D2' in cell E2, combining data into a single cell. The withdrawal in this example is now represented by a negative number.

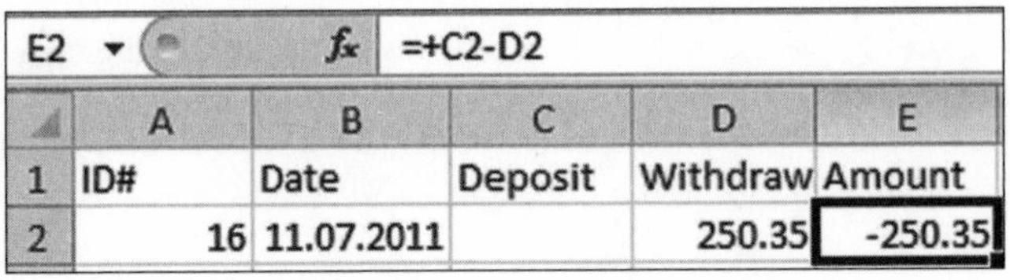

Figure 3-5: Combining data into a single cell.

E2	▼	f_x	=+C2-D2	
◢	A	B	C	D	E
1	ID#	Date	Deposit	Withdraw	Amount
2	16	11.07.2011		250.35	-250.35

Here's how to calculate the tax exclusive value from the tax inclusive value:

1. **Calculate the consumer tax Exclusive Amount by inserting a column beside the Inclusive Amount column and using the formula Inclusive Amount/(Consumer Tax+100)%.**

   Figure 3-6 shows an example of this calculation, including the formula required based on the Excel cells involved. In this example:

   Inclusive Amount: $500

   Consumer tax: 10%

   Exclusive Amount: 500/1.1 = 454.54

Figure 3-6: Calculating consumer tax Exclusive Amount.

C2 ▼			f_x	=+A2/(B2+1)
	A	B	C	
1	Inclusive Amount	Consumer tax	Exclusive Amount	
2	500	10%	454.5455	

2. **Copy the formula to the end of the data list by clicking the small black box at the bottom of the cell and dragging it down alongside the existing data.**

Don't apply the Exclusive Amount calculation where the Selling Price is already exclusive of consumer tax, or the consumer tax is 0.

Mapping tax rates

The tax rates of the raw data need to reflect Xero's own unique tax rates before importing. Refer to Chapter 2 for more detailed information on tax rates. To update the tax rates:

1. **Identify how the tax rates should be mapped from the old system to Xero default tax rates.**

   You may wish to seek specialist advice here.

2. **Update using the Find and Replace function.**

Importing Data into Xero

Once you've exported and prepared your data (see Appendixes A, B and C online at www.dummies.com/go/xerofd2e, as required), it's ready for importing. At this point, undertake one last review of the data and/or submit it to responsible parties for final approval. A cup of tea and fresh eyes may highlight issues to be rectified prior to import.

Once you're satisfied, follow the steps outlined in the following sections to import data into Xero.

Importing only up to 500 rows at a time is a good idea — doing so helps prevent any browser time outs.

Chart of accounts

Follow these steps to import your chart of accounts into Xero:

1. **From the Xero dashboard go to Settings⇨Chart of Accounts⇨Import.**

   The Import Your Chart of Accounts window opens (see Figure 3-7).

2. **Answer the two questions on the window.**

   - What system are you importing from?

     If you're using a UK, US or global version of Xero, you only have the single option of choosing Xero at this point. If you're importing from Sage (see Appendix B) or QuickBooks (Appendix C), or another system, choose Xero. (Jump online to www.dummies.com/go/xerofd2e to download Appendix A, B and C for free.) Yup! A little confusing, but if you've completed the Xero Chart of Accounts template (refer to the section 'Downloading Xero templates', earlier in this chapter), Xero is the option you need to select here. If you're using an Australian or NZ version of Xero, you're presented with three options here: Xero, MYOB or BankLink. If you're importing from MYOB (see Appendix A, also online at www.dummies.com/go/xerofd2e) select MYOB. If you're importing from Sage or QuickBooks, pick Xero. The other option is BankLink, another type of accounting software.

   - Does the file you are importing contain account balances?

     Select No. It is preferable not to import balances because some checks are not repeatable. If your data has balances, don't worry — Xero will ignore them if you select this option.

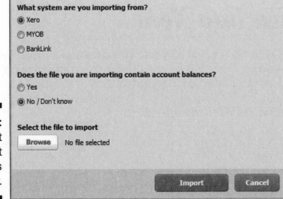

Figure 3-7:
The Import
Your Chart
of Accounts
window.

3. **Click the Browse button to select the required file and then click the blue Import button.**

   For example, you could select the AccountsImport.csv file in the DataReadyForImporting folder within the CONVERSION folder.

   Clicking the Import button brings up the Confirm Your Imported Accounts window, which provides a report on the impending import process. This is an opportunity to review the integrity of data prior to import.

4. **Review data integrity by clicking the View link beside each report line.**

   You're provided with an overview of the import, summarising what has been included:

   • New accounts

   • Updated accounts (the numbering may look odd, because the default Xero accounts will be archived, but don't stress — continue the process and you will see the new accounts added)

   • System and locked accounts that haven't been updated

   You're also given a summary of what has been excluded:

   • Accounts that can't be imported due to error

   • Accounts that are deleted or archived

   You have the option here to print errors and changes; however, the option only prints a list of the accounts that couldn't be imported due to errors, not a comprehensive overview of the import anomalies.

   Note: Xero only has a single consumer tax account in the Chart of Accounts. That is, all GST or VAT or sales tax (depending on where you're based) is funnelled into a single consumer tax account. When importing from MYOB into Xero, various consumer tax accounts are merged into Xero's single consumer tax account. Xero doesn't recognise consumer tax lines imported from other systems. A default one is automatically created within Xero and any existing consumer tax lines aren't used in future transactions.

   If further editing of the data is required, click the grey Cancel button.

5. **Click the green Confirm button to continue with the import process.**

6. **Allocate the bank and credit card accounts.**

   At the Confirm your Bank and Credit Card Accounts stage, five Account Type options are available: Bank, Credit Card, PayPal, Current Asset and Current Liability. Select the Account Type/s required and enter account details. Refer to Chapter 2 for information on account types.

Note: The sales and purchases accounts aren't imported during the importation of the chart of accounts — see the sections 'Sales' and 'Purchases', later in this chapter.

7. **Confirm the bank and credit card Account Types by clicking the green Save button.**

   You're returned to the Chart of Accounts dashboard and can view the imported accounts.

Contacts

Follow these steps to import contacts into Xero:

1. **From the Xero dashboard go to Contacts⇨All Contacts and then click on the blue Import button.**

   The Import Contacts window opens.

2. **Click the Browse button to select the required file and then click the blue Import button.**

   For example, you could select <Contacts>Import.csv file from the DataReadyForImporting folder within the CONVERSION folder.

   Select the option to Ignore Empty Fields — because this is new data, you have nothing to override.

   Clicking the Import button displays a report on the impending import process in the Import Contacts window.

3. **Review the report integrity.**

   If further editing of the data is required, click the grey Go Back button, and see the relevant appendix online at www.dummies.com/go/xerofd2e for your previous accounting system.

4. **Once satisfied, click the green Complete Import button.**

   The imported contacts are displayed in Xero.

When importing contacts into Xero, you may also be importing the bank details for those contacts. If this is the case and you've imported the Bank Account Number, double check it imports correctly. If it imports as something like 4.4444E+58 go back to the Excel spreadsheet and format the cell to be a number with no decimal places and try the import again.

Inventory items

Follow these steps to import inventory items detail into Xero:

1. **From the Xero dashboard go to Settings⇨General Settings⇨Inventory Items⇨Import.**

   The Import Inventory Items window opens.

2. **Click the Browse button to select the required file and then click the blue Import button.**

   For example, you could select the InventoryImport.csv file from the DataReadyForImporting folder in the CONVERSION folder.

   Clicking the Import button displays a report on the impending import process in the Import Inventory Items window.

3. **Review the report integrity.**

   If further editing of the data is required, click the grey Go Back button, and see the relevant appendix for your previous accounting system, online at www.dummies.com/go/xerofd2e.

4. **Once satisfied, click the green Complete Import button to import the data.**

   The imported inventory displays in Xero.

Sales

Once Xero is set up, you will receive payments against outstanding sales invoices, so they need to be in the system to reconcile against when the money is receipted. ***Note:*** Xero groups the invoices you issue under the Sales area (see Chapter 6 for more details).

In the lead-up to a conversion, I encourage clients to chase all outstanding sales, pay what bills they can, and review any potential bad debts. This assists with detoxing the data and minimises transactional data being brought across into Xero.

Australian and New Zealand users have the option of importing MYOB Service and Item Sales invoices, exported directly from MYOB. See Appendix A online at www.dummies.com/go/xerofd2e for more information on this.

Follow these steps to import sales details into Xero:

1. **From Xero's home dashboard go to Accounts⇨Sales and click the Import button.**

   The Import Your Sales Invoices window opens.

2. **Click the Browse button to select the required file and then click the blue Import button.**

   For example, you could select the SalesImport.csv file from the DataReadyForImporting folder in the CONVERSION folder.

   Clicking the Import button displays a report on the impending import process in the Import Your Sales Invoices window.

3. **Review the report integrity.**

   The import action can't be undone if you proceed so check this report extra closely. If further editing of the data is required, click the grey Go Back button, and see the relevant appendix for your previous accounting system online at www.dummies.com/go/xerofd2e.

4. **Once satisfied, click the green Complete Import button to import the data.**

   The imported sales are imported in Draft status and now display in Xero. You have the opportunity to enter additional data in each invoice, and approve them as outstanding. (See Chapter 6 for information on dealing with draft invoices.)

5. **Enter credit notes.**

   Credit notes or negative sales can be imported in the same way. See Chapter 6 for information on entering Credit Notes.

6. **Manually update any imported records where the consumer tax wasn't the standard rate.**

   Find the relevant imported invoices, click on them and update their details to reflect the correct allocation of consumer tax. See Chapter 6 for information on editing sales invoices.

7. **Correct any issues by sorting out individual issues or deleting and re-importing the data.**

   The imported invoices only have a single line of transactional details. If you need to add additional detail, such as a different Due Date, or additional transactional information, locate the invoice, click in to it to edit it and save it.

   To delete a draft invoice you don't need, click the check box to the left of it and click the red Delete button.

See Chapter 6 for more information on locating and editing sales invoices.

8. **Check the import balance matches the balances of the data imported.**

9. **Approve sales invoices individually or as a batch.**

   See Chapter 6 for details on approving sales invoices.

Purchases

Once Xero is set up you can make payments against outstanding bills, so they need to be imported into Xero so you can reconcile them when the money is paid. ***Note:*** Xero groups the bills you receive under the Purchases area (see Chapter 6 for more details).

Australian and New Zealand users have the option of importing MYOB Service and Item Purchase bills exported directly from MYOB. See Appendix A for more information on this, online at www.dummies.com/go/xerofd2e.

Follow these steps to import Purchase details into Xero:

1. **From the Xero dashboard go to Accounts⇨Purchases and click the Import button.**

   The Import Your Bills window opens.

2. **Click the Browse button to select the required file and then click the Import button.**

   For example, you could select the BillsImport.csv file from the DataReadyForImporting folder in the CONVERSION folder.

   Clicking the Import button displays a report on the impending import process in the Import Your Bills window.

3. **Review the report integrity.**

   The import action can't be undone if you proceed, so check this report extra closely. If further editing of the data is required, click the grey Go Back button, and see the relevant appendix for your previous accounting system, online at www.dummies.com/go/xerofd2e.

4. **Once satisfied, click the green Complete Import button to import the data.**

   The imported bills are imported in Draft status and now display in Xero. You have the opportunity to enter additional data in each invoice, and approve them as outstanding. (See Chapter 6 for how to deal with draft invoices.)

5. **Enter Debit Notes.**

   Debit Notes or negative bills can be imported in the same way.
   See Chapter 7 for information on entering Credit Notes. *Note:* Xero
   refers to debit notes as credit notes — don't get confused!

6. **Manually update any imported records where the consumer tax wasn't the standard rate.**

   Find the imported invoices, click on them and update their details
   to reflect the correct allocation of consumer tax. See Chapter 7 for
   information on editing bills.

7. **Correct any issues by sorting out individual issues or deleting and re-importing the data.**

   The imported bills only have a single line of transactional details. If you
   need to add additional detail, such as a different Due Date, or additional
   transactional information, locate the invoice, click in to it to edit it and
   save it.

   To delete a draft bill you don't need, click the check box to the left of it
   and click the red Delete button.

   See Chapter 7 for information on locating and editing bills.

8. **Check the import balance matches the balances of data imported.**

9. **Approve bills individually or as a batch.**

   See Chapter 7 for details on approving supplier bills.

Bank transactions

Perhaps you've decided on a conversion date and set up your bank
accounts in Xero; however, a gap occurs between the conversion date and
the date the bank feeds activate, or perhaps your bank doesn't offer bank
feeds. In this case, you can manually import statements — see Chapter 4 for
further guidance on how to do this.

Follow these steps to import Bank Transactions into Xero:

1. **From the home dashboard go to <Relevant Bank Account>, click the Manage Account button on the top right and select the Import a Statement link.**

   The Import Bank Transactions window opens.

2. **Click the Browse button to select the required file and then click the green Import button.**

For example, you could select the <Bank>Import.csv file from the DataReadyForImporting folder in the CONVERSION folder.

The Statement Import Options window opens (see Figure 3-8).

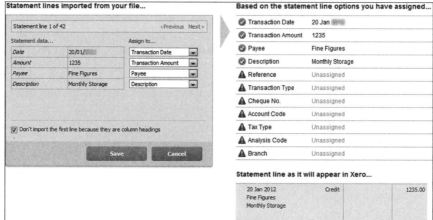

Figure 3-8:
The
Statement
Import
Options
window.

3. **In the blue Statement Lines Imported from Your File box, under the Assign To column click on the drop-down menu and select the Xero bank statement fields the imported data should be matched to.**

The available bank statement fields in Xero are Transaction Date, Transaction Amount, Payee, Description, Reference, Transaction Type, Cheque No., Account Code, Tax Type, Analysis Code and Region. A Xero field can only be selected once.

The table on the right highlights the outcomes of your selections. Use the Next option to see the potential treatment of the next imported transaction. The statement fields can be reselected until you're happy the transactions showing are correct.

4. **Check the box labelled Don't Import the First Line.**

You check this box because the first line is a column heading.

5. **Once you're satisfied the data suitably matches, click the green Save button.**

A pop up window confirms statement lines were imported.

6. **Click OK.**

   The Bank Reconciliation window opens, because the imported transactions need to be reconciled — see Chapter 8 for guidance on reconciling bank transactions.

7. **Process the other bank transactions files by repeating Steps 1 to 6.**

Manual journals

Xero does not recommend importing manual journals during the conversion process because, preferably, transactions should be allocated to the correct area rather than via a manual journal. If you do decide entering a manual journal is the best solution, remember that only a user with Standard user status and above can access the manual journal area.

To import manual journals into Xero follow these steps:

1. **From the dashboard go to Reports⇨All Reports⇨Journal Report and click the Manual Journals button, then click the Import button.**

   The Import Manual Journal window opens.

2. **Click the Browse button to select the required file and then click the blue Import button.**

   For example, you could select the ManualJournalsImport.csv file from the DataReadyForImporting folder in the CONVERSION folder.

   Clicking the Import button displays a report on the impending import process in the Import Manual Journal window. It stresses the action cannot be undone!

3. **Review the report integrity.**

   If further editing of the data is required, click the grey Go Back button, and see the relevant appendix for your previous accounting system, online at www.dummies.com/go/xerofd2e.

4. **Once satisfied, click the green Complete Import button to import the manual journal(s).**

   The imported data is classified as a draft manual journal on the Manual Journals dashboard.

5. **Post the journal entry by clicking on it, reviewing details are complete and correct, and clicking the green Post button.**

   This is a journal entry so debits must equal credits. Also check the consumer tax has been applied as required. The manual journal is now listed as a posted manual journal.

6. **Process the other imported manual journals by repeating Steps 1 to 5.**

Fixed assets

Only a user with Adviser status can tackle some of the processes related to Fixed Assets. To import fixed assets into Xero follow these steps:

1. **From the home dashboard go to Accounts⇨Fixed Assets and click on the Import button.**

   The Import Fixed Assets window opens.

2. **Click the Browse button to select the required file and then click the blue Import button.**

   For example, you could select the FixedAssetsImport.csv file from the DataReadyForImporting folder in the CONVERSION folder.

   Clicking the Import button opens the Import Fixed Assets window, which provides a report on the impending import process, and highlights the action can't be undone.

3. **Review the report integrity.**

   If further editing of the fixed asset data is required, click the grey Go Back button, and see the relevant appendix for your previous accounting system, online at www.dummies.com/go/xerofd2e.

4. **Once satisfied, click the Complete Import button.**

   The imported data is classified as a pending item on the Fixed Asset dashboard.

5. **Review the imported fixed assets by clicking on the individual asset in the Pending Items dashboard and updating the details as required.**

   See Chapter 14 for guidance on fixed asset details.

6. **Once satisfied, a user with Adviser status can move the fixed asset from pending to the Fixed Asset Register by clicking to open the fixed asset and clicking the green Register button.**

   The asset is now a part of the Fixed Asset Register.

7. **Check the details of the other imported fixed assets and register them by repeating Steps 5 to 6.**

Unpresented payments or uncleared funds

At conversion date the bank balance in Xero should match the Trial Balance from the old system. The Trial Balance is a standard document you should find in the Reports section of your accounting system. If it does, hurrah! Break out the chocolate and skip this section!

If the balances don't match, it may be because a supplier has been paid but the cheque or payment hasn't been presented on the bank statement or, vice versa, you've paid a client by cheque and it's not cleared yet. This payment or receipt eventually hits the bank statement, and the Xero bank balance. Follow these steps to prepare the accounts in anticipation of this:

1. **Identify the balance of unpresented payments or uncleared funds by running a bank reconciliation in the old system as at the conversion date.**

2. **Create an asset account in Xero called** Uncleared Funds **and a liability account in Xero called** Unpresented Payments.

   Refer to Chapter 2 for information on creating new accounts. Select the option Show on Dashboard. The goal of this exercise is to return the balance to nil, and once at nil, you'd remove this option from the two accounts.

3. **Enter the balances identified in Step 1 in the Uncleared Funds and Unpresented Payments conversion balance.**

4. **Pre-empt the transactions hitting the bank statement by entering the individual transactions identified in Step 1 as Spend Money and Receive Money transactions.**

   Allocate the Spend Money transactions to the Unpresented Payments account.

   Allocate the Receive Money transactions to the Uncleared Funds account.

   See Chapter 8 for information on Spend Money and Receive Money transactions.

   Consumer tax has already been reflected in your conversion figures, so allocate a not reportable tax rate to all transactions entered here.

5. **When payments are recognised in the bank statements, code them in Xero to the Uncleared Funds and Unpresented Payments account.**

6. **Check off the payments as they're recognised.**

   The amount entered into the conversion balance should be reduced to nil.

If that doesn't sort out your balances, check transactions prior to the Trial Balance bank balance haven't been included in Xero (which would mean they've been double counted). Double counted transactions need to be deleted — see Chapter 4.

Turning Off Your Old System

You and your staff may be feeling apprehensive about the big switcheroo — that is, moving your accounting operations entirely across to Xero. To ensure the move goes smoothly, you may need to manage staff expectations. If staff are involved in your accounting operations, incorporate them in the decision-making process, provide adequate training, and be prepared to answer their questions.

Questions staff (or you) may have may include the following:

✔ What if I need access to historical data?

✔ How can we move to the new system?

✔ When is the switchover date?

The following sections provide you with some answers.

Accessing historical data

You can still refer to the old system for detailed historical information. Although historical balances can be entered into Xero for comparative purposes, your old accounting system should be relied upon for a detailed history. Create a file directory entitled something like 'Historical Financial Data' and move all your historical information to the file for future access.

If you were using an accounting solution where you were paying an ongoing subscription fee to them, you no longer have to make this payment — nice to be saving some money, hey?! — but you should still be able to access your data. As time goes by, however, if you upgrade your computer you may no longer be able to install 'old' accounting software on a 'new' platform. You'll never have these problems with a web-based product like Xero, but they're unavoidable with desktop software.

Moving to the new system

You can approach pulling the plug in a couple of ways:

✔ **Set up Xero and switch over instantly:** This means you're no longer actively using the old accounting system, and you've focused all your energies on learning and using Xero.

✔ **Set up Xero but run the accounting systems in parallel:** This means energies are divided between working on the old and new system and on learning Xero — and you're probably going to spend extra time out of your day running two systems. However, it means you can compare reports produced. Once you're confident Xero is capturing all data, you can turn off the old system.

You need to decide what suits your style and method of operation. Make sure Xero meets your business requirements, and review what you expect in accounting software. Then focus on getting your Xero file set up, activating bank feeds, defining a clear switchover date, and working towards the goal of moving completely to Xero as swiftly as possible — like ripping a plaster off!

Confirming the switchover date

Ideally, you want to move to a new system at the start of an accounting period — or, even better, the start of a new financial year. Activating automatic bank feeds in some instances may take a few weeks, or even months, so if a suitable cutover date is looming in your calendar, start the process of setting up Xero early, with a focus on activating the bank feeds. Return to Xero as the impending day approaches to complete the set-up process, and switch over on the first day of the next period.

Chapter 4

Fine-tuning Your Set-Up

- -

- -

*I*met my husband-to-be during a glorious English summer. Our courtship involved touring the Cotswolds in a 1964 open-top white MG that he had impressively rebuilt with his own hands. Easy to understand how I fell in love with him! Without discounting the incredible talents of my husband, his being able to rebuild an MG was also because cars were created more simply in the sixties. The dashboard consisted of a speedometer, temperature indicator, oil pressure gauge, full beam indicator, a radio with speakers and a glove box. My husband used to say if you needed to know anything else about the car's performance, just listen! Compare the MG's dashboard to a car of today — modern cars have everything from a GPS navigational system to mobile phone connectors.

Simple or complicated, the purpose of a dashboard is to provide information in a single view, assisting you during the journey in reaching your destination. If you ignore the warning signs on the dashboard, the destination is unlikely to be reached. Xero utilises the concept of a dashboard to provide a quick overview and insights into how the business is performing; further dashboards then provide details on Sales and Purchases and other areas of the business.

As the user, you should review the dashboards to ensure the business is keeping on track and take note of any warning signs. If necessary, as with driving, you may need to make changes, deal with the issue, and return to the journey. Just as the little flashing oil bottle doesn't mean a genie has landed on your car, you shouldn't guess or disregard the signs Xero gives you! Know what indicators are good and what indicators require your attention.

In this chapter, I provide all the information you need to be able to read your business dashboards as quickly as you would the dashboard of your car. I also cover setting up bank feeds and bank rules, and making use of email templates.

Tools of the Trade: Understanding the Dashboard

When you log into Xero, you can't avoid the home dashboard! On the left side of the dashboard are the business accounts for banks, credit cards and online gateways that have been set up in Xero. For some people, this may be a very short (or very long) list! On the right side are overviews of (in this order):

- ✔ Accounts Watchlist — if you've not selected any accounts to show on the Dashboard Watchlist, this block won't display (refer to Chapter 2)
- ✔ Money Coming In
- ✔ Money Going Out
- ✔ Expense Claims

If you ever get lost in Xero and need to re-orientate yourself, return to the home dashboard by scrolling to the top of the screen and clicking Dashboard on the menu bar.

The following sections cover each of the main areas of Xero's home dashboard. *Note:* When I refer to bank accounts in the following sections, I mean this to include all bank, credit card and online payment gateway (such as PayPal) accounts — any accounts that you receive payments into.

Xero balance versus bank balance

On the left of the dashboard are the bank accounts that you've set up in Xero (refer to Chapter 2) and, from here, bank balances can be easily reviewed and reconciled.

The Statement Balance represents the actual bank account balance in your account, as per its last update within Xero. The Balance in Xero represents the balance of the transactions entered in the Xero bank account. Ideally, the two balances should be equal, and you should see a green tick and the word Reconciled. This means that all cash inflows and outflows from the account have been reconciled and coded within Xero. Alas, if the balances aren't equal, you need to reconcile — and reconciling on a regular basis is essential to ensuring the accounting records are accurate. See Chapter 8 for the full details.

If the accounts are reconciled but the Xero balance and the bank balance don't equal, it may be a timing difference. This always happens when I pay off my business credit card account from my business bank account. I reconcile the transfer in my bank account. The difference between the two balances is the transfer payment I made. The Xero balance recognises I've posted an entry to my credit card, but the credit card feed lags behind by about 12 hours. Once the transaction appears and is reconciled in my credit card, the balances match. (This normally sorts itself out within one business day.)

If the accounts are reconciled but the bank balance doesn't reflect your actual account balance, this could mean the opening balance was entered incorrectly and this is having a knock-on effect on the current balance. Review the opening balance and amend if necessary (refer to Chapter 2).

Other issues that could result in your bank balance not matching your actual balance could be missing or duplicated statement lines. Compare the bank feeds to your bank account and identify what's causing the problem. (For example, I had a client whose bank interest never appeared on her bank feeds — if you have multiple accounts, these accounts may have an inherent hierarchy that means interest only appears in the feed for one of the accounts, even if the other accounts aren't related to this bank account feed.) Let Xero customer care know if the issue occurs regularly but, if it's a one-off issue, isolate and import the missing statement line, or delete it. (See the section 'Managing bank feeds', later in this chapter, for more information.)

If all bank accounts are not selected to be displayed on the home dashboard, at the bottom of the accounts on the left of the dashboard is advice about how many of your bank accounts are showing on the dashboard and a link to the Manage Bank Accounts area.

Account Watchlist

The Account Watchlist is a snapshot of the monthly and year-to-date balances of accounts you want to keep an eye on. Any account (except bank, credit card and online gateway accounts) can be added to the Account Watchlist; however, adding more than ten may be overwhelming. It's difficult to interpret a deluge of information! This section provides some help on selecting which accounts to keep an eye on, and how to add them to your watchlist.

Selecting accounts to add to your watchlist

Only add to your watchlist the accounts that provide insights into business performance and any accounts that you need to track. This may include key sales accounts, payroll and tax liability accounts.

It's up to you to decide the ones that affect your business most — for example, perhaps your upcoming tax obligations or loan balances are most useful. Once set up, you can change the accounts on the watchlist at any time.

Adding an account to the Account Watchlist

You may want to add an account to your watchlist for a number of reasons — for example, to monitor a short-term loan you have for a new computer. To add an account to the Account Watchlist, follow these steps:

1. **From the Account Watchlist dashboard, click the Go to Chart of Accounts link.**

   The Chart of Accounts window opens.

2. **Select the account to be added to the Account Watchlist.**

   The Edit Account Details window opens.

3. **Check the box to the left of the Show on Dashboard Watchlist option at the bottom of the screen.**

4. **Click the green Save button.**

5. **View the added account by clicking Dashboard on the menu bar.**

   You should be able to see the added account on the watchlist.

If you no longer need to track the account, repeat the above steps but at Step 3 uncheck the box to the left of the Show on Dashboard Watchlist option at the bottom of the screen. This removes the account from the Account Watchlist.

Money Coming In

The Money Coming In dashboard is a mini summary of the Sales dashboard, showing draft invoices, overdue invoices and what money the business is currently owed. From here, you can quickly access the Sales dashboard and more detailed sales information, and add a new invoice.

See Chapter 6 for a detailed overview of Sales.

Overall, how are you feeling about Xero?

At the bottom right side of your Xero home screen is a *Yay!* face, *Meh* face and *Grrr!* face. If you click on any of these, a comment box appears inviting you to send Xero some feedback or even add a query. Xero Customer Care assigns a ticket based on your feedback and, if required, attempts to respond to your query or issue.

Money Going Out

The Money Going Out dashboard is a mini summary of the Purchases dashboard, showing draft bills, overdue bills and what money the business currently owes. From here, you can quickly access the Purchases dashboard and more detailed purchases information, and add a new bill.

See Chapter 7 for a detailed overview of Purchases.

Dealing with expense claims

The Expense Claims block is an overview of the Expense Claims dashboard, and the status of all expense claims can be seen here: Your Current Claim, All Current Claims, Awaiting Authorisation and Awaiting Payment. The block also provides quick access to adding a new receipt or viewing the Expense Claims dashboard.

See Chapter 7 for a detailed overview of expense claims.

Setting Up Users

A bookkeeper I consult for arrived at work on a sunny Monday morning. She started her normal work day but something wasn't right. She was confused but couldn't exactly work out what was wrong, so asked me to look at the file. I noted that a lot of changes had been made over the weekend by the business owner's spouse. It transpired the wife had had some spare time so she thought she would access the file and fix a few things up! It took a few days to undo all these 'fix ups'!

You may give some people access to Xero but still want to restrict what they can do and see, so they don't inadvertently create errors or access sensitive information. The following sections show you how to set user levels and how to add new users.

Understanding user access levels

When you set yourself or others up as users in Xero, you can achieve a level of protection by assigning access levels. You can choose between the following:

- ✔ **Read Only:** This level of access is useful for managers who want to view invoices, bills and reports but don't want to accidently change anything. Like a kid in a museum, the access allows them to view without touching!

- ✔ **Invoice Only:** This access is useful for administrative, sales or purchasing staff who enter invoices or bills. Furthermore, you can use four options within this type of access — you can specify whether staff with this level of access can only create the invoices and bills in draft format (this access is *Draft Only*), or can also approve and pay them (this access is *Approve & Pay*). As a user, staff with this access can also enter their own expense claims. Alternatively, staff can be given access to *Sales Only* or *Purchases Only*.

- ✔ **Standard:** This access is useful for the everyday user, such as the bookkeeper who needs to access a variety of areas. Some of the processes they can't do include publishing reports (except Bank Reconciliation Summary), locking down accounts, processing some aspects of fixed assets, and editing organisational and financial settings. An additional option is to allow Standard users access to Cash Coding (this access is called *Cash Coding*) or restricting access to this feature (this access is called *Non Cash Coding*).

- ✔ **Adviser:** This is like VIP access to all areas, and is useful for the management and tax accountant or the business owner who wants full access to the accounts. Adviser status includes everything a Standard user can access and more. Full access means you can publish reports, lock dates or prepare manual journals — practically anything you want to do!

The Standard and Adviser users can be given additional permission to:

- ✔ Add and remove users and change users' permissions
- ✔ Administer payroll, including preparing and posting runs
- ✔ Add and edit customer and supplier bank account details

Inviting other users to access Xero

One of the truly amazing features of Xero is, when you're setting up other people as users, you're inviting these people to access your data online in real-time. This means you can invite someone to review your data and help you interpret your dashboard, sort out a tricky transaction, or process end-of-year reports. You no longer need to save the file to a USB stick and mail it to the accountant, for your accountant to then waste time working out what software type and version is needed to open the file. With a simple email invite, your accountant can access your files within a few minutes, and be talking to you in real-time about your live data!

If you're set up on Xero but your accountant hasn't used it, still encourage your accountant to work directly within the Xero environment. I have worked with accountants who, even if they had never seen Xero before, were happy to give it a go and soon found it simple to navigate. The feedback from the accountants was they found doing what they needed to do within Xero easy, once they had a look around. (You could also let your accountant know that an excellent *Xero For Dummies* guide on the subject is available!)

Invite your accountant or adviser to access your Xero account by following these steps:

1. **From the home dashboard, go to Settings➪General Settings➪Users.**

   This brings up the Users dashboard.

2. **Click on the blue Invite a User button.**

   The Invite a User dashboard appears (see Figure 4-1).

Enter their details

First Name   Last Name   Email

Access to the accounts

Choose the user's level of access to this organisation's accounts:

	Bank reconciliation (?)	Invoices (?)	Edit settings (?)	View reports (?)	Publish reports (?)	Lock dates (?)
○ Read Only	✖	Read only	✖	Read only	✖	✖
○ Invoice Only	✖	Draft only ▾	✖	✖	✖	✖
● Standard	Non Cash Coding ▾	✔	✔	All Reports ▾	✖	✖
○ Adviser	✔	✔	✔	✔	✔	✔

☐ **Manage Users** Allow this user to add and remove users and change permissions

☐ **Payroll Admin** Allow this user full payroll access, including preparing & posting pay runs and payroll reporting

☐ **Contact Bank Account Admin** Allow this user to add and edit bank account details held for customers and suppliers

[Continue]   [Cancel]

Figure 4-1: The Invite a User dashboard.

3. **Enter the required details under Enter Their Details.**

   Include your accountant's name and email details.

4. **Select the Adviser option and check the Manage Users and Payroll Admin options.**

   Checking the Payroll Admin option gives your accountant full access to your accounts. *Note:* Your accountant may need to invite some of her own staff members to get their hands dirty and work in your file. Checking the Manage Users option allows your accountant to invite these users.

5. **Click the blue Continue button.**

   This brings up the Personalise Invitation and Send window (see Figure 4-2).

Personalise invitation and send

In order to give Your Accountant access to ▓▓▓ ▓▓▓ ▓▓▓ ▓▓ they need to accept an email invitation from you.

The invitation that will be emailed is shown here and can be changed before being sent.

Email message

> Hello Accountant,
>
> ▓▓▓ ▓▓▓ ▓▓▓ ▓▓ would like you to access their account at Xero. ▓▓▓ ▓▓▓ ▓▓▓ ▓▓ uses Xero to help manage their business.
>
> Please contact me if you have any queries,
>
> Your Name
> Your Details

Send Invite

Figure 4-2: The Personalise Invitation and Send window.

6. **Personalise your message to the invited user.**

   For example, you can add a reference to recent discussions about your business, and include your name and contact details.

   If the invited user isn't aware you're intending to send this invite, adding further explanation is useful, as is making a follow-up phone call.

7. **Click the green Send Invite button.**

Be aware that Xero is associated with one email address and the invite email is sent as if it is from that email address.

Clicking the Send Invite button brings you back to the Users Dashboard. Here, you see the status of the invite — either Pending or Active. If the invite recipient doesn't respond, you can click on the recipient's name, and then edit and resend the invite.

Once your accountant has accepted your invite, she can access your Xero file and any reports needed, including the Fixed Asset Register. She also has the ability to export all general ledger transactions.

You can follow similar steps to those outlined in the preceding list to invite other users into your Xero files. Just adjust the access option based on the person you're sending the invite to.

When sending out user invites in Xero, if you send an email to a non-existent email address, you're alerted via the email address used to log in to Xero. So check your email account first if you haven't had a response to an invite.

If your outsourced services such as your accountants want you to set up a single login (for example, 'The Brilliant Accountants') for all their staff to use, I encourage you to say no to this. You want anyone accessing your Xero file and financial data to be accountable and tagged in the audit trail. As the small business owner, you don't benefit from issuing one single login accessed by multiple people. If you were audited or reviewed by a court of law, a single login would be frowned upon.

Taking Advantage of Live Bank Feeds

If you're familiar with internet banking, you know that when you log into your bank account in the morning, you view transactions from the previous day. This information is the source of your bank feeds. Through permission-based, highly secure encryption, this data is sent into your Xero accounts under the guise of bank feeds.

When you log into Xero, the data in your Xero Bank Statement is essentially identical to what you see on your bank statement online bank transaction history as at the last bank feeds imported. No more data entry! And no more waiting for bank statements to arrive by mail so you can work on a bank reconciliation. The data you view on the dashboard is essentially live, and you can confidently make decisions using real-time data.

Note: Bank feeds can be set up for some bank accounts, credit card accounts and online payment facilities. For simplicity's sake, I refer to all three as bank feeds in the following sections. Major high-street banks typically have bank-feed capability, but some smaller institutions may have no feeds available. Most feeds are daily, or when manually refreshed. Fortunately, the number of bank feeds available seems to be increasing every day. I recently set up a client who used a small country bank that didn't have bank-feed capability when we set up her accounts. Within a few short weeks that had changed, and we were able to add the links and activate the bank feeds — revolutionising her accounting process.

Activating live bank feeds

Xero lets you activate live bank feeds from your bank, credit card and online payment options accounts.

Before starting the bank feed process, make sure the details you're about to enter absolutely match the details from your accounts. Ensure relevant parties at your bank are in receipt of permission documentation and are processing it. Things can occasionally take longer than they need while setting up bank feeds, and you may need to manage the process to keep it on track.

Bank accounts

Here's how to activate live bank feeds from your bank accounts:

1. **From the dashboard, click Accounts⇨Bank Accounts and navigate to the relevant bank account.**

   The window has two options: Get Bank Feeds or Manually Import a Statement. If you can't see the Get Bank Feeds option, you're not able to activate bank feeds. Double-check that you've entered the details correctly (refer to Chapter 2) and then check with your Xero advisory team. If the Get Bank Feeds option still doesn't appear, you need to manually import remaining data — see the section 'Manually Importing Statements', later in this chapter, for more.

2. **Click the green Get Bank Feeds button.**

   Because you haven't yet gone through your permission requirements, hitting this button at this stage takes you through to an information page. However, the bank you're with affects what happens after that. Most likely, you're able to link through to a Xero help area with the latest information on how to set up live bank feeds for that particular account, either through a partner bank feed or a Yodlee feed (see the sidebar 'Where do bank feeds come from?' for more). You may need to fill out a form and send it to Xero or your bank, or your bank may let you apply through online banking.

If it's a partner bank feed, once permission has been processed you receive a notification email from Xero and statement lines start importing — meaning you're done!

If it's a Yodlee feed, underneath the bank account you should see an 'Automatic bank feeds are available for this account' note along with the green Get Bank Feeds button.

3. **Click on the green Get Bank Feeds button (if required).**

   This now brings up the Setup Automatic Bank Feeds window.

4. **Enter your actual bank login and your bank password in the Your Bank Login and Your Bank Password fields.**

5. **Read the automatic bank feed terms and conditions and check the box to confirm.**

   You can access the terms and conditions by clicking the link.

6. **Click Next.**

   Xero is now connecting with your bank. This may take a few minutes. Read the prompts as they appear and act accordingly (these are different for different banks).

   Once a successful connection has been made, a green Start Bank Feed Now button appears.

7. **Click the green Start Bank Feed Now button.**

   An activation window opens.

8. **Select the matching bank feed from the drop-down menu.**

   You're given the option to import up to 90 days of transactions or transactions starting from a set date. Aim to import data back to your conversion date (the date you're starting your Xero file from). If this option isn't available, go as far back as you can, and then manually import remaining data. (See the section 'Manually Importing Statements', later in this chapter, for more.)

9. **Click the green OK button.**

Credit cards

Here's how to activate live bank feeds for your credit card:

1. **From the dashboard, click Accounts⇨Bank Accounts and navigate to the relevant credit card account.**

   If the credit card is linked to your bank account and you've already entered bank account passwords, you still need to enter passwords again. However, if you've never entered passwords for this institution, you need to refer to permission requirements at Step 2 in the section 'Bank accounts', for an appreciation of the security steps you need to go through.

2. **Click the green Start Bank Feeds Now button.**

   The Setup Your Bank Feed window opens.

3. **Select the matching bank feed from the drop-down menu.**

   Make sure you select the correct feed! Don't start importing your personal accounts.

   You're then given the option to import up to a maximum of 90 days or transactions starting from a set date. Aim to import data back to your conversion date. If this option isn't available, go as far back as you can and then manually import remaining data. (See the section 'Manually Importing Statements', later in this chapter, for more.)

4. **Click the green OK button.**

   You're notified when the transactions are ready.

Online PayPal payment options

PayPal is an international facility for online payments and money transfers. Like your bank accounts, PayPal is an independent to Xero, and as such your account with them needs to be separately established. At the time of writing, live bank feeds are only available for PayPal premier or business accounts. But the feeds are received twice a day! Here's how to activate live bank feeds for your PayPal account:

1. **Find the email 'Activate your PayPal account in Xero' sent when you included your PayPal account in Xero.**

   Refer to Chapter 2 for more on adding PayPal to your Xero set-up.

Where do bank feeds come from?

Recognising the sort of feeds activated within Xero is useful because sometimes issues are reported with feeds and knowing what feeds you're receiving means you'll be aware if any delays in the data have been announced. Two types of bank feeds are possible:

✔ **Partner bank feeds:** If you're required to complete a bank feed authority form, the feed is from a partner bank. (This means Xero has established a direct relationship with the partner bank.)

✔ **Yodlee feeds:** If you're able to activate the bank feed while logged into Xero, the feed is from Yodlee. Yodlee is an online banking solution service.

2. **Click on the first hyperlink in the email.**

   This takes you to Give Third-Party API Permission screen in PayPal, so you can update settings and allow Xero to access your data.

3. **Enter** `paypal_api1.xero.com` **in the Partner API Username field.**

4. **Check the 'GetTransactionDetails' and 'TransactionSearch' options, and click Submit to save the settings.**

5. **Verify that you own the PayPal email address by clicking on the second hyperlink on the email.**

   PayPal feeds should start in the next few days.

Organising bank accounts on your dashboard

To display bank accounts on the dashboard, click on Accounts⇨Bank Accounts and tick the checkbox beside Show Account on Dashboard. To conceal the bank account, untick the checkbox.

Prioritise the order of the dashboard bank accounts by following these steps:

1. **Select the bank account by clicking on it.**

2. **Drag the bank account to move it up or down and drop it into the required position.**

Managing bank feeds

Even once your bank feeds are all set up and seem to be working fine, you may notice some odd gremlins. You still need to keep an eye on your bank feeds and manage any problems. Some of the actions you may need to take include the following:

✔ **Refreshing Yodlee feeds:** Occasionally, you may notice that the Yodlee bank feed seems a little outdated. Refresh the bank feed and, shortly afterwards, you're notified that the bank feed has been refreshed. Some new unreconciled transactions may also pop up in your account. To refresh the bank feed click on Manage Account and click on Refresh Bank Feed.

- ✔ **Re-entering passwords for Yodlee feeds:** If your Yodlee bank feed banking passwords are changed, the connection to the bank feeds is affected, and you need to re-enter passwords. If you use a token or answer a security question every time you log in to your internet banking, your bank has Multi-Factor Authentication security functionality (try saying that quickly three times!). This means the bank feed in Xero needs to be refreshed on a regular basis. Realistically, refreshing the feed weekly is probably enough. This process can only be done by the user who entered credentials to activate the feed. Each refresh brings in transactions that have occurred since the last refresh, up to a maximum of 90 days with most banks (some banks only allow up to 30 days). A little bit of extra work, but it does provide peace of mind over the security of your bank feeds.

- ✔ **Importing duplicate transactions:** Importing data without inadvertently importing duplicate data can be tricky — even when you're being very careful with the date ranges. If you spot duplications, identify the data that needs to be deleted and see Chapter 8.

- ✔ **Deleting bank feeds:** To delete a bank feed completely, you need to delete the bank account from your Xero accounts — refer to Chapter 2.

Some bank feeds don't match up perfectly in Xero. Anomalies such as refunds, negative amounts and income from interest may be read incorrectly. Report the issue to the bank and to Xero, so each party can examine its matching process. If you don't use internet banking, a CSV file can be created by recreating the bank statement data in Excel and converting it to a CSV file. Or you can use a tool like the CSV Converter (available at csvconverter.gginternational.net), which converts .csv files so they're suitable for importing into accounting programs. Basic CSV files can then be imported into Xero. (Refer to Chapter 3 for more on CSV files.)

Manually Importing Statements

If your bank doesn't offer bank feeds, or if you're waiting for your bank feed to become live, you can manually import the bank data.

If you're just waiting for your Yodlee bank feeds to become active, bear in mind that the data can be back-dated. This means, if you can wait, all the data you need may become available and you won't need to manually import the data. Make a decision based on what suits you.

To manually import bank statements, follow these steps:

1. **Download the bank statements data from your online bank account in .OFX, .QIF or .CSV format and save it to your finance directory.**

   Ensure that you select the date range that you wish to import — ask your bank for help if you're unsure about the process.

2. **Within Xero, from the home dashboard, click Accounts⇨Bank Accounts and navigate to the relevant bank account.**

   The window has two options: Get Bank Feeds or Manually Import a Statement.

3. **Click the Manually Import a Statement link, click the green Browse button and select the file to be imported.**

4. **Click the green Import button.**

   Voila! All statement lines are imported just as if they were an automatic feed. Takes a little bit longer but still works a treat.

Bank Rules

Bank rules govern the treatment of imported bank transactions. Set up correctly, they improve productivity by automatically creating the transactions that match imported bank feeds. To complement this, Xero learns transactions as you go, and starts suggesting matches without a predefined bank rules.

Bank rules do have some limitations; they can't, for example, be set up to transfer between banks accounts. Some people also have the misconception that bank rules result in automatically reconciling the transactions — quick and easy confirmation is still required for each individual line, however. Although matches for transactions are suggested, now and then a suggestion is incorrect and needs to be edited or ignored.

Setting up bank rules

The simplest way to set up bank rules is during the reconciliation process, because the bank rule template automatically fills with suggested fields. However, in this section I take you through a cleanskin bank rule, so you can grasp how they are created and how to edit them if you ever need to.

So reap the rewards of setting up correct bank rules in the initial months to improve ongoing coding and reconciliation. (See Chapter 8 for guidance on reconciliations.)

Set up bank rules on bank feeds not on imported bank statements, because the fields of the bank feeds may be slightly different.

Here's how to create a bank rule:

1. **From the home dashboard, go to the centre of the screen and click on the Manage Account button, and select the Bank Rules link from the drop-down menu.**

   The Bank Rules window opens, where existing bank rules can be viewed.

2. **Click the Create Rule button and select Spend Money Rule from the drop-down menu.**

   The Create Rule window opens. This bank rule template has a seven-part wizard to work through.

3. **Set criteria for the bank rule by working through the drop-down fields at part one of the Spend Money Rule wizard.**

   Figure 4-3 shows these fields. For example, if you were creating a bank rule for petrol expenses, you'd need to choose the option All from the drop-down options offered in the 'When money spent on the bank statement matches [All/Any] of the following conditions . . .' line. At the first field on the next line, you'd then select Any Text Field; at the second field, you'd select Contains and, in the final field, you'd enter the text PETROL (or something equally generic, to catch all petrol purchases).

   Opting for Contains rather than Equals within part one of the Spend Money Rule wizard allows the rule to be as flexible as possible, while still correctly capturing the maximum number of transactions.

   Additional criteria can be added using the Add a Condition button, if relevant.

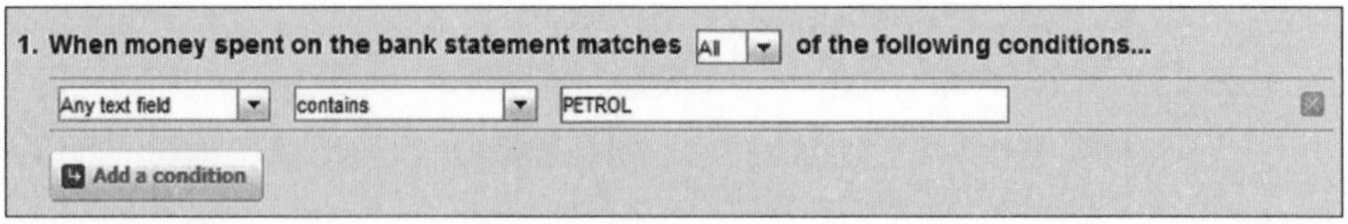

Figure 4-3: Part one of the Spend Money Rule wizard.

1. When money spent on the bank statement matches [All ▼] of the following conditions...

| Any text field ▼ | contains ▼ | PETROL | ⊠ |

➕ Add a condition

4. **In part two of the Spend Money Rule wizard, select The Contact Will Be An Existing or New Contact option, and enter a generic term in the text field.**

   Figure 4-4 shows these options selected in the Spend Money Rule wizard.

Figure 4-4: Part two of the Spend Money Rule wizard.

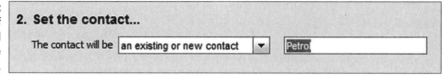

2. Set the contact...

The contact will be | an existing or new contact ▼ | Petrol

Save time by using generic terms. For example, you don't need to create a new contact for every petrol station you make a purchase at. Keep it simple and create a generic contact for regular little expenses like petrol, office stationery and milk by just using the generic term in the text field of part two of the Spend Money Rule wizard.

If a new contact is entered here, it is created as a new contact.

5. **Include a fixed value in part three of the Spend Money Rule wizard (as required).**

   In this example of a petrol expense, part three of the wizard can be skipped because the transaction has no fixed value (the amount you spend on petrol may vary each week). If the expenditure included a fixed component, the value of this component can be defined here.

6. **Allocate the transaction detail at part four of the Spend Money Rule wizard.**

   See Figure 4-5. For the petrol example, in the Description field enter Petrol Expenses; start typing in the account name in the Account field, and Petrol Expenses autofills. (Refer to Chapter 2 for more on adding Petrol Expenses to your chart of accounts.)

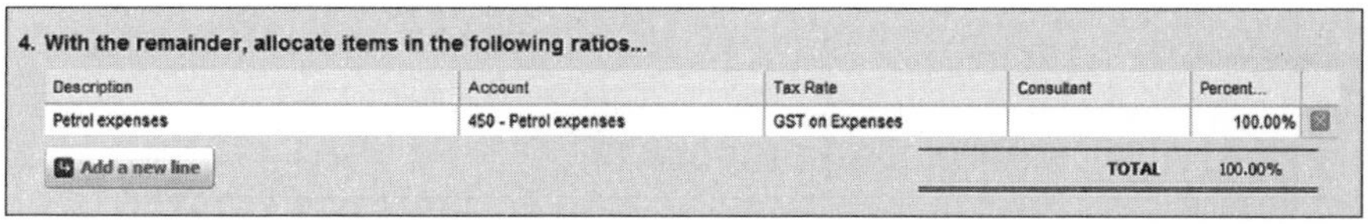

Figure 4-5: Part four of the Spend Money Rule wizard.

4. With the remainder, allocate items in the following ratios...

Description	Account	Tax Rate	Consultant	Percent...
Petrol expenses	450 - Petrol expenses	GST on Expenses		100.00%
Add a new line			TOTAL	100.00%

In the Tax Rate column, select the appropriate tax rate and allocate the required percentage. For this example, you'd leave the percentage at 100 per cent, so the entire transaction is allocated to petrol expenses.

The percentage column is useful if something is partially used for personal use and you're able to determine an average split — that split could be added here. For example, in Australia I keep a detailed log book to determine that 20 per cent of my car use is personal and 80 per cent is business. So instead of 100 per cent in the percentage column of the petrol expense line, I enter 80 per cent, add an extra transactional line and allocate the remaining 20 per cent to my personal loan account.

Tracking options can also be selected here, which allow you to departmentalise different transactions, hence enabling reporting on specific areas of the business. (Tracking is explained in further detail in Chapter 12.)

7. **Select From the Reference from the drop-down menu at part five of the Spend Money Rule wizard.**

   Figure 4-6 shows this part of the wizard.

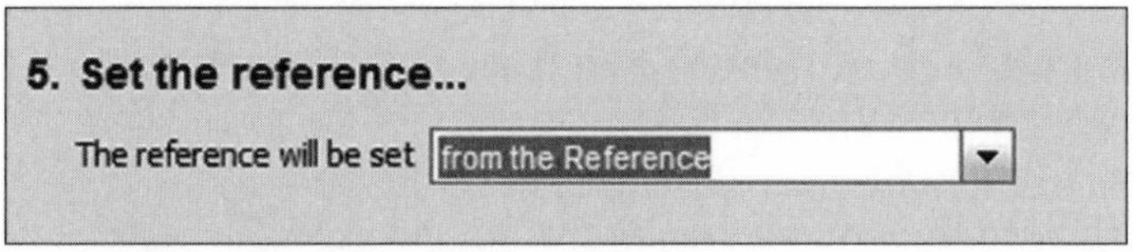

Figure 4-6: Part five of the Spend Money Rule wizard.

5. Set the reference...

The reference will be set | from the Reference | ▼ |

8. **Select All Bank Accounts from the drop-down menu at part six of the Spend Money Rule wizard.**

   Figure 4-7 shows this part of the wizard.

   Unless you have specific reasons, always opt for all bank accounts here. Otherwise, you can select specific accounts. For example, if insurance paid out of Account A is always car insurance and insurance paid out of Account B is always professional indemnity insurance, that could be specified here in the reference and on individual bank rules.

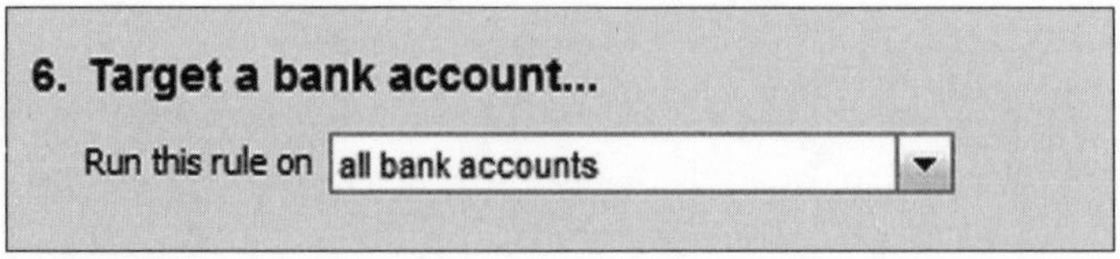

Figure 4-7: Part six of the Spend Money Rule wizard.

6. Target a bank account...

Run this rule on | all bank accounts | ▼ |

9. **Clearly name the bank rule at part seven of the Spend Money Rule wizard, including the customer/supplier and adding the typical type of deposit/expense**

   This allows you to locate it in the bank rules list later on. For example, enter 'Petrol Station — PETROL EXPENSE' in the text field.

10. **Click the green Save button.**

    If you created a bank rule to match an existing transaction, when you save the rule and return to the bank transaction window, an OK button should be between the two matching transactions. If not, the criteria of the bank rules may not entirely capture the transaction. Have you included payee name? Have you been too specific, thus deselecting the transaction? Review the template and edit the options selected.

You can also use this process to set up Receive Money rules. You just select Receive Money Rule at Step 2 in the preceding list, and then the process mirrors that of a Spend Money Rule.

You can also set up bank rules during the reconciliation process, because the fields on the Bank Rule template automatically fill with suggestions, and you can then edit and save these suggestions, rather than create the rule from scratch as I've shown here.

Managing bank rules

To access a list of active bank rules, go to the reconciliation screen, click on Manage Accounts button, and click on Bank Rules. Bank Rules are applied according to the order in which they sit on this list.

To edit a bank rule, click on the link in the bank rule name and the Edit Rule window opens. Edit accordingly and save. To change the order shown, click, drag and drop the bank rule.

To delete a bank rule, click in the checkbox and select the red delete button.

Take care not to create duplicate bank rules. View Xero in two browsers, or even on two monitors, and have the bank rules screen open as you process bank reconciliations.

Using File Storage and the Xero Inbox

All Xero solutions come with file storage of 1 GB and up. (These are soft limits and, because online storage is cheap, I expect these limits will increase over time.) This storage offered by Xero means you can upload practically all types of documents to Xero and associate them directly with the relevant financial information in your Xero file. Within the File Storage area you can also create new folders, so you've the choice of attaching information to transactions or filing it away.

Here are some examples of how you can use Xero's online storage feature:

- ✔ Attach a car lease document to the Contact who you have the lease with.
- ✔ Attach a telephone bill to the actual telephone expense.
- ✔ Attach calculations on a spreadsheet to a Manual Journal.
- ✔ Avoid collating and submitting supporting documentation to the accountant at the end of the year, because they're already attached to the transactions. (See Chapter 6 for more on attaching a document to an invoice.)

I've even heard of one cheeky accountant who uses Xero to store the final back-up file from an old accounting solution. Imagine that!

The quickest way to upload documents to Xero is by utilising the Drag and Drop method, and the following steps show you how. In the example used in these steps, I show you how to attach an electricity bill PDF to a Xero bill recording the electricity expense.

Here's how to upload a file to Xero:

1. **Open your Xero Purchases dashboard and the file directory where your documents are stored and arrange them side by side on your screen.**

   Have the file directory area on one side of your computer screen and the Xero Purchases dashboard on the other side.

2. **Locate the required PDF in the file directory.**

   In this example, you would locate the PDF file for the electricity bill.

3. **Locate the required transaction in the Xero Purchases dashboard.**

   Go to Accounts⇨Purchases⇨See all and search for the relevant transaction. In this example, you would locate the electricity bill transaction.

4. Click on the required transaction in Xero to open it.

In this example, you would click on the electricity bill. See Chapter 7 for further guidance on locating purchases.

5. Left click on the required file located in your file directory and drag it across to the open electricity bill in Xero.

In this example, the required file would be the PDF of the electricity bill.

A grey '+Upload Files' window opens. Release your mouse, and the PDF attaches itself to the bill in Xero.

You can also email documents directly to the Xero Files area. Here's how:

1. Click on the folders icon at the top right of the screen to locate your unique Xero email address.

This opens up the Files area, and on the right you can see email address. Every Xero file has an email address associated with it — likely something long and quite complicated. This address can be used to email and upload documents directly into the Xero Files directory.

2. Save your Xero email address to your email management solutions contacts area, with the name 'Xero Inbox'.

3. Attach a document to an email and send the email to your unique 'Xero Inbox' email address.

Within moments the attached document arrives in the Files area Inbox (see Figure 4-8). From here, it can be attached to a new transaction. You can also attach the document by accessing the Files area from within a transaction.

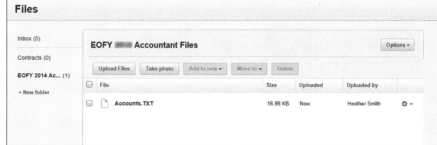

Figure 4-8: Files storage area.

Giving documents you're uploading to Xero recognisable names helps when you retrieve and file them, especially if you're completing your filing a little while after you originally sent the file.

The Files area can be accessed by all users with Invoice Only access and above, so don't leave confidential information here. A user can only access files attached to a transaction if they have permission to access that transaction.

Xero doesn't have an inbuilt feature for downloading several attachments at once. Quick Win Developments (www.quickwindevelopment.com) offer an Excel Integration Tool as a Xero add-on that allows you to download several attachments in one go. Another option is to upload financial documents to Receipt Bank (www.receipt-bank.com), which can then extract the required data and push a summary of this data, along with the document, directly into the selected transaction type in Xero — saving you coding hours.

Part II
Daily Activities

Five Ways to Maximise Your Time while Using Xero

✔ **Checklists:** Develop checklists of activities that need to be undertaken in Xero. Identify what needs to be done and when, define schedules and delegate responsibilities.

✔ **Training:** Provide staff members with training to optimise their time using Xero. Instructing staff on standard procedures like uploading bills or adding contact details can improve the workflow procedure for the business.

✔ **Invoice promptly:** Review and send out online sales invoices on a timely basis. This minimises time wasted trying to remember all the details that should go on the invoice, and should help with cash flow.

✔ **Go mobile:** Install the mobile version of Xero on your iPhone or android device, and actively use it to reconcile, issue invoices and contact business associates, while on the go.

✔ **Focus:** While online, it's tempting to let yourself get distracted (and start searching for dinner recipes, perhaps) while reconciling! Turn off email notification, shut down social media sites, utilise time-sensitive site blocking tools, and stay focused on working through the required tasks in Xero.

Get your staff involved in the collaborative aspects of Xero! Check out a free online article about introducing your staff to Xero at www.dummies.com/extras/xero.

In this part ...

- ✔ Figure out how easy it is to set up and use contact information for customers, suppliers or employees.

- ✔ Turbo boost your cash flow through creating, approving and sending invoices, and actively following up on outstanding debts. Also get the lowdown on how to streamline invoicing through using recurring invoices and bills to improve productivity.

- ✔ Get familiar with the ins and outs of billing electronically. Unfortunately, you have bills to pay — but at least I show you how to easily enter, approve and pay them, as well as how to electronically process payments.

- ✔ Learn to reconcile! Once you get your head around reconciling you will love to do it first thing in the morning (I promise!). Done correctly, reconciling accounts ensures your financial records are accurate and up to date, which means you're producing useful information for making key business decisions.

- ✔ Discover how to use Spend Money and Receive Money, including processing direct payments, prepayments and overpayments.

Chapter 5

Managing Your Contacts

*W*hat would your business be without contacts? Customers to buy from your business, suppliers to sell to your business, and employees to work within your business. Details of contacts can be set up in Xero and linked to all transactions. Capturing comprehensive information about contacts enhances your understanding of them and can improve relationships. For example, knowing which suppliers tend to discount their products towards the end of the financial year, or offer discounts or free products if you buy in bulk, improves your bottom line. End result? Boosting your business!

In this chapter, I cover adding and managing all possible contacts for your business — customers, suppliers and employees. I also show you how you can use Xero's Smart List functionality to generate targeted email lists from your existing customer base.

Note: If converting to Xero from another accounting program, you can import your existing contact list into Xero. Refer to Chapter 3 for more information.

Setting Up Customers

Businesses rely on customers in some shape or form to inject income into the business. Customers may be people, other businesses, government bodies or other entities.

To create a new customer contact in Xero, follow these steps:

1. **Click Contacts on the home dashboard menu and select Customers from the drop-down list.**

   The Contacts dashboard opens at the Customers tab.

2. **Click the blue Add Contact button.**

   The Add Contact window opens. (This is a large window with multiple sections.)

3. **Add the relevant details in the Contact field.**

   This text field and the Contact Person field are shown in Figure 5-1. Enter the business name or, if a sole proprietor, enter the first and last names.

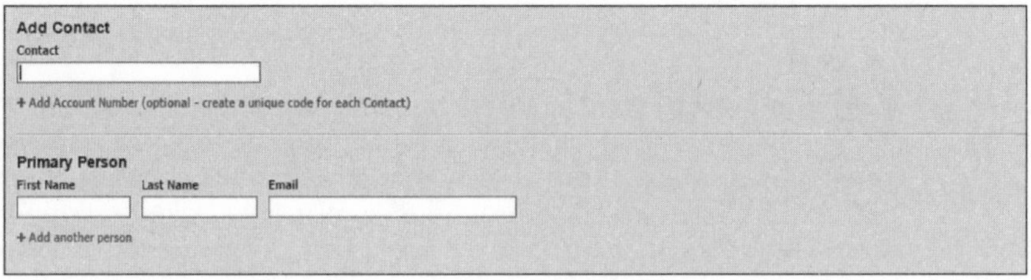

Figure 5-1:
The Add
Contact and
Contact
Person
section of
the Add
Contact
window.

> **Add Contact**
> Contact
> [   ]
> + Add Account Number (optional – create a unique code for each Contact)
>
> **Primary Person**
> First Name   Last Name   Email
> [   ]   [   ]   [   ]
> + Add another person

4. **Add details of the key Primary Person for this customer.**

   Enter the first and last name of the person you deal with most often at the business, and the direct email address. *Note:* If the business is a sole proprietor, this information may be a repeat of what you entered for Step 3.

5. **Click the + Add Another Person hyperlink to add details of additional people associated with the contact.**

   Up to five additional people can be added to the contact.

   To the right of the added person's email address is a checkbox; check this box if you want them included in emails sent from Xero.

6. **Enter the relevant details in the Contact Details text fields.**

   These text fields are shown in Figure 5-2. Type in the contact information as required, remembering to capitalise the Town/City text.

If the address is the same as the postal address, click the Same as Postal Address link and the fields autofill.

The first field for Australian and New Zealand users is Find Address. Start entering the actual business address — for example, 299 Junction Road — and Xero's in-built tool suggests possible complete addresses. Select from the choices offered and the rest of the fields autofill!

Enter the contact details of the person who approves invoices in the Attention field. This may be a repeat of the contact person information from Step 3. Also, the Direct Dial field is meant to refer to the phone on the desk in an office situation but you can use it for any extra contact information you have. Better to have more ways to contact customers who may become elusive when payment is due!

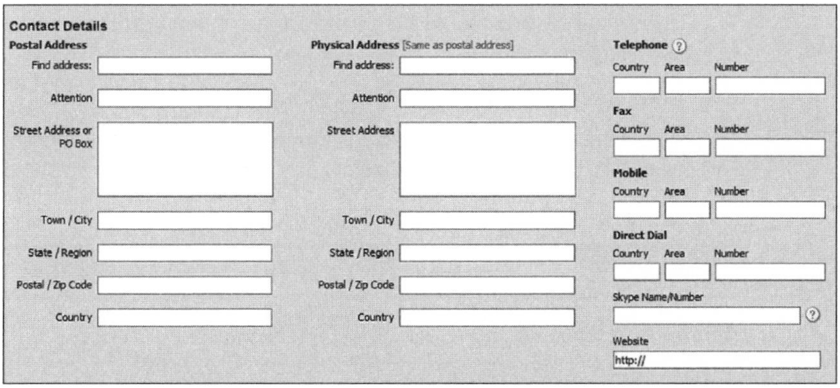

Figure 5-2:
The Contact
Details
section of
the Add
Contact
window.

7. **Enter the contact's default account settings for Sales and Purchases in the Financial Details block (if required).**

You have the option of associating a single default general ledger Sales and Purchases account and Tracking category to every contact. For example, if you sold training services to a school and on all new invoices you wanted the Account field for this sales line to populate as 'Training Services Sales', you'd use this feature.

To allocate a default Sales account, go to the drop-down menu below For Sales Default Account (see Figure 5-3). Continuing on with the preceding example, you'd select Training Services Sales. Likewise, to allocate a default Purchases account, go to the drop-down menu below For Purchases Default Account, and select the required account.

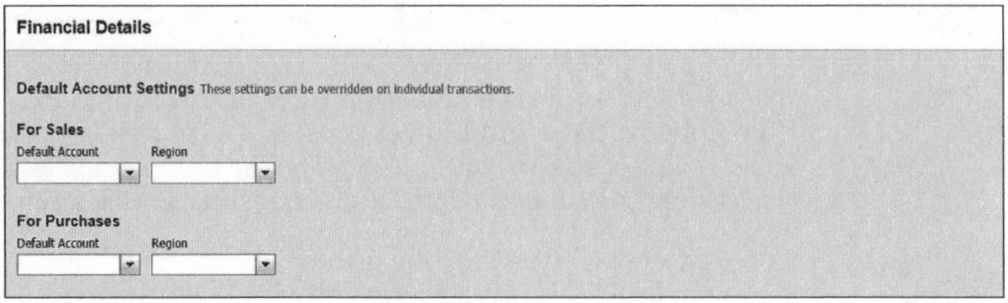

Figure 5-3:
The
Financial
Details
block of the
Add Contact
window.

Financial Details

Default Account Settings These settings can be overridden on individual transactions.

For Sales

Default Account | Region

For Purchases

Default Account | Region

Beside the Default Account field, you can also select a Tracking category to associate with the Contact against both income and expenditure. See Chapter 12 to learn more about Tracking Categories.

The default Account and Tracking settings can be overridden on individual transactions. Refer to Chapter 2 for adding new general ledger accounts to Xero.

8. **Enter the contact's default tax details in the next block.**

   The fields available will depend on the country your Xero file is associated with (see Table 5-1).

Table 5-1	Xero Contact Tax Details by Region			
Australia	*New Zealand*	*United Kingdom*	*United States*	*Global*
ABN	GST Number	VAT Number	Tax ID Number	Tax ID Number
Sales GST	Sales GST	Sales VAT	Sales Tax	Sales Tax
Purchases GST	Purchases GST	Purchases VAT	Purchases Tax	Purchases Tax

9. **Enter the contact's default discount details as a percentage in the next block. (Note that this step is optional.)**

   This default discount rate can be overridden on individual transactions.

10. **If you have Xero Premium edition, select the default currency, if different from the file's base currency, from the drop-down menu.**

11. **Enter the contact's bank details in the Batch Payments block.**

    Batch payments are typically made to a supplier (see Chapter 7 for more). The fields available will depend on the country your Xero file is associated with (see Table 5-2).

Table 5-2		Xero Bank Fields by Region		
Australia	*New Zealand*	*United Kingdom*	*United States*	*Global*
Bank Account Number	Bank Account Number	Bank Account Number	Bank Account Number	Bank Account Number
Bank Account Name	Bank Account Name	Bank Account Name	Bank Account Name	Bank Account Name
Details	Particulars Code Reference	Details	Details	Details

You may have two separate bank reference numbers associated with your bank details. For example, if your bank account is in Australia, you have a six-digit BSB number as well as a bank account number. In this case, all the numbers are added to the Bank Account Number field. Enter all the numbers, with no spaces, and remember to include zeros at the start of the number if relevant.

In the Reference/Details field of the batch payments section enter '<Your business name>'. The reference appears on the contact's bank statement and may help them identify the transaction.

12. **Select the default invoice branding for the contact from the Invoice Branding drop-down menu.**

    If you can't see this option, you currently only have a single invoice associated with Xero. You can make changes to Xero's default invoice branding and customise branding themes. Chapter 6 tells you more.

13. **Enter your bill due date requirements in the Bills Default Due Date (Optional) field.**

    You have a number of options here. For example, if you want bills paid within seven days (an option that works for most businesses), you can do this by entering '7' in the first field and selecting Day(s) after the Bill Date from the drop-down menu. The due date will automatically be seven days after the bill date. However, if you've agreed on specific terms with a contact, enter those terms here.

14. **Enter your sales invoice due date requirements at the Sales Invoice Default Due Date (Optional) field.**

    As with the preceding step, you have a number of options here. Entering '7' in the first field and selecting Day(s) After the Invoice Date from the drop-down menu means the due date will automatically be created at seven days after the invoice date.

Contacts can be both suppliers and customers! As you work through the steps of creating a new contact, you may be wondering why I refer to the customer as a 'contact' — why do I keep using the word *contact*? Great question. Thanks for asking. Once saved, the newly created contact is in limbo. Within Xero, it is merely defined as a

Making use of History & Notes

Take a look at the History & Notes section at the bottom of the contacts window. You can see two buttons: Show History (# entries) and Add Note. Whenever you (or someone else) change any details for a contact, Xero automatically generates History Notes, which detail the changes, when they were made and who made them, as well as other details. When you click Show History, any History Notes for the contact pop up. The Add Notes option is useful for adding your own notes — you can use it to record details of conversations, coffee preferences, birthday information, anything! When a period is locked, History & Notes is still accessible.

To view activity associated with History & Notes, users with Adviser status can go to the Adviser tab, and select History & Notes Activity. The History & Notes Activity dashboard opens (see the following figure) and at the top are three drop-down search options: Period, Items and User. If you wanted to know who in the last month had added Sales Invoices, from the Period drop-down menu select 'Last Month', from the Items drop-down menu select 'Sales Invoice' and click the blue Update button to filter the results that match the search criteria. The matching data is listed under column headings Date, Item, Action, User and Notes. You can click in via the Item column to view individual underlying transactions.

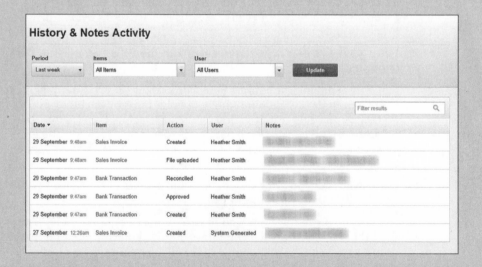

Contact. It isn't until a sales invoice is created that the contact is listed as a *Customer*. But wait there's more! A purchase invoice can be raised against the very same Contact and it is also now listed as a *Supplier*. A single contact can be both a customer and a supplier.

15. **Enter the contact's Xero Network Key in the key field.**

   If contacts also use Xero, they can supply a *Xero Network Key*, a long alpha-numeric number. To help clients locate their Xero Network Key in their Xero file, ask them to go to the home dashboard, and click on Settings⇨General Settings⇨Xero to Xero. Then click on the Send Xero Network Invite button and email the invite to you! More information about how the Xero Network Key enables Xero to Xero communication is provided in Chapter 6.

16. **Save the new Contact by clicking the green Save button.**

   A sparsely populated Individual Contact's dashboard appears. Interactive details of Receivable Invoices, Payable Invoices and a graphical representation of activity over the past 12 months can be viewed on the this dashboard (shown in Figure 5-4) once additional transactions have occurred. From here, you can click the + New button to create sales invoices, repeating sales invoices, bills or repeating bills. Click on Send Statement to send a statement from this area.

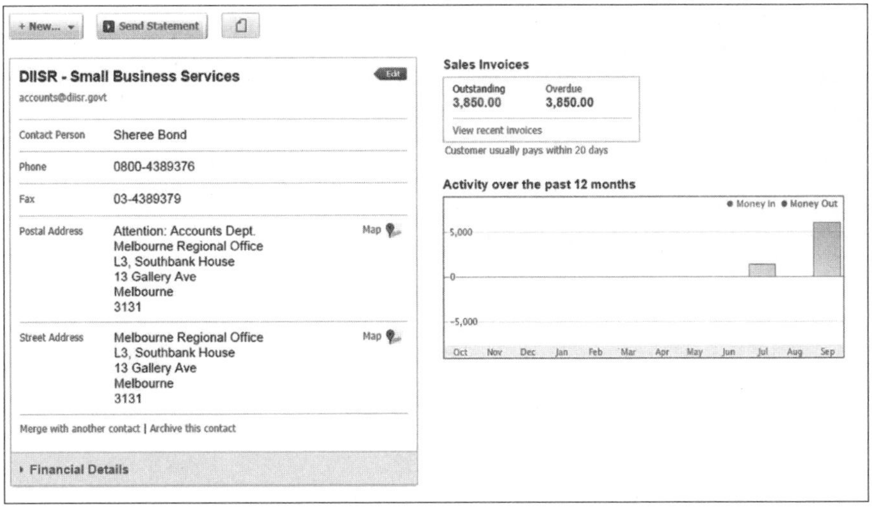

Figure 5-4:
The
Individual
Contact
dashboard.

Taking advantage of free or cheap calls

When entering contacts into Xero, a field on the Contact Details section allows you to include the contact's Skype name and number. Skype is a popular software application that provides free or cheap voice over internet calls (VOIP). Entering the Skype name and number for your contacts means these contacts can be called using Skype via Xero.

To enable this feature, install the free Skype software (see www.skype.com for details), activate Skype, set up a Skype account, and click on the blue Skype logo on the Contact Details window to call the contact. Just remember the Skype logo (and the functionality of this feature) isn't viewable while contacts are in edit mode.

Setting Up Suppliers

To add suppliers into Xero simply create a new supplier contact card by following the steps outlined in the preceding section. Too easy?! Seriously, suppliers and customers are set up using the same steps!

Tweaking Your Contacts after Set-Up

After you've added all your customers and suppliers into Xero (refer to preceding sections), you may still need to fine-tune your set-up, or streamline how you find and manage your contacts. The following sections show you how.

Finding your contacts

Yikes! You may have so many contacts that finding a specific contact is difficult. Locate an individual contact by clicking Contacts on the home dashboard menu and selecting All Contacts from the drop-down menu. This brings up the Contacts dashboard (see Figure 5-5).

From here, you can locate the contact by one of three options:

✔ Click on the contact link listed on the dashboard.

✔ Click on the tab of the first character of the contact to access a customised list, and then click on the contact link.

✔ Enter any part of the contact name, email address or contact account number in the search field on the right and click the blue Search button. From the suggestions click on the contact link.

Figure 5-5:
The
Contacts
dashboard.

Whichever method you use, the individual contact's dashboard appears.

Managing your contacts

Contacts never stay still for long! Their details are always changing and need to be updated. Edit contact details by following these steps:

1. **Click Contacts on the home dashboard menu and select All Contacts from the drop-down menu.**

   The Contacts dashboard appears (refer to Figure 5-5).

2. **Find and click on the contact you need to edit.**

   Refer to the preceding section for options on how to do this.

3. **Click on the small blue Edit button on the individual contact's dashboard.**

   The contact details appear in editable format.

4. **Make the required changes and then click the green Save button.**

Grouping your contacts

Contact groups can be created for customers and suppliers (but not employees; see the section 'Setting Up Employees', later in this chapter). You can create quite a number of groupings, and contacts can be assigned to more than one group. Groups may be formed around different payment terms, franchisees, new clients, overseas contacts — anything that suits your business requirements.

To create a new Contact Group from the home dashboard, select All Contacts from the drop-down menu. On the Contacts dashboard, click the New Group button, and then enter the group's name. Click OK to save the new group.

To add contacts to a group, simply tick the check box beside the contacts' listing, click the blue Add to Group button, and select an existing group or create a new group.

To remove contacts from an existing group, from the Contacts dashboard, click on the Group tab, tick the check box beside the contacts listing, and click the blue Remove from Group button.

Merging your contacts

Ooops! You've just realised two contacts in Xero are actually the same person or business. Sometimes a number of Contacts are created in error. For example, transactions are processed against different contacts and then you realise they should all be mapped against a single primary contact. Not to worry! To merge contacts and transactions into a single primary contact, follow these steps:

1. **Click Contacts on the home dashboard menu and select All Contacts from the drop-down menu.**

   The Contacts dashboard appears (refer to Figure 5-5).

2. **Find the contacts that need to be merged.**

   Refer to the section 'Finding your contacts', earlier in this chapter, for options on how to do this.

3. **Check the box to the left of the secondary contacts that are to be merged into the primary contact.**

   Don't select the primary contact. Leave that for the following steps.

4. **Click the blue Merge button.**

   The Merge Contacts window appears.

5. **Select the primary contact that the other contacts will be merged into by entering the contact into the Find Contact field.**

6. **Confirm the merger and click the green Save button.**

   You can't go back once you click Save, so make sure you want to do this! The merged contacts are archived, and the transactions are merged into the single contact.

If you've set the period or end-of-year lock dates (refer to Chapter 1), after the contact merges the original transaction prior to the lock date is still tagged to the original contact. However, when you drill down on the Contact name, you link directly to the merged contact details.

Unpicking accidentally merged contacts

Even though you can't unmerge your contacts (refer to preceding section), if you do realise you've merged in error, you can attempt to repair the damage and reallocate key information.

Start by creating the new Contacts you need to allocate the transactional information to (refer to the earlier section, 'Setting Up Customers'). Then refer to historical records, report back-ups or financial information to identify what transactions relate to which Contact. Next, edit the transaction to correct the tagged Contact (see Chapter 6 for editing Sales transactions and Chapter 7 for editing Purchases transactions). If you've a lot of transactions to work through, this will be a time-consuming process, so consider how far back historically you really need to go.

Archiving your outdated contacts

Contacts can't be deleted, but they can be archived — which means they can be restored if needed. To archive a contact follow these steps:

1. **Click Contacts on the home dashboard menu and select All Contacts from the drop-down menu.**

   The Contacts dashboard appears (refer to Figure 5-5).

2. **Find the contact you want to archive.**

   Refer to the section 'Finding your contacts', earlier in this chapter, for options on how to do this.

3. **Check the box to the left of the contact and click the grey Archive button.**

   The Archive Contacts window appears.

4. **To confirm the contact should be archived, click the green Yes button.**

Egads! You made a mistake and archived a current contact. Not to worry — archived details can be restored. From the Contacts dashboard, click on the Archived tab, tick the check box beside the contact's listing and click the Restore button.

Setting Up Employees

Xero has limited payroll functionality (visit www.dummies.com/go/ xerofd2e for more information). Users who want a robust payroll may want to look at an add-on solution (see Chapter 16 for more on this). This section works through the process of setting up a new employee.

This section is only relevant for New Zealand, UK and global users (outside of the United States and Australia). The Australian and US version of Xero has a comprehensive integrated payroll solution and although if you have this version you can still set up employees using the following instructions, don't! Setting employees up within the payroll area is more efficient, which isn't covered in this book. Ask your Xero advisory team for more information and check out www.dummies.com/go/xerofd2e for online resources that focus on this area.

To create a new employee, follow these steps:

1. **Click Contacts on the home dashboard menu and select Employees from the drop-down menu.**

2. **Click the blue Add Employee button.**

   The Add Employee window appears.

   Only users with Payroll Admin access can view the Employee window (refer to Chapter 4 for how to set up access levels).

3. **Add the employee's details in the first block.**

   Enter the employee's first and last name, and a personal email address. Avoid entering employees' work email addresses, in case they leave and you still need to communicate with them.

4. **Add Employee Contact Details.**

   Similar information is required as when adding customers or suppliers (refer to the section 'Setting Up Customers', earlier in this chapter, for more).

5. **Add the employee's tax details in the Employee's Details block.**

   The tax fields you're required to fill out will depend on the country your Xero file is associated with (see Table 5-3).

Table 5-3	Xero Employee Tax Fields by Region	
New Zealand	*United Kingdom*	*Global*
IRD Number	National Insurance Number	Employee Tax Number

6. **Add the employee's wage rate details in the Ordinary Rate field.**

   The rate of pay can be overwritten during a pay run.

7. **Add employee payment details in the Payment Details block.**

   In the Reference/Details field, enter '<Your business name> WAGES'. The reference appears on the employee's bank statements if payments are

Connecting with contacts while you're cruising

While crossing the Sydney Harbor on a ferry (or cruising all sorts of places), you can touch base with your contacts using Xero Touch on your mobile device! You just need to download and install the Xero app for your iPhone, iPad or smart phone, and then tap on the Xero icon to open the app. You're asked to enter your email address and password, and then you're prompted to create a four-digit passcode, which saves your details and makes future log-ins quick and easy — when you return again to Xero Touch, you just need to tap and enter the passcode to access Xero. Furthermore, iPhones with fingerprint sensors also allow you to log into Xero Touch using Touch ID.

The Xero Touch dashboard displays a summary of Accounts, Invoices, and Expenses, with four icons along the base: Dashboard, Invoices, Expenses and Contacts.

All active bank, credit card and PayPal accounts are listed in the Accounts section. Additional information includes current balance, number of unreconciled transactions and last date the bank feed updated. Click through on an individual account to access the reconciliation area. Here you have similar features available for reconciling as you do in the desktop version of Xero (see Chapter 8 for guidance on reconciling).

The Invoices section lists a summary of the Draft, Overdue and Unpaid invoices, and allows you to add additional invoices. Click through the detail of each individual invoice (see Chapter 6 for guidance on sales invoices).

The third section on the Dashboard is entitled Expenses and lists outstanding expense claims, and includes the option of adding expense claims. (See Chapter 7 for guidance in entering Expense Claims.) *Note*: Xero Touch does not upload expense information into the Purchases or Spend Money transactions, only Expense Claims.

Tap the Contacts icon and a search screen appears. Enter the name of a contact and the screen autosuggests existing contacts. You can then click the desired contact and drill through to the contact information. You can't edit the contact details, but you can do a few neat things: Tap a phone number to call contacts, tap an email address to email them, or click the street address and you're taken to a Google map from your device. How geekilicious is that?!

Additional notes can also be added to the contact's details — just click the blue History & Notes link at the bottom of the screen, click the blue Add a New Note link, enter notes in the blank screen, and then click the blue Add button. The screen returns with the new note added. Click the Contacts button at the top of the screen and then the Dashboard icon at the bottom of the screen to return to the dashboard.

made via Xero batch payment facilities (see Chapter 7 for more on batch payments).

8. **Click the green Save button.**

   Employee records can't be merged or added to contact groups; however, they can be edited and archived.

New employees can also be created during a Pay Run. (Jump online and visit www.dummies.com/go/xerofd2e for more information.)

You can import contact details from other accounting packages. Refer to Chapter 3 for more information.

Utilising Smart Lists CRM Functionality

Smart Lists is an advanced search tool for your existing customer base that can help you create targeted customer profiling based on each customer's history with your business. The tool, available on Xero's home dashboard under Contact, allows you to run a conditional search that generates a specific selection of contact details — which, for example, can then be used in an email marketing campaign. It's like a small in-built customer relationship management (CRM) system.

Say a jeweller wanted to identify clients who had previously purchased a wedding ring from the business so she could send these customers an annual email. The jeweller could use Smart Lists to identify these customers, using the search term 'wedding ring'. From the generated results, they'd also know the year of the wedding anniversary — meaning they could suggest the appropriate traditional and modern gift options for the specific anniversary the couple were celebrating. Statistically, targeted and insightful emails to an existing client base are more likely to generate additional sales.

Here's how to create your own Smart List:

1. **From the home dashboard, select Contacts⇨Smart List.**

   On the left are some example Saved Searches. Click on them to see the results for your own business.

2. **Click on the New Smart List button on the top left.**

   On the right of this button, conditions for the new list can be added.

3. **From the drop-down menu beside Find Customers Matching All/Any of the Following Conditions, select All.**

4. **Click the +Add a Condition hyperlink and from the drop-down options select 'Invoice'.**

   Once 'Invoice' is selected, the following fields appear: Invoice, Any, More Than, Dollar Value, Ever.

   If you have the multi-currency option, you also have the option to select currency type, beside Dollar Value. Work your way through the drop-down criteria and choose options that are of interest to you.

5. **Click the blue Run Search button.**

   The result of the search appears in the table below.

6. **Tick the box beside the hyperlink Select All [#] Customers.**

   Customers identified through a Smart List search can be identified for debt collection, contacted via a targeted marketing campaign and sorted into a contact group.

Once you have the results from a Smart List search, you can use this list of contacts to create a new Contact Group within Xero, or add it to an existing Contact Group. Here's how:

1. **At the Smart List search results page, select the results and click the Add to Contact Group button.**

   The Add to Contact Group window opens.

2. **Choose whether you want to add the list of contacts to an existing group or create a new Contact Group.**

   To add the list to an existing group, tick the box next to this group. (Refer to the section 'Grouping your contacts' for more on Contact Groups.) To use the list to create a new group, click on the +Add to a New Group option.

To export Smart List search results as a CSV file, click the Export button at the top of the search results page. From the drop-down menu select CSV. The CSV file transfers to your computer and you can locate it in your Downloads file.

Constant Contact (www.constantcontact.com) is an online marketing tool with options that include email marketing. You can export your Smart List search results to Constant Contact to take advantage of these options when marketing to your existing contacts. To export search results to Constant Contact you need a Constant Contact account. Once you have that sorted, click the Export button on the Smart List search results page and from the drop-down menu select Constant Contact. ***Note:*** Email information needs to be complete for this to work.

Chapter 6

Managing Your Sales

· ·

· ·

I had a customer who sold medical equipment and who was most pleased with himself. His small business had generated significant sales. Closer inspection, however, revealed a majority of the sales were to a single customer and much of the sales income was still outstanding. This raised concerns for me, and I suggested that, rather than continue selling to the customer, he should put his energies into actively chasing the money for the outstanding sales. The objective of a sale should always be having cold hard cash deposited in your business bank account. Other aspects of sales are nice (such as goods or services going out from your business), but your focus should be moving customers to opening their wallet and giving your business cash.

In this chapter, I take you through Xero's invoice lifecycle — going from the draft invoice to awaiting approval, approved, sent to the client, awaiting payment and overdue. I cover all the ways Xero makes invoicing your customers — and getting them to actually pay up — easier, including making use of the Sales dashboard, issuing invoices, recording payments and creating statements. I offer guidance on cash transaction and provide help on more advanced functions such as invoice branding and invoicing groups. I also provide help on using Xero's email templates to chase overdue invoices.

Cash accounting is when income and expenditure are recognised when cash is received or paid. *Accrual accounting* is where income and expenditure are recognised when the actual transaction occurs — that is, the date of the transaction, not when the cash is received or paid. Many micro and small business owners have company taxes prepared on an accruals basis but prefer to look at review reports on a cash basis. Perhaps looking at reports on a cash basis gives them a more realistic view of what is happening in their business. If you're operating a simple cash business such as a shop, you don't need to issue invoices through Xero for each individual invoice, but you do need to record the takings through Xero so they match up with your bank statements. See the section 'Recording income for a simple cash business', later in this chapter, for more.

Navigating the Sales Dashboard

The Sales dashboard is a reflection of your business, and understanding what it tells you about sales and customers is critical to the ongoing success of your business. Key areas on the Sales dashboard allow you to proactively invoice, chase incoming money, recognise significant debtors and stay mindful of debtor exposure, and all should be monitored regularly. When you have strategic planning sessions, you can use the knowledge gained from your Sales dashboard to analyse key aspects of your business.

Spend time understanding the tools available on the Sales dashboard to help you understand and improve cash flowing into the business. Ask yourself questions about your business and the sales being tracked. Do you service a few big elephants (and so are dependent on their continued support), or lots of little fish? Are all your eggs in one basket? Using information from your Sales dashboard, you may decide you need to expand or contract your customer base.

Access the Sales dashboard from the home dashboard by clicking Accounts⇨Sales. The Sales dashboard (see Figure 6-1) is split into three blocks: Buttons, menu bar and charts.

Figure 6-1: The Xero Sales dashboard.

The first block of the Sales dashboard contains four buttons: New, Send Statements, Import and Search. The New button gives you a few invoicing options: Click through to create a New Invoice, Repeating Invoice, Credit Note, Invoice to Contact Group (an option if you have existing Contact Groups; refer to Chapter 5) and Add a contact group. The Send Statements button allows you to drill down to the Statements window. The Import button takes you to the import process (covered in Chapter 3). Clicking on the Search button opens the search pane. Here you can enter number, reference, contact name, amount, date criteria, and the unsent option to search for invoices.

The second block of the Sales dashboard contains a combination of seven small and large tabs: Paid, Repeating, See All, Draft, Awaiting Approval, Awaiting Payment and Overdue.

The balances of key stages of the invoice lifecycle — draft, awaiting approval, awaiting payment and overdue — are highlighted. (Remember that your cash flow is improved the more quickly your invoices move through these stages.)

Here's how you can explore the Sales dashboard:

- View all paid invoice information by drilling down through the Paid tab. Paid invoices can be printed or emailed from this area.

- Sort columns by clicking on the row headers. Select an invoice by checking a single box or multiple boxes to the left of the invoice(s).

- View the invoice detail by clicking on the relevant invoice row. Return to the Sales dashboard by clicking on the Sales link in the top left corner. (The Sales link is teeny-tiny, but will be there!)

- View all repeating invoice information by drilling down through the Repeating tab. Repeating invoices can be edited or deleted from this area.

- View all summarised invoice information by drilling down through the See All tab.

- View a summary of draft invoices by drilling down through the Draft tab. A *draft* invoice is where the information has been saved, but no journal entries have been created against it. Draft invoices can be submitted for approval, approved, deleted, printed or emailed from this area.

- View a summary of invoices awaiting approval by drilling down through the Awaiting Approval tab. Invoices awaiting approval can be approved, deleted, printed or emailed from this area.

✔ View a summary of invoices awaiting payment by drilling down through the Awaiting Payment tab. Invoices awaiting approval can be approved, deleted, printed or emailed from this area. Red due date text indicates invoice collection has passed its due date. Additional notes can be attached to the invoice in the Expected Date column.

✔ View a summary of overdue invoices awaiting payment by drilling down through the Overdue tab. A search block appears above the list of overdue invoices to assist in finding invoices. Enter known criteria about the invoice and click the blue Search button to filter your invoices.

The third block of the Sales dashboard contains two areas: Money Coming In and Customers Owing the Most. The latter option can be shown as a list or pie chart.

To export all Sales Invoices in CSV format, drill down through Accounts⇨Sales⇨See all and click the Export button. The CSV file downloads to your Downloads file area.

Money Coming In

The Money Coming In bar chart represents current net monthly outstanding invoices determined by the due date. Each colour block within the month represents the main outstanding customer.

Here's how to explore the Money Coming In bar chart:

1. **Hover over the colour blocks to view a summary of outstanding invoices, including contact name and phone details.**

2. **Click to drill down to invoice details.**

   The chart highlights long-term outstanding debtors and, hopefully, encourages you to chase payments!

Customers Owing the Most — list

The Customers Owing the Most list provides a summary of the top five outstanding and overdue amounts owed by customers. You can click on any row to drill down to an individual customer statement, or click on the All link to drill down to the Statement window listing all customer statements.

Customers Owing the Most — pie chart

The Customers Owing the Most (or *debtor exposure*) pie chart reflects the net amount owed by your top five outstanding customers in relation to all monies owed. Each piece of the pie represents a different customer. Hover over the pie pieces to view a summary of the outstanding invoices, including contact name and phone details, and highlight the debtor exposure in the list on the right.

The charts on Xero's Sales dashboard let you know who owes your business money, but you still need to proactively communicate with customers to remind them of any outstanding payments. Send statements, emails or text messages, or make phone calls — the squeaky wheel gets the oil!

Mastering Basic Invoice Functions

Invoicing is extremely important but it can drain a considerable amount of administrative time, so try to keep this function as simple and automated as possible. Maximise money coming in to the business by ensuring detailed invoices are sent out on a timely basis directly to the person responsible for approving the payment of the invoice. Maintain comprehensive contact details and ensure you invoice the entity to pay the bill.

The following sections cover all you need to know to invoice your customers effectively, from creating new invoices to sending them out to customers, with lots of productivity tips thrown in along the way.

Creating a new sales invoice

Follow these steps to create a new invoice:

1. **From the Sales dashboard select + New Invoice.**

   The New Invoice window appears (see Figure 6-2).

   The invoice number automatically fills for a new invoice. The Invoice Prefix and Next Number generated can be customised in the Invoice Settings area — see 'Setting up the basics', later in this chapter, for more on this.

2. **Enter the contact name in the To field.**

   If the customer is already in your Xero file, start typing the first three letters of the contact name and Xero autosuggests contact names, and the associated primary contact person's first name, last name and email address. Select the relevant contact, or type in the name of a new contact. Refer to Chapter 5 for guidance on adding Contact details.

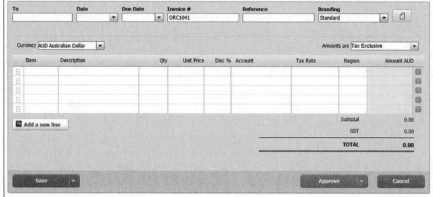

Figure 6-2:
The New
Invoice
window.

3. **Fill out the Date box.**

4. **Fill out or accept the suggestion for the invoice Due Date box.**

If you've defined a customer's payment terms within the Contacts area (refer to Chapter 5 for more), the Due Date box autofills.

Keep payment terms as tight as possible. Offering extended credit terms is like loaning cash to another business. Can you really afford to do that? Payment up-front, or payment on the day of service, is ideal; however, net 7 or 14 days may be more realistic for your industry.

5. **Fill out the optional Reference field.**

This could be a purchase order number or the name of the contact who approved the invoice. If you don't have a name, contact the organisation and check who's responsible for approving the invoice. Don't send an invoice in hoping that someone will pay it! Help the business pay you by completing this field appropriately.

6. **Click on the document symbol and attach any relevant files**

The documentation you'd like to attach could be a copy of the purchase order or something else relevant to the sale. This attachment process directly associates the file with the invoice, and the attachment can be accessed when viewing the transaction. Once the document is uploaded, click on the gear icon at the right and select 'Include with invoice' to include a link to the document within the emailed invoice. For further insights into file storage within Xero, refer to Chapter 4.

7. Select the invoice design from the drop-down Branding field options.

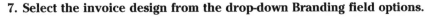

Xero offers default branding themes for invoices, but you can also customise these themes. See the section 'Designing clear invoices for a positive cash flow', later in this chapter, for more guidance.

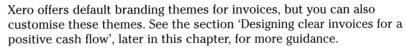

If you have Xero Premium edition, you can select the invoice currency from the drop-down Currency field options.

8. Select the consumer tax status of the invoice from the drop-down Amounts Are field options.

The three available options are as follows:

- Tax Exclusive: The transaction line amounts are exclusive of tax allocated from the tax rate column. The calculated consumer tax is added at the bottom to the invoice subtotal to sum to the total figure.

- Tax Inclusive: The transaction amounts are inclusive of tax allocated from the tax rate column, and at the bottom of the invoice the included consumer tax is extracted and detailed between the invoice subtotal and total amount.

- No Tax: If this option is selected the default Tax Rates are replaced with the consumer tax rates for No Tax and no tax is allocated to the transaction. You can't change the tax rate defined in the Tax Rate column. If you switch back to a Tax Ex/Inclusive option, the consumer tax rates don't switch back — so be careful!

9. Enter or select the inventory item from the optional Item field.

The other fields populate with the item details.

Minimise time spent on data entry by creating detailed items for regular sales. See Chapter 13 for guidance on creating items.

Due date calendar shortcuts

You can speed up data entry when creating sales invoices by using shortcut keys in the due date field. Here are some possible shortcut keys and what they do:

- +[#]m: Adds a date [#] months after invoice date

- +[#]w: Adds a date [#] weeks after invoice date

- +[#]: Adds a date [#] days after invoice date

- [#]: Adds the [#] date in current month

- *[#]: Adds the [#] date in following month

10. **Enter a comprehensive narrative in the mandatory Description field.**

    Include as much information as possible, such as dates, contacts, work completed, items supplied. If you provide something on a complimentary basis, still include it here, highlighting what great value you are!

11. **Fill out the mandatory Quantity and Unit Price fields.**

    If the sale is for a fixed-price product, enter the quantity as 1, and the full price in the unit price column.

12. **Enter any discount to be applied to the row in the optional Disc % field.**

    If the customer has a predefined discount, it autofills here (but can be overridden).

    By entering the percentage discount in the row, the discounted amount is posted to the account. If you want to see the amounts separated, don't use the discount percentage option — run the discount as a separate row instead.

13. **Enter the account name or number and select the desired account from the suggested drop-down list for the mandatory Account field.**

    After an invoice has been issued and money receipted against it, the account and tracking fields are the only ones that can still be edited.

14. **Select the desired rate from the mandatory Tax Rate field.**

Making use of the Expected Date column for invoices awaiting payment

A customer called to tell me cash flow was tight and ask if it would be okay if she paid my invoice one month after the invoice date. While I prefer to receive payment on time, I understand the reality of business and was happy the customer talked to me about this issue. I told her I could agree to a late payment. To note this within Xero, I clicked on the Awaiting Payment tab on the Sales dashboard. I then clicked on the plus symbol in the Expected Date for the relevant invoice, which brought up the customer's name and contact details. In the Notes field, I left details of our conversation and, in the Expected Date field, I typed in +M, which meant a date one month after today's date autofilled the field. Clicking Save meant the new invoice date appeared in the Expected Date column. If I need to review the notes at a later date, I can just click again on the Expected Date field.

15. **Select from options in the drop-down menus in the available Tracking fields.**

    Tracking is optional and you won't see the field if the feature is not set up. See Chapter 12 for guidance on setting up Tracking fields. The Amount field can't be edited. The subtotal, consumer tax and total automatically calculate.

    Populate the remaining rows with sales information as needed. Within the invoice, you have the ability to drag and drop the individual lines. *Note:* In Figure 6-2 the Tracking field is called 'Region'. Your Tracking field could be labelled something different.

16. **Click the Add a New Line button (as required).**

    This allows you to add additional lines to the body of the invoice.

 If you work with multiple clients, and bill them based on the time you spend with them and on their projects, using a Time Tracking tool like MinuteDock can help you streamline your invoicing processes even more. MinuteDock enables you to capture the time you spend with different clients, collate the detail and push it through to Xero, generating a comprehensive invoice. See Chapter 16 for more on add-on solutions for Xero.

Saving, approving and cancelling invoices

The life cycle of an invoice can include being created as a draft, submitted for approval, awaiting approval, approved, awaiting payment and, finally, receipting payment. Xero also allows you to skip some of these steps and jump straight to the approval stage. This section covers each of the basic stages.

Saving

Instead of saving the invoice first, you can simply Approve it — see the following section for more. When saving an invoice after it's been created (refer to the section 'Creating a new sales invoice', earlier in the chapter, for more), you have a number of options:

✔ To save the invoice and continue working on it, click the drop-down arrow beside the blue Save button, and select Save (continue editing). The invoice is saved and remains open so you can continue working on it.

✔ To save the invoice as a draft, click the drop-down arrow beside the blue Save button, and select Save as Draft. (The invoice is now listed under the Draft tab.)

✔ To save the invoice and submit for approval, click the drop-down arrow beside the blue Save button, and select Save & Submit for Approval. (The invoice is now listed under the Awaiting Approval tab.)

✔ To save the invoice and then create a new invoice, click the drop-down arrow beside the blue Save button and select Save & Add Another.

Approving

Only users with Adviser, Standard or Invoice Only with the options Sales Only or Approve & Pay access can approve an invoice. Refer to Chapter 4 for more on setting user access levels.

When approving an invoice, you have a number of options:

✔ Simply approve the invoice by clicking the green Approve button.

✔ To approve the invoice and then create a new invoice, click the drop-down arrow beside the green Approve button and select Approve & Add Another.

✔ To approve the draft or awaiting approval invoice and view the next invoice (draft or awaiting approval respectively), click the drop-down arrow beside the green Approve button and select Approve & View Next.

Once you approve an invoice, Xero files it in the Awaiting Payment area.

Cancelling, deleting or voiding

Here's how to cancel, delete or void an invoice, dependent on the status of the invoice:

✔ If you want to cancel the invoice, during the original creation stage click grey Cancel button.

✔ To delete a Draft or Awaiting Approval invoice (without payment applied), from the Dashboard click Accounts⇨Sales and then drill down on either the Draft or Awaiting Approval option, check the box beside the relevant invoice and select the button labelled Delete. At the Confirm window, click the green OK button, and the status of the invoice reverts to Deleted.

✔ To void an invoice Awaiting Payment, or Paid, first any payment made against the invoice needs to be removed (see the section 'Removing allocated payments', later in this chapter. The status of both types of invoices now reverts to Awaiting Payment, with no assigned payment allocation. Click on the invoice detail, and select the Invoice Options button, and from the drop-down menu select Void. At the Confirm window, select the green OK button and the status of the invoice reverts to Deleted.

The details of a cancelled invoice disappear entirely, while the erased details of cancelled and voided invoices can be found by searching under the grouping labelled All.

If you click the Cancel button on an invoice, no confirmation window appears, so you don't have a chance to back out. The invoice is gone forever.

Sending an invoice to a customer

I prefer to email all documents, because emailing is quicker, traceable and environmentally friendly. However, some customers refuse to receive emailed invoices, using numerous excuses — they don't have a printer, or their printer isn't connected to the computer (seriously!). So you may need to use a mix of printed and emailed invoices. This section shows you how.

Printing customer invoices

Follow these steps to print customer invoices:

1. **Go to the Sales dashboard, drill down on the Awaiting Payment tab to find the relevant invoice and check the box to the left of the document.**

   A single invoice or multiple invoices can be selected and processed at the same time.

2. **Click the blue Print button.**

   The Confirm window opens.

3. **If the invoice has not been marked sent, click the Mark as Sent button; if the invoice has been marked sent, click the green OK button.**

   The Print Invoice window opens.

4. **Click the green Print Now button.**

   A PDF is created, which can then be printed in the PDF window.

Emailing client invoices

Emails sent from Xero are sent directly from Xero, so they don't need to go through your email software! Check out the section 'Defining your user email addresses', later in this chapter, to understand which address you're sending the email from. If you don't select the option at Step 9 in the following steps to be sent a copy of the email, you won't be able to access a copy of the sent email.

To email customer invoices follow these steps:

1. **Go to the Sales dashboard, drill down on the Awaiting Payment tab to find the relevant invoice and check the box to the left of the document.**

2. **Click the blue Email button.**

   The Send Invoice window opens filled out with the customer's details.

3. **Enter the email address in the To field (if required).**

   Multiple emails can be entered in this field, separated by a comma. If the To field was originally blank and you enter an email address at this stage, Xero automatically updates the contact details.

   If multiple invoices are selected, the email addresses for all invoices are listed. To instantly remove an invoice from this grouping, click on the cross on the far right.

4. **Select the Email template from the drop-down menu.**

   See the section 'Taking Advantage of Email Templates', later in this chapter, for guidance on customising the template.

5. **Accept or overwrite the text in the Subject field.**

6. **Accept or overwrite the text to the customer in the Message field.**

   Use the Message field as an opportunity to touch base with customers, and motivate them to pay you fast!

7. **Select the required Send option.**

   You can also choose to include an online link and PDF attachment of the invoice at this step — see the following section for further information.

8. **Check the Mark as Sent box.**

   If multiple invoices are selected, the Mark as Sent option is listed for all invoices.

9. **Check the Send Me a Copy box.**

   This creates an email copy of the invoice for your own records.

10. **Click the green Send button.**

    The invoice is emailed to the contact.

How online invoicing works

Emailed invoices have the option to include either a

- Link that can be tracked when viewed
- PDF attachment

Opting to include a link creates a live link of the invoice that customers can access through their browser. (See the section 'Setting up the basics', later in this chapter, for guidance on defining a link as a default option.)

You can view a live invoice link by diverting an invoice to your own email address — simply follow these steps:

1. **Create an invoice.**

   Refer to the section 'Creating a new sales invoice', earlier in this chapter for guidance.

2. **Email the invoice to your own email address.**

   Refer to the preceding section for more information on how to do this, remembering to insert your own email address in the To: field.

3. **Tick the box beside Include PDF Attachment, and tick the box beside Send Me a Copy.**

4. **Click Send.**

5. **Open the email and click on the link in the message of the diverted invoice.**

The invoice that you reach by following the live link is almost the same as the PDF that can be attached to the email — it's just better. The interactive goodness is found in the three coloured bars across the top.

Here's how you can explore the live invoice you sent:

✔ View outstanding bills by clicking on the Outstanding Bills link on the top cyan bar.

✔ View the net amount owing, and the number of days payment is overdue by, on the wide white bar, just beneath the top bar.

✔ Start the payment process via PayPal (or other payment service) by clicking the green Pay Now button. (Actual customers would then enter their PayPal details.)

✔ Convert the live invoice to a PDF by clicking the PDF button.

✔ Convert the live invoice to a CSV file by clicking the CSV button.

✔ Email the supplier (that's you, in this case!) by clicking the light grey Questions or Comments About this Bill? link. If you continue with this option, you'll receive an email, referencing the invoice. A system-generated note detailing the email message is added to the History & Notes section of the invoice.

✔ Save the online invoice directly into your Xero software.

If customers you're sending invoices to don't have Xero software, they can save the invoice as a notification. If you click Save on an online Xero invoice, you can create a Xero account to store all such saved bills in an area created specifically for them!

You can also check out the social media links that were added during the set-up process (refer to Chapter 2) by clicking on each of them via the online invoices.

Because the linked invoice is live, as the invoice updates — for example, with receipt of payments or changes to the invoice — the linked invoice also updates.

Notice the green tick beside invoices? A pale green tick indicates they've been sent. Dark green indicates the link has been clicked on.

Creating and sending invoices via your mobile device

While onsite with clients, or waiting to pick someone up from the airport, you can generate invoices and follow up on outstanding debts using Xero on your mobile device. That's a productivity booster and cash-flow improver in the palm of your hands! You just need to download the Xero app from the relevant App store — once you have, the basic process of using Xero mobile is pretty simple.

Here's how to use Xero mobile on an iPhone:

1. **Tap on the Xero icon on your mobile device and enter your four-digit passcode or use Touch ID.**

    The home dashboard screen opens with your company listed at the top, and icons to access Invoices, Expenses and Contacts at the bottom. *Note:* If you move away from the mobile version of Xero, when you return you need to re-enter your four-digit passcode.

2. **Click on the Invoices icon at the bottom of the screen and create a new invoice by clicking on the grey cross at the top of the screen.**

    The New Invoice screen opens. Refer to the section 'Creating a new sales invoice', earlier in this chapter for more.

3. **Click the grey Add button on the top right.**

    Five options appear: Approve & Send, Send Draft, Approve, Save as Draft, and Cancel.

4. **Click Approve & Send to email the invoice to your customer.**

    An email appears. Check the details.

5. **Swipe across the circle beside Send Me a Copy, to receive a copy of the email you're about to send.**

    Confirmation appears that an email will be sent to your default email address.

6. **Email the invoice by clicking Send on the top right.**

    The Invoices dashboard appears with the option to view a detailed listing of invoices under the columns headed Overdue, Unpaid and Draft. Click through an individual invoice to see underlying detail;

click the back arrow to return to the Invoices dashboard.

7. **Click the Dashboard icon at the bottom of the screen and then at the top left click the three horizontal grey lines and choose the Logout option in the next screen to securely log out of Xero.**

Here's how to use Xero mobile on an android device:

1. **Tap on the Xero icon on your mobile device, and enter your four-digit passcode.**

   The home dashboard screen opens. Across the top are four headings: Dashboard, Invoices, Expenses and Contacts. **Note:** If you move away from the mobile version of Xero, when you return you need to re-enter your four-digit passcode.

2. **Click on the Invoices heading at the top of the screen to access a summary Sales dashboard.**

   A summary of the overdue sales invoices appears. Take a few moments to explore the Sales dashboard. Click on Overdue, for example, to reveal a drop-down menu that allows you to access Unpaid, Submitted and Draft invoices. Click through an individual invoice to see underlying detail;

click the back arrow to return to the Invoices dashboard. Click on the magnifying glass on the top right corner to search for an invoice.

3. **Click the + on the top right and from the drop-down menu select Create Invoice.**

   The New Invoice screen opens. Refer to the section 'Creating a new sales invoice', earlier in this chapter for more. On the top right is a paperclip to facilitate taking a photo or adding a file to the invoice.

4. **Click Save on the top right.**

   Four options appear: Approve & Send, Approve, Send Draft, and Save As Draft.

5. **Click Approve & Send to email the invoice to your customer.**

   An email appears. Check the details; here you have the opportunity to add an email address or edit the email message.

6. **Click Send on the top right corner.**

   Confirmation appears on the screen that the invoice has been successfully sent.

7. **Click the Xero icon at the top of the screen and then on the top right click Logout to securely log out of Xero.**

Mastering More Advanced Invoice Functions

Invoice branding is not just about adding some creative flair — ensuring all required information is present and easy to read can help ensure your invoices are paid on time. You can customise the default branding theme in Xero and use other functions in Xero to save time when you're invoicing, such as using repeating invoices or invoicing groups. The following sections show you how.

Designing clear invoices for a positive cash flow

While I lived in Canada, I processed invoices at the local council office. The lack of information, or confusing information, on some invoices I tried to process amazed me. Basic information like banking details or who to contact if I had a query about the invoice weren't included on the invoice.

Your invoice branding — how you provide and present information on your invoices — can have a positive influence on your business's cash flow. The invoice design needs to be fit for the purpose intended — that is, alerting customers how to pay the money they owe you. Customer invoices, credit notes, prepayments and statements can be customised to suit your business branding. They can share the same theme, or multiple themes can be created.

Available within Xero are basic and comprehensive invoice customisation options. *Note:* Default branding themes can be assigned to individual customers.

Setting up the basics

Follow these steps to customise the basic elements of your business invoices:

1. **Click on Settings⇨General Settings⇨Invoice Settings and click the Default Settings button.**

   The Default Settings window opens. In the top block you can customise the default Bills and Sales Invoice payment terms. The payment terms can be customised for individual contacts and overridden during the creation of the bill or the invoice.

2. **Enter details in the Bill's Default Due Date (Optional) field.**

   For example, you can click in the Due field, enter '10' and then click on the drop-down menu and select Of the Following Month. This means the due date for future bills entered with no supplier payment terms defaults to the 10th of the following month.

3. **Enter details in the Sales Invoice's Default Due Date (Optional) field.**

   For example, you can click in the Due field, enter '7' and then click on the drop-down menu and select Day(s) After the Invoice Date. This means the due date for future sales invoices entered with no customer payment terms defaults to seven days after the invoice date.

4. **Enter details for the Automatic Sequencing block, if desired.**

   In the Automatic Sequencing block are three fields: Invoice Prefix, Credit Note Prefix and Next Number. You can customise the invoice and credit note prefix but it's not really necessary. If you don't have a burning desire to change it, just leave it.

5. **Enter the invoice number you want to generate when you create your first sale in Xero in the Next Number field.**

   If you're just starting out, you could leave this field and the invoicing would start at one. However, you may want to give the impression of being a business that has been in existence for some time, so you can enter a higher number in the Next Number field, and tell no-one!

6. **Check the box below Show Outstanding Bills.**

   Checking this box means that, when an invoice is sent from Xero, an online link to the invoice is created. Pretty exciting, huh? Refer to the section 'How online invoicing works', earlier in this chapter, to see this in action.

7. **Click the green Save button.**

   When customising invoices in Xero, don't accidentally send them to a real customer. Instead, set up a 'dummy' contact with your own email address, and test the invoice design out by emailing it to yourself.

Adding payment services

A number of different payment services can be customised to appear on online Sales Invoices. Like your bank accounts, the relationship with the payment service needs to be established outside of Xero. To add a Payment Service, click Settings⇨General Settings⇨Invoice Settings⇨Payment Services⇨+ Add Payment Services, then fill out the fields, and click Save. The payment can be added to invoice themes as you wish, via the customisation of invoices. Once a payment service has been added to an invoice the invoice theme names are listed beside the payment service in the Payment Services dashboard.

Customising the Branding Theme

To customise the default business invoice that is created when the file is set up, click on the button labelled Options on the right side of the Invoice settings window and then Edit. This opens the Edit Branding Theme window. In this section, I show you how you can work through this invoice branding, setting up a simple yet professional Standard themed invoice (of course, you're free to override any customisation suggestions).

Once you're finished customising your Standard themed invoice, you're given the option to upload your business logo, for use on the invoice. If you'd like to make use of this option, having your logo ready to go before you start the customisation process is a good idea. The format of the logo you're uploading to your invoice must be .jpg, .gif, or .png and the logo must be scaled to 400 pixels wide and 120 pixels high. (The file size must be less than 200kb.) If you're not sure about how the uploaded logo will look on your invoice, talk to your graphic designer (or whoever designed the logo for you) about possibly resizing your logo.

Here's how to set up a Standard themed invoice:

1. **Click on Settings⇨General Settings⇨Invoice Settings, click the New Branding Theme button and select Standard theme.**

   The New Branding Theme window opens (see Figure 6-3).

   Clicking the drop-down arrow beside the New Branding Theme button presents you with two options: Standard theme and Custom .docx theme. The simplest option to set up is a Standard theme so I recommend working through that one first.

New Branding Theme   ✕

Name	
Page size	⦿ A4
	○ US Letter
Top margin	1.35
Bottom margin	1.00
Address padding	1.00
Font	Calibri
Font size	9pt
Draft Invoice title	DRAFT INVOICE
Approved Invoice title	TAX INVOICE
Overdue Invoice title	TAX INVOICE
Credit Note title	CREDIT NOTE
Statement title	STATEMENT
Draft Purchase Order title	DRAFT PURCHASE ORDER
Purchase Order title	PURCHASE ORDER
Remittance Advice title	REMITTANCE ADVICE
Receipt title	RECEIPT

Measure in   ⦿ cm   ○ inches

☑ Show tax number
☑ Show column headings
☑ Show unit price & quantity
☑ Show payment advice cut-away
☑ Show tax column
☐ Show registered address
☑ Show logo
☐ Hide Discount

Show tax subtotals by
tax rates over 0%

Show currency conversion as
a single tax total

Payment Services

Terms & Payment Advice

Logo alignment
○ Left
⦿ Right

Show taxes as
⦿ Exclusive
○ Inclusive

Enter your contact details as they should appear at the top of all PDFs you print or send

Demo Company (AU)
23 Main Street
MARINEVILLE NSW 2000

[Save]   [Cancel]

Figure 6-3: The New Branding Theme window.

2. **Enter a name for your branded forms.**

   It won't be as hard as choosing a name for your first born, but you need to choose something. Keeping it simple is best — for example, use the prefix MAIN then the document's name.

3. **Select the typical page size for your invoices.**

   The choices are A4 or US letter.

4. **Select the measurement unit and enter the invoice border size.**

   Choose a measurement unit (centimetres or inches) you're comfortable with first, and then enter sizing for Top and Bottom margin, and Address padding. Ensure the margin size is at least 1 cm to give the invoice enough room to neatly print.

5. **Choose your preferred default invoice font in the Font field and select a font size.**

   The stylish people choose Trebuchet but, of course, the choice is up to you! Font selection is an important element of business branding so check with your design department when making this decision. My micro-business design department consists of one keen-eyed 13-year-old daughter! If you don't have a design department, have a look at the kinds of things you've had designed for your business in the past, such as your website, shop signage or even business cards, or throw it out on social media and let those you are connected with be your guide and choose a font that works in with your overall brand.

   When selecting the font size, only a few size options are available. Choose the maximum option of 11pt — anything less gets too hard for some people to read (and you don't want people using the excuse they can't pay you because they can't read the invoice!).

6. **Specify names for individual invoices.**

   You can adjust the names for the following (in the order shown on screen):

   - Draft Invoice
   - Approved Invoice
   - Overdue Invoice
   - Credit Note
   - Statement
   - Draft Purchase Order
   - Purchase Order
   - Remittance Advice
   - Receipt

Each naming field has 20 character spaces and already has a suggested name. To keep things simple, just add the overall name of your branded form (chosen in Step 2 of this list) to the start of each suggestion. So your draft invoice becomes *[NAME] DRAFT INVOICE* (and so on). Abbreviate the name if necessary to fit the field.

At the time of writing, Xero does not yet offer the option to produce sales quotes. This functionality is due soon but, in the meantime, a workaround is to create a new invoice branding theme called Quote and, at the Draft Invoice Title field enter 'Quote'.

7. **Move across to the second column and check elements that you want to appear on the invoice.**

   Select all the options you require and then remove ones that you decide you don't want.

8. **Select your Payment Services account from the drop-down options.**

   Adding a Payment Service here allows you to let clients pay invoices via your online payment service such as PayPal. (See the preceding section for more on adding Payment Services.)

9. **Enter when and how you expect to be paid in the Terms and Payment Advice box.**

   The field is limited to 1,000 characters. If you can't fit in everything you want to say, have your full terms and conditions on your website. That way, you can have the basics on your invoice and then include a link to them in this box.

The terms and payment information is important so, once you've included it, print out the invoice and make sure you've entered the information correctly and it can be easily read. And remember to keep payment terms as tight as possible!

10. **Select your preferred logo alignment (if required).**

    If you choose to upload a logo for your invoice, how to do so is covered after these steps — for now, you just have to pick which side of the page you want it to sit on. If you're not sure, select the right alignment.

11. **Select your preference at the Show Taxes As field.**

    Selecting the Inclusive option means all invoice amounts displayed are inclusive of consumer tax. With both options (Inclusive or Exclusive), the final invoice amount is shown inclusive of consumer tax.

12. **Enter your business contact details in the final box.**

    This may include your phone and email details.

13. **Check all your details and click the green Save button.**

    This saves your branding theme and the New Branding Theme window closes.

Congratulations! You've created a new invoice template. And the good news is you can have unlimited standard templates so, if your business has a number of identities (or different strands), you can create a different standard invoice for each identity.

Once the template has been created, you're given the option to upload a business logo by clicking on the Upload Logo hyperlink. If you want your logo to appear, click the link and follow the instructions for uploading the file.

Uploading a logo to your invoice means it's now a customised invoice. To save it, just click the Save button. The Invoice Settings window now displays the customised invoice template block. Any additional template blocks you create will also sit in this area. The customised invoice templates can be edited, copied or deleted, and the logo can be changed or removed from the Invoice Settings dashboard by clicking the Options button.

If you have multiple templates and want to change the order of the templates shown in the Invoice Settings window, hover on the top left corner, and click to grab the template. Move it where you want.

If you need to access the Invoice Settings after you've created your invoice, click on Settings on the Menu Bar and select General Settings. Under the heading Features select Invoice Settings. There you have further invoice customisation options.

Fancy schmancy invoice branding

If you want to take your invoice branding to the next level, you can design up to 15 DOCX invoice branding themes and use them with sales invoices, credit notes and statements.

Why on earth would you want 15 different themes? Well, if you sell different sorts of products, you can customise the invoice to the particular product. For example, when I sell one of my guides to starting a small business, I use an invoice that upsells appropriate products relevant to the purchase. Of course, it's perfectly acceptable just to use a single branded invoice — but it's nice to have options!

DOCX invoice branding allows you to work on invoices in a Microsoft Word format, which allows for greater scope of customisation. If you understand the concept of using mail merge features, you should be able to navigate your way around designing DOCX templates for your business.

To create a new DOCX branded template from the home dashboard, follow these steps:

1. **Go to Settings⇨General Settings⇨Invoice Settings, click the New Branding Theme button, and select the Custom .docx Theme option from the drop-down menu.**

   The New Branding Theme window opens.

2. **Name the new theme in the Your Title for the New Branding Theme field and click OK.**

   For this exercise, I'm calling the theme MAIN but you can choose to call it something else.

3. **Scroll to the bottom of the Invoice Settings screen to locate the newly created invoice theme.**

4. **Click the Download button from the <MAIN> Invoice Block to download a template file.**

   The <MAIN> Templates zip file downloads to your computer.

   The process used to open your zip file depends on your computer set-up. I simply double click on the zip file to open it.

5. **Open the Microsoft Word document called Invoice.**

   Now you have the opportunity to customise your theme: Text surrounded by « » is a field that merges with data from your accounting system. Plain text appears as it is.

   If during that process you think you lost the downloaded file, look in your downloads file directory — it should be there. If the invoice is in Protected View mode click Enable Editing to allow you to edit the document.

6. **Select fields as required to make adjustments.**

   Tinker with the invoice as you desire — you can change fonts, font sizes and other aspects of the invoice. Hover over and select the field «INVOICE TITLE» and change the colour of the text to a scandalous pink colour, if you want — because everything's always better in pink! (Or is it just me who thinks that?!)

   Many customisations can be incorporated into the invoice. Go as crazy as you think works, but make sure the invoice still does what it is supposed to — notify customers they owe you money and let them know how they can pay you! And don't feel that you are under time pressure to complete all your customisation. You can close Xero down and work on the invoice, and then log back in and upload it at a later date.

7. **Save the document to your computer.**

8. **Return to the Invoice Settings dashboard of Xero, and select the Upload button at the <MAIN> invoice block.**

   The Upload .docx Template opens.

9. **Click Browse (underneath the word Invoice), select the edited file and click Open.**

   Notice the chosen file now appears on the Upload .docx Template window, beside the Browse button.

10. **Click the green Upload button.**

    Voila! The customised invoice appears as a branded .docx invoice on the <MAIN> invoice block.

To customise the Credit Note, Statement and Purchase Order or to further edit the invoice, follow Steps 3 to 10.

Working with repeating invoices

Some customers I work with sign up their customers to fixed monthly subscriptions, meaning their customers are billed the same amount for this subscription every month. For these customers, I've set up a Repeating Invoice template, which automatically generates a new invoice based on a saved template periodically. So an automatic invoice is sent to the customer on the same day every month. I also use these templates for some of my own invoices and, once I've set them up, all I have to do is edit the Repeating Invoice templates annually for price increases — for the rest of the year, I can forget about them. My valuable time is used servicing the customer, not preparing invoices!

To create a repeating invoice, follow these steps:

1. **Go to the Sales dashboard, click on the drop-down menu beside the New Invoice button and select New Repeating Invoice.**

   The New Repeating Invoice window opens (see Figure 6-4).

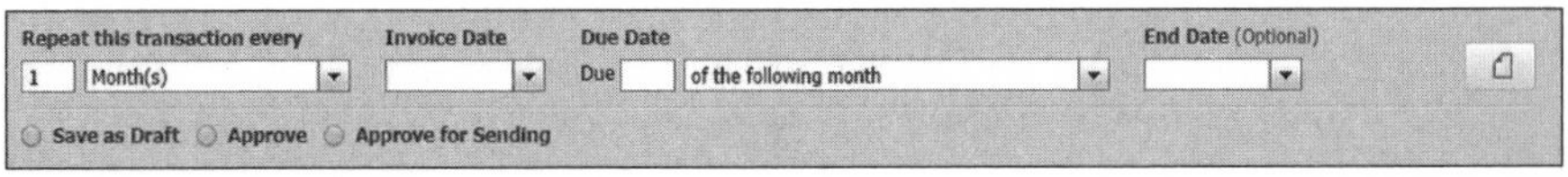

Figure 6-4:
The New
Repeating
Invoice
window.

2. **Fill out the Repeat This Transaction Every field.**

   You have a few options here. For example, if you want the invoice to repeat every month, enter 1 in the numeral field and select Month(s) from the drop-down menu.

3. **Select the original invoice date by clicking in the calendar field.**

4. **Define the repeating invoice due date.**

   Again, you have different options here. For example, if you want the invoice to be due on the 7th of the following month, enter 7 in the Due field and select Of the Following Month from the drop-down menu options.

5. **Fill out the optional End Date calendar field (if end date is known).**

6. **Select the Approve for Sending option.**

   Selecting this option means the invoice is automatically emailed to the customer every time it's created. *Note:* This does not mean that the template has been saved — you still need to complete the remaining steps.

   In the message the [Contact Name] will be the overall business name. You might like to override the name in this field with the first name of the person you are sending the invoice to (if you know it).

7. **Fill out the remainder of the body of the invoice following Creating an Invoice.**

   Use the reference field to give the invoice an identifying name.

8. **Save the template by clicking the green Save button.**

   The template is filed under the Repeating tab.

Invoicing contact groups

I visited a customer who wanted an easy way to process 750 annual membership renewals. To add further complexity, the customer offered five levels of membership pricing with dues increasing annually. My solution was to set up five different contact groups and, using Xero's Invoice to Contact Group feature, invoice each group. Voila! This created 750 individual annual membership renewal invoices easily and got rid of the nearly two days of creating and checking data that had been required when my customer was using another accounting system.

To invoice a contact group follow these steps:

1. **Create a contact group and allocate appropriate contacts to the group.**

   Refer to Chapter 5 for information on this process.

2. **Click the New button on the Sales dashboard and select the contact group.**

   This means the whole contact group is going to receive the invoice.

3. **Complete details on the invoice, for the group.**

4. **Select the blue Create Draft Invoices button.**

   The Draft invoices tab appears with draft invoices for all contacts in the group. Click on individual invoices to drill down and edit.

5. **Select all draft invoices, click the green Approve button, and click the green OK button.**

   Refer to the section 'Creating a new sales invoice', earlier in the chapter, for more.

That was crazy easy!

Managing credit notes

If the invoice needs to be changed after being issued to a customer — for example, because the amount billed was incorrect or has since been renegotiated — a credit note can be raised to formally recognise the change. The credit note can offset outstanding invoices, or accompany a refund.

To process a credit note, follow the steps outlined in this section.

Allocating a credit note for a specific invoice

Follow these steps to apply a credit note to an existing sales invoice:

1. **Go to Accounts⇨Sales⇨See All and click on the relevant invoice to open it.**

   If the invoice is approved, skip ahead to Step 3.

   If the invoice is Draft or Awaiting Approval, you can simply edit the invoice details to reflect the change, rather than undertaking the burden of creating a credit note. If you still want to use the invoice, go to step 2.

2. **Click the green Approve button at the bottom of the invoice.**

    Before an invoice can have a credit note applied against it, it needs to be approved.

3. **In the top right corner click Invoice Options and from the drop-down menu select Add Credit Note.**

    The New Credit Note window appears, mirroring the details of the invoice the credit note is to be applied against.

    Note: The Credit Note doesn't need to replicate the full amount of the invoice; it could be less, reducing the invoice. It could be identical, or it could be more — reflecting other amounts that need to be refunded and automatically raising a new credit note waiting to be applied to another invoice for the respective customer.

4. **Fill out the Date and Reference fields.**

    Enter a detailed reference of the relevant invoice in the Reference field.

5. **Amend the credit note details as required and click the green Approve button.**

    The credit note is applied to the invoice.

Processing a credit note where no invoice exists

The practicalities of business mean that sometimes customers, for whatever reason, realise they don't need what they've paid for. With your permission, they return it. Rather than give them a refund upfront, you can raise a credit note to be applied against a future purchases.

To create a new credit note without an existing transaction to apply it against, follow these steps:

1. **On the Sales dashboard click the drop-down arrow beside the + New button and select the Credit Note button.**

2. **Complete the details on the Credit Note screen.**

    To comply with taxation requirements, include comprehensive details about why the credit note is being issued. *Note:* The values are entered as positive.

3. **Save or approve the Credit Note.**

    Refer to the section 'Saving, approving and cancelling invoices', earlier in this chapter, for details on this.

    Because no existing outstanding customer invoice relates to this credit note, the credit note simply saves. If at a future date a customer invoice is approved, the Allocate Outstanding Credit? window pops up. Click the green Allocate button if the credit note should be applied to this invoice, and the Allocate Credit to Invoice dashboard opens.

4. **At the Allocate Credit to Invoice dashboard enter the amount of the credit note in the Amount to Credit field.**

5. **Click the green Allocate Credit button.**

   The credit is applied to the new Sales Invoice.

6. **Print or email the invoice.**

   Refer to the section 'Sending an invoice to a customer', earlier in this chapter.

Recording Payments

Receiving payment is always exciting! And recording payments received in a timely manner means you can be confident your reports showing invoices awaiting payment are correct. You are also well placed to follow up on outstanding debts in a timely manner.

In the following sections, I cover recording payments against sales invoices for a simple cash business, and recording the payment of multiple invoices using the batch deposit feature.

Receipting against sales invoices

To record a payment against a sales invoice, follow these steps:

1. **Go to the Sales dashboard and click the Awaiting Payment tab.**

2. **Click the required invoice to drill down to the detail.**

   At the bottom of the invoice is a Make a Payment block. A full or part payment against the invoice can be recorded here.

3. **Fill out the Amount Paid field.**

4. **Fill out the Date Paid calendar.**

5. **Select the general ledger account the money was paid into in the Paid To field.**

   Payment may be made to your bank, credit card or PayPal account, or any account set up to enable payments from the account. Refer to Chapter 2 for guidance on customising general ledger accounts.

6. **Fill out the optional Reference field.**

   For example, you could include the cheque number here.

7. **Click the green Add Payment button.**

   You're returned to the Sales dashboard. At the top of the screen is a green block, confirming the details of the payment receipted. Two hyperlinks also appear: View Invoice, a short cut to drill down and view the invoice details again, and Send Receipt. See the next section for guidance on sending out a receipt.

Sending receipts

A sales receipt formally acknowledges that customer payment has been received. Before you can send a receipt, you need to get your ducks in a row, as follows:

- ✔ Customise your receipts email template — see the section 'Taking Advantage of Email Templates', later in this chapter.

- ✔ Create a standard branded theme for your receipt – refer to 'Customising the Branding Theme', earlier in this chapter.

To send a receipt after receiving payment against a single invoice follow the steps outlined in the preceding section. At Step 7, once the payment has been added, click on the hyperlink Send Receipt and the Send Receipt window opens up similar to Figure 6-5. Jump ahead to Sending a Batch Deposit receipt to customers, and follow the instructions from Step 4 onwards. Payment can also be receipted during the reconciliation matching process, described in Chapter 8.

Recording income for a simple cash business

Clients of mine are the owners of a small independent grocery store. They sell an amazing array of imported and local foods, and many customers flock to their shop. When they review their takings at the end of the day, they have received a combination of cash, debit card, credit card, AMEX and Diners payments from their wonderful customers. They have also used money from their cash takings to pay for expenses, such as cash-on-delivery items.

Of course, they don't need to issue each customer an individual invoice from Xero, but the business still needs to account for the takings. To add to the complexity of this scenario, some payments take a few days to be received by the bank and some payments are subject to commission deductions. All this means the business is never exactly sure how much they're going to receive and when they're going to receive it in their bank.

To prepare for recording daily sales, I advised these clients to create a Cash Sales contact and then charge the daily sales to this contact.

If you operate a simple cash business and want to use the same approach, here's how:

1. **Obtain a copy of the cash register reading at the end of the day.**

   If you have multiple cash registers, you need the total for all of them. You may be able to get this information if you're using a network system; otherwise, add it up on a spreadsheet.

2. **Prepare a daily Sales Invoice charged to the Cash Sales contact, splitting out the different lines payment is going to be received from.**

   Payment could be received as cash, debit card, credit card and so on. Use the Unit Price field to enter the commission and bank charges as negative amounts deducted from the income.

3. **As payment is receipted in the bank, record payment against the invoice.**

   Payment may be receipted in several stages, via the cash banking.

Making use of batch payments

The batch deposit feature in Xero can be utilised when recording cheques to be deposited, or a single payment against multiple invoices. Using the feature creates a single transaction in the Xero file, which can then be reconciled against a single transaction in the bank feed.

Recording a batch deposit against sales invoices

To record a batch deposit as a payment against a sales invoice, follow these steps:

1. **Go to the Sales dashboard and click the Awaiting Payment tab.**

2. **Check the invoices to be included in the batch deposit.**

   Note: Overpayments cannot be recorded within a batch deposit, and Credit Notes cannot be included within a batch deposit. Refer to the section 'Managing credit notes' earlier in this chapter, to record the credit note against an invoice, where relevant.

3. **Select the Deposit button.**

4. **Fill out the Payment Date Paid calendar.**

5. **Fill out the compulsory Reference field.**

   Include summary details of the payment here.

6. **Select a Bank Account from the drop-down options.**

7. **Fill out the optional Reference/Cheque No field, against individual invoices in the batch.**

   Once all required fields are filled, the green Deposit button becomes active.

8. **Click the green Deposit button.**

   Once the deposit has been created, on the top right of the Batch Deposit appear the buttons Print Deposit PDF, Send Receipt and Options.

Locating a Batch Deposit

Once you've recorded the Batch Deposit, you might want to locate it so you can edit it, print the deposit slip or send a receipt. Here's how to locate a batch deposit:

1. **Go to Accounts⇨Bank Accounts and select the relevant bank account the batch deposit was associated with.**

2. **Click the Search button, on the right side, and search for** Payment: multiple items **in the Description or Contact Name field.**

   A list of Batch Deposits appears. Click through on the relevant one.

Printing a Deposit Slip for a Batch Deposit

A Deposit Slip can be printed off from a Batch Deposit, and presented to the bank with the cheques. Here's how:

1. **Find the applicable deposit.**

   Refer to the preceding section for help with this.

2. **Click on the relevant Batch Deposit, and select the Print Deposit PDF button on the top right.**

   The Print Deposit Summary button appears.

3. **Click the green Print Now button.**

   The Deposit Summary can be located in your download folder and can be printed from there.

Sending a Batch Deposit receipt to customers

A customer receipt can be printed or emailed from a Batch Deposit. Here's how:

1. **Find the applicable deposit.**

   Refer to the section 'Locating a Batch Deposit' for help with this.

2. **Click on the relevant Batch Deposit, and select the Send Receipt button on the top right.**

   The Send Receipt window appears (see Figure 6-5).

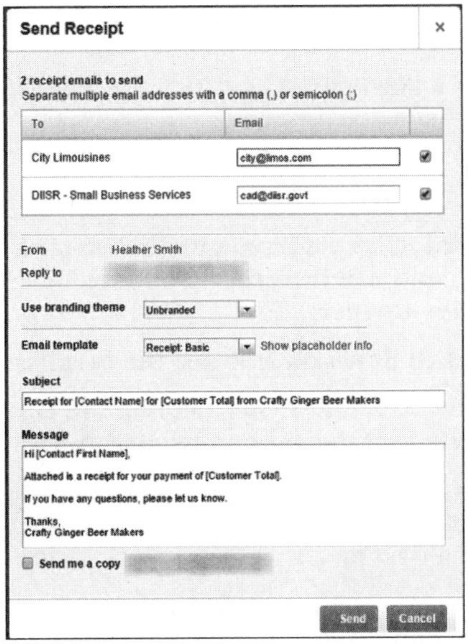

Figure 6-5: The Send Receipt window.

3. **Check the email recipients, listed in the Email field, are correct.**

   Edit or add additional email recipients, using a comma (,) to separate. Uncheck the boxes against customers you don't want to send a receipt to.

4. **Select a branded theme from the drop-down options and then click the Use Branded Theme line.**

   Refer to 'Customising the Branding Theme', earlier in this chapter, for direction on branding themes.

5. **Check and edit the Email template (if necessary).**

   See the following section for guidance on email templates.

6. **Check and edit the Subject Line and Message (if necessary).**

   The Subject Line and Message are sourced from the email template, so assess whether the template needs to be edited for future use, before making changes to this version. Remember this is an opportunity to thank a paying customer, and encourage them to re-use your services.

7. **Check the box beside Send Me a Copy.**

8. **Click the green Send button.**

   This sends the receipt to your customer.

Removing allocated payments

You may find you've assigned a payment to an invoice and then need to remove it, because you need to change the details of the invoice or the payment was allocated incorrectly. To 'unallocate' a payment follow these steps:

1. **Go to the Sales dashboard, click on Accounts⇨Sales, click the Search button on the right side, and use the criteria options that have appeared to search for the invoice.**

2. **Locate the invoice and drill down on it to see the invoice detail.**

3. **Click on the relevant Less Payment hyperlink and the corresponding dollar amount at the bottom of the column headed Amount.**

   The Payment transaction appears. If multiple payments have been assigned, multiple lines of payment transactions will appear, and each one needs to be individually removed.

4. **On the relevant Payment transaction, click on the Options button, and from the drop-down menu select Remove & Redo.**

   The payment is removed from the bill. If additional payments need to be removed, click your web browser's back arrow twice and then refresh the screen, to see the current transaction details. Repeat Steps 3 and 4 to remove additional payments.

Taking Advantage of Email Templates

I engaged a funky young local graphic designer to do some work for an organisation I was working with. Her work was superb and I would happily recommend her to other contacts — until I got a two-page email from her, consisting of unrelenting personalised abuse advising me I was late in paying her bill. I pay my bills on a timely basis. All my bills! So this was a shock to me. I reviewed incoming correspondence and it turned out I had received an email from her but it included a foreign attachment created in specialised graphic software. Unbeknown to me I didn't have the required software so I couldn't read her attachment, and had no idea it was an invoice. Sadly, her unnecessary email destroyed our professional relationship and any future business dealings. If only she'd thought about how to chase outstanding invoices while in a calm frame of mind.

Recognising businesses need to deal with similar situations, Xero allows you to create customisable email templates to deal with typical business scenarios, such as the following:

✔ Here's your invoice!

✔ Here's your invoice — it's due for payment soon!

✔ Here's your invoice — payment is overdue!!

✔ Hey! Have you forgotten about my invoice?

✔ Has your dog eaten my invoice???

Documents can be emailed to contacts directly from within Xero. You don't need to have an email system on your desktop — you can log in to Xero anywhere in the world, email contacts, and opt to have a copy of the email sent to you. Draft templates are created by default, and this can be overridden to suit your requirements.

Defining your user email addresses

I've a client who oversees the operations of three separate businesses. She has a separate email address for each business, but accesses each of the three Xero business files with the same email log-on — her own personal email address. When she generates correspondence from the Xero business file, or receives email replies, she wants them to be associated with the individual business email address — not her personal email address.

Xero can be customised so her user name is associated with a different email address from within Xero. This means all correspondence sent from the individual Xero files can reflect the different businesses. This avoids confusion and tames email correspondence — and customers never know BrazilianBetty@Dmail.com is the logged-in user sending invoices from the business Xero file!

To add an email address to your user profile, follow these steps:

1. **Go to Settings⇨General Settings⇨Email Settings.**

   The Email Settings window opens (see Figure 6-6). The top bar informs you the name of the logged in user and the email address any replies from the correspondence will be sent to. (Replies will be sent back to this address even if they are sent from a different address.)

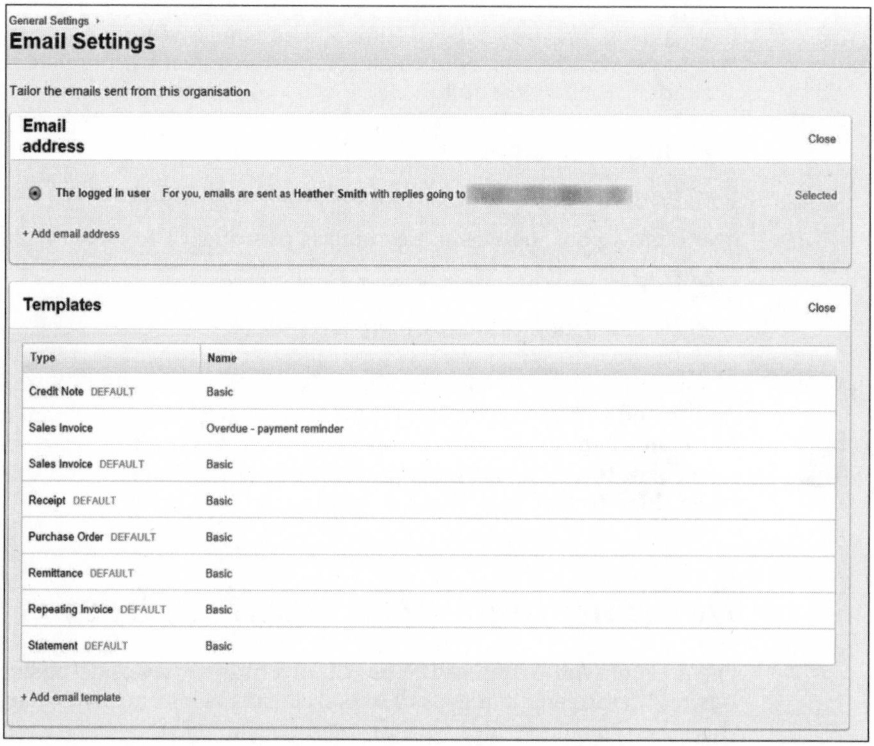

General Settings ›
Email Settings

Tailor the emails sent from this organisation

Email address   Close

⦿   **The logged in user**   For you, emails are sent as Heather Smith with replies going to   Selected

+ Add email address

Templates   Close

Type	Name
Credit Note DEFAULT	Basic
Sales Invoice	Overdue - payment reminder
Sales Invoice DEFAULT	Basic
Receipt DEFAULT	Basic
Purchase Order DEFAULT	Basic
Remittance DEFAULT	Basic
Repeating Invoice DEFAULT	Basic
Statement DEFAULT	Basic

+ Add email template

Figure 6-6: Email Settings window.

2. **Click the blue Edit hyperlink at the end of the bar, and then click + Add Email Address hyperlink.**

   The Add a New Reply Email Address window opens. Enter the preferred email address in the Reply To email address field. Enter the name in the Name field and click the green Add Email button. The email holder receives an email from Xero notifying them their email address has been added and, once they approve it, the preferred email address can be linked to any outgoing correspondence from the Xero file.

Refresh the screen, select the default email address for the organisation and select the green Save button.

Creating a new email template

To create an email template to follow up on an overdue invoice, follow these steps:

1. **Go to Settings⇨General Settings⇨Email Settings⇨Template and click the + Add Email Templates hyperlink.**

   The Add an Email Template window opens.

2. **Select Sales Invoice from the Type drop-down menu.**

   Other options here relevant to the Sale area include: Credit Note, Sales Invoice, Remittance Advice, Repeating Invoice, Statement and Receipt.

3. **Enter the name FollowUp in the Name field.**

   This indicates that the email template is suitable to send with an overdue invoice.

4. **Leave the box next to Default unchecked.**

   If you tick the box next to Default, this template would then become the default email sent with all invoices — which you don't want in this case because this email is only suitable to send when invoices are overdue.

5. **Complete the Subject Line and Message Body fields.**

   Insert the words 'FOLLOW UP:' at the start of the invoice message before working on the body of the message.

Placeholders can be inserted into the template. They autopopulate with relevant data when the email becomes live. For example, the placeholder [Invoice Total] populates with the actual numerical total of the invoice. Pretty awesome! Each template type has its own relevant placeholders that can be used to customise the message body of the invoice. So check out the options that work best for you.

Here's some sample text you could use in the message body:

> Dear [Contact Name],
>
> I wanted to check that you have received Invoice [Invoice Number] for [Invoice Total].
>
> Can you please reply to this email to let me know that you have received the invoice?

Thank you,

<enter your name here>

[Trading Name]

6. **Click the green Save button.**

The email template has been saved and can be selected when you email an invoice.

Deleting a template

If you need to delete an email template, follow these steps:

1. **Go to the Email Settings window, click on the link, and at the bottom select Delete Template.**

The Delete Email Template confirmation window opens.

2. **Click the blue Yes button.**

Connecting with contacts via social media

If you thought invoicing couldn't get any better (refer to preceding sections if you need convincing), the cherry on the top of email templates is the ability to personalise invoicing with social media. For social media addicts like me this feature is pretty cool. Yes — you can tweet me to tell me you have paid my invoice, from within the invoice! What a connected world we live in!

To add social media links to your invoicing, follow these steps:

1. **Click on Settings⇨General Settings⇨Organisation Settings, scroll to the bottom of the page, click + Add contact field, select required options from the drop-down list and enter your social media links in the fields.**

Note: Mobile, fax and DDI information can be added via this process.

2. **Enter the vanity name of the business's social media sites in the relevant fields.**

If you don't want an icon on your invoice, don't complete the field. If you have your own personal social media presence, think about whether you want to include it here. Do you want businesses knowing the real you?

Following Up on Outstanding Debtors

Receiving monies owed to the business in a timely manner is critical for the survival of your business. And you can utilise a number of features of your accounting system to help you follow up with outstanding debtors, including the following:

- ✔ Xero's home dashboard highlights what money is owing. You can then drill down through the graphs to detailed invoicing information.

- ✔ The Sales dashboard highlights overdue invoices, and provides the contact details of who to call about the invoice.

- ✔ The Contacts area allows you to maintain comprehensive information about customers, including communication details — keep in mind that having multiple avenues you can use to contact customers when invoices are unpaid is very useful.

- ✔ The History & Notes area automatically maintains an audit trail against the contact. Furthermore, additional notes can be manually added. This can help you profile the payment habits of customers — for example, if they typically don't pay during school holidays, invoice them early!

Refer to Chapter 5 for more on contacts and the History & Notes section.

As well as the features in the preceding list, Xero also offers two types of statements that can be sent to customers as a reminder monies are outstanding, covered in the following sections.

A review of your overdue accounts, and areas within Xero such as your Aged Receivables report, should be undertaken on a monthly basis. See Chapter 10 for details on this.

A debt tracking add-on like Debtor Daddy (www.DebtordDaddy.com) sends out multiple email reminders to outstanding debtors automagically.

Your accounting system is essential for keeping on top of outstanding debts; however, the personal touch always works a charm when getting people to pay up, and remain your customers. Hiding behind terse emails is not a nice way to run a business. Keep communications civilised and professional and always check the basics first — for example, make sure customers actually have your invoice before you scream at them about a missed payment! Also make sure your recording of payments received is up to date (refer to the earlier section 'Recording Payments'), so you can be sure your statements are accurate.

Making use of statements

Statements let customers know what invoices have been issued and how payment has been receipted. Two types of statements are available in Xero: Activity and Outstanding.

Activity statements are issued for a defined period, and display all activity for that period. They're useful if you want to detail how payment has been applied to previous outstanding invoices.

Outstanding statements are issued as at a defined date and display all outstanding activity as at that date. These are useful if you simply want to let customers know how much is outstanding without confusing them with the detail.

If I'm chasing payment from a customer, and I've sent the customer multiple invoices, to avoid any confusion I send the customer an activity statement so she can reconcile what she has paid me to date.

Once you've sent a statement (Activity or Outstanding), the contact's History & Notes section is updated to reflect this. Live links are not an option with statements.

Creating an Activity statement

To create an Activity statement, follow these steps:

1. **Go to the Sales dashboard and click the Send Statement button.**

2. **Select Activity from the Statement Type field.**

3. **Enter the From and To period in the calendar fields and click the blue Update button.**

   This assigns the statement period.

4. **Click the check box to the left of the customer row for the required customer(s).**

   One or many customers can be selected at this point.

5. **Print or email the statement.**

   Follow the same steps as for printing or emailing invoices (refer to the section 'Sending an invoice to a customer', earlier in this chapter, for more information).

Creating an Outstanding statement

To create an Outstanding statement, follow these steps:

1. **Go to the Sales dashboard and click the Send Statement button.**
2. **Select Outstanding from the Statement Type field.**
3. **Set the date in the calendar field and click the blue Update button.**
4. **Click the check box to the left of the customer row for the required customer(s).**

   One or many customers can be selected at this point.
5. **Print or email the statement.**

   Follow the same steps as for printing or emailing invoices (refer to the section 'Sending an invoice to a customer', earlier in this chapter, for more information).

Chapter 7

Managing Your Payables

. . . .

. . . .

I work with a client who leads an active and generous life. While she often posts funny photos of herself on Facebook, showing her enjoying her next crazy adventure, she has always worked hard — really hard! She sent her kids to private school, owned a lovely house and led an enviable life — and then, in a matter of a few months, lost everything. What happened? It sounds very simple, but she lost track of the bills. She overlooked paying suppliers, and soon unpaid suppliers stopped providing stock — and she was no longer able to run her business.

Inspirationally, the story has a great ending. She refocused her energies on understanding her numbers, took over the bookkeeping, and embraced her business reports. Over time, she repaid her debts — all of them — and slowly rebuilt her business. She's now re-engaged a bookkeeper; however, at any point in time, she prides herself on knowing exactly how much money she owes her suppliers.

Xero can help you avoid the same pitfalls. In this chapter, I provide everything you need to understand your own debts, starting with working your way through Xero's Purchases dashboard. I provide tips on utilising purchase orders, keeping track of bills and paying them in a timely manner, and finish off with advice on entering your expense claims into Xero.

Navigating the Purchases Dashboard

If all your bills are processed through the Purchases area (see the sidebar 'Understanding your records' for more on this), the first thing you need to know to manage your payables is: What do I owe? Xero gathers all that information on the Purchases dashboard, which you can access from the home dashboard by clicking Accounts⇨Purchases. (Figure 7-1 shows the Purchases dashboard, highlighting the features that are available if you process all bills through the purchases area.)

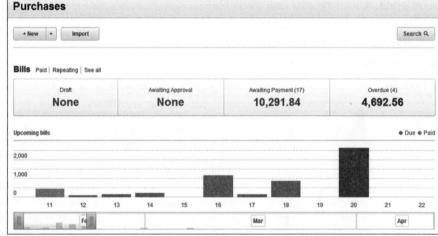

Figure 7-1: The Purchases dashboard.

If you process all bills through Xero's purchases area, the Purchases dashboard is split into three blocks: Buttons, menu bar and a bar chart.

The first block of the Purchases dashboard contains three buttons: New, Import and Search. The New button allows you to click through to create a New Bill, Repeating Bill, Credit Note and Purchase Order. The Import button begins the import process (covered in Chapter 3).

Clicking on the Search button opens the search pane. Here you can enter bill amount, reference, contact name and dates criteria to search for bills or purchase orders.

Understanding your records

The information available in Xero's Purchases dashboard depends on how you choose to process bills. If all payments originate through transactions imported via the banks (either through live bank feeds or manually importing statements — refer to Chapter 4), you're unlikely to have any data here. If occasional payments, such as tax payments, payroll or capital purchases are made via the Purchases area, you can access some limited information. If all bills are processed through the Purchases area, you can access lots of information through the Purchases dashboard, giving you insight into when and to whom you owe money. This can assist in cash flow planning and future negotiations with suppliers.

Businesses using cash accounting may never need to look at Xero's Purchases area. (*Cash accounting* is where income and expenditure are recognised when cash is actually received or paid.) In Australia, many micro and small businesses adopt cash accounting, so they don't really need to enter purchases in advance of paying them — instead, they pay the bill and record the transaction when it appears on their bank feed. Interestingly, I find UK accountants

are often obsessed with entering supplier bills. When I suggest to them that they're creating extra work for themselves, after a thoughtful discussion, many start to agree with me. If your purchases are made against bank cards — so they're easily recognised and reconciled within Xero (see Chapter 8) — maybe you too don't need to use the Purchases dashboard. Of course, if following this method, you need to keep tight control of your finances and know exactly how your cash flow is looking.

If you're using accrual accounting, or want to include comprehensive details within Xero of the big ticket items you've purchased, or want complete control of your spending, read on. (*Accrual accounting* is where income and expenditure are recognised when the actual transaction occurs — that is, the date of the transaction, not when the cash is received or paid.) If not, this chapter may not be relevant to you and you can skip to a chapter more applicable to your business methods.

Remember: Your focus should always be on creating accurate records, not creating extra work!

The second block of the Purchases dashboard contains seven tabs: Paid, Repeating, See All, Draft, Awaiting Approval, Awaiting Payment, and Overdue. Here's how you can explore this area:

- ✔ View all paid bill information by drilling down through the Paid tab. Paid bills can also be printed from this area.
- ✔ Sort columns by clicking on the column headers.
- ✔ Select bills by checking a single or multiple boxes to the left of the bills.
- ✔ View the bill detail by clicking on the relevant bill row. Click on the document symbol to see details of any files attached to the bill transaction. (Click on the teeny-tiny Purchases link in the top left corner to access a different view of the Purchases dashboard.)

✔ View all repeating bill information by drilling down through the Repeating tab. Repeating bills can be edited or deleted from this area. The area provides an overview of the details of repeating templates.

✔ View all summarised bill information by drilling down through the See All tab.

✔ View a summary of draft bills by drilling down through the Draft tab. Draft bills have been saved, but no journals have been created against them. Draft bills can be submitted for approval, approved, deleted and printed from this area.

✔ View a summary of bills awaiting approval for payment by drilling down through the Awaiting Approval tab. Bills awaiting approval can be approved, deleted and printed from this area.

✔ View a summary of bills awaiting payment by drilling down through the Awaiting Payment tab. Bills awaiting payment can be printed, paid in a batch or scheduled for payment from this area.

Click on Accounts⇨Purchases to return to the high level view of the Purchases dashboard. The third block of the Purchases dashboard contains a bar chart displaying upcoming bills, representing the current net monthly outstanding bills determined by the due date. In other words, it highlights outstanding creditors. Paid bills are indicated by green bars, with cyan indicating unpaid bills. Underneath the chart is a stretch bar.

Here are some ways you can explore the bar chart and stretch bar of the Purchases dashboard:

✔ Hover over the block to view a summary of the outstanding bills.

✔ Grab the stretch bar and pull it to view an extended period.

✔ Click each of the bars of the bar chart to drill down to bill detail.

Interpreting icons

Getting to know the icons used in the Sales & Purchases area is useful, and can help you move quickly through your payments. Here's a list of the icons Xero uses and what they mean:

✔ File Symbol: A PDF or image is stored within Xero

✔ Small face: The contact paid is an employee

✔ Rectangle with yellow dot: A credit note has been applied

✔ Yellow CR: Credit note

✔ Slash through icon: The transaction has been voided

✔ Red Cross through icon: The transaction has been deleted

Managing Your Supplier Bills

The mining boom has brought many interesting businesses to Brisbane, Australia (where my business is based). One such business, and a client of mine, is an export business that helps other businesses source large pieces of mining equipment. Everyone in the office speaks French, they make the strongest coffee imaginable and tell me where to find authentic French food in Brisbane. (You may be surprised to find out that Brisbane has a thriving French community!) For this business's owner, monitoring current and future purchases is a critical part of running his business. It helps him forecast cash flow expenditure and claim back consumer tax in a timely manner.

A respectful relationship with suppliers, which includes paying them according to their payment terms, is critical for business success. Tracking purchases via Xero's Purchases dashboard helps you know what you owe and when it's due, and can help you maintain and nurture these relationships.

The life cycle of a bill in Xero can include being created as a draft, submitted for approval, awaiting approval, approved, awaiting payment and, finally, applying payment. Xero also allows you to skip these steps and jump straight to the approval stage. The following sections cover each of the basic stages. I also cover how to generate a purchase order, which you can use to detail agreed spends for products or services.

Creating a new bill

When you receive an invoice for payment, you need to 'create' that invoice as a bill in Xero. Follow these steps to create a new bill within Xero:

1. **Go to the Purchases dashboard and select + New.**

   The New Bill window appears (see Figure 7-2).

2. **Enter the contact name in the From field.**

   If the supplier is already in your Xero file start typing the first three letters of the contact name and Xero autosuggests contact names and their associated primary contact person's first name, last name and email address. Select the relevant contact, or type in the name of a new contact. (Refer to Chapter 5 for guidance on adding Contact details.)

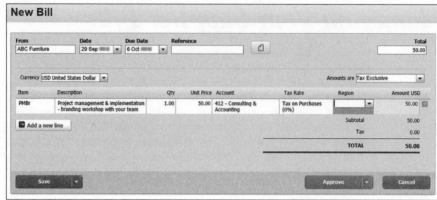

New Bill

From	Date	Due Date	Reference		Total
ABC Furniture	29 Sep ▬ ▾	6 Oct ▬ ▾		🗋	50.00

Currency USD United States Dollar ▾   Amounts are Tax Exclusive ▾

Item	Description	Qty	Unit Price	Account	Tax Rate	Region	Amount USD
PMBr	Project management & implementation - branding workshop with your team	1.00	50.00	412 - Consulting & Accounting	Tax on Purchases (0%)	▾	50.00

➕ Add a new line

	Subtotal	50.00
	Tax	0.00
	TOTAL	**50.00**

Save ▾   Approve ▾   Cancel

Figure 7-2:
The
New Bill
window.

If an existing unbilled Purchase Order has been assigned to the supplier, notification appears above the bill, and you can save time by bringing the Purchase Order details into a Bill. If there's a single unbilled Purchase Order, click the blue Copy Line Items hyperlink, and at the Copy Purchase Order to Bill window, check the box Mark as Billed and click the green OK button. If there are multiple unbilled Purchase Orders, select View as a List and a new tab on your browser open at the Purchase Orders dashboard, where you can select from the Purchase Order you may wish to convert to a bill. Discard the original bill you were working with. See the section 'Generating a purchase order', later in this chapter.

3. Enter the Date in the date calendar box.

4. Enter the bill Due Date.

5. Enter the optional bill Reference field.

Purchase bills are not automatically numbered. You can use the text field for a mnemonic reference, or to repeat the supplier bill number or the name of the contact who issued the bill.

6. Scan a copy of the bill to your computer and attach it to the transaction via the document symbol.

The scanned copy is stored in a retrievable format.

Many countries allow records to be stored in digital format, and the practice is environmentally friendly too! Just check with your country's tax regulations to make sure maintaining digital records is acceptable.

Select the bill currency from the drop-down Currency field options.

7. **Select the consumer tax status of the bill from the drop-down Amounts Are field options.**

   The three options are Tax Exclusive, Tax Inclusive and No Tax (refer to Chapter 6 for an explanation of these options).

8. **Enter or select the inventory item from the optional Item field.**

   The other fields populate with the item details.

9. **Enter a comprehensive narrative in the mandatory Description field.**

   Include as much information as possible, such as dates, contacts, work completed and/or items supplied. Keeping serial numbers and warranty information here is also useful for future reference. Because this field is mandatory, if you've nothing to say just add a full stop.

10. **Fill in the mandatory Quantity and Unit Price fields.**

    If the sale is for a fixed price product, enter the quantity as 1, and the full price in the unit price column.

11. **Enter the account name or number and select the desired account from the suggested drop-down list for the mandatory Account field.**

    After a bill has been issued and money paid against it, the Account and Tracking fields are the only fields that can still be edited.

12. **Select the desired rate from the mandatory Tax Rate field.**

13. **Select from options in the drop-down menus in the available Tracking fields (if available).**

    Tracking is optional and you won't see the field if the feature is not set up. See Chapter 12 for guidance on setting up Tracking fields. The amount field can't be edited. The subtotal, consumer tax and total automatically calculate. Populate the remaining rows with purchase information as needed. *Note:* In Figure 7-2 the Tracking field is called 'Region'. Your Tracking field could be labelled something different.

14. **Click the Add a New Line button (as required).**

    This allows you to add additional lines to the body of the bill.

15. **Save the bill.**

    Xero gives you a number of options:

    • If you want to just save the bill, click the blue Save button.

    • To save the bill as a draft, click the drop-down arrow beside the blue Save button, and select Save as Draft. (The bill is now listed under the Draft tab.)

- To save the bill and submit for approval, click the drop-down arrow beside the blue Save button, and select Save & Submit for Approval. (The bill is now listed under the Awaiting Approval tab.)

- To Save the bill and then create a new bill, click the drop-down arrow beside the blue Save button, and select Save & Add Another.

Approving and cancelling bills

A lawyer I know spent a few weeks in bed recovering from a severe bout of pneumonia. As he lay there, with nothing to do but think, he mulled over his business performance. He wondered why the cash situation was so tight when he had been so busy. When he returned to work, he took a careful look at the books. The amiable bookkeeper, who regularly baked scrummy cakes for the office, had been siphoning off a considerable sum of the money from the business. Combining a gambling habit with forged cheques and erasable ink sooner or later ends up with a visit to jail.

Any bank accounts through which cash leaves the business should be appropriately approved. In a micro or small business, approval of all payments may be the responsibility of the owner. In a larger business, different approval levels may be in place — for example:

- ✔ A junior manager is responsible for approving payments up to $1,000.
- ✔ A senior manager is responsible for approving payments up to $5,000.

The active word in the preceding examples is **responsible**. Approving payments should be treated with the utmost of importance and undertaken in a considered manner. Anything less may have a detrimental effect on cash flow. Within Xero, users who can approve a bill are those within the following user levels:

- ✔ Adviser
- ✔ Standard
- ✔ Invoice Only with the Option to Approve & Pay or Purchases only

Approving

When approving a bill, you have a number of options:

- ✔ Simply approve the bill by clicking the green Approve button.
- ✔ To approve the bill and then create a new bill, click the drop-down arrow beside the green Approve button and select Approve & Add Another.

✔ To approve the Draft or Awaiting Approval bill and view the next bill (Draft or Awaiting Approval respectively), click the drop-down arrow beside the green Approve button and select Approve & View Next.

Once a bill is approved it is filed in the Awaiting Payment area.

Cancelling, deleting or voiding

Here's how to cancel, delete or void a bill, dependent on the status of the bill:

✔ If you want to cancel the bill during the original creation stage, click grey Cancel button.

✔ To delete a Draft or Awaiting Approval bill, from the Dashboard click Accounts⇨Purchases and then drill down on either the Draft or Awaiting Approval option, check the box beside the relevant bill and select the Delete button. At the Confirm window, click the green OK button, and the status of the bill reverts to Deleted.

✔ To void a bill Awaiting Payment or Paid, first any payment made against the bill needs to be removed (see 'Removing allocated payments', later in this chapter). The status of both types of bills now reverts to Awaiting Payment, with no assigned payment allocation. Click on the bill detail, select the Bill Options button, and from the drop-down menu select Void. At the Confirm window, select the green OK button and the status of the bill reverts to Deleted.

The details of a cancelled bill disappear entirely, while the erased details of deleted and voided bills can be found by searching under the grouping labelled All, and checking the Include Deleted & Voided tick box.

If you click the Cancel button on a bill, no confirmation window appears, so you don't have a chance to back out. The bill is gone forever.

Generating a purchase order

While living in Cheltenham, I worked for an organisation that closely monitored promotional spends against budget. This process involved raising a detailed internal purchase order. The purchase order needed to be authorised by appropriate personnel, and my role involved checking the proposed account allocations.

A purchase order is a document detailing agreed spends for products or services. Internally, it monitors and controls spending; externally, it provides suppliers with authorisation to deliver their good and services.

The Purchase Orders dashboard is found below the Bills dashboard on the Purchases dashboard. It's quite sparse until you've created some purchase orders, but this section covers what it can include once it's populated.

The high-level Purchase Orders dashboard is split into two blocks: Buttons and a menu bar. Click the blue See All hyperlink to see a detailed Purchase Orders dashboard. At the top is a button for creating new purchase orders and across the top are five tabs: All, Draft, Awaiting Approval, Approved and Billed (see Figure 7-3).

Figure 7-3:
The
Purchase
Orders
dashboard.

Clicking the + New Purchase Order button brings up the Purchase Order form (see Figure 7-4). The steps for creating a new Purchase Order mirror the steps for creating a new bill — refer to the section 'Creating a new bill', earlier in this chapter. However, you need to be aware of the following three different options:

- ✔ **Delivery Date:** This field offers a pop-up calendar and above it are four blocks: Today, + 7days, + 14 days and + 30 days. Click the + 30 days and the field populates with a delivery date 30 days after the Purchase Order date.

- ✔ **Order Number:** This auto generates from the default invoice settings. Refer to Chapter 6 for more insight into this.

- ✔ **Theme:** Check if your existing themes are appropriate. If they're not, you may need to create a dedicated purchase order template. Further information about themes and templates can be found in Chapter 6.

The block at the base of the Purchase Order includes fields for the Delivery Address, general contact details and Delivery Instructions.

The Delivery Address and Attention fields populate from the Organisation Settings existing information. To change the Delivery Address click on the drop-down options and select from None, + Add new address, + Add one-off address, + Search from contacts, Postal and Physical.

The Delivery Instructions field is a 500-character text field where you can include specific instructions for the delivery company — so, for example, you can let the delivery person know to bring your goods to the red door at the back of the building while navigating the guard dogs!

Like a bill, a Purchase Order can be saved or approved.

Although a little less exciting than cicadas emerging from underground after 17 years, understanding the life cycle of the Purchase Order is worthwhile. If you opted to save the Purchase Order as Draft, under the Draft tab, you have the option to Submit for Approval, Approve, Print, Send or Delete it.

At any stage in the Purchase Order's life cycle, you can click on the Purchase Order, click the Options button, select Copy to...and copy the contents to a draft Bill, Purchase Order or Sales Invoice.

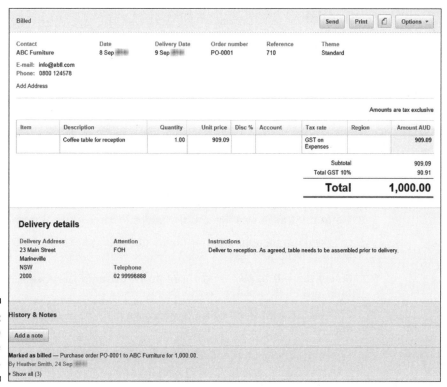

Figure 7-4:
The
Purchase
Order form.

Once a Purchase Order is Awaiting Approval, under the Awaiting Approval tab you have the option to Approve, Print, Send or Delete it (refer to Figure 7-3).

Under the Approved tab, you have the Billed, Print, Send or Copy To options. The Billed option marks the Purchase Order as billed, but does not create a bill from this. Once a Purchase Order has been marked as billed, under the Billed tab, you have the option to Print, Send or Copy the order.

Making Payments

You can use Xero two ways to make payments: Recording individual payments or scheduling recurring payments. The following sections take you through these options. You can make payments to bills directly from within your Bank Reconciliation screen (see Chapter 8). However, where a delay might occur between when you make the transaction and when it hits the bank — for example, payment via cheque — it's important to record the transaction immediately and Xero will find the match once it clears from the bank account.

Before processing payments, you need to have set up your bank accounts in Xero — refer to Chapter 2 for more on this. When preparing to make a payment, check that enough money is available in your business accounts. Check your bank account directly — the business account balances on the Xero dashboard may not include recent transactions.

Recording an individual payment

To record a full or partial payment against a bill, follow these steps:

1. **Go to the Purchases dashboard and click Accounts⇨Purchases.**

   Bills need to be approved for payment before payment can be applied against them.

2. **Select the bill to pay by drilling down through the Awaiting Payment tabs and click through to the detail of the bill.**

   The bottom of the bill features the Make a Payment block (see Figure 7-5).

Figure 7-5:
The Make
a Payment
block.

Make a payment ⑦

Amount Paid	Date Paid	Paid From	Reference	
2,500.00	13 Feb ▼	091 - Business Sav ▼	Deposit	**Add Payment**

3. **Fill out the Amount Paid field.**

4. **Fill out the Date Paid calendar field.**

5. **Select the general ledger account the payment is to be made from using the drop-down list in the Paid From field.**

   Payment may be made from your bank, credit card or PayPal account, or any account set up to enable payments from this account. Refer to Chapter 2 for guidance on customising general ledger accounts.

6. **Enter a useful reference in the optional Reference field**

7. **Check the box beside the Pay by Check field (if required).**

   Only US users have this feature (see the sidebar 'Payments made by check' for more).

8. **Click the green Add Payment button.**

   At the top of the screen, a green tick appears, with confirmation details of the payment and a blue Send Remittance Advice link. See the section 'Sending remittance advice', later in this chapter, for guidance on how to do this.

   If the Pay by Check field was selected, the Pay by Check window opens.

   The information on the check autofills and the check number and Pay To field can be overridden. For traceability, adding further information to the optional Memo field is good practice.

9. **Click the blue Edit link to add or edit recipient's address details.**

10. **Click the drop-down arrow at the Check Style field to select a check style (if required).**

    See the section 'Stylising your check', later in this chapter, for information on different check styles.

11. **Select your print and/or save options.**

    You have three options: Save & Print PDF, Save and Cancel. To print a check, click Save & Print PDF and, at the Print Check window, click Print now.

    The PDF of the check downloads to your computer's download file. To finalise payment, email or mail it to the client.

Payments made by check

A check is a document authorising the bank to pay the named recipient money from the payee's account. Two common spellings for this document are used: cheque (UK spelling) and check (US spelling). Because the feature in Xero is only available to US users, and it's labelled **Check**, that's the spelling I'm using here.

US users can access the Checks dashboard to search and review checks, establish their current status, print to PDF, and void or delete checks if they are no longer valid or were created in error. When voiding a check there is the option to choose the date you want the check to be voided on. From the Checks dashboard, you can also access the Spend Money button. To access the Checks dashboards go to Accounts⇨Checks.

Recording batch payments

Recording batch payments may not be as enticing as a batch of warm and gooey chocolate-chip cookies, but using this feature within Xero can really reduce processing time.

Creating a new batch payment

To record batch payments, follow these steps:

1. **Check single or multiple bills to be paid in the Awaiting Payment area of the Purchases dashboard.**

2. **Click the Batch Payment or Make Payment button (for US users).**

   The Confirm window opens.

   For US users, the Make Payment window opens with three options: Pay By Check, Batch Payment and Cancel.

3. **Click the green OK or Batch Payment button (for US users).**

   The New Batch Payment window opens (see Figure 7-6).

4. **Enter the date payment will be made in the mandatory Payment Date calendar.**

5. **Select the account payments will be made from in the mandatory Bank Account field at the top of the window.**

6. **Enter supplier bank account details in the Bank Account column.**

   Once a bank account has been allocated to a supplier payment, this account will save and be available the next time you make a batch payment. If you intend to use this process to transfer payments electronically, you must complete this field — see the next section.

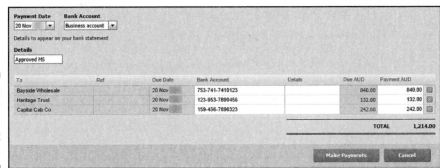

Payment Date	Bank Account						
20 Nov ▼	Business account ▼						
Details to appear on your bank statement							
Details							
Approved MS							

To	Ref	Due Date	Bank Account	Details	Due AUD	Payment AUD	
Bayside Wholesale		20 Nov	753-741-7410123		840.00	840.00	☒
Heritage Trust		20 Nov	123-953-7890456		132.00	132.00	☒
Capital Cab Co		20 Nov	159-456-7896323		242.00	242.00	☒
					TOTAL	**1,214.00**	

Make Payments   Cancel

Figure 7-6: The New Batch Payment window.

7. **Enter a payment or supplier reference in the optional Details field.**

8. **If required, override the amount to be paid in the Payment column.**

   The amount outstanding for the bill autofills in the payment field; however, if you're simply making a part-payment or deposit, override the amount.

9. **Click the green Make Payments button.**

   The batch payment is created.

Exporting a batch file to your bank

If you've never created a bank file, take a few moments to get your head around the process; it may save you a huge amount of time! A bank file is a file that can be uploaded to your internet banking. Payments are processed in Xero, and details of those payments (including full bank account details) are exported via a bank file. You then import the bank file into your online banking. But don't worry — importing the file does not result in payments going out from your account like automatic balls from a baseball-pitching machine. Once the bank file is imported, you can see full details of pending payments and authorise them accordingly.

Note: Prior to being able to upload files to your bank, you need to contact your bank and let staff know you want to upload electronic bank files. Staff can then enable this feature. Depending on the bank, staff may need to provide you with a security code device and a direct entry user ID, and let you know if you need to include a self-balancing transaction.

After a payment is processed within Xero (refer to preceding sections), follow these steps to export a bank file:

1. **Click Export Batch File from the batch payment window.**

   The bank file is downloaded to your computer.

   Note: For this to work, business bank details and supplier bank details need to be entered into Xero.

2. **Manually upload the file to your online internet banking.**

   Some financial institutions require you to use a banking security token at this stage. It generates a unique security code every few seconds. You need this code when you log in, along with your username and password.

3. **Authorise the payments from within your internet banking.**

After processing the bank file, you don't need to store it, just delete it.

If you didn't create a bank file immediately after the batch payment was processed, you can return later to the payment. Locate it under the relevant bank account's Account Transactions tab and click on the relevant payment (the Description is Payment: Multiple Items). At the top, you can access the Export Batch File button, and work through the preceding steps.

Removing allocated payments

You may find you've assigned a payment to a bill and then need to remove it, because you need to change the details of the bill or the payment was allocated incorrectly. To 'unallocate' a payment follow these steps:

1. **Go to the Purchases dashboard, click on Accounts⇨Purchases, click the Search button on the right side, and use the criteria options that have appeared to search for the bill.**

2. **Locate the bill and drill down on it to see the bill detail.**

3. **Click on the relevant Less Payment hyperlink and the corresponding dollar amount at the bottom of the column headed Amount.**

   The Payment transaction appears. If multiple payments have been assigned, there will be multiple lines of payment, and each one needs to be individually removed.

4. **On the Payment transaction, click on the Options button, and select Remove & Redo from the drop-down menu.**

   The payment is removed from the bill. If additional payments need to be removed, click your web browser's back arrow twice and then refresh the screen to see the current transaction details. Repeat Steps 3 and 4 to remove additional payments.

Mastering Other Payment Considerations

As well as the basic functions of entering and approving bills, and making payments, with Xero you can also master some more advanced options, such as working with repeating bills, scheduling payment and sending remittance advices. The following sections cover these aspects and more.

Printing bills

You're unlikely to need to print the bill created in Xero on a regular basis, but if you ever need to, follow these steps to print your record of the supplier bills:

1. **Go to the Purchases dashboard, drill down on the Awaiting Payment tab to find the relevant bill and check the box to the left of the document(s).**

    A single bill or multiple bills can be selected and processed at the same time.

2. **Click the blue Print button.**

    The Confirm window opens.

3. **Click the green OK button.**

    The Print Bills window opens.

4. **Click the green Print Now button.**

    You see a status window telling you that Xero is creating a PDF.

5. **Print the PDF by clicking the Print icon in the upper-left corner.**

Working with Repeating Bills

Unfortunately, many business bills arrive on an all-too-regular basis, but utilising Xero's Repeating Bills function, which automatically generates new supplier bills based on a saved template, makes this a little less burdensome.

Once you've defined a Repeating Bill template, an automatic bill is created and saved as a draft or approved (as per the requirements you've defined within the template). Templates can be edited if terms change. All this results in you being able to use your valuable time to earn money rather than prepare bills!

To create a Repeating Bill, follow these steps:

1. **Go to the Purchases dashboard, click on the drop-down menu beside the + New button and select the Repeating Bill option.**

   The New Repeating Bill window opens (see Figure 7-7).

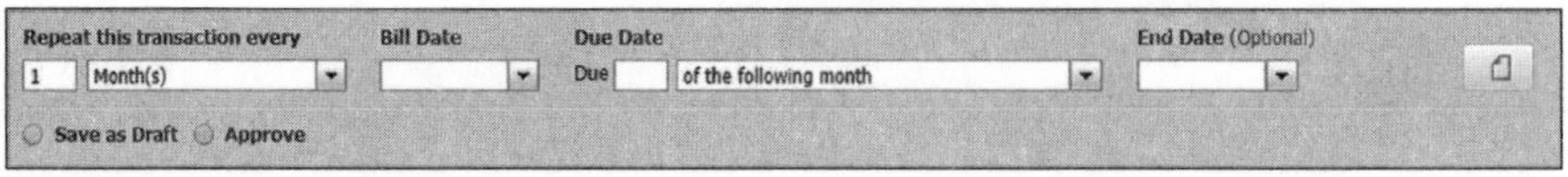

Figure 7-7:
The New
Repeating
Bill window.

Repeat this transaction every		Bill Date	Due Date		End Date (Optional)	
1	Month(s) ▾	▾	Due	of the following month ▾	▾	⌁
○ Save as Draft ○ Approve						

2. **Fill out the Repeat this Transaction Every fields.**

   You have a number of options here. For example, if you want the bill to repeat every month, enter 1 in the numeral field and select Month(s) from the drop-down menu.

3. **Select the original Bill Date by clicking in the calendar field.**

4. **Define the repeating Bill Due date.**

   Again, you have a number of options here. For example, if you want the bill to be due on the 7th of the following month, enter 7 in the Due field and select Of the Following Month from the drop-down menu.

5. **Fill out the optional End Date calendar field (if end date is known).**

6. **Click the file symbol and attach files relevant to the recurring transactions.**

   If the recurring transaction was for car lease payments, for example, you could attach the original supporting lease document here, and it would be associated with every transaction — without using up any extra storage space.

7. **Select the Save as Draft or Approve option.**

   Selecting this option tells Xero whether you'd like the bill saved as a draft or approved when it generates, based on the dates you have entered.

   Where the bill is the same every repeat instance, you would choose the option to approve. Where the bill might vary in value every instance — for example, a phone bill — you would choose to save it as a draft.

8. **Fill out the remainder of the body of the bill by following the steps outlined in the section 'Creating a new bill', earlier in this chapter.**

   Use the reference field to give the bill an identifying name.

9. **Save the template by clicking the green Save button.**

   The template is filed under the Repeating tab. When the bill is created, it indicates that it has been generated from a repeating transaction.

Scheduling payments

A business I worked for in London struggled to pay its bills. Suppliers sat in the reception area throughout the working day, desperate to collect what was owed to them. The situation was very depressing. As money was made available, it was released and applied to outstanding bills. The members of the Accounts Payable department had to pay close attention to who was to be paid. Suppliers with goods and services that were needed to keep the business operating were prioritised. Future payments were grouped together in bundles of £10,000 lots, so the business could easily identify and pay critical payments quickly. Batching future payments enabled the business to protect their cash flow during difficult times.

While this wasn't a happy scenario for the suppliers, the payment system kept the business afloat and people employed.

Xero's Schedule Payments feature enables you to develop a program of planned payments, helping you manage your cash flow. You're able to see the total payments due on a particular day, and you can click on the date to see a list of scheduled payments planned for that day. Follow these steps to schedule future payments:

1. **Check single or multiple bills to be paid in the Awaiting Payment area of the Purchases dashboard.**

2. **Click the Schedule Payment button and select the intended date in the calendar box.**

   The Planned Date column fills out with the selected data. Hovering beside the planned date reveals a blue plus and minus option and a red cross. Clicking the blue plus and minus options increases or decreases the date by one day. The date can be overridden by clicking it and selecting another date from the calendar box or erased by clicking the red cross.

Once you've entered future payments, a Schedule of Planned Payments block appears on the Purchases dashboard, with the payments grouped by payment dates. Each block clearly details the date and the total group payment. Click on the block to drill down to see the batch payments for that date.

Stylising your check

I was once told if you stamped the correct details on a cow, you could use the mammal in place of a typical paper-based check. Far easier to customise checks in Xero, and send them as payment!

Note: Only US users can access the Checks dashboard in Xero and customise a check.

To customise a check, follow these steps:

1. **Go to Settings⇨General Settings⇨Check Styles.**

   The Check Styles dashboard appears.

2. **Click the Options button on the right.**

   Four options appear on the drop-down menu: Edit, Alignment, Copy and Upload Logo.

3. **Click Edit.**

   The Edit Check Style window appears.

4. **In the Name field, enter Company Check.**

   See if the address details are correct and leave all the other information as is.

5. **Click the green Save button.**

6. **Set the check's print area alignment in relation to the paper, by clicking the Options button and selecting Alignment**

   The Check Alignment window opens (see Figure 7-8).

   Note: After the first time of drilling through to Options (refer to Step 2), two additional options appear here: Remove Logo and Delete.

7. **Align the check portion as required and click the green Save button.**

   Click in the Check area to activate the ability to edit the alignment. You have the option to click on the directional arrows, or enter absolute point values in the Top(y) and Left(x) box. Repeat this exercise for the Voucher area. Click the blue Reset button, if you need to start afresh.

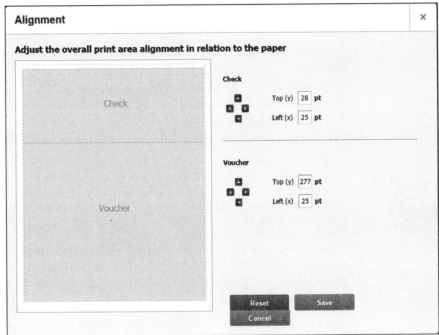

Figure 7-8:
The Check
Alignment
window.

The check doubles as a remittance advice, because it has room at the top for the check details and at the bottom is a voucher, with the reason for the payment. The recipient can give the check to the bank, and retain the voucher for record-keeping purposes.

8. **Upload a logo to the stylised check by clicking the Options button and selecting Upload Logo.**

9. **Click Browse, select the logo, click Open and click the blue Upload button.**

Sending remittance advice

A remittance advice notice lets your suppliers know that you've processed a payment against their bills, so they stop chasing you for payment! The notice details the supplier bills that payments have been applied against and can assist suppliers during their reconciliation process.

Send a remittance advice immediately after payment has been made by following these steps:

1. **Click the Send Remittance Advice link or the Send Remittance button.**

   The Send Remittance Advice link appears at the top of the screen after making an individual payment and the Send Remittance button appears after making a batch payment.

   Clicking the link or the button opens the Send Remittance Advice window.

   If you need to resend a remittance advice, or didn't send it directly after payment was made, access the Purchases Dashboard and search for the relevant paid bill. Drill down to the detail, and click the blue Payment link on the bottom left. The Transaction: Payment window opens. At this stage you also have the option to View Remittance PDF, but it's preferable to email it. Click Options⇨Send Remittance to access the Send Remittance Advice window. (This option isn't available for US users.)

2. **Fill out the Email Address field.**

   Once an email address is entered as part of the remittance advice process, it is added to the contact details.

3. **Edit the email Subject field and Message body as necessary.**

4. **Check the Send Me a Copy box.**

   This allows you to maintain a digital copy of correspondence.

Remittance advices are useful for reconciling purposes but, once I have receipted and reconciled payment, I shred any printed versions. I hate unnecessary paper!

Managing credit notes

If a change to a supplier bill occurs, you may request the supplier issues a credit note. The credit note can offset outstanding bills, or accompany a refund. (If you have accounting knowledge, then, yes, technically this is known as a debit note — don't get confused by Xero's terminology!)

To process a credit note, follow these steps:

1. **Go to the Purchases dashboard, click the drop-down arrow beside the + New button and click the Credit Note button.**

2. **Complete the details on the Credit Note screen.**

   Include a reference to what bill it is applied against, and enter positive values!

3. Save or approve the Credit Note.

Follow the same steps as with saving and approving bills (refer to the section 'Approving and cancelling bills' earlier in this chapter, for more details).

If no outstanding supplier bill exists, the Approved Credit Note simply saves, and is listed on the Awaiting Payment grouping on the dashboard. If, at a future date, a bill is approved against the supplier, an Allocate Outstanding Credit? window opens, where you can select Allocate (or Skip if you don't want to allocate now). Select Allocate and a window very similar to Figure 7-9 opens.

If, however, an outstanding supplier bill does exist, the Allocate Balance on Credit Note appears automatically appears.

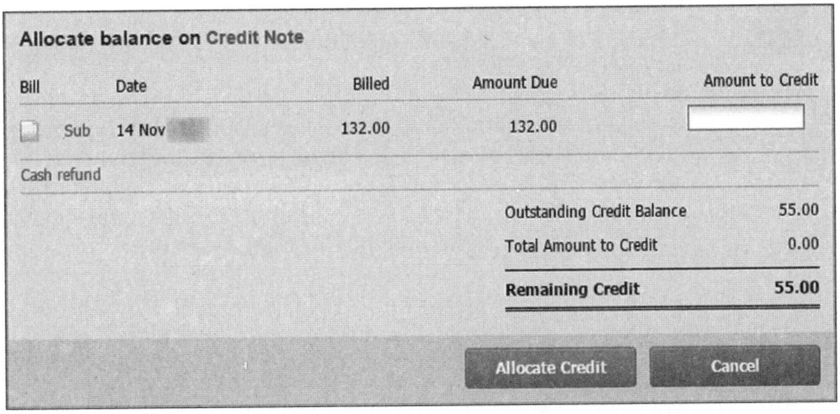

Allocate balance on Credit Note				
Bill	Date	Billed	Amount Due	Amount to Credit
Sub	14 Nov	132.00	132.00	
Cash refund				
			Outstanding Credit Balance	55.00
			Total Amount to Credit	0.00
			Remaining Credit	**55.00**
			Allocate Credit	Cancel

Figure 7-9: The Allocate Balance on Credit Note window.

4. If the credit note should be applied to this bill, allocate the amount accordingly.

In the example shown in Figure 7-9, the value of the credit note can be split across individual bills or treated as a cash refund. Once you enter the full credit amount against a bill, the Remaining Credit balance becomes zero.

Where a new bill was raised against an existing credit note, you only have the option to allocate the credit note amount to the recently raised bill.

5. Click the green Allocate Credit button.

The amount is applied to the Bill. *Note:* The amount allocated cannot be greater than the invoice.

Entering Expense Claims

In an ideal world, you're able to enter all business transactions through your business accounts and avoid cash transactions altogether; however, this rarely ends up being the case. Say, for example, an employee of your business fills the business car up with $50 worth of petrol and then pays for it personally — so spends personal money on behalf of the business. The employee charging the purchase to a company credit card, so it then goes through the normal payment process, is preferable, but in real life that may not be feasible. Instead, the employee needs to claim the money back from the business and the payment needs to be processed as an ad hoc expense claim.

Processing expenses though Xero means your employees are responsible for entering their own expenses and are no longer bound to one petty cash tin (perhaps kept at head office or locked away somewhere else). And accounts staff are freed of the time-consuming task of processing an old-fashioned nasty petty cash tin!

Xero's Expense Claims dashboard (accessed via the bottom right corner of the main dashboard) is where you process such claims. All claims need to go through the same process. A new expense claim is first added as a Draft claim. It then needs to be submitted for approval, then approved and authorised for payment. Finally, the claim is paid.

The Expense Claims dashboard (see Figure 7-10) contains four headings summarising the current status of expense claims, and an Add Receipt option.

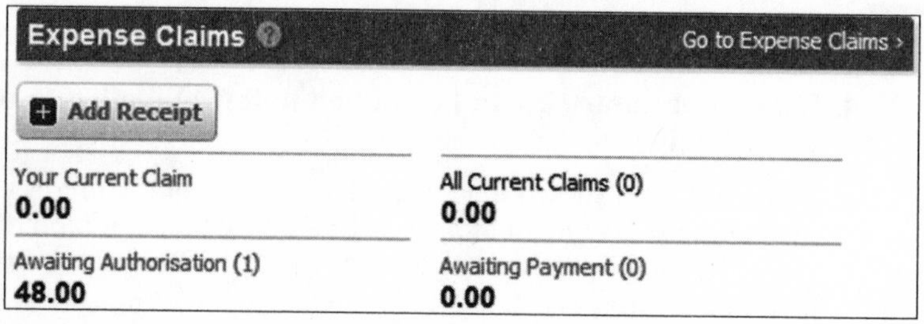

Figure 7-10:
The Expense Claims dashboard.

Expense Claims	Go to Expense Claims ›
+ Add Receipt	
Your Current Claim	All Current Claims (0)
0.00	**0.00**
Awaiting Authorisation (1)	Awaiting Payment (0)
48.00	**0.00**

Here's a summary of the four headings on the Expense Claims dashboard, and the information they provide:

✓ **Your Current Claim:** This field is context sensitive to the user who has logged into Xero, so if you're logged in, this field shows any expense claim you've lodged that's still current. If you're peeking over the shoulder of another user, this field displays that user's current expense claim.

✔ **All Current Claims:** This field is the total of all current expense claims in the business for all users. If you're a micro business with only one user, this amount always equals the total shown under Your Current Claims. At this stage, you can't access the underlying detail for the expense claims of other users.

✔ **Awaiting Authorisation:** This field details the total expense claims awaiting authorisation. The user must have the required authority level (assigned via their user role within Xero) to authorise and approve the expense claim.

✔ **Awaiting Payment:** This field details the total expense claims awaiting payment.

Clicking the hyperlinks on the Expense Claims dashboard takes you through to the Expense Claims summary area.

Several people may be involved in the processing of expense claims: The user who makes the claim, a first level manager who authorises the claim, a second level manager who approves the claim and the financial controller who makes the payment. Of course, if your business is very small, you may be wearing all the hats and performing most or even all of these roles.

Adding a new expense claim

The process of claiming an expense starts with the user entering the payment as a New Receipt in Xero.

To enter a New Receipt, do the following:

1. **Scan your receipt.**

   You don't need to be able to upload a copy of your receipt to Xero to process your claim, but storing receipts safely is always a good idea — rather than leaving them on the car dashboard to fade away! Xero allows PDF, jpg, png, and gif digital formats for the scanned receipts.

2. **Go to the Expense Claims dashboard and click the Add Receipt button.**

   The New Receipt window opens (see Figure 7-11). Multiple expenses can be entered and processed as a single batch at a later date.

New Receipt

Receipt from	Date	Reference			Total
					0.00

☑ Include Tax   Line item amounts are: ○ Tax Exclusive ⦿ Tax Inclusive

Description	Quantity	Unit Price		Amount AUD
	1.00	0.00		0.00

Account ⊙	+Add	Tax Rate	Region	+Add

⊕ Add a new line

	Subtotal	0.00
	GST	0.00
	TOTAL	**0.00**

Save & Add Another Receipt   Save   Cancel

Figure 7-11:
The New
Receipt
window.

3. **Attach a scanned copy of the receipt to the transaction by clicking on the blue 'Attach a File' hyperlink below Attachment.**

The source document is stored online in a retrievable format. This is an efficient method of storing source documents and legal in many jurisdictions. Check your own local laws and requirements. This step is optional but it's a good habit to adopt.

4. **Enter the relevant receipt data and save the transaction.**

The Receipt From field is linked to your Contacts, so you would enter the supplier name here. If you have more than one receipt to enter, select the blue Save & Add Another Receipt button, return to Step 1 and repeat the process. To record a single receipt (or once you've entered your last claim) click on the green Save button.

Saving your last claim takes you to an expanded view of the Current Claims window, listing a summary of current expense claims. ***Note:*** The status of the claim at this stage will be Draft, and the claim now needs to be approved (see the section 'Submitting a claim for approval', later in this chapter).

Making mobile expense claims

Keep on top of expenses while enjoying a latte by scanning and uploading expense receipts to Xero on your mobile device. (Now, to me, this sounds geektastic!)

Many of my clients tell me they don't want their employees messing around allocating account codes to receipts — so they don't let employees use this feature. I'm here to tell you the process is quick and easy, and the employee doesn't need to touch account numbers. Once uploaded, you or your bookkeeper can access the updated information within a matter of seconds, code it, and approve or forward it to managers for approval. Employees on offsite projects can submit expenses in a timely manner, ensuring pesky receipts don't go missing, and income isn't missed because the expenses aren't on-charged to clients!

So flatten your receipts and grab your mobile device — here's how to upload the basics of an expense on your iPhone:

1. **Tap on the Xero icon, enter your four-digit passcode or fingerprint and click the Expenses icon at the bottom of the screen.**

   The Current Claim dashboard appears.

2. **Click the blue Claim Your Purchases button in the centre of the screen.**

   If you're adding subsequent purchases after this, you'll just need to click a grey cross on the top right.

   A receipt entry form appears.

3. **Enter the receipt supplier in the From field.**

   The field draws from your existing list of contacts so you may be able to select an existing contact.

4. **Click the blue Add an Item hyperlink to add specifics about the receipt.**

   On the next screen you can add Description, Quantity, Price, Account, and Job details. On the top right, select the grey Done link.

   If you don't know the account or job code, leave it blank. (However, I suspect many employees are in a better position to know what account the expense should actually be allocated to than the bookkeeper, so allowing them to code expenses could be another time saver.)

   Note: The use of *item* here does not refer to, and cannot access, Inventory items. This process is for simple receipts only; detailed purchases should run through the Purchases area accordingly.

5. **Click the grey Add Files button and then Take Photo, and take a photo of the receipt.**

   The image of the receipt attaches itself to the claim. In many jurisdictions this is a legally acceptable storage method for paper receipts. (If unsure, check with your accountant.)

6. **Click the Details link, and edit the tax status of the Amounts and Date field, if required.**

   You can add supplementary information about the receipt in the reference section.

7. **Click the grey Add button**

   And you're done.

Here's how to upload expenses on an android device:

1. **Tap on the Xero icon on your mobile device, and enter your four-digit passcode.**

   The home dashboard screen opens. Across the top are four headings: Dashboard, Invoices, Expenses and Contacts. *Note:* If you move away from the mobile version of Xero, when you return you need to re-enter your four-digit passcode.

2. **Click on the Expenses heading at the top of the screen to access an Expenses dashboard revealing any Current Claims.**

3. **Click the + on the top right and from the drop-down menu select Add Receipt.**

   A numbered Receipt screen opens. Refer to the section 'Adding a new expense claim', earlier in this chapter, for more. The fields available are From, Description, Total, Categorise to an Account and Details. After the initial information has been added, Add Another Item appears, and additional details with individual coding can be added. On the middle left is a camera symbol to facilitate taking a photo or adding a file to the receipt.

4. **Click the tick on the top right corner to save the receipt.**

5. **Click the Xero icon at the top of the screen and then on the top right click Logout to securely log out of Xero.**

What I've shown in the preceding steps is the bare basics, to get you (and your employees) in the habit of recording expenses straightaway. You can complete more fields in this type of expense claim — refer to the section 'Creating a new bill', earlier in this chapter, for guidance.

Submitting a claim for approval

Once the claim has been entered (refer to preceding sections), it needs to be submitted for approval, as follows:

1. **Go to the Expense Claims dashboard and click on the Your Current Claims link.**

   This brings up the Current Claim table (see Figure 7-12).

2. **Select the check box to the left of the expense claims that you want to submit for first level approval and click the Submit for Approval button.**

   A confirmation box opens, informing you that you have selected items to be submitted for approval.

3. **Click OK.**

   This moves the claim to the Awaiting Authorisation area in the Expense Claims window.

To view a summary of the claims awaiting authorisation, click on the Awaiting Authorisation link on the Expense Claims dashboard. *Note:* If you selected multiple expenses for approval at the same time, they're batched together in a single claim, so you'd only see one line here.

The claim still needs to be approved so the expense can be paid and included in the business financial statements — see the following section.

Figure 7-12:
The Current
Claim table.

Add Receipt							
Current Claim	Previous Claims				Awaiting Authorisation (1)	Awaiting Payment (0)	Archive
Submit for Approval	Delete	1 item selected					1 receipt | 50.00
☑ Receipt ▾		Receipt From	Receipt Date	Date Entered	Items	Status	Amount
☑ 2		Claimant's name	12 Feb 2013	12 Feb 2013	1	Draft	50.00

Reviewing and authorising the claim

Once an expense claim has been created and submitted for approval (refer to preceding sections), a first level manager needs to authorise the claim.

Users with Read Only and Invoice Only (Draft Only or Sales Only) roles (refer to Chapter 4) can't authorise expense claims in Xero.

To select the transaction that needs to be authorised, click the Awaiting Authorisation link on the Expense Claims dashboard. This takes you to the Awaiting Authorisation table (see Figure 7-13). Select the expense claim to be approved by clicking the check box to the left of the Receipt and click the Approve button. (I know this is a little bit confusing — this transaction was sitting under the Awaiting Authorisation link, so you probably would expect an Authorise button instead — but an Approve button it is!)

After clicking the Approve button, the status for the claim changes from Awaiting Review to Approved.

At the Awaiting Authorisation stage, you or the first level manager who's reviewing the claim can decline or delete the expense claim — if, for example, you decide it's not an appropriate business expense.

Figure 7-13:
The Awaiting
Authorisation
table.

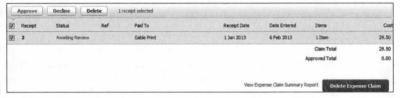

Once the claim has been approved, it can be authorised by the second level manager.

To authorise a claim, go to the bottom of the Expense Claims screen on the home dashboard and click on the Awaiting Authorisation link. Click though on a claim to see the underlying detail. Below this detail, the Authorise Expense Claim block appears with two fields to complete: Payment Due Date and Reporting Date (see Figure 7-14).

Even though you're processing the claim now, the expense may actually have occurred earlier in the year. To be correctly reflected in your financial reports, you can make the date in the Reporting Date field in the Authorise Expense Claim block different to the Payment Due Date (the date the payment is actually made).

Complete the two fields and click the blue Authorise button, and claims are now ready for payment (covered in the following section).

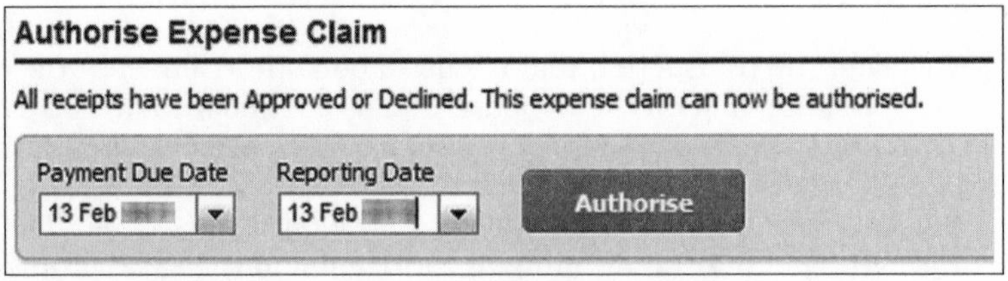

Figure 7-14:
The Authorise
Expense
Claim
block.

Authorise Expense Claim

All receipts have been Approved or Declined. This expense claim can now be authorised.

Payment Due Date Reporting Date
13 Feb ▼   13 Feb ▼   **Authorise**

Paying the claim

Finally you're ready to pay the expense claim. Click on the Awaiting Payment link on the Expense Claims dashboard to view a list of expense claims awaiting payment. Click anywhere along the row to drill down to see the detail of the expense claim you wish to pay.

To complete the payment, you need to fill out the following four fields at the bottom of the Expense Claims window:

  ✔ **Amount Paid:** This is the actual amount the claimant will be paid. *Note:* The expense claim can be partially paid, with the unpaid amount remaining in Xero as awaiting payment.

  ✔ **Date Paid:** This is the actual date the expense payment will be paid.

  ✔ **Paid From:** This is the account the expense claim will be paid out of.

  ✔ **Reference:** For audit purposes, always include a detailed reference.

After completing the four fields, click the green Paid button. The processed expense claim now sits in the archive summary area within Xero and the claimant needs to be reimbursed for the claim, if that hasn't already happened.

At the very bottom of many of the Xero windows sits the History & Notes area, which details the history of user activity in this area. You (and other users) can also add explanatory notes to this area, and these notes are tagged with the date and the user name. They are excellent for audit tracking because they cannot be edited or deleted.

Chapter 8

Reconciling Your Bank Accounts

- -

In This Chapter

▶ Getting ready to reconcile

▶ Ticking off your correctly matched transactions

▶ Looking at transactions that don't seem to match

▶ Making use of the Cash Coding spreadsheet

▶ Going through your imported bank statements and locating transactions

▶ Accessing Spend Money and Receive Money functions

▶ Knowing how to correct your mistakes

- -

*R*econciling your accounts involves matching cash movements from your bank statement with transactions recorded through Xero. Reconciling on a regular basis is an essential part of ensuring the accounting records portray an accurate reflection of your business finances — you don't want to waste time entering reams of incorrect data and producing gobbledegook. Instead, you want to produce accurate information such as management reports that you can use in your business to assist with business decisions and save valuable time — so, for example, you're not chasing outstanding debtors when the Aged Receivables report is incorrect.

As well as clarifying your business's accounts, reconciling helps you recognise and deal with fraud, errors, bank charges, bank interest, unpresented cheques and money received. Once you have conquered reconciling, not only are you in a position to make better-informed decisions, but you also feel the immense satisfaction of knowing that your financial records are accurate, complete and up to date.

This chapter explains how to reconcile bank accounts in Xero, including accepting transactions that Xero has matched up correctly and troubleshooting those transactions it hasn't. I also cover cash coding and how to process spending and receiving money transactions. Lastly, I show you how to fix any errors you make along the way.

Note: Businesses may use a number of financial facilities to process transactions: bank accounts, credit card accounts and payment gateways such as PayPal. Rather than constantly repeating this long list of possibilities, I simply use *bank account* to cover any sort of financial facility your business could use.

Preparing to Reconcile

Reconciliation is pretty easy with Xero, but a little bit of preparation makes it even easier. Make sure that you have everything on hand, including:

- ✔ Cheque books
- ✔ Deposit books
- ✔ Receipts
- ✔ Remittance advices
- ✔ Statements
- ✔ Supplier invoices

You should also have handy any notes from colleagues explaining transactions. For example, you may assume money received by a landlord from a tenant is rental income; however, if it is actually a bond or deposit payment you need to treat the transaction quite differently. These notes are important because they provide further guidance on how to accurately code the transaction (see the section 'Taking Advantage of Cash Coding', later in this chapter, for more on this).

The corresponding detailed transactions automatically feed in from your bank once activated or they can be imported. (Bank feeds and manually importing statements are covered in Chapter 4.)

Any transactions that don't pass through your bank accounts, such as cash payments for expenses, won't be captured with this reconciliation process. Instead, you can enter those transactions via Expense Claims, covered in Chapter 7.

Reconciliations should be done in a timely manner. Once you have your accounts set up in Xero and are taking advantage of automatic bank feeds (refer to Chapters 2 and 4), reconciling your main accounts on a daily basis is hard to resist. If you have the time and the inclination, go ahead — once people get in the swing of it, many find momentum builds up and they happily reconcile daily. A client of mine who recently set up his business accounts on Xero told me the first thing he did when he got out of bed in the morning was reconcile his business accounts — doing so gave him such a feeling of a satisfaction. (Of course, he could have even stayed in bed to do his bank rec, via the mobile app — refer to Chapter 1 for more.)

You may not wake up with the same ambition, of course. When deciding what accounts to reconcile when, keep the following in mind:

✔ If you want accurate Aged Receivable reports, you need to reconcile all bank accounts that take in customers' payments. Typically, this is your main business bank accounts (including credit card accounts and online gateways — and it's these accounts this chapter is focused on). Reconciling these accounts means the Money Coming In dashboard is up to date, and you're able to follow up on money you're owed. Businesses focused on maintaining a positive cash flow (and, over the long term, all businesses should be) may reconcile these types of accounts in-house on a daily basis.

✔ If you want accurate tax reports, all reports that have tax-related transactions passing through them need to be reconciled. This may include high-interest accounts, loan accounts and credit card accounts, but may not include some accounts. For example, a foreign currency account may not have a consumer tax passing through it, so you don't need to reconcile it to prepare an accurate consumer tax report. Most businesses reconcile these types of accounts on a weekly or monthly basis.

✔ If you want accurate financial reports, all accounts, including any owner's loan accounts and clearing accounts need to be reconciled.

Accounts such as suspense or clearing accounts are really easy to neglect. Do so at your peril! Depending on your reporting requirements, you may choose to reconcile any remaining accounts every three months; however, I recommend you make sure all accounts are reconciled at least once a month.

Reconciling accounts other than your main business accounts is covered in Chapter 10.

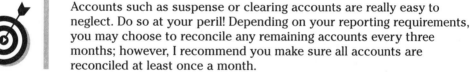

A comment on business bank accounts

Keep your business bank accounts as simple as possible! One of my clients set herself up on Xero over about a month, and every few days she kept discovering another account. Once her accounts were fully set up, the dashboard showed her the tangled web of bank accounts and added level of complexity she had created for herself. To simplify her business, she shut down nearly half of the bank accounts. Moving from a shoebox to Xero can highlight how complicated your business banking is. So keep your business banking simple, maintain as few bank accounts as viably possible, and take this opportunity to review what accounts you actually need.

Automagically Reconciling Accounts

Three bookkeepers walked into a small business. One of them sat down and processed the paper records manually and, at the end of the day, she waved and said, 'I'll see you tomorrow'. The second bookkeeper sat down at a computer and manually entered data into a desktop accounting package. At the end of the day, she waved and said, 'I'll see you next week'. The last bookkeeper sat down at her computer, opened up a Xero file, created some bank accounts with activated bank feeds, and reconciled the accounts in Xero. After a couple of hours she waved and said, 'I'm finished. Let me show you how to reconcile — it's easier than a game of space invaders. You just need to check the matches, click to reconcile and call me when you have any problems. I can remotely log in and help wherever you are, so you'll probably never see me again! Toodle Pip!' Seriously?! If you get your files set up correctly (as I show you throughout this book), it can be that easy!

The reconciliation process in Xero involves matching cash flows from your bank statement with transactions recorded through Xero. If Xero manages to match things up correctly (based on how you have set your files up), you can just whiz through your reconciliation, accepting these matches. Ideally, accepting Xero's suggested matches should clear the bulk of your reconciliation.

Understanding the hierarchy for matching

Xero works through a preferential process when suggesting matching transactions for reconciliation purposes. Understanding how Xero handles matches is useful so you can work quickly within the system.

Initially, Xero matches by amounts and reference. If the bank statement amount equals a transaction already entered in Xero, a match highlighted in green is suggested. If multiple Xero transactions exist that could match the transaction from the bank feed, an Other Possible Match(es) Found link appears. Drill down to select the correct matching transaction. Secondly, Xero refers to the first bank rule in the list of bank rules that matches the criteria. If you created a bank rule, and it doesn't seem to match as expected, check the list of bank rules (go to Dashboard⇨Bank Accounts⇨Bank Rules) and identify what rule may be jumping ahead in the matching process. Edit or rename the bank rule if necessary. (Refer to Chapter 4 for more on bank rules.) Finally, Xero remembers historical reconciliations and autosuggests a similar treatment, although the suggestion isn't highlighted. If Xero doesn't identify a possible match, a match isn't suggested!

Autosuggestions can't be edited; however, you can update them to reflect the most recent match. I've a client who reconciled a transaction using an incorrect tax code, so all future matches autosuggested re-using the same incorrect tax code. Once we intervened to reconcile using the correct tax code, all future autosuggestions were correct — phew!

Accepting transactions Xero has matched correctly

You don't have to guess how many transactions you need to reconcile, because Xero has the number staring you in the face in a big blue button when you open your dashboard. In Figure 8-1, the dashboard's Reconcile # Items button says I haven't done my homework on 28 transactions. Subtle! The easiest way to whittle down that number is to first accept all the transactions Xero has matched correctly.

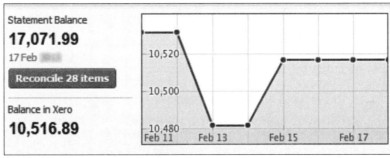

Figure 8-1: The bank account on the dashboard.

Here's how:

1. **Open at the home dashboard and click on the blue Reconcile # Items button.**

   This button highlights the number of transactions waiting to be reconciled.

   The first time you access the Xero reconciliation area, you'll see a Getting Started box at the top of the screen. This has some help information about the topic.

2. **Scroll down to the row of four tabs and click on Reconcile.**

   The row of four tabs gives you the following options: Reconcile, Cash Coding, Bank Statements and Account Transactions. If you have any transactions to reconcile, the Reconcile tab tells you how many by including the number within round brackets on the tab.

Note: You only see four tabs here if you have Adviser status or have been given access to cash coding in Xero. If you don't have this status, you won't see the Cash Coding tab. Refer to Chapter 4 for more about status levels.

By default, the Reconcile tab should be active. If it's not, click on it to reveal all the information included on this tab.

Clicking on the Reconcile tab drills down to the bank account area, detailing transactions that are yet to be reconciled. On the left side is the header *Review your bank statement lines . . .* and under this are the transactions from your bank account. (These statement lines are created when you import your bank statement or through automatic bank feeds — refer to Chapter 4 for more.) On the right, underneath the heading *. . . then match your transactions in Xero*, are the transactions to be confirmed in your Xero software.

Xero tries to match up the transactions from your bank statement and your transactions in Xero in pairs, which saves you a massive amount of time. However, you have the final say when confirming these suggestions; that's the reconciliation process!

At the base of the reconciliation window is a Suggest Previous Entries checkbox. Leave this box ticked if you want Xero to suggest how the transactions should be reconciled.

3. If unsure, explore a bank transaction.

Clicking on the blue More hyperlink opens the Statement Details pop-up window (see Figure 8-2). This provides further information on the transaction that the bank has collected, including as much of the following as is available: Transaction Date, Payee, Reference, Description, Transaction Amount, Transaction Type, Cheque No and Analysis Code.

This additional knowledge may assist you in the reconciliation process by helping you work out whether or not transactions have been matched correctly and whether you should go ahead and accept this matching.

Don't worry if all the fields aren't filled in within the Statement Details window. As bank institutions become more in tune to what businesses need, and what bank feeds can include, they're likely to provide more complete information.

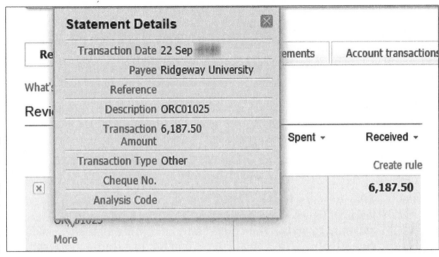

Figure 8-2:
The
Statement
Details
pop-up
window.

Click on the X in the upper-right corner to close the Statement Details window.

4. Reconcile any transactions that Xero has matched correctly.

When you're satisfied the transactions accurately match up, record them by clicking the blue OK button in the middle, shown in Figure 8-3.

Once you click the button, a tick pops up, replacing OK. The box turns green and the matched transactions fade away, indicating that they have been reconciled.

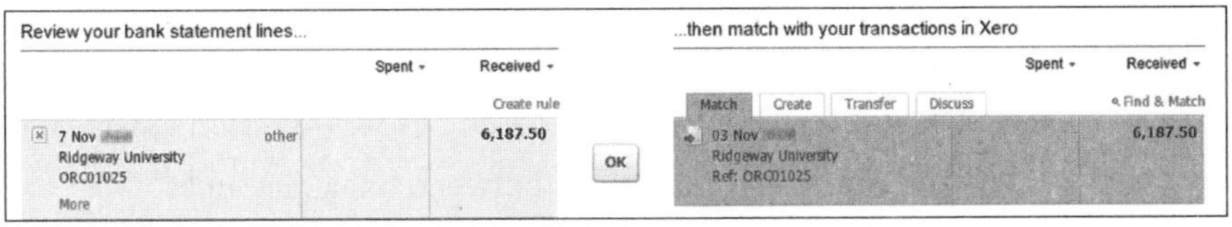

Figure 8-3:
The OK
button in
the middle
of matching
transactions.

5. Repeat Step 4 as often as needed.

Go through the entire list and reconcile all transactions that match correctly. (That's the easy part done.)

Busy? Let your team do the work

If you have your Xero account linked to your Xero advisory team, they're able to see the total number of unreconciled transactions in your business and react accordingly. Depending on the support agreement you have with your advisers, they may simply send you an email reminder or they may offer more detailed assistance to help you reconcile any outstanding transactions. If you'd like to see how to link Xero to an advisory team, and how the support package you choose can affect your monthly charges, check out Chapter 1.

After setting a business up, I typically find Xero takes about six weeks to learn all the regular transactions. Until that happens, the automagic of Xero can only go so far. Sometimes, after accepting all the transactions matched correctly by Xero, you still have outstanding transactions that need to be reconciled. In this case, you have to hunt for the matching information for payments in or out. This involves using the tabs in transaction boxes shown on the right side of the Reconcile tab — the Match, Create, Transfer and Discuss tabs — and the Find & Match function. How to use these features is discussed in the following section.

Tweaking Transactions to Reconcile

When you're reconciling, the columns of transactions don't always automagically match, and intervention is necessary. Xero offers a number of options that enable you to enter different types of transactions:

- ✔ **Match:** For when you need to match multiple transactions or create new transactions, or a mix of both.
- ✔ **Create:** For when you don't think the transaction exists in Xero.
- ✔ **Transfer:** For transactions between bank accounts.
- ✔ **Discuss:** For sending an SOS to your Xero advisory team — you can use this tab to add comments and seek input.

Each of these options can be seen in Figure 8-4 and are discussed in the following sections. But first, I cover Xero's hierarchy system for making matches.

Match	Create	Transfer	Discuss		Find & Match
Who	Name of the contact...		What	Choose the account...	▼
Why	Enter a description...				
Region	▼	Tax Rate	▼		Add details

Figure 8-4:
The transaction box.

Matching misfit transactions

Sometimes Xero can't find a simple match between the transactions shown in your bank statement and the transactions recorded through Xero. This can occur with split payments, for example. Perhaps you're focused on attaining bonus points on your credit card for your next holiday adventure, and so process numerous individual business payments against a personal credit card. You then withdraw the money to pay for these payments in one lump sum from your business account. The individual transactions need to be selected to match the single transaction reflected in the bank statement. Making a part payment can also create problems.

Here's how to get your existing transactions to play nice and match up:

1. **Find the four tabs within the transaction box and click the Match tab.**

   The Find & Match button appears.

2. **Click the Find & Match button.**

   While this may seem a pointless step, you must take it to access the Find & Match window, shown in Figure 8-5. At the top of the window, under the heading *1. Find & select matching transactions*, is a table with a list of possible transactions from Xero that may match or partially match the bank transaction.

3. **Narrow down the possibilities by using the search fields and clicking the blue Go button.**

   If a number of possibilities are displayed, the Match Options fields allow you to search by name or reference number, or by amount, to further refine your options. Possible matches to your search are returned in the 'Find and select matching transactions' table.

   Note: If you have multi-currency features, two check boxes may be available below the search area: Show Received Items to reveal bills, and Show Base Currency items only. Check or uncheck them as relevant.

1. Find & select matching transactions ⓘ

	Date	▲	Name	Ref/Number	Spent	Received
☐	21 Dec		Central Copiers	945-ORC	163.56 AUD	
☐	9 Jan		SMART Agency	SM0195-70135	2,000.00 AUD	
☐	7 Feb		Net Connect	O721-003	54.13 AUD	
☐	8 Feb		PowerDirect	C-20112	108.60 AUD	
☐	9 Feb		SMART Agency	SM0210-70209	2,500.00 AUD	
☐	14 Feb		PC Complete		2,166.99 AUD	

☐ Select all on this page   Showing 1 - 30 of 30

Match options

Search by name or ref/num

Search by amount

[   ] [Go]

Clear search

☐ Show Received Items
☑ Show AUD items only

2. View your selected transactions. Add new transactions, as needed.

No transactions have been selected

Create new transaction

⊞ New...   ▾

3. The sum of your selected transactions must match the money spent. Make adjustments, as needed.

No transactions selected   ⊞ Adjustments ▾

Must match: Money Spent `4,500.00 AUD`   0.00 AUD ⚠ Total is out by: 4,500.00

[Reconcile]   [Cancel]

Figure 8-5:
The Find
& Match
window.

4. **If the relevant transaction(s) are displayed, check the box to the left of each transaction and the line is highlighted.**

   If the sum of the selected transactions matches the amount shown in the bank statement, the Reconcile button at the bottom of the screen turns green.

5. **If you agree with the reconciliation, click the green reconcile button.**

   Congratulations! You've just cleared another transaction from your reconciliation list.

6. **Repeat these steps as appropriate.**

It may not always be so easy to select the transaction (or group of transactions) that match up to the payment shown on your bank statement. The payment made through your bank may be a part payment, or you may need to create a new transaction within Xero through the Transfer Money or Spend/Receive Money functions. (See the following sections for more on part payments and transferring money, and see the section 'Using the Spend Money and Receive Money Options', later in this chapter, for more on this topic.)

Processing part payments

Say you've committed to purchase goods for $1,000. You make a 30 per cent deposit up-front, with final payment due on delivery. You enter the $1,000 bill into Xero, within Purchases, and make a $300 payment against the outstanding debt through your business bank account. So, according to Xero, the transactions don't match up. To enlighten Xero, you need to split the allocation of the transaction.

To allocate this split transaction, follow these steps:

1. **Within the Find & Match window, go to the table at the top part of the window and check the box to the left of the relevant transaction.**

   Split appears next to the transaction as a hyperlink.

2. **Click on the blue Split hyperlink.**

   The Split Transaction window opens (shown in Figure 8-6).

Split transaction   ☒

Split this transaction if you need to record a part payment.

Balance	AUD 6,187.50
Part payment	500.00
Remaining amount	AUD 5,687.50

✓ **Split**   **Cancel**

Figure 8-6:
The Split
Transaction
window.

3. **Allocate the relevant portion of the transaction in the blank field.**

   Notice the remaining amount balance adjusts accordingly.

4. **Click the green Split button.**

   This records the transaction through Xero and means the transaction within Xero now matches the one shown on your bank statement and the Reconcile button at the bottom of the screen turns green.

5. **If you agree with the reconciliation, click the green reconcile button.**

   Another one down! (Is it time for chocolate yet?!)

6. **Repeat these steps as appropriate.**

Transferring money

If you can't find a match for a transaction showing on your bank statement with a transaction, set of transactions or part payment within Xero, you may realise that it doesn't yet exist in the Xero account you're reconciling and you need to add one or several more transactions. This brings you to the second part of the Find & Match window, signposted with the heading *2. View your selected transactions*. Clicking the New button to the right of this brings up two options: Spend Money and Transfer Money.

When I worked for a construction company in Singapore, every night our savvy accountant rang the bank, agreed a rate and transferred huge sums of money into a high-interest earning account overnight. The money worked hard while we slept! She then transferred it back in the morning. You may not have huge sums to transfer to a high-interest account, but if you do have excess money, your cash flow can benefit from utilising these sorts of account. When you transferred money between bank accounts (so the movement of cash shows on your bank statement), you also need to enter the transaction in Xero — using the Transfer Money option.

If you realise a transaction isn't a simple transfer, you may need the Spend/Receive Money options. Jump ahead to the section 'Using the Spend Money and Receive Money Options' section for a full explanation.

If you just need to transfer money from one account in Xero to the one you're reconciling, follow these steps:

1. **Click the New button on the Find & Match window.**

   This brings up the Spend Money and Transfer Money options.

2. **Select the Transfer Money option.**

   This brings up the New Transfer window (shown in Figure 8-7). The Date and the From Account fields are filled by default with the matching information. Select an account and enter the transfer amount. If you want to add Tracking categories, click +Add Tracking and the fields appear.

   The Transfer Money option can only be recorded between accounts set up as Bank Accounts, Credit Cards or Online Payment Accounts within Xero.

3. **Click the green Transfer button.**

   If the amounts match, the Reconcile button at the bottom of the screen turns green.

4. **If you agree with the reconciliation, click the green reconcile button.**

   Another transaction disappears from your reconciliation. (Just like chocolate disappears from your cupboard . . .)

Note: If you know you need to enter a money transfer through Xero, you can jump straight to doing so by using the Transfer tab (see the 'Transfer' section, later in this chapter, for more). This takes you through a slightly different process to the one described in the preceding list, but performs the same function.

Create

After Match (refer to preceding section), the second option available if you need assistance matching transactions is Create. If you do not think the transaction exists in Xero at all, you can create it under the tab of the same name. Figure 8-8 shows the Create tab and the three available fields within it: Who, What and Why.

To create a new transaction in Xero to match the transaction showing in your bank statement, follow these steps:

1. **Click the Who field and enter the business or individual name.**

   From the bank transaction you may be able to identify the required name and, as you start typing, the field fills with suggestions if the name or similar names have been used previously. If you're dealing with a new contact, enter the new name.

Once you've typed a new contact name into the Create window, it automatically gets added to Xero. So make sure you use the specific name of the person or business rather than something generic — so your bank's name, for example, rather than just 'bank fees'. If at a later date you need to edit the name, you can find it in Contacts. (You can find out more about contacts in Chapter 5.)

2. Click the What field and enter the account details.

Select the relevant general ledger code from your chart of accounts or start typing the name of the account. As you start typing, auto-suggestions pop up in the field, or you can access a full list of options by clicking on the drop-down button.

3. Click the Why field to enter more detail.

If you're using a Fixed Asset account code, entering some information in the Why field is mandatory. If not, once you've filled in the Who and What fields, the OK reconciliation button appears, meaning you've added enough information for Xero to match this transaction and reconcile it. However, for the purpose of maintaining a detailed trail of what you have done — otherwise known as an audit trail — filling out a reason for the transaction in the Why field area is a good idea.

If you're using Tracking options, they'll be available at the bottom of the Create box to be selected and associated with the transaction. (Find out more about tracking options in Chapter 12.)

4. Check the tax rate applied to the transaction.

You can override the account's default tax rate, which Xero will automatically apply to the transaction, if necessary.

5. Click the Add Details button (if required).

This opens up the Spend Money window, which you may require if the transaction is more complicated than a simple transaction match — say, you need to split payments over a number of transactions. Here, you can split out the money as necessary. (See the section 'Using the Spend and Receive Money Options' later in this chapter for a full explanation.)

6. Click OK to record the matching transactions.

Transfer

This option allows you to record a transfer that has already occurred between accounts set up as Bank Accounts, Credit Cards or Online Payment options accounts within Xero. If you wanted to record a transaction to an account that was not set up in this manner you would need to use another method.

After clicking on the Transfer tab, the Select a Bank Account option appears. Clicking on the drop-down menu shows you the available accounts that have been set up in Xero. Select the relevant option and the reciprocal match is highlighted on the other account. If you need to add tracking categories, refer to the section 'Transferring money', earlier in this chapter, for guidance in how to do that.

Discuss

The Discuss tab can be used when you're unsure how to code a transaction, such as a personal expenditure transaction. You can detail your queries in the text box under the Discuss tab (shown in Figure 8-9). Your Xero adviser can then go online, review the transaction, correctly code it or advise you what to do. You can revisit and code the transaction. After a number of transactions have been coded correctly in Xero, the software becomes increasingly intuitive and starts to suggest further matching transactions.

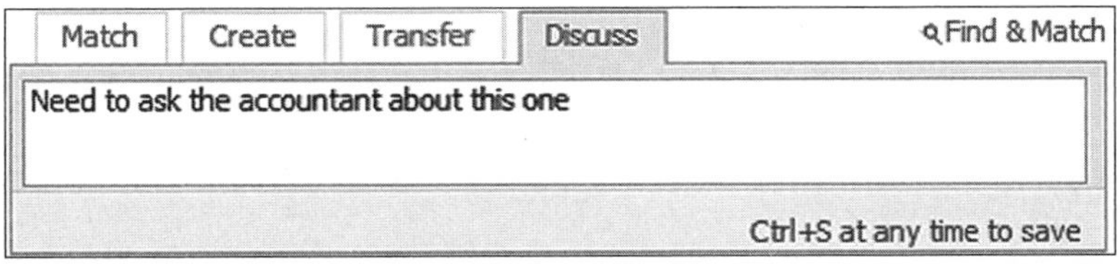

Figure 8-9:
The text box
under the
Discuss tab
option.

Match	Create	Transfer	Discuss	⚲ Find & Match

Need to ask the accountant about this one

Ctrl+S at any time to save

Reviewing other possible matches

When the transaction on the right side of your reconciliation screen is shaded green, you may also see a blue hyperlink suggesting that other possible matches exist. To drill down to the other possible matches, click on the hyperlink. You can then select the relevant one and, once you are satisfied, record the transaction by clicking OK.

At the very bottom of the reconciliation screen is a Suggest Previous Entries checkbox. While ticked, Xero autopopulates possible matches with suggested transactions it's learned. While unticked, Xero will only suggest exiting matches and bank rules. If you (or any other users accessing your Xero file) have a tendency to be overzealous playing this game of snap, leaving this checkbox unticked may be safer, to help avoid potential errors.

Taking Advantage of Cash Coding

The Xero account window includes four main tabs: Reconcile (covered earlier in this chapter), Cash Coding, Bank Statements and Account Transactions. The Cash Coding area isn't as pretty as the main reconciling window — it's formatted more like an Excel spreadsheet. However, using the spreadsheet format means the Cash Coding area is the ultimate processing spot for cash transactions in Xero, allowing for manoeuvrability and quick data entry options. Yes! You can reconcile even faster! Once your bank rules are set up (refer to Chapter 4) and you're using your shortcut keys (see the sidebar 'Taking advantage of shortcut keys'), jump into the Cash Coding area and you'll be zipping along!

Only users with Adviser status or Standard users who have been given access by their adviser in Xero can access the Cash Coding area. In fact, if you don't have this status, you won't even see the Cash Coding tab on the account window.

Getting familiar with Cash Coding

The Cash Coding table (shown in Figure 8-10) contains exactly the same unreconciled data as the Reconcile tab area; the data is simply in a spreadsheet format. Across the top of the table are various column headings, including Date, Payee, Reference, Description, Account, Tax

---

Taking advantage of shortcut keys

If you are within the Xero Cash Coding spreadsheet, you can use a number of shortcut keys to help you quickly navigate around an active cell:

✔ Tab: Move forward to the next cell

✔ Shift+Tab: Move back to the previous cell

✔ Enter: Move down one row

✔ Shift+Enter: Move up one row

You can also use shortcut keys when editing data within Xero, as follows:

✔ + key: Copies Account, Tax Rate and Tracking fields from the row above, into the row beneath

✔ Shift+Down arrow: Ticks current row, and moves down to the row beneath

✔ Alt+Down arrow: Converts a Payee name that is in all CAPITALS to proper case

Utilising shortcut keys can really improve your productivity. In my travels, people who use shortcut keys are usually faster than people like me who use the mouse.

Rate, Spent and Received. No invoice, bills or matching transactions are highlighted here, but bank rules do apply. Visit the Reconcile tab first, reconcile invoices and matching transactions and then pop into Cash Coding if you're an expert.

Figure 8-10:
The Cash
Coding
table.

		Date▲	Payee	Reference	Description	Account	Tax Rate	Region	Spent	Received	
		13 Feb	Truxton Property Manag...		Rent				1,181.25		
		14 Feb	SMART Agency		70135 70209				4,500.00		
		14 Feb	Jakaranda Maple Systems		DEPOSIT ADV					2,000.00	
		14 Feb	NAB		Bank fee				15.00		
		14 Feb	Copper St Bakery		Eft				15.75		
		14 Feb	7-Eleven		Misc corner store	453 - Office Exp...	GST on Exp...		15.50		
		15 Feb	Copper St Bakery		Eft				11.90		

Reconcile (26) **Cash Coding** Bank statements Account transactions

Uncheck all Discard changes Shortcut keys Displaying all 26 ▶ Show more

Most of the columns on the Cash Coding table are self-explanatory. All fields are editable except the Date, Spent and Received fields so, apart from these, you can click in and out of the fields as you wish, entering additional business data.

When entering data to the Cash Coding table, a good place to start is the Payee field. Tab across to this field, selecting the correct Payee. Then move to the Account field. Once the Account has been entered, the default tax rate automatically fills in. If a discussion note was entered on the Reconcile window, it appears as a tiny icon in the Date column. Hovering over the icon reveals the entered text.

At the far right side of the table are two boxes: A forward slash and a cross. The forward slash opens up a Spend Money or Receive Money window. The cross turns red, and whenever anything turns red in Xero it alerts you that you now have the option to delete the transaction (if required — a warning message will appear to help ensure you don't delete anything by mistake).

Once the transaction details have been entered, the transaction can be ticked and reconciled. But the reconciling goodness does not end there! (See the following section for more.)

Clicking on each individual column heading of the Cash Coding table allows you to sort the fields within that column.

Understanding bulk coding

Bulk coding enables you to reconcile transactions at Xero-hero speed — however, you can also make mistakes at high-speed too! Make sure you know what you are doing before giving this a go. By selecting a number of transactions and making a change to a single transaction in that group, the same change repeats across all checked transactions. Sorting transactions allows for even more efficient coding.

To quickly bulk code a number of similar purchases made at the same store, follow these steps:

1. **On the Cash Coding dashboard, sort the Payee data by clicking the header of the Payee column.**

2. **Check the box to the left of all the similar transactions.**

   All lines are highlighted.

3. **Allocate the same account to all similar transactions by clicking the Account field of the first highlighted row and selecting the account the selected transactions are all to be allocated to.**

   Notice the Account and Tax Rate filled in for all highlighted transactions. This is bulk coding at its finest!

4. **If you need to enter unique Reference, Description and Tracking information for individual transactions, uncheck the transactions and enter relevant data in the fields.**

   Otherwise, you could continue to use the bulk-coding feature and enter duplicate information.

5. **To reconcile the transactions, check the box to the right of them and click the Save and Reconcile Selected button.**

Bulk coding does not just apply to transactions from the same payee. Perhaps you spent a week at a conference and all expenses for the week have to be allocated to the same expense account and the same tracking account. Select all the transactions, make the change in a single account, click Save and Reconcile and voila! Batched, matched and neatly reconciled.

If you don't know what account or what tax code to code the transaction, ask your Xero advisory team or accountant. Leave a note for them in the Discuss box. (Refer to the section 'Discuss' earlier in this chapter.)

If you make a mistake, you can click on the Discard Changes button at the top of the table and reverse the changes that were just entered. If only everything in life was that easy.

The number of transactions displayed on the Cash Coding grid can be increased or decreased. Scroll to the middle bottom of the screen and a double sided arrow appears. Click on the pull-down bar and drag it up or down as required. This customisation doesn't stick, however — you need to re-do it for each visit to the Cash Coding dashboard.

Viewing Bank Statements

The Bank Statements tab in your Xero account window (shown in Figure 8-11) lists the start and end date and balance of all imported statements. If your bank feeds are automatic, you probably don't need to visit this area at all, unless you're investigating a gremlin. So, if you're happy with your figures, don't even waste your time looking here!

However, if you manually import bank statements or if something has gone amiss with your bank reconciliations, reviewing the Bank Statements area is worthwhile. After clicking on the tab, go over the information provided. If a gap appears between start and end dates or balances, or transaction dates overlap, you have an issue that requires further investigation. Maybe a statement is missing or duplicate information was imported during a manual import, and now the statement needs to be found or duplicates deleted.

Figure 8-11: The Bank Statements tab.

Reconcile (28)	Cash Coding	**Bank statements**	Account transactions			
Imported Date ▾		**Start Date**	**End Date**	**Start Balance**	**End Balance**	**Status**
9 Dec		1 Dec	7 Dec	(558.98)	4,094.12	Unreconciled
8 Dec		5 Dec	6 Dec	(3,449.58)	(558.98)	Reconciled
6 Dec		27 Nov	5 Dec	1,053.45	(3,449.58)	Reconciled
28 Nov		8 Nov	27 Nov	1,130.25	(884.55)	Reconciled
8 Nov		28 Oct	7 Nov	(1,889.76)	1,130.25	Reconciled
28 Oct		8 Oct	27 Oct	2,041.53	(1,889.76)	Reconciled

To see the transaction details that were imported with the bank statement, click in the bank statement rows. Within the detail area you can delete individual transactions, or delete the entire bank statement, if indeed it was imported in error.

Viewing Account Transactions

The Account Transactions tab (shown in Figure 8-12) details the account transactions that have been created in Xero. To the left of the transaction details, Reconciled (in green) indicates the transaction has been reconciled while Unreconciled (in orange) indicates an unreconciled transaction, which may highlight the need for further investigation. Reconciled (in black) means the transaction has been manually marked as reconciled.

Viewing pages of data

When using Xero to view a table with a lot of information, you have a couple of different options for organising the information. At the bottom of the webpage displaying the table are two drop-down box options:

✔ **Page # of # (# total items):** Tells you the page you are on, and the total number of lines associated with this table.

✔ **Showing X items per page:** Tells you how many items are being shown per page. You have the option to change this, and can choose to show from 10 to 200 items.

Just don't get confused — *items* here doesn't refer to inventory items. Instead, the term just refers to the transactions that can be viewed on the page.

Figure 8-12:
The Account
Transactions
tab.

	Date	Description	Reference	Spent	Received	Status ▲
☐	15 Sep	Nowtown Reader's Group			100.00	Unreconciled
☐	29 Sep	Prepayment: PP team	PP456	1,000.00		Unreconciled
☐	29 Sep	Prepayment: PP team	PP789		1,000.00	Unreconciled
☐	29 Sep	Overpayment: OP team	OP456	100.00		Unreconciled
☐	29 Sep	Prepayment: Notown News	1234	100.00		Unreconciled

Using the Spend Money and Receive Money Options

I work with a lovely not-for-profit organisation and, because every payment has to be approved by the board, the accounts department are always late paying bills. One time, they overpaid my invoice. I contacted them and suggested I hold on to the extra and apply any future work I did for them against the overpayment. This meant that I didn't have to waste admin time repaying them, and I didn't have to chase them for payments for a while. Two wins for me!

The Spend Money and Receive Money options can be used to record overpayments, as well as direct payments and prepayments. The Spend Money option can be used to enter cheque transactions, for example, and the Receive Money option can be used to record cash deposited in the bank. Processing via these options means a transaction already exists in Xero to match, once the bank transactions hit Xero.

To access the Spend Money and Receive Money area, click on the bank account, and then on the Manage Account button on the far right side. The Edit Account Details window opens (shown in Figure 8-13), giving you quite a lot of useful options, including the Spend Money and Receive Money options.

Figure 8-13: The Edit Account Details window.

Click the Spend Money link to access the Spend Money window (Figure 8-14). At the top right corner of this window, a drop-down menu is provided, which allows you to select how the money was spent, from the following options:

- ✔ Direct Payment
- ✔ Prepayment
- ✔ Overpayment

Direct payment

You can record cheque payments via the Spend Money Direct Payment option. Select Direct Payment on the drop-down menu and a pale-blue background appears with standard entry options. Grab your cheque book, enter the information and save the transaction.

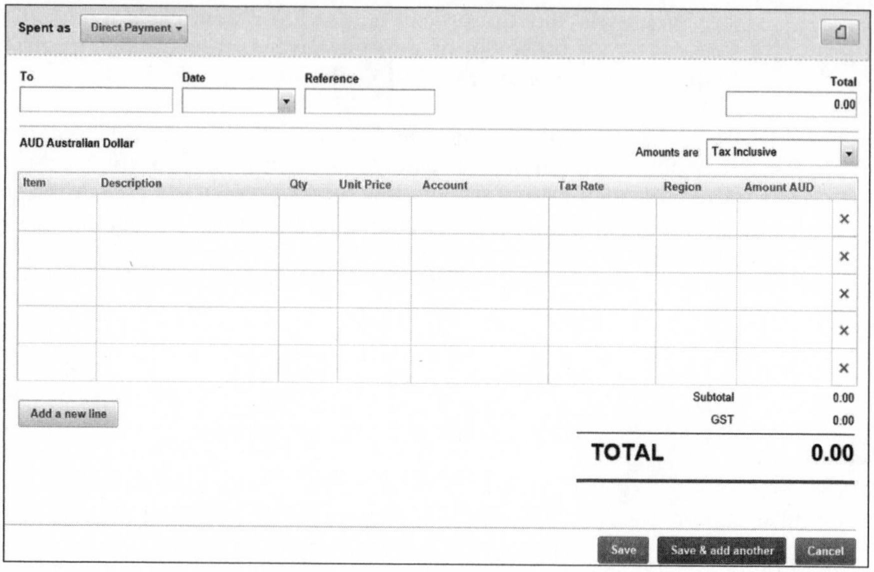

Figure 8-14:
The Spend
Money
window.

If you've deposited money into your bank, you can record this by selecting Receive Money⇨Direct Payment on the drop-down menu. Grab your deposit book or check your statement online, enter the data associated with the deposit(s) and save the transaction. If you're recording multiple payments in a single deposit, still record them separately and make a note of the group deposit. The Receive Money area has the option to re-order lines, and once the transaction is recorded, a receipt can be issued via email or PDF to the payee.

Prepayment

If you've made a payment in advance to a supplier, you can record this by clicking on the arrow to the right of Direct Payment, and selecting Prepayment from the drop-down menu. A pale-salmon background appears with standard entry options. Here you can fill in the transaction and save the entry. After saving the transaction, the amount exclusive of tax can be seen on the Profit and Loss in expenses.

Overpayment

An overpayment may occur when you're paying a supplier and round up the invoice amount, which in turn overpays the bill. Or, alternatively, when you receive money from a client greater than the existing invoices for this client.

You can record the overpayment via Spend or Receive Money, and when future work is undertaken with the supplier or customer, the overpayment can be applied to the invoice or bill when it is raised.

Identify the details of the overpayment and record it by clicking on the arrow to the right of Direct Payment and selecting Overpayment from the drop-down menu. A pale-salmon background appears with limited options, and a pre-filled Account and Tax Rate. So you can't actually do too much here — just add the description, date, amount (tracking option if relevant) and save. After saving the transaction, the amount can be seen on the Balance Sheet in accounts payable.

Underpayment

An underpayment may occur when the money coming in for an invoice is slightly less than expected. It may be due to banking charges on the transaction or the client mistakenly underpaying an invoice. Your options are the following:

- ✔ If you have an ongoing relationship with the client, prompt the client to pay the underpayment with the next payment.

- ✔ If your records are kept on a cash basis, you could choose to edit the original invoice so it matches the actual payment. (To do so, go to the Sales dashboard⇨Awaiting Payment tab. Locate and select the invoice, click the Invoice Options button, select Edit and make the changes. Then click Update the Invoice and reconcile the transactions.)

- ✔ Use the underpayments feature to process the adjustment to the liability account.

To process an underpayment follow these steps:

1. **From the accounts reconciliation window, identify the incoming money and click the Find & Match link on the top far right side.**

   The reconciliation block opens.

2. **Find the original invoice in the Find & Select Matching Transactions block and select it by checking the box.**

   Use the search function to the right of the block to assist in finding the original invoice if you need it. Scroll down the block, and you can see red text highlighting how much the total is out by.

3. **To process the underpayment click the Adjustments button, select Minor Adjustment, and enter the underpayment in the field that appears.**

The red alert text disappears, and the green Reconcile button is highlighted.

4. **Click the green Reconcile button to record the underpayment and reconcile the transaction. The underpayment is coded to a Rounding current liabilities account.**

Processing prepayments and overpayments

Once recorded (refer to preceding sections), the prepayment and overpayment are processed by applying them to a Purchase or Sales Invoice from the same supplier. When a new Purchase or Sales Invoice is created and approved for a client with an outstanding Prepayment and/or Overpayment, the Allocate Outstanding Credit window opens up and you have the option to allocate the amounts.

Searching for a transaction

You may realise that you've entered a Spend Money or Receive Money transaction incorrectly, and need to edit the transaction to correct it. Or, even worse, you may just kind of have this feeling that something is wrong but may not realise what you're looking for. So you first need to find the transaction.

Make a note of everything and anything you know about the transaction — the available search fields are the following (listed in the order shown):

✔ Description

✔ Contact name

✔ Amount or amount range

✔ Date or date range

Jot these down on some notepaper. Then, with the gusto of Captain Cook or Christopher Columbus, start searching for the transaction. Start at the Dashboard tab and then click on the Manage Account button on the right side of the relevant bank account. When the Manage Account window appears, click on Account Transactions to access the search box. This brings up a list of transactions, with a Search button at the top right side.

Clicking on the Search button opens up various field options: Description or Contact Name, Minimum Amount, Maximum Amount, Exact Amount, Start Date, End Date, Exact Date (see Figure 8-15).

Figure 8-15:
The search box located within the Account Transactions window.

Enter what you know about the transaction, and the list of filtered information returns possible candidates. If you don't know what account the transaction occurred against, you'll need to repeat this for all accounts, until you locate the transaction. Click on the transaction that needs editing. To convert the transaction into an editable format, click on the Options button on the right side and select Edit Transaction. Once you have made any necessary changes, record the revised transaction by clicking the green Update button on the bottom right of the screen.

Fixing Errors

Everyone makes mistakes, and chances are at some point you will too — maybe you were overzealous, or were advised how to treat something incorrectly and you now need to retrospectively amend the transaction. No worries! Xero allows you to fix errors.

If you've already locked off an accounting period or submitted your reports to the Tax Office, you may not want to make changes in Xero within that date period. Check with your Xero advisory team if you're concerned.

If you (or someone in your business) got trigger happy, you may find that bank transactions have been reconciled incorrectly. This can happen in one of two ways: Transactions of the same amount have been matched incorrectly and, therefore, need to be unreconciled; or a transaction was created and was incorrectly coded, and so needs to be deleted.

Resolving the difference between Xero balances and bank balances

The reasons behind any differences between Xero balances and bank balances are explored in Chapter 4; however, because resolving these differences is a problem many users face, exploring how to resolve the issue in further detail is worthwhile.

Run through these steps and you should get to the bottom of your differences:

1. **Refresh the bank feed by clicking Manage Account⇨Refresh Bank Feed.**

   This step only needs to be performed if using Yodlee feeds.

   You may have to re-enter security details. Refreshing the bank feed option is not available for all accounts.

2. **Reconcile outstanding transactions.**

   Hey, that's what this chapter is about! (Refer to earlier sections for more.)

3. **Identify the actual difference between the balances and see if it rings any bells.**

   If you run the amount through your head, you may be able to recognise what the transaction relates to.

   Refer to the section 'Create' if the amount relates to a transaction that's missing from Xero.

4. **Confirm whether a known issue with the Xero bank feed exists.**

   Take a look at www.xero.com/blog/bank-feed-status to find out more about bank feed issues. Otherwise, contact Xero Customer Care (support@xero.com).

5. **Identify if transactions have been allocated to the account, but not yet reconciled.**

   From the dashboard, identify the bank account in question. Click on Manage Account ⇨ Account Transactions and then click on the Status hyperlink until the small black arrow beneath it is facing upwards. The word Unreconciled in the status column indicates an unreconciled transaction.

   Alternatively, you can run the Reconciliation Report, accessed from Manage Account menu, to identify transactions not yet reconciled.

6. **Establish whether the transaction is correctly allocated to the account.**

   If necessary, click on the transaction to view more details.

   If the transaction's recently dated, the issue may just be timing, and you need to wait for the matching transaction to feed in.

   If the transaction may be a duplicate created in error, make a note of the date and amount, and click on the Search button and enter in the identifying details you have.

   To delete an erroneous transaction, see the section 'Removing and undoing a bank transaction', later in this chapter.

   If you can confirm the transaction is correctly allocated but for some reason bank feed has not fed in correctly, click into the transaction, and click the Options button on the top right. Select Mark as Reconciled from the drop-down option, effectively forcing the reconciliation.

   Note: The Mark as Reconciled option may first need to be enabled — which you can do under the '?' option on the top of the screen.

7. **Go to Settings ⇨ General Settings ⇨ Conversion Balances to check the opening bank balance is correct.**

   An incorrect opening bank balance may be creating the difference. Only Users with Standard access and above can change Conversion Balances. Check with your Xero adviser if you're unsure about this area or refer to Chapter 2 for more details.

8. **Compare the bank feed transactions line by line with the real bank statements to identify any lines missing from the import.**

   Add individual transactions with the Spend and Receive Money options. After you've saved the transaction, drill back into it, click the Option button in the top right corner, select Mark as Reconciled, and then confirm on the pop-up window to again Mark as Reconciled.

   If bulk transactions are missing, identify the date range and import them again — refer to Chapter 4 for how to do this.

9. **If issues are ongoing, contact Xero customer support and, if required, deactivate the feed, refresh the screen and immediately reactivate it.**

   Contact Xero customer support to see if they can identify the issue. You can then deactivate and reactivate the feed via the Manage Account button. Also let your bank know you are having issues with the bank feed.

Unreconciling a bank transaction

To unreconcile the transaction, start at the main dashboard, click on the bank account and tab across to the list of account transactions. Find the transaction and drill down into it — on the top right you can see options where you can edit this transaction.

Unreconciling a previously reconciled account removes the association between the transaction and the bank statement line it was reconciled against. It doesn't delete the transaction or the bank statement line.

Removing and undoing a bank transaction

To delete a transaction, you first need to locate it — refer to the section 'Searching for a transaction', earlier in the chapter, for more. Once you've found the problem transaction in the list of possibilities (see Figure 8-16 for an example), click in the checkbox next to the transaction that needs to be deleted and click the Remove & Redo button. A confirmation window appears, asking if you really want to remove and redo the transaction. To confirm you're sure, click Yes.

Figure 8-16: Deleting a transaction.

What happens in life happens in Xero

Some small businesses run a bank account that's a little bit business and a lot personal, and they occasionally pay for business items using cash and they don't want to use the Expense Claims feature in Xero. This section outlines how I deal with this scenario.

Only transactions that specifically relate to the running of your business should go through your Xero account for that business. Ideally, you should have a business bank account that all business transactions go through, and this is certainly what Xero would advise. However, in reality accounts and transactions can get a little complicated, so having a method to sort out the mess is worthwhile.

Read through the following steps and think about whether the method outlined may work for you — it's a little bit tricky so not everyone's cup of tea.

Here's how to sort out business transactions from a mixed-use bank account:

1. **Add the 'mixed' bank feed to Xero.**

   Refer to Chapter 4 for help with adding bank feeds to your accounts. In this example, I call mine the '*Name* Loan Account', where *Name* refers to the individual partner.

2. **Add a liability account and check the box Enable Payments to this Account.**

   Refer to Chapter 2 for more on adding new accounts. I call mine the '*Name* Loan Account'.

3. **Reconcile business transactions that feed through in a normal fashion.**

4. **Delete non-business transactions via the bank statements Dashboard area.**

   Go to Dashboard⇨Manage Accounts⇨Bank Statements and click in on the Bank Statements with the yellow box to the left of them. A table of the detailed transactions appears. Check the box to the left of the transactions to be deleted, and click the Delete button.

   Instead of deleting non-business transactions, you can also allocate them to Drawings, which still allows for the account to be reconciled.

5. **Add cash transactions via the Spend and Receive Money functions and mark them as reconciled.**

   Refer to the section 'Using the Spend Money and Receive Money Options' more on these functions.

   Keep in mind that it doesn't matter the transactions did not go through the real bank account; this bank account ends up a mixed bag of transactions. Refer to 'Resolving the difference between Xero balances and bank balances' for guidance on marking transactions as reconciled.

6. Add and reconcile a transaction to bring the balance to zero.

This enables the financial reports to recognise all transactions that have passed through the account. Reconciling this account needs to be done regularly, to reflect accuracy in the financial reports; however, if you're not too concerned because the amounts are small, you can just do the reconciliation periodically when you need to submit the reports.

Part III
Making the Routine, Routine

Five Ways to $timulate Ca$h Flow

✔ **Issue a call to action:** Customise all documents sent out from Xero to include branding and details of the services and products your business offers. You'll remind customers to re-order from you, and you might turn suppliers into new customers.

✔ **Briskly follow up on money owed:** Reconcile regularly, and actively review your aged receivables reports. Use a variety of methods to follow up on late and slow payments, including, email, statements, phone calls and snail mail. Various add-on solutions, such as Satago, can automate this process for you.

✔ **Review credit terms:** If possible, ask for payment up-front, or reduce payment days offered. Offer multiple ways for customers to pay you; provide them with your bank details, and use online gateways like eWay or PayPal.

✔ **Make use of cash flow reporting:** Implement cash flow reporting to understand the upcoming money you'll have in the business, and determine how you can optimise positive cash balances and deal with negative cash balances. Cash flow reports can be developed by extracting data from Xero and manipulating spreadsheets, or you can use an add-on solution like Float.

✔ **Be submissive:** Avoid late fee penalties and interest charges by utilising Xero to prepare all tax declarations on a timely basis.

Want to make sure your bank reconciliations are reliable? To find out more about checking and refreshing bank feeds, head to www.dummies.com/extras/xero.

In this part . . .

✔ Customise reports to generate useful information and work in with how you use them in your own business. Add summaries, footnotes and charts to Xero too.

✔ Learn about key activities you can carry out regularly, such as reconciling and reviewing business information, and following up on outstanding debts.

✔ Discover how Xero can assist you in reporting on consumer tax relative to the jurisdiction you're in — information is included for New Zealand, the United States, Australia and the United Kingdom.

✔ Understand how your tax accountant can work collaboratively with you on your Xero accounts throughout the year — you'll benefit from receiving timely advice rather than ending up in a mad rush at the end of the financial year. Tax-related activities are explained, including how the single ledger system works, and how to enter manual journals, publish end of year reports, and work with a locked account.

Chapter 9

Generating Reports

. . . .

. . . .

Many business owners think accounting is simply about meeting tax obligations. Unfortunately, you do need to be concerned about tax and that's why a great tax accountant is a vital component of your business advisory team. However, tax isn't the only thing accounting is concerned with — and it shouldn't be your only concern either. The really exciting aspect of using an accounting package like Xero (imagine I'm jumping up and down on a soapbox, yelling this in delight) is that it enables you to produce timely and accurate management reports that can help you make informed decisions.

In this chapter, I show you how to take advantage of all the reporting options Xero offers, including customising reports, knowing which version of a report to use when, and exporting data to view in other applications.

Understanding the Reports Available in Xero

Some people run their small business on the assumption that a positive bank balance means the business is healthy — and that's all they need to know. Don't be like them. Take a moment to think about what information, and in what form, would really help you make decisions and, in turn, improve the performance of your business.

Xero offers a wide range of available reports, and is always updating the kind of reports offered. To see the kind of reports you can access, go to the main dashboard and click on Reports⇨All Reports to access the Reports dashboard.

New generation of reports

Xero is improving existing reports to offer additional data, sorting and filtering options. To access this new generation of reports, go to the top of the Reports homepage and drill down using the Try Out the New Reports hyperlink. Here you'll find the latest new generations of reports offered by Xero and can explore them to see if they unlock further useful information and insights into your business finances and operations. For example, the new generation report offered for the existing Aged Payables report allows you adjust the Display options to suit your needs (see the following figure).

Keep checking these new reports, as Xero has indicated this is where they plan to focus their attention on improving reporting functionality. At the time of writing, the new generations of reports on offer relate to Accounts, Invoicing, Fixed Assets and Profit and Loss reports. The new generation Aged Receivables Detail Report includes the option of the field 'Invoice Seen'. You can customise to include this field, and detect whether the client has seen the outstanding invoice. If the invoice has not been viewed, there could be an issue with the email address, and you may need to make a phone call.

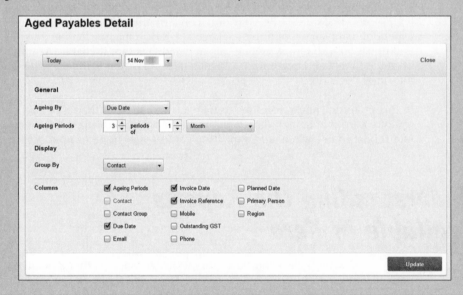

Accessing Xero's business reports

You can access a number of useful reports from Xero's Reports homepage. (*Note:* The reports you can access depend on your user role — refer to Chapter 4 — and the features you're using.)

Performance Reports show how the business is performing on revenue or expenses. Options Xero offers include

- ✔ **Budget Summary:** A summary of the monthly budget

- ✔ **Budget Variance:** Your monthly income, expenses and profit compared to budget

- ✔ **Executive Summary:** Includes monthly totals and some common business ratios; forms part of Xero's Management Reports

- ✔ **Expense by Contact:** Where the business incurred expenses, by contact

- ✔ **Income by Contact:** Where business income has come from, by contact

- ✔ **Inventory Items Summary:** A detailed view of sales and purchases for each inventory item

- ✔ **Profit and Loss/Income Statement:** Income, expenses and profit for a month (or year); forms part of Xero's Management Reports

- ✔ **Sales by Item:** Where business income has come from, by inventory item

Position Reports show how the business is positioned on assets, liabilities and equity, as follows:

- ✔ **Aged Payables:** Who the business owes money to; forms part of Xero's Management Reports

- ✔ **Aged Receivables:** Who owes the business money; forms part of Xero's Management Reports

- ✔ **Balance Sheet:** The assets, liabilities and equity of the business at a point in time; forms part of Xero's Management Reports

- ✔ **Depreciation Schedule:** Schedule of depreciation for every fixed asset in your asset register

- ✔ **Fixed Asset Reconciliation:** Summary of your fixed asset balance compared to your Fixed Asset Register

- ✔ **Movements in Equity:** Shows any changes in business equity during the year

Cash Reports show how cash levels are changing, as follows:

- **Bank Reconciliation Statement:** Reconciliation of bank accounts in Xero with the business statement balance
- **Bank Summary:** Summary of all money received and spent for each bank account
- **Cash Summary:** Amount of cash received and spent in a given month; forms part of Xero's Management Reports

Detail Reports show details of transactions in your accounts, including the following:

- **Account Summary:** Monthly balances over time for a single account
- **Account Transactions:** Summary of all transactions and journals in Xero
- **Customer Invoice Report:** Lists the people who owe the business money
- **Detailed Account Transactions:** Lists in detail all transactions entered into Xero, including invoices and bills, spend and receive money, payments and journals
- **General Ledger:** Summary of the debit and credit movements of individual accounts, and access to the General Ledger Exceptions report, highlighting transactions that deviate from the average
- **Journal Report:** Details the journal entries entered into General Ledger, and can be filtered to show cash journals
- **Supplier Invoice Report:** Lists the people the business owes money to
- **Tracking Summary:** Summary of account balances for each item in a tracking category (see Chapter 12 for more on tracking in Xero)
- **Trial Balance:** Balance for all accounts at a point in time

Specific reports are also available based on the country your business is based in, such as a Sales Tax Report or 1099 Report for US businesses, an Activity Statement for Australian businesses, or a GST or VAT Return report for NZ and UK businesses, respectively.

Foreign currency reports show how currency fluctuations have affected your foreign currency transactions. (These reports are only available to those on Xero Premium using multi-currency features — see Chapter 15.)

Pay Run reports show details of your pay run transactions. (Only users with Payroll Admin status can see these reports — see www.dummies.com/go/ xerofd2e for more.)

Selecting your favourite reports

When I'm working with a client, I like to present them with the following reports:

- ✔ Aged Receivables, as at the date of the end of the last month
- ✔ Aged Payables, as at the date of the end of the last month
- ✔ Balance Sheet, as at the date of the end of the last month
- ✔ Cash Summary reflecting the last period
- ✔ Profit and Loss (Accruals) reflecting the last period

I recommend that you make use of Xero's tracking features (see Chapter 12 for more on these). If these have been used by my client, I also provide copies of the Balance Sheet and Profit and Loss reports filtered by what's being tracked.

Of course, I encourage you to choose other reports that suit your needs and add these to your list of favourites!

For quick access within Xero, you can select key reports to appear in the drop-down list from the menu bar on Xero's main dashboard. To add and remove reports from the drop-down list, go to the Reports dashboard and click the star to the left of the required report's name. A blue star means the report appears from the drop-down Reports menu. A clear star means the report doesn't appear on the drop-down menu.

Sorting and filtering

Once you've generated a report within Xero, you usually have a number of sorting and filtering options. The options can be utilised to update and organise the information the report presents.

Not all reports have all the options listed in this section! Check what's available for the report you've generated by accessing the report and viewing the block at the top, then click the More Options link if it's available.

The options available usually include the following:

- ✔ **Sorting:** Sort by account name or account code.
- ✔ **Filtering:** Sort by tracking categories (see Chapter 12 for more on tracking).

✔ **Date Range:** Compare a number of different date ranges, including year to date, month to date, as at, and specific date ranges. And the data range can extend back over the life of the data file!

✔ **Cash Basis:** By default all reports are presented on an accruals basis. The cash basis option lets you display the report on a cash basis. Smaller businesses and some countries' tax systems tend to look at the reports on a cash basis — just make sure you don't get the two options confused! (Refer to Chapters 6 and 7 for more on cash versus accrual accounting.)

✔ **Show budget:** Compares the data to the relevant budget period. (See Chapter 10 for further information on budgeting.)

Customising Reports

Customise your reports so they do what they're supposed to do — help you understand the performance of your business. Use them to ascertain what you can do to set and achieve business goals and move the business in the direction you want.

Reports can only be customised in Xero prior to being Published — see the section 'Understanding Xero's Different Reporting Options', later in this chapter, for more on the different versions of reports available, and which users can access them.

Customising report layouts

Xero allows you to customise the layout of your reports — meaning the placement of accounts can be altered or grouped and subtotalled by a customised layout template.

Layout Options are like filters for reports, defining how they're presented. This is useful if you're highlighting different aspects of the information to different entities. For example, an organisation that approves grants may be happy to simply see a summarised view of a report, while a human resource manager may want to see the full details of personnel spending but isn't interested in seeing details of other parts of the business.

Xero also allows you to group similar accounts together, and display a summary of their balance on reports. For example, I like to break the businesses operating expenses into four groups: *Promotion*, *People*, *Place* and *Provisions* (refer to Chapter 2 for what expenses are included in each group). Rather than see the full details of staff expenditure, including wages, amenities and training, I can group the accounts so the net balance is displayed as a People subtotal on the Profit and Loss report. I can group accounts for all four groups, so when I look at the operating expenses, I only see subtotals for each of the groups and can then drill down if I need further detail.

Once created, layout templates can be shared with other users who access the file. Your Xero advisory team can share templates with you too.

The following reports can have their layout customised:

✔ Profit and Loss

✔ Balance Sheet

✔ Budget Variance

✔ Tracking Summary

In this section, I cover some of the layout customisation options available through Xero.

Creating a custom report template with Layout Options

The following steps outline how to customise report layouts:

1. **Click on Reports⇨All Reports and then the name of the report you want to customise.**

   For example, click on Profit and Loss to bring up this report.

   You can only customise report layouts for Profit and Loss, Balance Sheet, Budget Variance and Tracking Summary.

2. **Click the blue Layout Options button at the base of the report and select Create New Layout.**

   The New Layout window opens, asking you to complete the Layout Details (see Figure 9-1).

3. **Fill out the Layout Name field.**

   This gives the layout template a name — for example, you could choose *Management*.

4. **Fill out the optional Layout Description field (if desired).**

   Here you can describe the purpose of the template — for example, *Report for general management*.

5. **Check the Default box.**

   This makes this the default layout for all who view the report.

Layout Details

Layout Name

Layout Description (optional)

☐ Make this the default Profit & Loss for all users

6. **Click on the Add Group button and fill out the Group Name field.**

   This allows you to create and name a new group of accounts. For example, if you wanted to group all expenses relating to people on the Profit and Loss report, you could choose *PEOPLE* for the group name.

7. **Select your required option from the Place In drop-down menu.**

   For example, for a group showing expenses relating to people, you need to select the Less Operating Expenses option.

8. **Check the Show Summary Only box.**

   This means a subtotal of the accounts within the group is displayed.

9. **Click on the green OK button.**

   This saves the newly created Group.

10. **Check the box beside required accounts to add these to the group.**

    For example, to group expenses relating to people, you need to select the accounts for wages, amenities, training, and any other accounts showing people-related expenditure.

11. **Click the Move Selected Accounts button and choose the required group from the drop-down menu.**

    The group you created in Step 6 comes up as an option on the drop-down menu.

12. **Click the green OK button.**

    The selected accounts are now tiered underneath the required group and, when viewed in the actual report, only the net amount is displayed.

13. **Click the green Save button.**

    You can also click Save at any point as you work on the layout template, to ensure you don't lose your work.

Additional accounts can be added to the grouped accounts, or new groups created (for example, for Promotion, Place and Provisions groupings) by following Steps 6 to 12 in the preceding list. Group settings can be edited by clicking on Edit Group, making the required changes and clicking OK to save the changes.

Viewing reports using the layout template

Once you've created a new layout template (refer to preceding section), you can view a report using the template. From the Reports dashboard, click on the report and select the Layout Options button. From the drop-down menu, select Choose Layout and from the Choose Layout window, select the template layout to apply to the report.

Editing and deleting layout templates

To edit the layout template, click on the blue Layout Options button at the base of the report and select Edit this Layout. From there, click on the red Delete Layout button at the base of the page to delete the entire layout template. Click on the blue Edit Group link beside the group to edit the accounts within the group, and click on the blue Delete link to delete the group.

When is a profit not a profit?

Most small-business people are at least kind of familiar with the Profit and Loss report. They open up the report and have a Zen-like moment when they spot the one figure at the bottom of the report they understand: Profit. But take a closer look at your Profit and Loss report and you can actually see three separate lines of profit: Gross Profit, Operating Profit and Net Profit. Each one can tell you something about the business.

Gross Profit represents the pure profit from selling products or services — that is, sales income less direct costs. If I bought a can and sold a can, the difference would be gross profit. If you aren't making a profit at the gross profit level, you aren't going to make a profit at the bottom line! The next level of profit is Operating Profit. This should represent Gross Profit *less* the operating expenditure of the business. To me, Operating Profit truly reflects the profit of running the business. The final line of profit is Net Profit, which includes all of the legitimate income and expenses for the business that aren't necessarily a part of running the business. For example, income may also include bank interest, and expenses may also include home office expenses or the expenses of running the business owner's other car. These are income and expenses that may not necessarily go with the business if the business is sold.

Adding reporting 'bling': Summaries, footnotes and charts

Anyone allocated an Adviser role in Xero (refer to Chapter 4 for user roles) has the ability to add summaries and footnotes to reports. When saved, these appear on draft or published reports.

Summary notes

The summary notes you choose to add to reports could be generic and could apply to all customers. For example:

- ✓ Due to Easter, two public holidays occurred in the month

- ✓ Interest rates were cut by 25 basis points

- ✓ Elections to be held in the following month

These notes highlight aspects of the economy that may or may not impact the business. Notes specific to each company could also be included, enhancing the user's understanding of your reports. A summary for a company that sold solar-related items, for example, may include

- ✓ Government rebates for solar installation were withdrawn during the month.

- ✓ Average rainfall was lower than average for the month.

- ✓ Temperatures were unexpectedly higher than average for the month.

To add a summary, open a report and click the blue Add Summary button. A rich text editor opens up. Numerous formatting features are available — including bold, italics, tables, numbering and bullet points. Go wild! The summary can be copied from another document and added, using the shortcut keys Ctrl/Cmd+V. Save the summary using the green Save button and return to edit it by hovering across the summary and clicking directly into it. Delete the summary by clicking the cross at the top right corner.

Footnotes

If you have Adviser access, you can add extra detail to reports to assist or explain transactions. Simply click the drop-down arrow to the right of the data and add a footnote. Numbered notes appear at the bottom of the page.

Changing views

Xero allows you to view data within reports in different ways — by drilling down for more detail, stepping back for a wider view, or looking at the data visually using charts.

Drilling down on report information

To see further detail about individual transactions in a report within Xero, hover over the data and click on a link to drill down to an underlying transaction. *Note:* This doesn't always work; if you click and the link ends with '*false);*', the underlying detail can't be accessed.

Hover just to the right of entries on reports and a small drop-down arrow appears. Click on the arrow to highlight additional links and drill down on the links to access the information.

Adopting a wider view

Access an expanded view of the report by clicking on the Wide View button on the top right corner. To return to normal view, click the Standard View button.

The shortcut keys to access the wide view are as follows:

- ✔ **PC users:** Ctrl + Shift + F
- ✔ **Mac users:** Cmd + Shift + F

Displaying charts

For those with Adviser status, some reports have the additional option of displaying charts. When viewing the report, if you see a Show . . . button (or something like it), click on it and an interactive chart appears (see Figure 9-2). Click the cross on the top right corner to hide the chart.

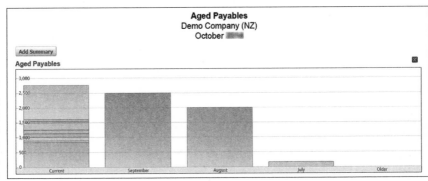

Figure 9-2: The Aged Payables interactive chart.

Understanding Xero's Different Reporting Options

Reports can be produced within Xero in various formats: Draft, published, printed or exported. A Standard user can access and run all reports under the Reports menu, but they can't process a draft or published report; only an Adviser can do that.

Draft

Reports can be created or viewed by users with Adviser status, and saved in draft format, capturing a snapshot of the business at a point in time. The draft version of the report includes any notes and annotations made on the report for other users to review.

Draft reports can be saved, viewed, edited and deleted. Only users with Adviser status can save, delete or publish a draft report.

To save a report as draft, open the report and click on the blue Save as Draft button. To access draft reports from the Reports dashboard, click on the Draft tab and select the report to view and/or edit. To delete a draft report, view the list of Draft reports and click on the cross to the right of the report.

Published

Publishing a report fixes it at a point in time, including any summary notes, annotations and criteria changes (where relevant). Published reports can be saved, viewed and deleted. Although they themselves can't be edited, if you have the Adviser user role, you can copy and edit them. To do this, just click on the Copy & Edit green button.

To save a report as published, follow these steps:

1. **Open the report and click on the green Publish button.**

   The report template window opens with three blocks of criteria to customise: Title & Details, Contents; Cover & Table of Contents; and PDF Preferences.

2. **Override the information in the Title & Details block, if necessary.**

   The Title, Subtitle, Report Date, Author and Published date appear on the summary listing on the Reports dashboard under the Published tab.

The Title, Subtitle, Report Date and Author appear on the contents page, and the Title, Subtitle, and Report Date appear in the footnotes of the report.

3. **Check Show Cover Page and Show Table of Contents Page as required.**

   The table of contents is useful when reports are connected (see the following section for more on this).

4. **At the PDF Preferences block, click the tiny colour block under the heading Border Colour.**

   A colour chart opens and you can select the colour branding of the report. This is an opportunity to brand the report your business colours. Next to the tiny colour block you can see the default hex code (a *hex code* is a method for specifying colours used on a web page) for reports is #00A0C6. If you have a business brand colour, find out what its hex code is and enter it here.

5. **Enter any additional information in the Report Footer Text**

   Footer text could be a disclaimer, a note that reports aren't audited, contact details, or a reminder that it's your birthday soon — just to check who's carefully reading these reports! The footer text appears in a block at the bottom of the report.

6. **Click the Publish button.**

To access published reports from the Reports dashboard, click on the Published tab. To delete a published report, view the list of Published reports and click on the selected report. When the report opens, select the red Delete Report button.

Once published, the report can be exported to PDF, Microsoft Excel, Google Docs (see the section 'Exporting Reports', later in this chapter), archived or copied to a new report and edited.

Connecting reports

To enhance user's understanding of the data behind the reports, reports can be connected. For example, say you review the Aged Payables report and identify a customer who owes a significant amount of money. From the Aged Payables report, you can click on the customer's name, drilling down to see the detail of their invoices. You can then click the Add to Report button, and the reports are now linked. Numerous reports can be associated with the primary report.

Connecting reports is a pretty neat trick but — alas — this feature is only available to users with Adviser status in Xero.

Once the primary report is published, you can access the linked reports when viewing the primary report in Xero via tabs at the top of the reports. When the primary report is published to PDF, the linked reports are included with the published report. When the primary report is published to Microsoft Excel, the linked reports are included as additional sheets. (See the section 'Exporting Reports' for more on publishing reports in different formats.)

Archived

Published reports can be archived. To archive a published report, from the dashboard, click on Reports⇨All Reports⇨Published, then click on the published report to open it. Scroll to the bottom of the screen and select the grey Archive Report button. Pretty quickly, the report is archived.

To access archived reports from the Reports dashboard, click on the Archived tab. A user with Adviser status can delete an archived report.

To delete an Archived Report, from the Published tab on the Reports dashboard, click on the Archived tab and then click on the archived report to open it. Scroll to the bottom of the screen and select the red Delete Report button. Status update: Gone!

Exporting Reports

To export a report, open the required report, customise it, scroll to the bottom, and click the blue Export button to see the export options. Reports can be exported in three formats — Microsoft Excel, PDF and Google Docs — as follows:

✔ **Microsoft Excel:** Selecting the option to export a report in Excel format means Xero downloads an editable Microsoft Excel file, inclusive of live formulas, to your computer. Click on the download, or find it in your download files, enable editing and start playing with it!

Exporting to Excel allows data to be easily manipulated to suit your needs, but it does mean any charts within the report won't be included in the download.

> ✔ **PDF:** A PDF file (a Portable Document Format file) is an un-editable file format. Selecting the option to export a report in PDF format means Xero downloads a PDF file to your computer. Click on the download, or find it in your download files, to view it. If the report contained a chart, it appears very nicely on the PDF file. The PDF files exported from Xero are small in size and can be emailed easily.
>
> *Note:* Only whole dollar amounts are exported in the PDF — that is, the cent amounts from any figures drop off.
>
> ✔ **Google Docs:** If you use Gmail, or have your email hosted through Google Apps, you have the option to export reports to Google Docs. The report is accessed online, can be edited like a typical spreadsheet, and can be shared with others. When you export the report from Xero to Google Docs, you then need to log in to your selected Google account and confirm Xero is a trusted site.

If you have numerous email addresses hosted through Google Apps, you need to log into Google with the email address you want associated with the downloaded document.

Accessing Management Reports

In addition to the reports you generate yourself in Xero, any users with Adviser status can access a predefined management pack of reports, for a selected period. The report includes the following (in this order):

- ✔ Executive Summary
- ✔ Cash Summary
- ✔ Income Statement/Profit and Loss
- ✔ Balance Sheet
- ✔ Aged Receivables
- ✔ Aged Payables

This report provides a good representation of the business's performance. If you export it to Excel, a corresponding report is created — useful for those who like manipulating data! See Chapter 12 for more on Xero's management report pack, and how to use it within your business.

Chapter 10

Mastering Your Weekly and Monthly Tasks

. . . .

. . . .

A recent client of mine has an interesting lifestyle business model — he imports a container of shoes and travels the country selling them at markets. One day, he arrived at my door with shoeboxes (oh, the irony!) filled with several years' worth of paperwork and receipts relating to the business — mostly just dirty, scrunched-up, faded bits of paper. What joy! It took my assistant hours just to flatten and sort all the information.

I completely understand that earning money and running your business is critical for business survival. Nevertheless, regular tasks need to be undertaken in the business, to ensure records are up to date, the Tax Office is kept happy and you have access to information about your business operations. I don't care who does this! It could be you, your assistant, a contract bookkeeper or a virtual assistant. But you (and/or your staff and advisers) need to develop and agree to processes that are undertaken regularly to ensure complete, accurate and reliable records are produced on a timely basis.

The complexity of your business determines the level of the weekly and monthly tasks you need to carry out, and whether you need to invest in additional solutions. In this chapter, I provide a general overview of the tasks a typical business needs to do on a regular basis, guiding you through reports you may need to submit for tax purposes. I also provide an overview of using budgets within the business. You can then adapt the tasks covered in this chapter to suit your business requirements.

Confirming Accounts are Complete

Reliable report preparation requires all accounts to be complete for the relevant period. I had a client working in the promotional industry who thought his accounts were all in order, and that he just needed a little extra assistance. I took a quick look and asked him why his bank charges were $70,000. We quickly worked out these charges were incorrect (surprise, surprise!). Whenever my client had an unknown transaction, he just allocated it to bank charges. The transactions incorrectly allocated to bank charges needed to be correctly allocated before any reports could be relied upon.

To ensure records are complete, check the following:

✔ All transactions for the reporting period have been entered

✔ Bank reconciliations are up to date

✔ General ledger exceptions — transactions that are extraordinary or unusual, in the business's records

 When you're reviewing information, look at it with all the knowledge that you have about the business, but also ask yourself does the data seem 'reasonable'? By that I mean does it seem fair and sensible for your business? I sometimes suggest to a client to look at reports with 'blurred eyes', to more easily identify numbers that seem too large or too small in comparison to the numbers around them. For example, bank charges of $70,000 would only really be reasonable if the business turnover was in the billions!

Reconciling Bank Accounts, Credit Card and Online Payment Gateway Accounts

Weekly tasks include some time spent reconciling your bank accounts, credit card and PayPal accounts. Refer to Chapter 8 for details of how and when to reconcile these accounts. If your accounts are reconciled in Xero, but the bank balances do not match, initially check the conversion balance was entered correctly (refer to Chapter 2) and then review the Bank Reconciliation Summary. (Access this by clicking Reports⇨All Reports⇨Bank Reconciliation Summary, and then selecting the relevant bank account.)

The Bank Reconciliation Summary compares your Xero bank statement balance to the conversion balance in Xero of the transactions (plus Outstanding Payments, Less Outstanding Receipts Plus Un-Reconciled Bank Statement Lines). *Note:* For some banks, where the statement balance is imported, it also includes these balances. The report runs for individual accounts and on any date. When accessing this report, you can also click on two additional tabs, revealing the Imported Statement Lines and the Statement Exceptions report. (The Statement Exceptions report highlights transactions that don't match a normally imported statement — for example, manually reconciled transactions, duplicates or deleted entries.)

On a day-to-day basis, if you need to investigate why bank accounts aren't reconciling, these reports can assist in identifying issues that may cause a discrepancy. Using the reports, you can crosscheck the detail within Xero to your actual bank account detail. Duplicate or manually entered transactions may need to be dealt with (refer to Chapter 8).

Speed up processing by having multiple Xero screens open at the same time. To view separate Xero files simultaneously, open them in different browsers, such as Google Chrome and Internet Explorer.

Reconciling Your Clearing Accounts

A clearing account is an account used to temporarily contain a transaction that's eventually coded to another account. For example, the other day a client accidentally paid an invoice twice, so I allocated the receipt of money to the clearing account, and when I refunded the payment, it was refunded from the clearing account. The net effect was zero! Using the clearing account meant I could avoid allocating the transaction to income, and distorting income figures for that period. To check the account is running smoothly, you need to reconcile your clearing accounts at least monthly. Refer to Chapter 2 for guidance on setting up a clearing account in your chart of accounts.

To reconcile clearing accounts, follow these steps:

1. **Click on Reports⇨All Reports⇨Account Transaction.**

2. **Enter the relevant criteria and update the report.**

   The information to enter or select is as follows:

   • **Account field:** Select the clearing account to reconcile.

   • **Date range:** Enter the period under review. If this is the first time reviewing the account, the From date needs to be the conversion date — that is, the date you started to use Xero.

   • **Cash basis:** Check this option if you're running the business on a cash basis.

3. **Check the closing balance.**

   If the closing balance is nil, the account is reconciled. Congratulations! (If the balance isn't nil, work through the tips following this list.)

4. **Click the Publish button.**

5. **Enter the clearing account name and date range in the Title field and click the Publish button again.**

   For example, I would enter 'Clearing Account 1/10/2014–31/12/2014' to indicate the Clearing Account is reconciled from 1 October 2014 to 31 December 2014. The report is listed on the Reports dashboard under the Published tab, and can be referred to at a later date.

If the closing balance for your clearing account isn't nil (meaning the account isn't reconciled), try these tips:

✔ Export the report to Microsoft Excel or Google Docs (refer to Chapter 9 for guidance on exporting reports). Once you can open the report in spreadsheet format, you can more easily see (and delete) matching transactions. Keep in mind that a few transactions may equal a single transaction, so you may need to juggle with the number to match them.

✔ Check your unmatched transactions. Unmatched transactions are referred to as unreconciled transactions and if you don't know what they relate to, you may need to investigate further. For example, check they've been entered correctly. Identify any transaction coded elsewhere and re-code them to the clearing account in Xero.

Reconciling Your Consumer Tax Control Account

Consumer tax collected and consumer tax paid (this includes GST, VAT and sales tax) by your business is allocated to a single consumer tax control account within Xero. When consumer tax is reported by the business, it again hits the consumer tax control account. As all consumer tax obligations go in and out of the single account, you can easily determine what consumer tax you owe to, or are owed by, the Tax Office.

Reconcile your consumer tax account on a monthly basis by following these steps:

1. **Check your organisation's Financial Settings are correct.**

   From the home dashboard, click Settings⇨General Settings⇨Financial Settings. (Refer to Chapter 2 for further information.)

2. **Check that all Consumer Tax Statements up to the last reporting period have been published.**

   Check the Published tab on the Reports dashboard to check what's been published and when.

   Some taxation authorities require submissions to be made in round or whole numbers. If this is applicable to your business, ensure the published reports meet these requirements.

3. **Generate the Consumer Tax Reconciliation report via the Reports dashboard.**

   Make sure the report is from the start of the required tax period, and include the conversion balance if relevant.

   This report can only be accessed by the users with Adviser status or Standard users with the All Reports option within Xero, and is only available if the Financial Settings indicate the business is reporting consumer tax. The report reflects cash or accruals basis, depending on the Financial Settings.

4. **Check the closing balance.**

   Hopefully the unfiled consumer tax is negligible for periods that have been processed — any other amount indicates the consumer tax in the records doesn't match what was paid for the period. (See the Tip later in this section for what you can do if the closing balance isn't nil.) Amounts manually entered in the adjustment or filed fields are not retained in the report.

Xero's Consumer Tax Reconciliation report details:

- ✔ **The reporting period:** The GST, VAT or sales tax period as defined by the Financial Settings.

- ✔ **Tax collected:** Total consumer tax collected, sourced from all transactions dated in the respective period.

- ✔ **Tax paid:** Total consumer tax paid, sourced from all transactions dated in the respective period.

- ✔ **Tax on imports:** Sourced from all transactions dated in the respective period coded to GST/VAT or sales tax on imports, or GST/VAT or sales tax on capital imports.

- ✔ **Adjustments:** This figure can be manually entered, but must be a figure your relevant Tax Office has agreed to. Don't just enter your own adjustment figure here.

- ✔ **Filed:** This autofills from consumer tax reported on the published Activity statements. The entry can be overridden or, if upon reviewing the report you realised published Activity statements are incorrect, the published Activity statements can be deleted and republished with the actual figures reported to the Tax Office.

✔ **Unfiled:** This provides a running balance of consumer tax collected *less* consumer tax adjustments and consumer tax filed. In some countries, the Tax Office only transacts in whole numbers, so any balances here may be due to rounding.

Assuming you are running the report for published periods only, if the closing balance for your Consumer Tax Reconciliation report isn't nil, you can review the report and identify the difference. If this difference is only small, don't worry about it. If it is significant, try to identify where the difference is and what caused it. You may need to speak to your Xero advisory team and/or the Tax Office in your country of business about submitting a revised consumer tax report.

Ideally, information for Xero's Consumer Tax Reconciliation report is sourced from the accuracy of other published reports. If you have manually entered data, publish the report for future reference.

Reviewing Your Business Information

You need to perform a number of different business-review tasks on a regular basis. Reviewing your business information, such as your General Ledger Exception report, your invoicing, and your aged receivables and payables should be performed on at least a monthly basis.

Spend time looking at your business information while you're sharp and productive (usually first thing in the morning for most people). Make sure you allocate enough time to check and analyse reports, but don't think you have to get through everything in one session. Spend 90 minutes working on your review, take a break and have a cuppa, and then start again. Hitting your records in regular 90-minute power sessions can help keep your records up to date and in tiptop condition!

General Ledger Exceptions report

As the name suggests, the General Ledger Exceptions report highlights extraordinary transactions, or unusual variations, in your business records. These can be transactions that have been coded differently to the default tax code of the account they were posted too, or transactions that are 2.5 *standard deviations* higher or lower than the norm. That's a fancy way of saying they're a certain amount higher or lower than the average transaction posted to the account. (For example, a transaction of $60,000 appearing in an account where the average transaction is $200.)

Xero's General Ledger Exceptions report can be accessed from the home dashboard, by clicking Reports⇨All Reports⇨General Ledger and then clicking on the General Ledger Exception tab.

Select the relevant period and review the highlighted transactions to check whether you consider them to be correct. Transactional information provided includes: Date, Type, Reason, Transaction, Reference, Debit, Credit and Consumer Tax.

Invoicing

Ideally, getting paid up-front for the products or services you provide is the best solution but it's not always possible! If you work with certain customers on an ongoing basis, keeping detailed records of what to bill them is vital. This can be done by creating a draft invoice and repeatedly editing and saving it during the period you work with the customer (on, say, a project that continues over many months), until it's time to invoice the customer. To ensure positive cash flow for your business, invoicing needs to be undertaken on a timely basis.

If you're working on a long-term project with a customer, don't wait till the end of the project to invoice them. For example, your terms could include invoicing them with a running total at the end of every month. Establish invoicing terms and invoice regularly!

If your customer is a bigger fish than you, and in a stronger position to dictate payment terms, clearly understand the terms and enter them in the customer's Contact details at the Sales Invoice Default Due Date field in Xero. And make sure you fit in with their terms to your advantage. If, for example, their terms are payment 60 days after end of month, make sure you send your invoices out at the end of the month, rather than at the beginning of the following month. It could mean the difference of 30 days for receiving payment! (Of course, the typical payment terms of Xero users are 7 days, 14 days or 30 days.)

Establish and maintain a regular time of the week or month for:

- ✔ Updating invoicing details
- ✔ Reviewing and approving draft invoices
- ✔ Issuing invoices

Refer to Chapter 6 for everything you need to know about creating and issuing invoices in Xero, including adding details to particular invoice fields.

Aged Receivables

If all outstanding invoices have been entered and bank reconciliations are up to date (refer to Chapters 6 and 8), the Aged Receivables report should be reviewed to follow up with customers who owe the business money. This outstanding invoice information can be found on Xero's home dashboard, within the Money Coming In block. For more detail, you can access three Aged Receivables reports. The classic Aged Receivables report is accessed via the main dashboard area. The other two reports are available by clicking 'Try out the new reports' to access new generation Summary and Detail Aged Receivables reports.

Chase outstanding invoices by following these steps:

1. **View the Aged Receivables report and identify debts that have been outstanding the longest.**

   All current sales are listed on the Aged Receivables report. Identify outstanding debts by referring to transactions in the 'older' column on the right. Jot them down on a piece of paper.

2. **Access the detail for customers with the longest outstanding debts.**

   On the classic Aged Receivable report, click the drop-down arrow to the right of the invoice amount and select Show Invoices. Right-click and, at the drop-down arrow, select something similar to 'Open in new tab' to access the detail of the invoice with this customer.

   On the new generation Aged Receivables Detail report, hover over the line detailing the invoice, right-click and select something similar to 'Open in new tab' to see the detail.

   Using the method outlined in this step means you never have to close the main report, and you can repeatedly access the detail underlying.

3. **Apply any available outstanding credits against the relevant invoice by clicking the blue Credit this Invoice link, entering the amount in the Amount to Credit field and clicking Allocate Credit.**

   If the credit amount is for a specific invoice, it should be matched against that invoice. After applying the credit, you return to the invoice detail.

4. **Check the top left corner of the invoice for a dark green tick and the word Sent.**

   This tick and Sent should appear beside Awaiting Payment, and they indicate the invoice has been emailed. If Sent doesn't appear here, perhaps the customer hasn't received their copy of the invoice. If the green tick is faded, the email link of the invoice has not been clicked on by the client. You need to review how you're issuing invoices to this customer. Get in contact with them and confirm the email or mailing address you should be sending invoices to. (Aghhh! Drives me crazy, but some people still prefer to receive invoices by snail mail.)

5. **Once you've established the invoice has been sent, and you believe the customer has seen the invoice, call the customer's accounts payable department (or whoever is in charge of paying invoices).**

   Put on your friendly yet professional voice for the call. Confirm the customer has the invoice, ask if any issues exist with it, and establish when they intend to pay. Keep the conversation jovial, establish a connection and, once you've found out the person's name, add it to the notes section of the Contact details in Xero (if this is new information).

   The Money Coming In block on Xero's home dashboard shows invoices due for payment, so you can check the ones that will be overdue soon. If I have spare time, I make my phone call to the person in charge of making payments before my invoice is overdue, to sort out any discrepancies ahead of time.

6. **Repeat Steps 2 to 5 for the remaining debtors identified in step 1.**

   Depending on the number of debtors in your report, you may need to increase the number of debtors you review each month.

Send out Activity statements to your customers through Xero on a monthly basis. Doing so is quick and easy, and provides another method of keeping in front of your customers. (Refer to Chapter 6 for guidance on sending out Activity statements.)

The Smart List feature (refer to Chapter 5 for guidance on how to use this feature) empowers you to create a list of outstanding debtors, and export the customer details to an online tool such as Constant Contact (www.constantcontact.com). This tool can then send out emails about the outstanding invoices. As well, various add-ons are available that plug into Xero, review aged receivables and automagically contact customers about outstanding debts, utilising emails, SMS and old fashioned telephone calls. See Chapter 16 for more on add-ons.

Aged Payables

If all outstanding bills have been entered and bank reconciliations are up to date (refer to Chapter 8), the Aged Payables report reveals who the business owes money too. The outstanding billing information can be found on the home dashboard, within the Money Going Out block, and in more detail on the Aged Payables report located on the Reports dashboard.

Understanding the 'dudes you owe money to'

An established Brisbane designer told me that, when she was dealing with family illness, her suppliers kept her business afloat and provided her with immense emotional support during the difficult times. Life never stays the same, and now life is good again — in fact, it's better, because she has a really strong bond with her suppliers. The 'dudes you owe money to' can't be defined so simply. They're an intrinsic part of your business success. Treat them with respect, pay them on time and communicate with them if payment is going to be late.

Follow up on outstanding bills by following these steps:

1. **View the Aged Payables report and identify the five bills that have been outstanding the longest.**

   These will be in the columns on the right. Jot them down on a piece of paper.

2. **Identify if any credit notes have been received, or if any invoices have been issued to the contacts whom you owe money to and apply these to the relevant bill.**

3. **Prepare and process payments.**

   If payments are likely to be delayed, communicate this with the contact. In some instances, this may hamper future supply of materials; however, communicating this information may also keep important channels open and enhance relationships.

Reporting to the Tax Office

During the 1990s I lived through several Canadian winters with my young children. When we visited local shops, I'd zip my son into a thickly padded winter suit, clip him into a pram, step outside, pick up the pram and tramp through thick snow carrying the pram, my son, handbag and anything else needed for a trip to the shops. Once safely inside the shop doors (and central heating), clothes had to be hurriedly stripped off or we would overheat! Quite a bizarre daily ritual for a girl used to the sun and heat of Australia's Gold Coast!

Whenever I purchased something in Canada, I never knew quite what I would pay. I could pay shelf price, or shelf price plus PST (Provincial State Tax) or shelf price plus GST (Goods and Services Tax) or a combination of

PST and GST — and it seems they now have HST (Harmonized Sales Tax). It was so confusing.

Don't let complex regulatory requirements dampen your entrepreneurial spirit. Xero has adapted its software to different jurisdictions and, depending on the option chosen when setting up the data file (refer to Chapter 2), features are available to suit your needs.

The following sections cover reporting in different countries. If your business is a micro-multinational, you may need to read more than one section; if, however, you're focused on local operations, just check out the section relevant to you.

Note: Over the next few pages I outline what features are available, where they are and how to use them, but I can't tell you what to enter. Why? Firstly, you should seek specialist advice specific to your own circumstances and, secondly, this book would be out of date in a nanosecond if I tried to cover governments' changing tax laws!

Prior to preparing a return for the Tax Office, double check that your financial settings are correct — found at Settings⇨General Settings⇨Financial Settings. (Refer to Chapter 2 for assistance in completing the financial settings, or speak with your tax accountant.)

Australian reporting

Businesses based in Australia report to the Australian Taxation Office (ATO). Depending on their operations and registration with the ATO, they may report on GST (Goods and Services Tax), PAYG (Pay As You Go) tax withheld, PAYG Instalments, FBT (Fringe Benefits Tax) and WET (Wine Equalisation Tax). This is done via Instalment Activity Statements (IAS) and Business Activity Statements (BAS). Many combinations of registration options are possible, so not all IAS and BAS look the same.

If your business operates in the building industry, you're also required to submit a Taxable Payment Annual Report to the ATO.

IAS preparation

An IAS is a form used to report PAYG tax withheld, PAYG Instalments and FBT. It is prepared on a monthly or quarterly basis and can only be prepared by users with Adviser status or Standard users with the All Reports option in Xero.

A business does not necessarily need to be registered for GST to prepare and submit an IAS; however, if you are not registered for GST, do not select None from the drop-down menu at the GST Accounting Method field (refer to Chapter 2 for more). You must select either Cash Basis or Accruals Basis to access your IAS in Xero.

To complete the IAS, follow these steps:

1. **Confirm accounts are complete for the relevant period.**

2. **Process all payroll for the period and print the Payroll Activity Summary report.**

   Make a note of payroll information for the reporting period, because this field doesn't autofill.

3. **From the home dashboard, access the IAS by clicking Adviser⇨Activity Statement, entering the relevant period, selecting Instalment Activity Statement and clicking the Update button.**

   Standard users with the All Reports option need to click Standard Users⇨Reports⇨All Reports⇨Activity Statement.

4. **Fill out the required fields in the IAS.**

   You need to fill out the following fields in the IAS (using information from your Payroll Activity Summary report):

   • W1: Total Salaries

   • W2: PAYG Withholding

   • W4: Amounts where no ABN is quoted

   • W3: Other Amounts

   • 7 or 5B: Deferred company/fund instalment or Credit from PAYG income tax instalment variation (the ATO will advise you if an amount needs to go in either of these fields)

5. **Publish the IAS.**

Refer to Chapter 9 for guidance on publishing reports.

After publishing your IAS within Xero, you still need to submit the IAS to the Tax Office. The document can't be printed from Xero and submitted. The information from the report needs to be entered onto the ATO business portal (bp.ato.gov.au) or onto the ATO's paper copy of the form and submitted.

BAS preparation

A BAS is a form used by a business registered for GST in Australia to report GST, PAYG tax withheld, PAYG Instalments, FBT and WET. It may be prepared on a monthly, quarterly or annual basis, and can only be prepared by users with Adviser status within Xero.

To complete the BAS, follow these steps:

1. **Confirm all accounts are complete for the relevant period.**

2. **Process all payroll for the period and print the Payroll Activity Summary report.**

   See www.dummies.com/go/xerofd2e for guidance on payroll. Make a note of payroll information for the reporting period, because this field doesn't autofill.

3. **From the home dashboard, access the BAS by clicking on Adviser⇨Activity Statement, entering the relevant period, selecting Business Activity Statement and clicking the Update button.**

   Standard users with the All Reports option need to click Standard Users⇨Reports⇨All Reports⇨Activity Statement.

4. **Fill out the required fields in the BAS.**

   The GST fields auto-populate in the BAS. You need to fill out the following fields in the BAS (using information from your Payroll Activity Summary report):

   • W1: Total Salaries

   • W2: PAYG Withholding

   • W4: Amounts where no ABN is quoted

   • W3: Other Amounts

   • 7 or 5B: Deferred company/fund instalment or Credit from PAYG income tax instalment variation (the ATO will advise you if an amount needs to go in either of these fields)

5. **Request another Adviser reviews the report (if required) by clicking on You Can Ask Your Adviser or Accountant to Review It in the green box above.**

   This option appears once the report data is prepared. If you click this link, the request review window opens.

6. **Select the Adviser to review the BAS from the drop-down list, enter a message in the field box and click Send.**

   An email is sent to the adviser, requesting a review of the BAS and including instructions on where to find the report.

7. **Once satisfied all details are correct, publish the BAS.**

    Refer to Chapter 9 for guidance on publishing reports.

After publishing your BAS within Xero, you still need to submit the BAS to the Tax Office. The document can't be printed from Xero and submitted. The information from the report needs to be entered onto the ATO business portal (bp.ato.gov.au) or onto the ATO's paper copy of the form and submitted.

The data for the GST Reconciliation report within Xero is sourced from the published BAS in Xero — another reason you should publish the report!

Taxable Payment Annual Report

Australian businesses operating in the building industry are required to submit a Taxable Payment Annual Report (TPAR) to the ATO, declaring payments made to contractors.

Before accessing the TPAR report, create a new Contact Group called Contractors and add to it all contractors that need to be reported on. (Refer to Chapter 5 for more on setting up Contact Groups.)

To then access the TPAR report, from the dashboard click Reports⇨All Reports⇨Taxable Payment Annual Report. Click on the blue Set up Rules button, and the Taxable Payments Rules window opens up.

In the Payments To field, click on the drop-down menu and select the Contact Group Contractors. In the Paid From field, click on the drop-down menu and select the general ledger code associated with contractor payments. If necessary add further rules to filter to the requirements. Click the green Save button and, if required, update contractor contact details (refer to Chapter 5).

Once the report is updated, click the green Export ATO Format button. The Confirm Your Details window opens. Confirm the details by clicking the green Confirm button. The report is exported to your desktop, and from there can be uploaded to the ATO portal.

New Zealand reporting

Businesses based in New Zealand report to Inland Revenue depending on their operations and registration. They may report on GST, FBT (Fringe Benefits Tax) and ESCT (Employer Superannuation Contribution Tax). The GST is reported via the GST Return and Provisional Tax Return.

A GST Return is a form used to report GST and is prepared on a monthly, bimonthly or half-yearly basis. It can be prepared by users with Standard and Adviser status within Xero.

To prepare your GST Return, follow these steps:

1. **From the dashboard, access the GST Return by selecting Reports⇨GST Return.**

   Across the top appears a block, headed up Enter your GST details.

2. **Enter your businesses GST details in the Enter your GST details block.**

   The available fields are as follows:

   - **Registration number:** Your business's GST registration number

   - **Accounting basis:** Choose between Invoice Basis and Payments Basis

   - **Filing frequency**: Monthly, Two Monthly or Six Monthly

   - **Next Period Due:** Various period options. depending on filing frequency

   Editing your GST details only needs to be done once, but they can be updated at any time. Once information has been entered in all fields, the save button activates. Click the blue Save button to save selected options.

   The GST Returns dashboard opens. Across the top of this dashboard are tabs for Due Now and Final Reports and on the far right is an Edit GST Details hyperlink. The relevant draft GST returns populate under the Due Now tab. If no GST return appears, click on the hyperlink Preview period so far, to view the data that has populated the return to date. Click through a Draft GST Return to access three report tabs: GST Return, Provisional Return and GST Audit Report.

   These reports are used as follows:

   - **GST Return:** An online worksheet for the GST portion of the Inland Revenue's GST and Provisional Tax Return.

   - **Provisional Return:** An online worksheet for the provisional tax portion of Inland Revenue's GST and Provisional Tax Return.

   - **GST Audit Report:** Provides summaries of the individual GST transactions that are reflected in the GST Return. From this report, you can drill down to the transaction detail.

   If the GST basis has changed, Xero is not able to calculate the adjustments required so you need to do this manually. Also, the GST in this report is sourced from GST allocated to transactions during the relevant period. GST coded purely to the GST account is not reported here. The figures on the GST Return can't be edited unless they are sourced from adjustment fields.

3. **Review the accuracy of the GST Return, Provisional Return, and GST Audit Report.**

4. **To finalise the report, click the green Save button and select Save Final.**

   The Prepared By window pops open.

5. **Beside the Author field, click on the drop-down options, choose the relevant Author and then click the green Save button.**

   The finalised GST return report appears with the GST Return and Provisional Return Tab at the top of the GST Returns dashboard. From here, you can check the report.

6. **Once satisfied the report is correct, click the Publish button, complete fields as necessary to publish the report (see Figure 10-1), and click the Save button.**

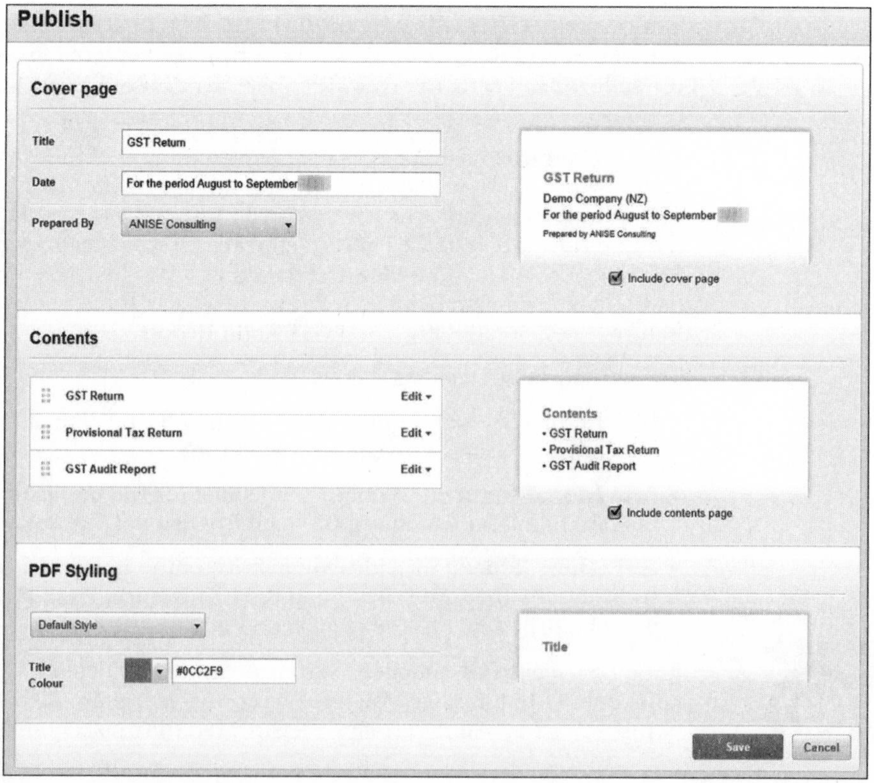

Figure 10-1:
The Publish window for the GST Return.

For future GST reports to be correctly generated, the current GST Return must be published in Xero! But publishing your report in Xero isn't the same as filing it with Inland Revenue. You must transfer the information from the GST Return form and file according to Inland Revenue requirements.

If you realise that the GST Return needs to be amended, you can delete the published report, and then rerun the GST Return report, adjust it and publish it.

US reporting

Businesses based in the United States report to the federal Internal Revenue Services (IRS) and also a state-based department of revenue. Each state has different rates, jurisdictions and requirements. Depending on their operations and registration, they may periodically file Sales Tax reports.

Within Xero, three tax reports are available for US users: Sales Tax Report Summary, Sales Tax Audit Report and Form 1099.

To view the Sales Tax Report Summary, from the home dashboard click on Reports⇨Sales Tax Report. A window then pops up with date range options and three options to define how the report is shown: Tax Rate, Tax Component and Account Type Show. The report summarises the financial settings of the business, and the taxes by Tax Component for the period.

The Sales Tax Audit report appears as the second tab, detailing the taxes by Tax Component for the period. Prepare, review and publish the report as is required by your jurisdiction. You must transfer the information from the Sales Tax Report form and file according to IRS and state requirements.

Xero US edition has Form 1099, which can be used to report different sorts of income to the IRS. *Note:* Only users with Adviser status can set up Xero's Form 1099, and only those on standard and premium plans have access to Form 1099.

The following steps show you how to set up your Form 1099 in Xero, using the example of reporting income paid to contractors. To set up Form 1099, follow these steps:

1. **Create a Contact Group for contractors who may need to be reported via Form 1099.**

   Corporations should not be included in this group. Refer to Chapter 5 for guidance on creating Contact Groups in Xero.

2. **From the home dashboard, go to Reports⇨All Reports⇨1099 Report (under Tax Report).**

   The first time you access the 1099 report, a set-up screen appears with guidance.

3. **Click the blue Set Up Rules link.**

   The 1099 Rules window appears.

4. **Select the contractors Contact Group in the Payments To drop-down field.**

   This is the group set up at Step 1.

5. **Select All Accounts in the Paid From drop-down field and select Box 7: Non-Employee Compensation in the Report As drop-down field.**

6. **Click the Add Rule button (as required).**

   This allows you to add extra rules to meet your 1099 report requirements. If unsure, speak to your Adviser about what additional requirements may be necessary.

   To reset the rules, click the Reset All Previously Edited Box Types link and deselect payments.

7. **Click the green Save button.**

   This saves the 1099 Rules. A summary of contractors and transactions captured by the rules appears on the 1099 Reports dashboard. Any transactions not meeting the IRS threshold are filtered out.

8. **Check for red Missing Details text and add text as required.**

   If the Missing Details text appears, click through and enter the required contact details, including Tax Id Number of the contact.

9. **Click the green Save button to update details.**

   Repeat Steps 8 and 9 for all contacts with missing details.

10. **Review included transactions by going to Reports⇨All Reports⇨1099 Report and clicking on an individual contact.**

    The transactions for the contact appear at the bottom of the screen.

11. **Untick any transactions not required in the 1099 Report.**

    PayPal, credit cards and foreign currency payments are excluded from the transaction list.

12. **Click the green Save button to update details.**

13. **Click the green Use e-File Services button and click Track1099 to produce and file your 1099 Report online.**

    Xero is integrated with Track1099 (www.track1099.com) a company that can securely e-file Form 1099 to the IRS — helping you with your productivity.

    The first time you click on Track1099, you're taken to the Track1099 sign-up page for a Xero client. Once you've created an account with Track1099, you can import the Xero data.

    If you don't want to file the 1099 Report electronically, click the blue Export button, and export a CSV file.

Sales tax in the United States is not a one-size-fits-all topic, because of the different state-based reporting requirements. For further information and resources on US sales tax, check out Avalara's website (www.avalara.com/learn).

UK reporting

Businesses based in the United Kingdom report to HM Revenue and Customs (HMRC). Depending on their operations and registration with HM Revenue and Customs, businesses may report on VAT (Value Added Tax), PAYE Pay As You Earn, and Class 1 National Insurance contributions. Reporting is done via a VAT Return or a Flat Rate VAT Return.

To prepare your VAT Return within Xero, follow these steps:

1. **From the dashboard, access the VAT Return by selecting Reports⇨VAT Return.**

   The VAT Return dashboard opens. Across the top are two tabs, as follows:

   • **VAT Return:** An online worksheet for the VAT portion of the HM Revenue and Customs VAT Return.

   • **VAT Audit Report:** Provides summaries of individual VAT transactions that are reflected in the VAT Return. From this report, you can drill down to the transaction detail.

2. **Select the period month end from the Ending: field drop-down options and select Update to refresh the report.**

   The VAT in Xero's VAT Audit Report is sourced from VAT allocated to transactions during the period. VAT coded purely to the VAT account is not reported here.

3. **Review the accuracy of the VAT Return, and VAT Audit Report.**

4. **Once satisfied the report is correct, click the File VAT Now . . . button, complete fields as necessary to publish the report, and select the File and Publish button.**

   The File VAT Return window opens. To file the VAT Return online, register with the HMRC for online filing and obtain a Gateway ID and a password.

5. **At the File VAT Return window, check the box 'File now with HMRC', enter your HMRC Gateway login, confirm your 9-digit VAT number and click File & Publish.**

   The All Reports dashboard opens at the tab 'Filed with HMRC'. The column headed Status highlights the stage the filed VAT Return is at with the HMRC.

   You also receive an email confirming receipt of successful submission.

For future VAT Reports to be correctly generated, the current VAT Return must be filed in Xero! If you choose not to electronically file your VAT Return with the HMRC via Xero, you can still publish it and file it the regular way.

If you realise that the VAT Audit Report needs to be amended, you can delete the published report, and then rerun the report, adjust it and publish it. However, you can't file it with the HMRC for the same period a second time; you'll need to contact them about the adjustment.

Think globally, act locally

While Xero offers several country-customised versions, a global generic version, available for the rest of the world, is also available. Whether the user be in Port Perry (home of the best hot chocolates I've ever tasted) or Paris, they can access all the basic functionality of Xero, which includes bank feeds and online access. Users of the global Xero version need to be aware of three key aspects: Tax Rates, Tax Reporting and Add-ons.

Take, for example, Canada: Canadian consumer taxes are complicated because they differ across provinces and territories and may incorporate federal and provincial sales tax or a combination of both, known as a harmonized

tax. If the business needs to record a particular consumer tax, the tax needs to be defined as a tax rate. (For insights into setting up Tax Rates refer to Chapter 2.) Segregated tax information filters through to the Sales Tax Report and can be transposed on to forms for submission to relevant tax authorities.

If using the global Xero version and you have a particular requirement, such as you need to generate checks or run country-specific payroll, you can integrate a solution from the Xero Add-on marketplace (see www.xero .com/add-ons/ for further information). For guidance on using add-on solutions, see Chapter 16.

Recording payments to the Tax Office

After preparing a submission for your respective Tax Office, a payment or a refund is recorded. To enter the payment or refund in Xero, add the Tax Office as a contact in your file. Enter a payment as a bill (refer to Chapter 7 for guidance on entering bills) and enter a refund as an invoice (refer to Chapter 6 for guidance on entering invoices).

Entering either a bill or an invoice for your tax payment or refund helps ensure your Accounts Receivable, Accounts Payable and Bank Balance are correct. Don't be lazy and instead use Spend Money and Receive Money!

If different sorts of tax have been paid or refunded, split out the transaction and allocate accordingly, to ensure the accuracy of the account.

Taking Advantage of Xero's Budget Functions

When I lived in Cheltenham in the United Kingdom, I worked as a business-planning analyst for a FMCG (fast-moving consumer goods) company. I was responsible for developing budgets for the Private Label division. (Private Labels are products repackaged with home-label branding.) I dealt with a wide range of items, including cheese, chocolate, coffee and custard! Calculating cost price was challenging because each product had a slightly different recipe depending on its branding, and many ingredients were sourced from overseas, with freight and currency fluctuation implications. Every year, considerable time and effort went into developing an annual budget. Every month, actual results were compared to the annual budget forecast and anomalies were analysed and dealt with. Every quarter, the annual budget was revised to build in known changes (to the market for the goods but also to the overall market and economy), so actuals ended up being compared to both the annual budget and the revised budget!

Fortunately, not all budgets need to be as complicated as the preceding scenario. However, preparing budgets and forecasts of planned business income and expenditure, which also capture the macro economy and its potential effect on the business, is good business practice. A budget can incorporate planning for future financing, evaluating business performance, encouraging responsible spending and setting motivational goals.

Preparing and analysing a budget is like fine-tuning your own business radar. The process helps in understanding the business's operating environment, and what has led to current performance and outcomes. Sitting back and being happy with outstanding business performance isn't good enough! You need to understand what led to that outcome so you can repeat it again (and again and again).

In the following sections, I cover creating and reviewing a budget within Xero.

Initially, obtaining all the information required to prepare a budget may be difficult, so you can treat it as a work in progress. Add to the budget as you understand business transactions — just don't ignore it because you think it's too hard!

Creating a budget

To create a new 12-month annual profit and loss budget for the next financial year in Xero, follow these steps:

1. **From the main dashboard, click Reports⇨Budget Manager.**

   This opens the Budget Manager dashboard (see Figure 10-2).

Budget Manager

Select Budget	Start	Actuals	Period	
Overall Budget	Jan	3 months	12 months	Update

Overall Budget   Wide view

	Jan-	Feb-	Mar-	Apr-	May-	Jun-
Income						
Interest Income (270)	15	17	19	21	23	25
Sales (200)	9,606	9,846	10,092	10,292	10,492	10,692
Total Income	9,621	9,863	10,111	10,313	10,515	10,717
Less Cost of Sales						
Packaging (301)	448	469	471	474	477	480
Purchases (300)	5,016	5,141	5,270	5,325	5,380	5,435
Selling Fees (302)	44	45	46	47	48	49
Total Cost of Sales	5,508	5,645	5,787	5,846	5,905	5,964
Gross Profit	4,113	4,218	4,324	4,467	4,610	4,753
Less Operating Expenses						
Bank Revaluations (497)	0	0	0	0	0	0
Income Tax Expense (505)	0	0	0	0	0	1,280
Realised Currency Gains (499)	0	0	0	0	0	0
Unrealised Currency Gains (498)	0	0	0	0	0	0
Total Operating Expenses	0	0	0	0	0	1,280
Less Overheads						
Advertising (400)	160	164	168	172	176	180
Bank Fees (404)	25	25	25	25	25	25
Cleaning (408)	0	0	0	0	0	0
Consulting & Accounting (412)	512	525	538	538	538	538
Depreciation (416)						

Import   Export   Save   Cancel

Figure 10-2: The Budget Manager dashboard.

2. **At the Select Budget field, click on the drop-down menu and select Add New Budget.**

   The Add New Budget window appears.

3. **Fill out the Name field.**

   Use something clear and simple, such as *Annual Budget [year]*, replacing *[year]* with the relevant year.

   If you've set up tracking in Xero (see Chapter 12), you can filter the budget by the tracking categories here. If you want to amend the tracking options, or create a copy of the budget for another purpose, click on the blue Edit link beside the name of the budget on the dashboard.

4. **Click the green Save button to save the budget's name.**

5. **Click on the Start field's drop-down list and select the month your financial year starts in.**

6. **Click on the Actuals field's drop-down list and select 12 months.**

   Once selected, your business's actual data for the last 12 months fills out on the left of the spreadsheet.

7. **Click on the Period field's drop-down list and select 12 months.**

   Once selected, blank fields for 12 months open up to the right of the spreadsheet. This is where you need to enter your budget figures.

8. **Click on the blue Update button to update the criteria selected.**

   Review the data using the horizontal and vertical scroll bars. At the far right is a total column, summing the full 24 months of data.

9. **Enter data by cell or column, as follows:**

   • **Enter data in the first blank cell and click the green arrow that appears beside the cell and the month heading.**

     The Apply Formula window opens, displaying short-cut options to adjust and copy the cell's data for future months.

   • **Enter data in a column and click the green arrow that appears beside the month heading.**

     The Apply Formula to All Accounts window opens, displaying short-cut options to adjust and copy the column's data for future months, or to clear all data.

   As you're entering budget data, intermittently click the green Save button to avoid timing out and losing data.

10. **Save, Delete or Cancel, as required.**

    The budget is saved by clicking the green Save button, deleted by clicking the red Delete button and editing is discarded by clicking the grey Cancel button.

Data can be manually entered in each cell, copied across other cells or columns through using the short-cut options, or added to CSV spreadsheets (such as Microsoft Excel spreadsheets) and imported into the budget.

Improve your productivity by downloading a template customised to the criteria of your newly created budget in Xero. Access the template by clicking the blue Import button on the Budget Manager dashboard, which brings up the Import a Budget screen. From here, click the Download Template button. The template will download to your Downloads folder and can be used to develop a budget within a CSV spreadsheet (such as an Excel spreadsheet). You can then import this file back into Xero at the Import a Budget screen. Click the blue Browse button, select the saved spreadsheet and click the blue Import button. (Refer to Chapter 3 for information on working with CSV files.)

Reviewing and editing your budget

Once you've created a budget (refer to preceding section), you need to review it on at least a monthly (if not weekly) basis, looking at budgeted versus actual figures. After reviewing your budget, you may need to edit it to more accurately reflect expectations for the business in the current climate.

To edit an existing budget in Xero, go to the Select Budget field on the home dashboard, click on the drop-down arrow and select the required budget. The Budget Manager dashboard appears and you can edit fields as required.

Xero offers reports such as the Budget Variance report, which details budgeted versus actual performance and helps give you a better understanding of your business — see Chapter 12 for more.

Setting a Period Lock Date

Lock dates prevent users from altering accounts prior to and inclusive of the set date. Once the period lock date has been set by an Adviser, only users with Adviser status in Xero can edit accounts prior to and inclusive of the date. Advisers can also change the period lock date, selecting an earlier or later date.

To lock down accounts at the end of a period, click Settings⇨General Settings⇨Financial Settings. From the Period Lock Date drop-down menu, select the date and click Save. (For more on end of financial year reporting, and year end lock dates, see Chapter 11.)

Chapter 11

End of Financial Year Reporting

A tax accountant once told me he'd saved his client $40,000 in taxes. He didn't really save the client money. He did what a good tax accountant is supposed to do — review the business to legitimately minimise tax expenses. Tax is a significant expense — if not the single largest expense — for many businesses. A tax bill has sent many a business into bankruptcy. Scary, huh! So you need to give your business's preparation for the end of financial year the attention it deserves. With Xero (and your reliable Xero advisory team) by your side, all processes become a lot easier. You'll be back to the money-making side of your business in no time!

In this chapter, I cover everything you need to know about the tasks you and/or your bookkeeper can undertake for the end of the financial year, and provide lots of tips for working with your tax accountant, helping you perform the Martha Stewart of all spring cleans of your accounts. I include information on the preparation your business can do in-house, including reconciling, reviewing and tidying up your records. I then outline what your tax accountant does with the data file at the end of the financial year.

Like regular cleaning that you perform year-round, you should take advantage of the collaborative nature of Xero and review any issues as they arise with your accountant on a regular basis throughout the financial year. However, for any issues you've been putting off, you have the opportunity to sort them out now or make a note and alert your tax accountant to them — hence the *spring clean* nature of this activity.

Getting Ready for the End of Financial Year

In Australia around the middle of the year, a commercial runs on TV wishing everyone a 'Happy EOFYS!' (*EOFYS* here stands for *end of financial year sale*). So what is the end of the financial year, and what does it mean for the small-business owner? The financial year is a 12-month period of a business's accounting records. A business financial year may not align with the governing country's financial year or a calendar year. If the business has ties with an international organisation, all associated businesses may opt to report across the same period. Or it may make more sense to align with a different period — for instance, many school-related operations, such as school canteens, align their financial year to the school year.

The end of financial or fiscal year is an important date in the accounting and business calendar. Business-owners need to plan, prepare and deal with the end of financial year, empowered with the trusted advice of their tax accountant.

Note: The collaborative nature of Xero allows you to work with your accountant throughout the year — the strategies covered in the following sections are an opportunity to pull everything together and finalise the year.

Finding out where you're at

In Chapter 10 I cover developing an annual budget and then reviewing your budget regularly and revising forecasts accordingly. In this section, I cover finalising your budget and forecast in the lead-up to the end of financial year.

About two months prior to the end of financial year, you should prepare a forecast of the full-year results and review your financial accounts. Using Xero's Budget Manager function, you can easily create a suitable forecast for this purpose.

Here's how:

1. **From the dashboard, click Reports and go to the Budget Manager, click in the Select Budget field and select + Add New Budget.**

2. **Name this budget FORECAST 201X and click the green Save button.**

3. **Select the Start date as two months before the end of the actual year.**

   If the financial year ends in June, the selected date would be May.

4. **In the Actuals field select 12 months, in the Period field select 3 months.**

   In the Period field, '2' would have been okay, but that's not an option.

5. **Click the blue Update button, and Export the data to excel.**

You can now tinker with the spreadsheet — add in an averaging formula, for example, for the last two months and so creating a 12-month forecast. You can then add an extra column at the end and tally the data for the 12-month period. Just make sure you don't overstate the tally — only grab 12 months!

Refer to Chapter 10 for more information on Xero's Budget Manager, and ask your accountant for assistance if required.

Xero is a cloud-based solution, so trusted advisers who you've given Xero access to can jump in to your Xero file and collaborate with you in the budget development.

Being prepared early

Empowered with your actual results for the first ten months of the financial year and your forecasts for the last two months, make an appointment to speak with your tax accountant. In particular, discuss the following:

- ✔ Do your accounts have any issues that you need assistance with? Perhaps you have something like a pesky amortisation loan. Can your accountant sort out any issues prior to the end of the year?
- ✔ Do any tax-mitigating strategies need to be implemented during the current financial year?

Communicating with your accountant, be it via Skype, email exchanges or a face-to-face meeting, primes you for the approaching end of financial year.

A few other chores that can be done prior to the end of the financial year include

- ✔ If you've not been working with your accountant on a regular basis, book an appointment around the end of the financial year with members of your Xero advisory team — especially if you think you're going to need additional support at the end of financial year.
- ✔ Review the Aged Receivables report (refer to Chapter 10). Talk to your tax accountant to establish if you should identify customers who owe the business money and then urge them to make payment before the

end of the financial year. (You may have to write off any long overdue debts — see the section 'Processing a bad debt' for more.)

✔ Start preparations for a stocktake on the final day of the year — if your business holds stock. (See Chapter 13 for more on managing inventory and Chapter 16 for inventory management add-on solutions.)

Reconciling tax payments for the year

If your business has made consumer tax payments during the year, you need to reconcile and review the full year's submissions and payments and correct the final payment for the full year. Yikes! Why might you need to do this? If the period wasn't locked down, transactions may have been accidently changed. Or incorrect figures could have been submitted to the Tax Office. Errors do happen — take this as an opportunity to correct them. Refer to Chapter 10 for guidance on reconciling consumer tax payments, and instead of reviewing a reporting period, review an entire year.

Your tax accountant is also likely to review and reconcile this account, and identify any adjustments required.

Processing a bad debt

Your business made a sale or you invoiced a customer for certain services and all efforts have been made to collect the outstanding debt but you realise it's futile — you're more likely to see pigs fly than receive the payment. In this case, writing the invoice off as a bad debt is necessary to ensure your financial records correctly reflect the reality of the situation. Take a look at your bad debts quarterly and take a good look before the end of the financial year.

Here's how to write off a bad debt:

1. **Open up the sales invoice that needs to be written off and make a note of the number and date.**

   Refer to Chapter 6 for more information on accessing sales invoices.

2. **Apply a credit note to the invoice by clicking Invoice Options and selecting the Add Credit Note option from the drop-down list.**

3. **Enter the last date of the reporting period in the Date field.**

4. **Enter the original invoice's number and date in the Reference field.**

5. **Process the bad debt according to the accounting basis used.**

   How you process the debt depends on whether you use an accruals or cash basis, as follows:

   - **Accruals basis:** If the business operates on an accruals basis, create an expense account called Bad Debt (refer to Chapter 2 for guidance on creating accounts). Make a note of the tax rate, change the account to the bad debts account and change the tax rate to the original tax rate amount.

   - **Cash basis:** If the business operates on a cash basis, use the same account and tax coding from the original invoice. (This will have been auto populated for you — so, in fact, do nothing else.)

6. **Apply the bad debt to the invoice by clicking the green Approve button.**

   The outcome of this within the accruals method is the invoice is closed off; the Profit and Loss/Income statement displays the income and the bad debt expense as separate lines that offset each other. The consumer tax nets itself off in the Balance Sheet and the Consumer Tax report reflects the consumer as a sales and purchases line.

   The outcome of this within the cash method is the invoice is closed off; no trace of the transaction comes up in the Profit and Loss statement displays. The consumer tax nets itself off in the Balance Sheet/Income and the Consumer Tax report.

Preparing Accounts for Your Tax Accountant

During the year, hopefully you've taken advantage of the collaborative nature of Xero and liaised with your accountant to iron out and deal with any issues in your Xero file. However, when it comes to the end of the financial year, and as company taxes need to be prepared, you still need to review a few aspects of your Xero data file. This gives you a better understanding of your business and cuts down on the time your accountant takes (and charges) to prepare everything that's required. In this section, I take you through some areas of Xero that may need to be reviewed or worked on before you ask your accountant to access Xero and undertake the end of financial year review.

Your tax accountant can help you with many of the chores discussed in this section and, yes, your tax accountant's fee is tax-deductible! But if you have the time and energy, you can do some of the basic housekeeping yourself. (If not, hire a good bookkeeper to do it for you, rather than leaving it all for the accountant.) You're just throwing your money away if, for example, you ask your tax accountant to review your accounts while a balance is still showing in the suspense account, bank accounts are unreconciled and accounts have been left forlorn and forgotten. The other danger is that, if you hand everything over to your accountant, he may end up making some assumptions or needing to ask you about issues he can't sort out.

The following list outlines some of the areas that often pop up as issues when I do end of financial year reviews. Keep a record of your own issues that you need to alert your accountant about as you work through the points in the list.

Here are some actions you may need to perform before asking your accountant to finalise your accounts:

- ✔ Clear transactions allocated to any suspense or miscellaneous account so the balance is zero and so your records are complete and accurate.

- ✔ Review the General Ledger Exceptions report for the full period. Look for account balances that seem out of the ordinary or unexpected. Check whether you can understand or explain the balance. Compare the balance to the previous period — are they comparable? If it's reasonable to expect a deviation of, say, 10 per cent year on year, anything different should be reviewed.

  At the time of writing, Xero doesn't yet include a function that lets you search the whole general ledger (although this is in the works). A workaround is to run the Detailed Account Transaction report and search using Ctrl + F (PC) or Cmd + F (Mac); however, you can only search for specific data, not a range of data. From the home dashboard, click Reports⇨All Reports to access the Detailed Account Transaction report. For more advanced searching and filtering options, you can export the file to Excel.

- ✔ Upload any important source documents — like car lease agreements — and attach them to the relevant transaction, so tax accountant can easily review them (refer to Chapter 4 for more on file storage).

- ✔ From the home dashboard, go to the top active bank account and click Manage Account⇨Reconciliation Report to access the Bank Reconciliation Summary. Review the summary for all bank, credit card and online payment gateway accounts like PayPal, as at the end of the financial year. The Balance in Xero and the Statement Balance should equal. If they do, as in Figure 11-1, publish the reports as at the last day of the financial year. (Refer to Chapter 10 for guidance on what to do if the balances don't reconcile — that is, they're not equal.)

Figure 11-1:
Bank
Recon-
ciliation
Summary
displaying a
reconciled
account.

Bank Reconciliation Summary
Business Savings Account
(UK)
As at 17 February

Add Summary

Date	Description	Reference	Amount
	Balance in Xero		0.00
	Statement Balance		0.00

✔ From the home dashboard, go to the top active bank account and click Manage Account⇨Reconciliation Report and click the Statement Exception tab. This report identifies transactions that may cause the reconciliation to be out of balance. The report highlights the source of the transaction — auto (bank feed) or manual — and the reasons for the discrepancy, including duplicate or deleted entries. Review the exception statement for all bank, credit card and online payment gateway accounts like PayPal, as at the end of the financial year.

✔ Review the balances of the consumer tax account and payroll liability accounts (if relevant — refer to Chapter 10). Do they seem 'reasonable'?

✔ Review the Aged Receivables report from the Reports dashboard. Do you need to write off any accounts to bad debts?

✔ Review the Aged Payables report from the Reports dashboard. Do you still owe money to creditors and need to deal with this?

✔ Review fixed assets — from the home dashboard, go to Accounts⇨(Fixed Assets. Have any assets been purchased or sold during the year? Are they reflected on the Fixed Assets dashboard? Make a note of anything you need to mention to the accountant. (See Chapter 14 for guidance on dealing with fixed assets.)

Ideally, your tax accountant, with Adviser status, is processing the business's Fixed Asset Register within Xero. Doing so is simpler and fully utilises this feature in Xero. However, if you've still not brought your Fixed Asset Register details into Xero, take this opportunity to check if your accountant can give you a depreciation schedule so this schedule can be entered into Xero. (Also continue to encourage your accountant to work directly into Xero, rather than use an external solution — and buy a copy of this book too!)

✔ Review the Balance Sheet as at the date of the end of the year, as compared to the previous year (if you have those accounts). Do the balances seem reasonable? Do the suspense, miscellaneous or historical adjustment accounts have balances? Can you explain these balances? If questionable balances exist, click and drill down to review them. (To access the report, click Reports⇨All Reports⇨Balance Sheet.)

✔ Review the Profit and Loss/Income Statement report for the full financial year, compared to the previous year (if you have those accounts). Do the balances seem reasonable? Do any suspense or miscellaneous accounts have balances? Can you explain these balances? (To access the report, click Reports⇨All Reports⇨Profit and Loss/Income Statement.)

✔ Review the 'reasonableness' of other reports that you use on a regular basis.

✔ Review data from any add-on solutions. If you're using a program to assist with stock management, for example, you need to undertake a physical stocktake, update the stock values, and review work in progress. (See Chapter 13 for guidance on updating stock figures.)

✔ Perform a back-up of Xero data by exporting a detailed General Ledger report for the full financial year and save it to Microsoft Excel. Access the General Ledger report from the home dashboard — click Reports⇨All Reports⇨General Ledger. Select the correct date range and the Show YTD option so opening and closing balances and a running balance appears on report. Then click the Update button, scroll to the bottom of the screen and click the white Export Detailed General Ledger to Excel button in the middle. (Just don't get confused and click the blue Export button on the right.)

✔ Prepare your consumer tax report for the final period of the year (if relevant).

✔ Finalise and enter any payments that need to be made. After reviewing the consumer tax account, liaise with your tax accountant to clarify any payments that need to be made to taxation authorities. Likewise, after reviewing payroll liability accounts, payments may need to be made to the relevant authorities.

Once you've run through the areas for review in the preceding list, let your accountant know you're ready for him to work his wonders on your Xero data file.

Alert your accountant to any issues you've not talked to him about during the year that he should be made aware of, like the purchase of a new fixed asset or significant changes to operations. Ask him for feedback on your record keeping — could you make any improvements or do anything differently?

The benefits of some extra Xero housekeeping

I always like to practise what I preach. Even though I review my accounts regularly, here are some extra things I noticed when performing my own end-of-year housekeeping (covered in the section 'Preparing Accounts for Your Tax Accountant'):

✔ I had 10 cents sitting in a liability account so I (with my Adviser status) prepared a manual journal (see the section 'Entering manual journals', later in this chapter, for guidance on using manual journals) to transfer the balance to a petty cash account. An extra 10 cents in my petty cash account isn't a major concern and it clears a bothersome liability account.

✔ I also had a balance in the Overpayments account. I clicked on the amount and drilled down to see details of the account for the full year. I realised I needed to refund the overpayment and repaid my customer to clear the balance. (Refer to Chapter 8 for more on this.) The payment happened after the end of period date, but at least I knew it was sorted out.

✔ My electricity account seemed lower than previous years. I reviewed the bills and realised I'd missed entering a quarter that I had not paid using my business bank accounts. I located the bill and added it to Xero. I then set the bill up as a repeating draft bill so I'd never miss it again! (Refer to Chapter 7 for information on setting up repeating bills.)

✔ I had a balance in my reimbursable expenses clearing account. I realised I hadn't properly allocated a parking expense to the account, so I edited the invoice, and changed the account allocation.

Helping with Tax Accountant Tasks

When I initially review a customer's data, I check to see if the end of financial year has been finalised in the records by the tax accountant. Customers may have paid a tax accountant a lot of money to prepare financial accounts; however, frequently the job is unfinished. Telltale signs include no depreciation accounts and no manual journal entries on the last day of the end of the financial period.

What happened? It's likely the tax accountant extracted data from the business owner's system, reviewed it, made various assumptions, applied various tax laws, prepared the end of financial year reports and gave them back to the business owner in a folder or on a USB stick many months after the end of the financial year. If I'm lucky, the business owner has spent a couple of hours entering the end of year adjustments directly into the accounting system.

Alas, many don't understand or have the time to do this step and, year on year, layers of incompleteness build into their business records. (And the tax accountant probably charges a little bit more every year, because the poor business owner's accounts aren't up to date — and the cycle goes on!)

With Xero, you can make this process run a lot more smoothly. This is because your accountant can work with you through the year, directly within Xero, using Xero's single ledger accounting system. (So no more USB sticks months down the track.)

In the following sections, I cover the advantages of enabling your accountant to access your Xero data directly in more detail. If your accountant still prefers to finalise your accounts in another program, I also cover exporting Xero data for your accountant to import into another specialised tax software program. I also cover the whole process of finalising end of financial year accounts, from entering manual journals to working with a locked account.

Enabling your tax accountant to work directly in Xero

Xero introduces the concept of a *single ledger* accounting system. This is a system where both your accountant and you (as the business owner) can access and work on the same data. Your tax accountant finalises the end of year accounts directly into your business's Xero file. No time is wasted extracting or re-entering data, and no danger exists of the accountant working on the wrong data file, or the file getting lost on a USB stick.

Xero's single ledger accounting system means, as a business owner, you're better positioned to reflect on what adjustments have been made. (Shhhh! By this I really mean question the assumptions made by your tax accountant.) I'm one of those obsessive-compulsive people who questions and analyses everything. I want to understand, for example, why two cars are being depreciated differently, or why a certain business expense has been omitted from the records. Sometimes I pick up areas where an accountant has made the wrong assumption. But also, knowing the answers to these types of questions helps you run your business better — if the business can't legitimately claim an expense, you need to know that for future years, so you don't mistakenly overspend. (Yes, I am talking about entertainment expenses!)

Your tax accountant accesses Xero in the cloud. He can be at your office, his office or halfway around the world — it's all in the clouds, so your accountant could be anywhere! He enters the end of financial year adjustments directly into source documents, and general journals directly into Xero's single ledger via a manual journal and, therefore, the business owner's financial reports become the prepared financial reports.

Exporting general ledger transactions

Typically, your tax accountant prepares the business's tax reports in specialised software — either Xero Practice Manager or other software used by accounting practices. The Xero data may need to be exported and then imported into this software so he can prepare the tax requirements for your business and generate reports to be submitted to the relevant tax office.

In New Zealand and Australia, if your tax accountant is a Xero partner, they can perform tax processing on their side of the Xero platform via the Practice Manager.

My accountant, for example, exports the data from Xero and imports the data into Handiledger. This system then autofills Australian Taxation Office forms. Your accountant is likely to use their own Handiledger-style system, which autofills the relevant taxation forms for your country.

Extracting data from Xero is quite simple — although you can only do so if you have Adviser status within Xero. To extract data, follow these steps:

1. **From the home dashboard, click Adviser⇨Export.**

   The Export Transactions window opens up.

2. **Select the appropriate software file format for exporting.**

3. **Select the date range for the full year in the From and To fields.**

4. **Export the general ledger transactions by clicking the blue Download link.**

   The file saves to the file downloads directory.

Once data has been exported, your accountant can log into his own accounting system and import the downloaded Xero general ledger transactions.

Entering manual journals

I adored my accounting teacher. She neatly filled the blackboard with journal entries and trial balances. These days, you could spend your entire career working on accounting software and never see a general journal entry. They are there, happening behind the scenes, allocating debits and credits to the relevant ledgers, but you don't see them as such. However, on a few rare occasions, an entry is made that looks like a good old-fashioned general journal entry — a *manual journal*. A manual journal could be entered to

- ✔ Finalise the end of the financial year requirements
- ✔ Add Tracking to conversion balances (see Chapter 12)
- ✔ Distribute profits or allocate dividends
- ✔ Sort out minor rounding issues

Users with Standard user status and above can enter their own manual journal in Xero by following these steps:

1. **Access the Manual Journal dashboard by clicking Reports⇨All Reports⇨Journal Report and click the Manual Journals button and create a new journal by clicking the New Journal button.**

   A general journal template opens (see Figure 11-2).

2. **Clearly describe the purpose of the journal in the Narration field.**

   Use something like 'EOFY G/J financial year prepared by [accountant's name]'. So, as shown in Figure 11-2, my narration would say *EOFY 20XX/XX prepared by Dickensons*.

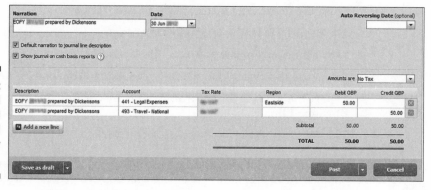

Figure 11-2:
Xero's end
of financial
year general
journal entry
template.

3. **Check the Default Narration to Journal Line Description box to allow the description to autofill all transaction fields.**

   Override fields as required.

4. **Record the date of the manual journal in the Date field.**

   This date should be the last day of the financial year.

5. **Define the accounting basis the journal is to use.**

   Check the Show Journal on Cash Basis Reports box if you want the journal to reflect a cash and accrual basis; leave the box blank if you want the journal on an accrual basis only.

6. **Specify whether the values entered in the journal are Tax Exclusive or Tax Inclusive by selecting the drop-down option from the Amounts Are field.**

   If your business isn't registered for consumer tax, don't select the No Tax option in the Amounts Are field, which intuitively seems to be the correct choice. If you do, you won't have the option to select the correct tax rate or the ability to exclude the transaction from the consumer tax reports.

   Lines of the journal entry are detailed in the block beneath the Amounts Are field. Each line should include a Description, Account and Tax Rate (tracking categories are optional — see Chapter 12). The line values must be allocated to either the debit or credit column.

7. **Add extra lines to the journal entry by clicking the Add a New Line button.**

8. **Delete lines of the journal entry by overriding the entry or clicking on the cross to the right of the entry.**

9. **Leave the Auto Reversing Date field blank.**

   The entry will not be reversed. (The automatic option to reverse journal entries is useful for businesses running on an accruals basis that need to create a journal on the last day of the month, and then reverse it on the first day of the next month.)

10. **Click the blue Save as Draft button.**

    You can save an out of balance journal (that is, one where the debit and credit columns don't equal) as a draft. Sometimes journal entries are arduously long — you may need to take a water cooler break before you have them all fully entered.

    You can click the Save as Draft button at any time. If you're entering a long journal clicking this button regularly is a good idea to avoid timing out and losing work.

11. **Edit the journal entry (if required).**

    Access the journal entry from the home dashboard — click Adviser⇨Manual Journal⇨All, and click on the relevant journal. At the top right of the journal, click on the Journal Options button and access options to reverse copy or delete the journal if those actions are required.

12. **If you allocated a line to a suspense account, delete that journal line and continue to enter the rest of the journal.**

13. **Post the journal entry to the ledger by clicking the green Post button.**

A manual journal can't post to an Accounts Payable or Accounts Receivable account. In fact, the only time you can post directly to either of these accounts is when you are processing an overpayment (refer to Chapter 8) or entering a conversion balance (refer to Chapter 2).

Special Considerations

The following sections cover some extra areas you may need to look at before your accounts are completely finalised, depending on how your accountant works — end-of-year reports and account lock dates.

Publishing end-of-year reports

Once your tax accountant has posted any adjustments and finalised the accounts (but before you start whooping with joy), he should publish the Income Statement Duplicated or Profit and Loss/Income Statement and Balance Sheet report for the financial year through Xero, and triple-check that they agree with the business's financial reports submitted to your taxation authority.

If your accountant doesn't do these things you can publish the reports yourself and check the figures — refer to Chapter 9 for guidance on publishing reports. *Note:* Only someone with Adviser status can publish these reports.

Locking down accounts

Lock dates prevent users from altering any accounts prior to and inclusive of the set date. Once the End of Year Lock Date has been set, if you (or anyone else) try to enter transactions in the period prior to the lock date you're notified the accounts are locked, and the transactions must occur after the given date.

Here's how you lock down the accounts after submitting your business's tax reports (if you have Adviser status in Xero): Click Settings⮞General Settings⮞Financial Settings and then, from the End of Year Lock Date drop-down menu, select the date and select Save.

The date selected for the End of Year Lock Date is typically the last day of the financial year. Usually, the lock date is set when your tax accountant has finalised and submitted the accounts for the end of financial year submission.

Once the lock date has been set, you can edit it if you have Adviser status in Xero. So you can change it, make any necessary changes, and set it again. However, only do so if absolutely necessary. In most cases, avoid making any changes, especially after reports have been filed, because these changes then lead to inconsistencies in the figures.

If your tax accountant doesn't lock down the end of year period after the end of the financial year, make sure you do (or someone else on your Xero advisory team with the required permission does).

Handling your Xero file when you sell your business

If you sell your business, you may be wondering what you do with your Xero file. Don't give the file to the new owner of the business! You can extract records from the file for them, such as a Chart of Accounts, the customer list and some reports, but the file should remain with you.

If you're no longer running the business, you have two options regarding your Xero file:

✔ Finalise your accounts and the sale of the business with your accountant, download all necessary information from your Xero file, and then end your Xero subscription. The Xero data file is converted to read-only and stored on Xero servers. If you need to access the files again, you can pay Xero an activation fee and the file is re-activated.

✔ Keep the file going indefinitely by continuing to pay your Xero subscription. You could save money and downgrade to the Starter package. If you start or buy a new business, however, you'll still need to create a new ledger (and Xero file) for this new business.

Part IV
Getting the Most Out of Xero

Five Astute Ways to Use Business Intelligence

- ✔ **Communicate:** The business's key decision-makers should be given guidance on how to access reports in Xero, and trained in how to read the reports. You may also need to highlight specific features of reports, such as tracking options, so they understand how to interpret the data.

- ✔ **Extract and manipulate:** Many of the reports and data found in Xero are available to be downloaded into a spreadsheet format. An add-on like QuickWin Excel Integration Tools offers full data extraction from Xero. From there, analysis and modelling can be undertaken, enabling you to build dashboards, charts and your own KPI reports.

- ✔ **Data mine:** Many of the references and amounts in Xero can be clicked on, allowing you to drill down and see the detail behind the high-level information.

- ✔ **Take advantage of add-ons:** Embrace the add-on ecosystem around Xero to pimp out your business intelligence experience. Add-ons can extrapolate data from within Xero for analysis, or combine internal data with external data, such as from a customer resource management solution, to provide meaningful and useful real-time information.

- ✔ **Use the dashboards:** Each of the key areas in Xero has a dashboard, highlighting top-level information for the business. This can be quickly accessed and reviewed to ensure you are on track to achieve your goals.

Explore the full potential of cloud computing. Discover a free online article on using and integrating Xero's add-on features at www.dummies.com/extras/xero.

In this part ...

- Use your Xero dashboard, key metrics and tracking tools to navigate towards your business goals. (This also encompasses management, performance, position and detail reports.)

- Learn your way around the easy-to-use Budget Manager business tool. Once you do, you'll have the opportunity to create multiple budgets to complement your current environment and future goals.

- Add simple inventory items to make invoicing easier. Xero does not have an inventory management system, but you can add items that help set up all those recurring items on an invoice.

- Read all about how to set up and maintain assets in the Fixed Asset Register.

- Learn how you can use the Xero multi-currency feature if your business is exposed to multiple currencies.

- Discover the online networking capabilities of Xero, the cost benefits of using add-ons, and exactly which add-ons might be useful to you and your business.

Chapter 12

Monitoring Your Business

*I*n the mid 1990s, my husband and I ventured on a road trip from Toronto, Ontario, to Boston, Massachusetts. With a car, a credit card, a rough idea of how we would get there and a two-week time frame, we set off on our journey. The trip was pretty uneventful for the first few hours (you have to either travel on the main road or go swimming in the freezing cold Lake Ontario!). After crossing the border into the United States, we had time to explore and to deviate from our route when the fancy took us. So we changed course and spent a few days in Montpelier, Vermont (foodies' heaven!). Getting back on track, we made it to the beautiful city of Boston (and, disappointingly, found the worst bed and breakfast I have ever stayed in).

A business can be like a road trip — you may start with a particular destination in mind, but then change course and achieve something that you would never have contemplated at the start of the journey. And sometimes that's okay. However, when you can clearly define the destination for your business, you're likely to find navigating a course, and focusing all energies on reaching it, much easier.

In this chapter, I provide help on establishing a road map for your business and recognising metrics that can help keep the journey on track, using Xero's tracking and reporting functions. You can leverage information generated from Xero's transparent and accessible dashboards to support all business decisions. Monitor your business's journey, and readjust and refine as necessary.

Identifying Key Metrics

Business strategy enables you to understand what needs to be done to achieve your business goals and get the business where it needs to be. In the simplest of terms, outlining a business strategy means you've defined a vision for your business, recognised the current business position, and undertaken a gap analysis between where the business is now and where you want the business to be.

Identifying the direction the business needs to move in then assists in defining goals and formulating tasks that you (and other staff members) can work towards to achieve the business vision. All activities undertaken by you or staff of the business should align to the strategic plan, to ensure the focus and direction of the business is maintained.

Focusing yourself and your team on specific targets

To start thinking about ways you can move your business in the direction of achieving your goals and overall strategy, have a look at this example. A training organisation offers study packages that, when taken up, attract government funding. The funding is paid in instalments — at sign up, midway through the 14 training units and at signed-off completion. Students would frequently complete all aspects of training and assessment; however, they could only be signed off once staff had completed all administration requirements.

The manager of the training organisation realised his cash flow was directly linked to signed-off training units. So, he found ways to motivate lecturers to move their students through training units. He continually stressed the importance of training unit sign-off targets with staff. He publicly praised and rewarded lecturers who achieved high training unit sign-offs. By dangling this carrot he cultivated a motivated team focused on achieving a single target: Signed-off completed training units.

To identify this simple KPI, the manager reviewed the Sales By Items report in Xero (found on the Reports dashboard), and customised it for the relevant period. The Quantity Sold column reflected completed units for the period.

Not once did he mention cash flow, or profit and loss, or bank balances to the staff. Instead, he dissected the organisation processes and identified key targets that directly affected cash flow. He extracted an easily digestible concept and kept the lecturers focused on that simple target. Of course, he was concerned about the business's cash flow, profit and bank balances but was aware staff eyes would likely glaze over if they were provided with too much information or too many targets.

If you employ staff and you're trying to make sure their activities align with the overall goals and strategy of your business, find ways that engage and motivate them, and recognise their achievements (refer to the sidebar 'Focusing yourself and your team on specific targets' for more).

With this in mind, you can develop key performance indicators (KPIs) to help the business keep on track. *KPIs* are a quantifiable measurement that can be set as a target to assist the business in achieving goals. They don't necessarily need to be a dollar value — they could be average debtor or average creditor days, or number of invoices issued per month. My husband used to manage airline safety, and the numero uno performance measurement for his job was whether take-offs equalled landings!

Using Xero to set realistic targets and strategies

Xero can assist you in achieving your business strategy. Here's how: You define an inspiring strategy, break it down into goals and then use the rich transparent data available in Xero to set targets that align to those goals. Through regularly reviewing the data, you can refine your operations and fine-tune your business's KPIs to achieve desired outcomes.

It's not the largest of businesses that survive, or the most innovative, or those that spend the most on marketing. The businesses that survive are the ones most responsive to change. You need to adapt and refine your strategy to the ever-changing environment in which you operate.

Setting KPIs and rewarding success

When looking to set and track KPIs, keep it simple: Identify KPIs, focus staff on targets and reward success.

To identify KPIs for your business, have a think about what KPIs are most likely to assist you in achieving the main goals of your business. What KPIs are likely to assist you in the decision-making process and keep you aligned with the business vision? Your KPIs could relate to sales, cash on hand and return on investment.

For example, KPIs that align to your business vision, and ways you can use Xero to track these, could include the following:

✔ Achieving a monthly cash surplus of $10,000 for six consecutive months to fund extension plans. To review this KPI in Xero, from the dashboard go to Reports⇨All Reports⇨Cash Summary. Set the criteria to compare six months by selecting the previous month in the Date field. In the Period field select 1 Month, in the Compare With field select Previous 5 Periods and click the blue Update button to view the customised data. Scroll to the bottom of the report to see the Net Cash Movement for each month. This is the monthly cash surplus KPI. If the cash surplus is not meeting the desired goals, you need to increase cash coming into the business and decrease cash flowing out of the business. (See the sidebar 'The power of positive cash flow', later in this chapter, for more.)

✔ Maintaining a return on investment percentage between 20 and 25 per cent to meet investor requirements. To review this KPI in Xero, from the dashboard go to Reports⇨All Reports⇨Executive Summary. Set the criteria for the report by selecting the previous month in the Date field, and in the Show field select Summary and Ratios. Click the blue Update button to view the customised data. Scroll down the report to the line headed Return on Investment (p.a.).

The Return on Investment ratio (or ROI for short) is my all-time favourite ratio. I use it to analyse all business spending. You have to spend money to make money but, whenever you spend, you should ask yourself what income is generated as a result of the investment. A desirable return on investment should be higher than current bank deposit interest rates. If they're lower than these rates, you need to justify why — and question whether you'd be better off selling the business and depositing all the money in a bank. For example, at the time of writing, bank deposit rates in England are hovering around 1.7 per cent. If a car yard has £8 million invested in business assets, it needs to generate income of at least 1.7 per cent of the value of these assets to achieve a return on investment that outperforms bank deposit rates. Running a business involves high levels of risk and time commitment — so, ideally, the business owner would want the Return on Investment ratio to be significantly higher than the bank deposit rates.

Note: I selected the previous month in both scenarios because data for the current month is likely to be incomplete and reflect a distorted reality.

See the section 'Delving deeper into the Executive Summary report', later in this chapter, for more on tracking performance margins and variances.

The KPIs for your business need to reflect where your business is in the business cycle. (A *business cycle* refers to the general economic fluctuations of the business, reflected in the business moving between stages of expanding and contracting, with constant fluctuation between the two.) A start-up business is focused on expansion, for example, spending as much money as it can on promotion while trying to build up sales. (Facebook, now a billion-dollar enterprise, ran at a loss for five years!) A contracting business may have steady sales, with minimal money spent on promotion or seeking out new business activities. The KPIs you select should reflect where your business is in the business cycle.

Reviewing your business strategy

Gazing into my mystical crystal ball, I could ponder the optimal moment to review a business's strategy, goals and KPIs — but, alas, I dropped it and it broke.

Developing a business strategy is like setting a car's GPS. Just like you need to check that your GPS is actually sending you in the direction you need to go, reviewing goals and KPIs when implementing strategic change is essential. Adjusting your business's goals and KPIs helps you align the business and ensure it reaches its new destination.

Use the reports and customisation available in Xero discussed throughout this chapter to review your goals and KPIs, and do so on at least a quarterly basis.

The business landscape is constantly changing and new business models are emerging. Those who adopt rapid changes in innovation and technology leave other businesses in their wake.

Generating Useful Information

For information to be useful, it must be complete and accurate. Incomplete data is unreliable and can lead to unsupported decisions. (Review Chapters 10 and 11 for guidance on undertaking the required tasks to ensure your data is complete and accurate, and your financial records are complete.)

Within Xero, you have access to a plethora of reports, and if you feel comfortable swimming in the numbers and data, jump in and enjoy them. If, however, you're not sure where to start, read on. Don't be that person who erects blinkers and ignores their business reports!

If you're feeling reluctant about diving into Xero's sea of data, set yourself a daily 15-minute challenge. Allocate 15 minutes each day to work through an area, and continue in 15-minute blocks until you grasp the concepts. This is how I find time to learn something new — and it may take a few days of 15-minute challenges before I fully understand something. Sleep can also be immensely beneficial in the learning process. If I'm trying to learn something, I often find that the next morning a few of the pieces of the puzzle have fallen into place.

Make a cup of tea, settle yourself down and spend 15 minutes every day reviewing, understanding and identifying how you can use Xero's reports in your business.

Taking advantage of management reports

For a brief moment I lived in Wolverhampton in the United Kingdom. In the job I was working at, I was responsible for preparing MMRs — the monthly management reports. Every month, I produced a bound book of monthly reports that I would distribute to managers — whether they liked it or not — a few weeks after the end of the month. By the time I could distribute the reports, the next month was almost over and, overwhelmed by so much information, I swear some managers used the books to prop up their computers.

How times have changed — using a cloud-based real-time system, management reports can be accessed when the manager wants to see and review them. ***Note:*** Data needs to be completed for the period you're reviewing for the reports to be accurate.

Users with Adviser status in Xero have the ability to access a predefined six-page Management Report. This report is a neat compact set of management reports that highlights all the general areas a business should be aware of. The reports contained within the Management Report are the following:

- ✔ Executive Summary
- ✔ Cash Summary
- ✔ Profit & Loss
- ✔ Balance Sheet
- ✔ Aged Receivables
- ✔ Aged Payables

Figure 12-1 shows the first page of Xero's six-page Management Report — the Executive Summary.

Here's how to access the Management Report if you have Adviser status: From the dashboard click Adviser⇨Management Reports. From here, you have access to Xero's predefined selection of six reports. Click on the field beside Page 1 of 6 to select the individual reports.

If you have Standard user access in Xero, you can still access the individual reports on the Management Report from the Reports dashboard. Simply click Reports⇨All Reports and locate the required report.

Executive Summary
Michelle
For the month of August

Add Summary

	Aug	Jul	Variance
Cash			
Cash received	1,840.00	3,489.10	-47.3% ▼
Cash spent	1,758.35	0.00	0.0%
Cash surplus (deficit)	81.65	3,489.10	-97.7% ▼
Closing bank balance	9,384.48	9,302.83	0.9% ▲
Profitability			
Income	8,866.00	1,600.00	454.1% ▲
Direct costs	4,411.12	0.00	0.0%
Gross profit (loss)	4,454.88	1,600.00	178.4% ▲
Other Income	0.00	0.00	0.0%
Expenses	46.95	552.92	-91.5% ▼
Profit (loss)	4,407.93	1,047.08	321.0% ▲
Balance Sheet			
Debtors	10,240.90	1,885.00	443.3% ▲
Creditors	7,259.03	2,275.85	219.0% ▲
Net assets	14,547.96	10,140.03	43.5% ▲
Income			
Number of invoices issued	5.0	1.0	400.0% ▲
Average value of invoices	1,773.20	1,600.00	10.8% ▲
Performance			
Gross profit margin	50.2%	100.0%	-49.8% ▼
Net profit margin	49.7%	65.4%	-24.0% ▼
Return on investment (p.a.)	363.6%	123.9%	193.4% ▲
Position			
Average debtors days	35.8	36.5	-2.0% ▼
Average creditors days	50.5	127.6	-60.4% ▼
Short term cash forecast	2,981.87	(390.85)	862.9% ▲
Current assets to liabilities	2.3	3.0	-23.2% ▼
Term assets to liabilities			0.0%

This report uses the most up-to-date exchange rate data available to convert foreign currencies into New Zealand Dollar. Enter exchange rates for 31 August

Notes

1. Figures converted into New Zealand Dollar using the following rate:
   0.776572 AUD Australian Dollar per NZD. Rate provided by XE.com on 31 Aug

Save as Draft   Publish   Print   Export

Figure 12-1: The Executive Summary page of Xero's Management Report.*

*Appearance of the Executive Summary page is correct at the time of writing but is subject to change.

Delving deeper into the Executive Summary report

Access the Executive Summary report in Xero via the Management Report. From the home dashboard, click Adviser⇨Management Report. It opens at Page 1 of 6, which is the Executive Summary report. In the Date field enter the previous month, in the Show field enter Summary and Ratios and click the blue Update button to update the report. The far right column displays a current month versus prior month variance analysis, or the percentage change between the two months.

The power of positive cash flow

A positive cash flow is necessary for business survival — profitable businesses can go bankrupt due to a lack of positive cash flow. If you have concerns about your cash indicators after looking at your Executive Summary report in Xero, take a look at how cash flow can be improved. For example, you could:

✔ Identify and escalate collection disputes more quickly. To identify overdue invoices, from the home dashboard view the Money Coming In dashboard and click on overdue invoices to drill down to further detail on the invoice and customer contact information.

✔ Review customer credit terms. To edit all customer credit terms, from the home dashboard go to Settings⇨General Settings⇨Invoice Settings and click the Options button on the Standard themed invoices and then edit. In the Terms and Payment Advice block, update customer credit terms by minimising the number of days they have to pay — for example, to *Net 7 days* — and save the branding theme. The updated information is on all future invoices using this theme. Do this for all invoices used. Click the Default Settings button to set a default due date for all sales invoices.

✔ Review cash collection procedures. Review a typical invoice printout the customer receives and assess if payment details are clearly stated. To view an invoice, from the home dashboard click Accounts⇨Sales⇨Paid, double click on a typical invoice to open it, and select the Print PDF button and then the green Print Now button. The invoice PDF downloads to your computer; click on the file to open and view. If you decide the invoice could be improved, you need to update the invoice branding.

✔ Review supplier payment terms. Ensure the supplier's bill default due date is correctly entered in the contact details, and withhold paying supplier bills until close to their due date. To view the supplier's bill default due date, from the dashboard click Contacts⇨Suppliers and click on a supplier. Select the Edit button and scroll to the bottom of the information. At the Invoice Setting block, check the Bills Default Due Date field and, if required, customise it to the supplier terms.

Refer to Chapter 6 for information on using the Money Coming In dashboard and invoicing, and to Chapter 7 for more on paying suppliers.

The colours Xero uses for current month versus previous month variances give you a high-level understanding of the businesses performance: Green is good (for example, current income is above previous income), red indicates this area needs some attention (because, for example, current expense is higher than last month), and blue indicates no information is available, the variance is nonsense, or no change occurred.

In the following sections, I look at the individual blocks from Xero's one-page Executive Summary report in detail and identify how you can extract useful information that can assist in the decision-making process of your business. *Note:* The following sections only cover blocks of the Executive Summary. To see some of these elements in more detail, and customise them to your needs, see the section 'Customising the Management Report', later in this chapter.

Cash

The first block of the Executive Summary report highlights business cash variances and the cash flow being generated by the business. If the cash spent (flowing outwards) is greater than cash received (flowing inwards), you have a negative cash flow. When looking at this area, also check the closing bank balance shown, sourced from bank, credit card and online payment style accounts. If the bank balance is low, do you have access to funds in case of unexpected needs? Should you arrange a line of credit that can be drawn on in emergencies? In most cases, having a positive cash flow and bank balances to cover several months' expenses is desirable (refer to the sidebar 'The power of positive cash flow' for more).

Profitability

The second block of the Executive Summary report highlights significant figures from your business's Profit and Loss Statement.

The usefulness of the information that appears on your Profit and Loss Statement in Xero, and so on the Profitability area of the Executive Summary, depends of how accurately you've applied account types to the Chart of Accounts in Xero. (For more information, refer to Chapter 2, where I explain the different account types and how to apply them.)

If your gross profit line on the Executive Summary report shows a loss, this means you're actually losing money with every transaction — the more business you do, the more money you lose. You need to drill down into the data and identify what is causing the loss and take a course of action to avoid further loss (see the sidebar 'Addressing a negative gross profit' for more).

Balance Sheet

The third block of the Executive Summary report summarises the significant figures from your business's Balance Sheet. The Debtor figure in this block reflects who owes the business money and gives you an indication of how much money the business may receive in the future. Keep in mind that this figure may incorporate potential bad debts. So, when looking at this area of the report, ask yourself whether all of this money is guaranteed.

If you're entering bills into Xero prior to their due date, the Creditors figure in this block reflects who you owe money to. Does the business have the cash to make these payments?

Finally, the Net Assets line within this block is essentially the net worth of the company.

Income

The fourth block of the Executive Summary report highlights business income variances. Two performance indicators are available here: Number of Invoices Issued and Average Value of Invoices. What you want to see here is dependent on your business's operations. Are you looking for yield or volume?

Xero is designed for hundreds of invoices and bills each month, which doesn't suit some business models. If, in order to recognise bulk invoices, a summary invoice is entered in Xero, the metrics mentioned in the Income block of the Executive Summary report may not be representative of your reality.

If a stable business selling a stable product wants to improve its profit, it needs to increase either yield or volume, or both. Think about how this relates to the business you operate. For example, a hairdresser who sells her time by the hour can only sell a finite number of hours. She has little scope to increase her volume. To increase her profitability she needs to increase her hourly rate; her *yield*. To increase her yield even further, perhaps she can upsell exclusive salon-quality hair and beauty products. Without changing the number of invoices issued, by increasing her hourly rate and selling products she can increase the average value of each invoice.

Performance

The fifth block of the Executive Summary report is a high-level indicator of Performance margins and variances, as follows:

Addressing a negative gross profit

A cut and dry response to a negative gross profit isn't possible. Some business's pricing strategies incorporate a loss leader — for example, food stores may sell essentials like milk or bread at ridiculously low prices to attract customers into their store, where they can entice them with other profitable merchandise. (How often have you popped into the shops for milk, and left with a trolley full of groceries?!) However, your business needs some lines to be profitable for this strategy to work, so a gross loss at the high level shown on Xero's Executive Summary report is cause for concern.

Of course, another aspect of profitability is recognising that everything spent in the business comes off the bottom line.

Strategies to implement if you have concerns about your profitability include

✔ Increasing your selling prices

✔ Increasing the number of clients

✔ Increasing the dollar value of sales to existing clients

✔ Increasing the number of times existing clients return

✔ Increasing income streams or selling additional services

✔ Minimising expenditure by comparison shopping, negotiating purchases and planning for expenditure

✔ Reviewing expenses

✔ Reviewing security around cash-handling procedures

By the way — don't discount the effectiveness of the last point on this list. A franchised café chain I know of implemented some impressive cash-handling procedures. Staff have to undergo rigorous training in appropriate cash handling, and video surveillance monitors any areas in the café where a staff member could touch cash. If the cash drawer is open for longer than a minute, head office is alerted and the café manager is called. If expected benchmarks aren't achieved, a team from head office is sent to the store to observe the store, review procedures and re-train staff. The chain has 275 stores, so even if only, say, $5 was misappropriated from each of the stores, every day, the business would lose over half a million dollars over the year. Minor theft can easily affect cash flow and change the course of the business!

✔ **Gross Profit Margin:** This is calculated by dividing Gross Profit by Income figures sourced from the Profit and Loss Statement. This margin indicates how efficiently direct costs are being used by the business. A high gross margin provides a buffer for operating costs. A low gross margin indicates you need to review all aspects of the business involving income received and direct costs.

✔ **Net Profit Margin:** This is calculated by dividing Net Profit by Income figures sourced from the Profit and Loss Statement. It reflects the monetary value of sales income left after all expenses have been paid. Fingers crossed this figure is positive. A high net profit indicates sales income is high in relation to expenses. Maybe you're first to market and exploiting a competitive advantage? Watch this figure — over time, business expenses tend to blow out and this figure can slip unnecessarily.

✔ **Return on Investment (p.a.):** This represents Profit/Loss divided by Net Assets multiplied by 12, sourced from Profitability and Balance Sheet figures.

The figures in the Performance block of Xero's Executive Summary report are relative indicators of your business's performance and, ideally, you want to see improvement.

Position

The final block of the Executive Summary report highlights business Position variances, as follows:

✔ **Average Debtor Days:** This is calculated by dividing Debtors by Income multiplied by the days in the month, with data sourced from the Profit and Loss Statement and the Balance Sheet. The figure reflects the average number of days the business takes to collect payment from customers. The ideal figure here is zero! Essentially, however, the lower the better — if the figures are high, you could face the risk of bad debts in the account.

Keep your accounts in Xero up to date so your Management Reports are accurate and useful. I had a client who invoiced for a significant amount of work that they had performed unauthorised. No problem with the work, but without a purchase order in place, the customer refused to pay my client, and the invoice needed to be written off as a bad debt — otherwise, the information on the Management Report would always be distorted.

✔ **Average Creditor Days:** This is calculated by dividing Creditors by Purchases multiplied by the days in the month, with the data sourced from the Profit and Loss Statement and the Balance Sheet. If bills are entered prior to payment, this figure reflects the average time the business takes to pay suppliers. If your number here is low, maybe the opportunity exists to delay payments a little and improve cash flow? If your figure is high, do you have cash flow issues? Do you need to sort out a line of credit? Are you treating your suppliers with respect?

✔ **Short Term Cash Forecast:** This shows Debtors less Creditors, sourced from the Balance Sheet, and provides a quick snapshot of your business's cash flow. A positive result here is desirable. A negative result highlights concerns about paying suppliers — and, if you're unable to pay suppliers, you may run out of stock to sell.

✓ **Current Assets to Liabilities:** This is calculated by dividing Current Assets by Current Liabilities using data sourced from the Balance Sheet Statement. Commonly referred to as the *current ratio*, this figure indicates the *liquidity* of the business — that is, how quickly money can be accessed in the business. A high positive result (a figure above 1) is desirable.

Performance Management reports

Xero's performance reports show how the business is positioned based on assets, liabilities and equities. One of the performance reports is included in the six-page Management Report: The Profit and Loss Statement, which reflects the profit for a period in time (the classifications on the Profit and Loss Statement are outlined in Chapter 2). The report can be generated over more than one financial year, which is useful for project tracking.

The Profit and Loss statement can highlight that you are spending too much money in a particular area. It can also highlight areas where opportunities exist to leverage over-performing income streams.

Position Management reports

As with Xero's performance reports (refer to preceding section), its position reports show how the business is positioned based on assets, liabilities and equities. Three of the position reports are also included in the six-page Management Report: Balance Sheet, Aged Receivables and Aged Payables.

A *Balance Sheet* is a statement at a point in time of the business's assets, liabilities and equity. (The classifications on the Balance Sheet are outlined in Chapter 2.) For more on the Aged Receivables and Aged Payables reports, refer to Chapter 10.

Detail reports

Xero's detail reports show the detail of the transactions in the accounts. If you need to further examine why something has happened, you can turn to the detail reports.

Understanding what your accountant can do for you

Partners of Xero users (that is, accountants working with their clients in Xero) in New Zealand and Australia have access to the Report Packs feature, which enables the roll out of a customised set of reports across all clients. This is done through applying report codes across the charts of accounts for individual businesses. The charts of accounts for each business are then linked through to defined report pack templates and the findings can be passed on to clients.

This means your Xero partner could provide valuable information that's specific to,

and gathered from, businesses in your field or with your scope. For example, a Xero partner could create a Customised Report Pack for all sole trader clients, extrapolate insightful comparative information and efficiently help all the businesses via the same report pack.

At the time of writing, Xero has plans to roll access to Report Packs out to partners in the UK and the US, so for further information or to find out whether your Xero Partner offers this service, contact your Xero partner.

Customising the Management Report

The management reports covered in the preceding sections highlight the main reports you should be looking at on a regular basis. In this section, I cover customising particular sections of the Management Report to show the most useful information.

Only users with Adviser status can access Xero's six-page Management Report. To access this report if you have this status, go to the home dashboard and click Adviser⇨Management Report. The report opens at page one, the Executive Summary.

Here's how you can customise the Executive Summary:

- ✔ In the Date field, select the relevant month from the drop-down options
- ✔ In the Show field, select the Summary and Ratio from the drop-down options

Click the blue Update button to customise the Executive Summary.

To access the Cash Summary report page, click on the drop-down menu at the top of the Management Report and select Page 2 of 6. You can customise the Cash Summary report in the following ways:

- ✔ In the Date field, select the relevant month from the drop-down menu
- ✔ In the Period field, select 1 month from the drop-down menu
- ✔ In the Compare With field, select Average from the drop-down menu
- ✔ Check the Show YTD and Show Income % check boxes

Click the blue Update button to customise the Cash Summary.

To access the Profit and Loss report page, click on the drop-down menu at the top of the Management Report and select Page 3 of 6. To make this report more useful, click on the Common Formats tab, and click the Current and Previous 3 Months link.

To access the Balance Sheet report, click on the drop-down menu at the top of the Management Report and select Page 4 of 6. You can customise the Balance Sheet report in the following ways:

- ✔ In the Balance Date field, select the relevant month from the drop-down menu
- ✔ In the Compare To field, select Previous Quarter from the drop-down menu
- ✔ In the Compare Periods field, select Previous 3 Periods from the drop-down menu

Click the blue Update button to customise the Balance Sheet.

To access the Aged Receivables report, click on the drop-down menu at the top of the Management Report and select Page 5 of 6. Customise the Aged Receivables report as follows:

- ✔ In the Date field, select the relevant month from the drop-down menu
- ✔ In the Show By field, select Month Name from the drop-down menu
- ✔ In the Ageing By field select Due Date from the drop-down menu

Click the blue Update button to customise the Aged Receivables report.

It's all about the numbers!

With your accounting solution producing timely accurate and accessible data, exploring the add-ons available in the Xero ecosystem to see what other analysis options are available is worthwhile. For example, to build and review cash flow forecasts, consider Float or Calxa. To assess performance, monitor trends and KPIs, and identify improvement opportunities, look to management reporting and financial analysis tools such as Fathom or Smeebi.

You can also create visually appealing financial and management reports using software like Spotlight Tools or Crunchboards.

You can view social media and CRM analytics alongside your management information by integrating Grappster or Moxy Cloud Reporting into your Xero records. Customise your financial data within Microsoft Excel using Quick Win Excel Integration Tools, or Diga, and compare multiple Xero entities, such as in a franchise situation, by applying Fathom, Spotlight Multi, and Qvinci to all the relevant files. Visit www.xero.com/add-ons/category/reporting/ to view all the Xero reporting add-on solutions, and check out Chapter 16 for general information about the Xero add-ons available.

To access the Aged Payables report, click on the drop-down menu at the top of the Management Report and select Page 6 of 6. Customise the Aged Payables report as follows:

- ✔ In the Date field, select the relevant month from the drop-down menu
- ✔ In the Show By field, select Month Name from the drop-down menu
- ✔ In the Ageing By field, select Due Date from the drop-down menu

Click the blue Update button to customise the Aged Payables report.

The Aged Payables and Aged Receivables Reports are also available with more filtering options in the new generation of reports. To access go to Reports⇨All Reports and click on Try Out the New Reports. (Refer to Chapter 9 for more on trying out the new generation of reports in Xero.)

After customisation, the six-page Management Report is ready to be saved as a draft report, or published, printed or exported. (Refer to Chapter 9 for guidance on producing reports.)

Understanding Xero's Tracking Options

For Christmas, my daughter gave me an iPhone case with a circular turret filter attachment that fits across the camera lens. It has multiple crazy filters — reds, blues, yellows, swirls and love hearts. So taking the same portrait of Charlie my dog while changing the filter produces pictures with a different perspective.

Xero Tracking options work a bit like a camera filter. Using the same business data, they enable you to see information from different perspectives. The Tracking options also allow you to departmentalise different transactions, enabling reporting on specific areas of the business.

You can create up to two separate tracking categories, and define unlimited category options. All transactions can be allocated a tracking category, and this field can be edited for unlocked periods. For example, if your business operates over multiple states, you could track the state a transaction occurs in by setting up a Tracking category called *STATES* and the category options could be Alabama, Alaska, Arizona and so on (or New South Wales, Victoria and so on).

Tracking enables you to produce reports that compare the performance and profitability across different categories, and view the position of the category. Continuing with the STATES tracking category example, you or key members of your staff could use this information to manage businesses or staff located in different states, and reward and replicate good performance while identifying and adjusting poor performance. Furthermore, monthly budgets for Tracking categories can also be created.

In the following sections, I take you through all the options available using Xero's Tracking functions.

Using Tracking

To start you thinking about how you can use Xero's Tracking options to better understand your business, I can give you an example using a mining company. Mines are required to provide financial reports defined by individual projects and tenements. (*Tenements* are exploration licences.)

Here's how the company could use Tracking:

✔ Two separate Tracking categories can be set up to define the Project and Tenement options.

✔ A single invoice can have transactions allocated to both Project and Tenement simultaneously.

✔ If an invoice needs to be split across multiple tracking options, the individual line items of the invoice can be allocated to different options using a percentage ('%') rather than a unit ('1') in the Unit Price field to easily enable this allocation. For example, one line could list the quantity as 0.85 (85 per cent) and the next line could list the quantity as 0.15 (15 per cent) totalling 100 per cent. With the Unit Price the same at each line, you can easily allocate the percentage.

Reports can be produced to reflect Project performance and Tenement performance as required.

Working out what your business should track

Deciding what areas of your business you need to track through Xero is a good thing to ponder over a coffee (with your management accountant, if you have one!).

A good place to start is by looking at whether your business has preordained groupings. Would information identified by such groups as geographical areas, sales staff, events, promotions, cars, wholesale versus retail, rental properties, grants, or expenses that need to be on-charged be useful?

You're able to apply two tracking categories to transactions. Think about how you could use this feature in your business. For example, you could compare how

- ✔ Grants are applied to different geographical areas
- ✔ Different events affect retail sales
- ✔ Staff perform over different projects
- ✔ Sales staff perform during different promotions

With the insights gained through using Xero's Tracking options, you may recognise, for example, that particular sales staff need additional training, events that aren't resulting in sales need to be cancelled, or some areas are missing out on grant funding.

Setting up Tracking

To set up Tracking options, follow these steps:

1. **Access the Tracking dashboard from the home dashboard and click on Settings⇨General Settings⇨Tracking.**

   The Tracking dashboard appears.

2. **Create a new tracking category by clicking the Add Tracking Category and fill out the Tracking Category Name field.**

   If you want to track sales across different states, for example, you could enter **STATES** in the Tracking Category Name field.

3. **Add Category options for the three available fields.**

   If adding states, you could enter **Alabama** in the first field, **Alaska** in the second and **Arizona** in the third.

   Both the Tracking Category Name and Category Options fields allow for more characters than you could possibly want. So you don't have to use abbreviations if the full name works better for you.

4. **Add more category options by clicking on the Add Another Option button and filling out the new field that appears.**

   See Figure 12-2 for where the Add Another Option button appears. Repeat this step for any additional category options required. (Remember — the number of additional categories you can add is extensive but don't go crazy — too many would be unmanageable.)

5. **Click the green Save button.**

   This saves the newly created Tracking category.

Figure 12-2:
Xero's
Tracking
Category
window.

Editing, deleting and applying Tracking options

If you need to edit specific Tracking category names or options in Xero, you can do so from the main Tracking dashboard. Simply access the name or option that needs editing, click the Rename link, edit the field, and click the Rename button to save the changes. This updates all existing transaction entries. *Note:* Tracking options cannot be combined.

To delete a Tracking name or option completely, access the specific tracking option that needs deleting from the Tracking dashboard and click on the cross to the right. If the Tracking category has been used against any transaction, it will be archived. Click OK and the Archive tab appears, with the archived transaction listed underneath. This transaction is still viewable on reports and can be restored from the Archive area, but it cannot be allocated to any new transaction. If the Tracking category has never been used, you simply confirm the deletion by clicking Delete when the confirmation window pops up. All reference to the deleted name or option disappears from Xero.

Tracking options can be applied to new transactions or retrospectively to existing transactions. Apply tracking allocations by accessing a transaction, clicking in the Tracking column and selecting the option from the drop-down menu.

Continuing the example from the preceding section, say you have created a tracking category called STATES and have added the names of all relevant states as category options within it, so you can track your sales by the states they took place in. If you know a sales transaction relates to a sale that took place in Alabama, click on the tracking column within the transaction and select 'Alabama' from the drop-down menu.

You can then finish processing the transaction as normal.

Reviewing Tracking reports

One specific report in Xero is dedicated to Tracking: The Tracking Summary report. To access this report from Xero's home dashboard, click Reports on the menu bar and click All Reports⇨Tracking Summary Report. The report displays a single tracking option by a selected Account group for a defined period. You can use this report to identify how tracking is allocated to accounts.

Other management reports that filter by tracking category include:

- ✔ Account Transaction
- ✔ Balance Sheet
- ✔ Bank Summary
- ✔ Budget Variance
- ✔ Cash Summary
- ✔ Depreciation Schedule
- ✔ Fixed Asset Reconciliation
- ✔ Income Statement/Profit and Loss

To view customised tracking on the Balance Sheet, follow these steps:

1. **From the home dashboard, click on Reports⇨All Reports⇨Balance Sheet.**

2. **At the Balance Date field, select the current month and year.**

3. **At the Compare To and the Compare Periods fields, select None.**

4. **Access Tracking criteria by clicking on the More Options link.**

5. **At the Sort By: field select Account Name.**

   The next two fields are the tracking fields: Filter by [Category Name 1] and Filter by [Category Name 2].

6. **Click on the Tracking field and select the Tracking option from the drop-down menu, and then repeat at the next Tracking field.**

7. **Update the report criteria by clicking the blue Update button.**

   The Balance Sheet report displays a single list of numbers that meet the tracking criteria.

Identify transactions that don't have a tracking account assigned to them by selecting the Unassigned option at the two tracking fields and clicking Update. You can drill down on the numbers to see further detail, edit the transaction and assign the tracking option. Of course, not all transactions need to have a tracking option assigned to them, but if you're relying on Tracking information, reviewing unassigned accounts to ensure information is complete is good business practice.

To view customised tracking on the Income Statement/Profit and Loss report, follow these steps:

1. **From the home dashboard, click on Reports⇨All Reports⇨Income Statement/Profit and Loss.**

2. **Click on one of the tracking name links on the customisation dashboard.**

   Choose between Compare [Category Name 1] or Compare [Category Name 2]. The report updates immediately.

   The Income Statement/Profit and Loss report displays a comparative list of numbers that meet the selected tracking criteria.

If using lots of tracking options in one category — for example, the 50 states of America — viewing reports online can be overwhelming. Exporting the report in spreadsheet format makes it easier to tackle the comparative information. To do this, generate the desired report in Xero, click the blue Export button at the bottom of the screen and then select Excel to download the spreadsheet to your computer. After opening in Excel, you can also click the cell beneath the heading of the first tracking option and select the Freeze Panes option. The headers remain fixed in place as you scroll to the right, making it easier to read the report.

Tracking conversion balances

If you moved to Xero from another system and have existing Tracking balances, you may want to enter these balances in Xero so the Tracking reports balances are complete to date. To enter the Tracking balances follow these steps:

1. **Identify existing Tracking balances as at conversion date, split out by account.**

   Refer to Chapter 2, where I explain conversion dates and accounts, for more on this.

   Using the example of tracking a state from America, the data for the Tracking Option *Alabama* could include:

   • Account type

   • Account name

   • Amount

   • Income: Consulting income, $1,500 (CR)

   • Direct costs: Consulting COS, $700 (DR)

Tracking options can be allocated to all account types, and the Net Income/Loss automatically calculates. You need to be able to identify whether the account balance is debit or credit in nature and, ideally, the debit amounts should equal the credit amounts. However, if a difference does exist, it's allocated to the automatically created Tracking Transfers liability account. Don't stress if this happens — the allocation isn't creating any new transactions in your system but is simply accounting for what has not already been allocated.

The Tracking allocations opening balance is entered via a manual journal. Users with Adviser or Standard status in Xero can enter a manual journal.

2. **Check the respective Tracking option exists in your data file by clicking Settings⇨General Settings⇨Tracking.**

    If the Tracking option is not listed, refer to the section 'Setting up Tracking', earlier in this chapter, for guidance.

3. **If you have Adviser or Standard user status, you can create a new journal from the home dashboard by clicking Reports⇨All Reports⇨Journal Report and then clicking the + Add New Journal link.**

    A new manual journal template opens.

4. **In the Narration field enter text to describe the purpose of the journal.**

    For example, possible text could be *Tracking option opening balance of Alabama*.

5. **Check the Default Narration to Journal Line Description box to allow this description to autofill all transaction Description fields.**

6. **Record your conversion date in the Date field.**

7. **Check the Show Journal on a Cash Basis Reports box to define the accounting basis the journal is to use.**

8. **Specify the values entered in the journal are Tax Exclusive by selecting the drop-down option from the Amounts Are field.**

9. **At the journal line click in the Description field to activate the default narration to automatically fill the field.**

10. **Click in the first Account field, start entering the account description and select the correct account from the drop-down options.**

    In this scenario it would be Consulting Income, and as it's selected the tax code autofills the Tax Rate field.

11. **Click in the Tax Rate field, and select a consumer tax rate that is not reported.**

12. **Click in the Tracking field, and select the Tracking option that the opening balances are being entered for.**

    In this scenario, the option would be Alabama.

13. **Enter the account balance in the relevant Debit or Credit column.**

    In this scenario 1500 is entered in the Credit column.

14. **Drop down to the next line and repeat Steps 9 to 11.**

15. **Leave the Tracking field blank, because this line is not allocated to a tracking code.**

16. **Enter the account balance in the opposite column that was selected at Step 13.**

    In this scenario 1500 is entered in the Debit column.

For the tracking conversion to work, the two entries in the Credit and Debit columns must result in the total debit and credit balance at the bottom of the journal being equal. If the total balances are not equal, review the steps, and check amounts entered are identical and no consumer tax has been inadvertently generated by the transaction. The net effect on the general ledger and the tax account is zero, and the conversion tracking balance is allocated.

17. **Add extra lines as necessary to the journal entry by clicking the Add a New Line button.**

18. **Post the journal entry to the ledger by clicking the green Post button.**

    To check the process worked, click Reports⇨Balance Sheet, select the criteria Compare [Tracking option] and compare it to the original numbers for the conversion date. In this scenario the criteria would be Compare Alabama. If Asset and Liability balances were entered, the Balance Sheet also needs to be reviewed. To check the Balance Sheet click Reports⇨Balance Sheet. For the criteria select the Balance Date as at the conversion date, click the More Options link and at the Filter By field select the relevant Tracking option.

Maintaining Budget Control: Budget Manager

In Chapter 10, I describe how to create an annual budget and review forecasts using Xero's Budget Manager. Xero also allows you to produce a Budget Variance report to help you review budget figures against actual results — and so helping you to explain the past and understand the future of your business.

You can access the Budget Variance report from the Reports dashboard. Once you have it open, select the Actual vs Overall Budget criteria.

You can then select the Wide View link at the right corner to see the full report on screen, if necessary.

Xero's Budget Variance report shows the following:

✔ The 'Actuals' column is the actual results for the month.

✔ The 'Budget' column is the budget figures for that month.

✔ The 'Var' is the dollar value of the difference between the actual results and budget figures.

✔ The 'Var%' is the percentage difference between the actual results and budget figures.

Xero uses colours to help you quickly identify differences between forecasts and actuals, with green indicating a positive difference (actuals were higher than forecasts) and red a negative difference.

Read together, the 'Var' and 'Var%' columns highlight the difference between actual results and what was budgeted. Ideally, you want the variance in either direction to be minimal. While a positive variance may be great, it may also suggest that the budget wasn't challenging enough for the business and you may need to increase it to keep yourself (and staff members) motivated. Red (negative) variances are cause for concern and should be reviewed, understood and dealt with if necessary.

Sometimes reviewing variances on a year-to-date (YTD) basis is more useful, because the budget may have been simply calculated and split across 12 months, leading to wide distortions. In particular, you should use variances on a YTD basis if you didn't have specific details to set your budget on a monthly basis. (A large business should have the resources to develop a budget on a monthly basis; however, a smaller business averaging out figures across a year is totally reasonable.)

If variances are minimal, congratulations! This demonstrates budget preparations were acutely aligned with business operations, and you should have added confidence the year should continue as the budget has mapped out.

Reviewing budget information assists you in developing your budget for next year, and helps plan the business's journey. For example, reviewing the budget helps you decide whether you have the capacity to employ additional staff, the funds to move from serviced offices to a rented office, or the capacity to deal with planned promotions.

Chapter 13

Managing Your Inventory Items

· ·

In This Chapter

▶ Working out how inventory items can be organised and maintained

▶ Establishing an inventory item within Xero

▶ Organising items in your inventory

▶ Changing inventory values and quantities after stocktake

▶ Finding out about add-on solutions

· ·

I worked with a client who ran a galvanising business — customers would send the business their steel for the business to then dip the steel in hot vats of molten zinc to prevent corrosion. If zinc levels in the vats dropped, additional zinc was added to refill the vat. (Sounds a bit like a scene from an action movie, doesn't it? 'Ve vill drop you in zee hot vats if you don't tell us your secrets!') The galvaniser's customers retained ownership of the steel, so the value of the steel never needed to be recorded as inventory. The zinc was purchased and melted (and so used by the business), so never sold in the format it was purchased. Xero's inventory system suited this business perfectly. Zinc was purchased via a bill, and the galvanising process was charged via an invoice.

In this chapter, I introduce you to the Inventory Items dashboard in Xero, where items are created and pricing is set. (Details of how invoices and bills are dealt with are provided in Chapters 6 and 7.)

Xero offers a simple inventory solution — it doesn't claim to offer an inventory management system. What it offers is useful for monitoring and processing services. If you're in that space where you have a trivial amount of physical inventory, Xero's Inventory Items solution may work for you, with some of the workarounds covered in this chapter. Even if you don't use inventory, understanding how items are used can help save data-processing time. However, if you have a retail store or significant physical inventory to manage, don't try to get Xero to manage business processes it was never meant to. Instead, integrate Xero with one of the many add-on inventory management solutions available. (I cover these add-ons briefly in this chapter, and in more detail in Chapter 16.)

Understanding Inventory Items

From Xero's home dashboard, you can access the inventory functions by clicking Settings⇨General Settings⇨Inventory Items. From here, items can be created, imported, exported or searched for. A list details the Item Code, Item Name, Cost Price and Sales Price. Clicking column headers sorts the columns.

I cover creating an inventory item later in this chapter, so you can skip ahead if you like. However, if you'd prefer to get more of an understanding of inventory and how it's reported, read on.

Periodic and perpetual inventory

Two methods of managing inventory are generally accepted: Periodic and perpetual.

A *periodic* inventory system doesn't keep a count of the inventory as it is purchased or sold. Inventory is recognised as a direct cost when it's purchased, and sales income when it's sold. A stocktake is needed to update the value of any inventory reported on the balance sheet.

A *perpetual* inventory system undertakes continuous counts of inventory within the business, updating inventory values, and applying the cost of the item against the sale price in the month it's sold.

Xero allows you to adopt a periodic inventory system. If you need to know the levels of your stock on a regular basis, your business requires a perpetual inventory management system. I recommend you consider utilising an add-on inventory management solution (see the section 'Accessing Add-On Solutions', later in this chapter, and Chapter 16).

Defining inventory accounts

Grouping different sorts of items helps you in your decision-making process around inventory, giving a clearer idea of income, cost of sales and gross profit at a group level. You can easily monitor the performance of inventory items using Xero's Tracking feature (covered in Chapter 12).

However, Xero only allows two Tracking categories, and perhaps you've used them already — maybe you're tracking sales by sales location and by sales staff. If so, here's a workaround that gives you additional reporting functionality. *Note:* If you have an available tracking category, use that! Only use this suggestion if you're using tracking categories elsewhere.

The method suggested in this section of grouping inventory accounts isn't suitable for a retail store!

One of my client's income streams is self-publishing books; she has self-published three books, and each book is defined as a different grouping. This means inventory can be spilt into three groups: book 1, book 2 and book 3. Her Chart of Accounts includes additional general ledger accounts to reflect the inventory groupings, as you can see in Table 13-1.

Table 13-1	Example of Grouped Inventory Accounts		
Group	*Sales Income*	*Direct Cost*	*Asset*
Book 1	Book 1 income	Book 1 direct cost	Book 1 inventory
Book 2	Book 2 income	Book 2 direct cost	Book 2 inventory
Book 3	Book 3 income	Book 3 direct cost	Book 3 inventory

When items are created, setting up inventory groupings means transactions are automatically posted to the appropriate account. This is easy to set up and quickly generates useful information. (Refer to Chapter 2 for guidance on setting up general ledger accounts, and to Chapter 9 for more information on grouping similar accounts.)

When it comes to considering the best inventory groupings for your business, the process may take some thought and it could be something that you come back to. At a minimum, I suggest three groups, and probably at a maximum ten groups. Detailing each individual item in the Chart of Accounts isn't required, and doing so means your reports become noisy and you're unable to glean useful information. By setting up the Chart of Accounts with basic groupings, you can view inventory at a group-detail level, or create subtotals and view the information at a summary level.

If you are using Xero without an add-on, Inventory Asset accounts have to be manually updated following stocktakes. Transactions involving inventory items (such as sales) don't update the Inventory Asset account unless directly posted to the Inventory Asset account.

Setting Up a Xero Inventory Item

In order to set up inventory items within Xero, gather together details relating to the items, including description, and purchase and sales information.

Creating inventory items

To create a new item, follow these steps:

1. **From the home dashboard click Settings⇨General Settings⇨Inventory Items.**

   This takes you to the Inventory dashboard.

2. **Click the + New Item button.**

   The New Inventory Item window opens (see Figure 13-1).

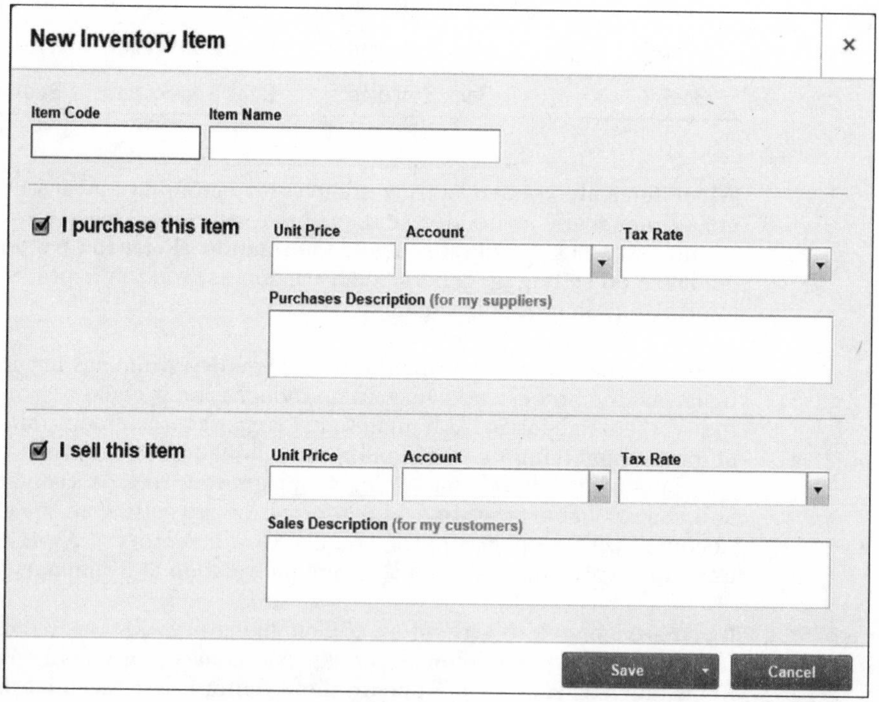

New Inventory Item	✕

Item Code　**Item Name**

☑ **I purchase this item**　**Unit Price**　**Account** ▾　**Tax Rate** ▾

Purchases Description (for my suppliers)

☑ **I sell this item**　**Unit Price**　**Account** ▾　**Tax Rate** ▾

Sales Description (for my customers)

Save ▾　Cancel

Figure 13-1: Setting up a New Inventory Item.

3. Enter the item code in the mandatory Item Code field.

Think about how you plan to name inventory items — make sure they're identifiable and easy to find. Mnemonic codes that utilise informative alphanumeric combinations are useful when deciding on a naming convention. For example, using *AU*, *USA* or *NZ* to suffix an inventory item could indicate a source country. When products are sourced from a single main supplier, consider using the supplier number as the item code or name. ***Note:*** Some reports display item lists in item code/name order. If the item code/name starts with zeros, the zeros are dropped from the code when exported to Excel. This may have knock-on effects elsewhere.

4. Fill out the Item Name field.

5. If the item will be purchased, complete the next five steps; otherwise, jump to Step 11.

If you're using inventory items to record standard service descriptions to quickly populate your invoices, you don't need to enter purchase details and can skip to Step 11.

6. Leave the box beside I Purchase this Item checked.

The purchase detail fields remain.

7. Enter the unit price of up to four decimal places in the Unit Price field.

Some businesses have contractual purchase agreements in place. It's useful to enter the agreed price here, as a crosscheck that supplier bills are indeed correct.

8. Select the purchase account from the drop-down Account field.

Refer to the section 'Defining inventory accounts', earlier in this chapter, when selecting an account.

9. Select the default tax rate from the drop-down Tax Rate field.

This rate can be overridden when processing a bill.

10. Enter a detailed item description in the Purchases Description field.

The description automatically appears on bills and can be overridden. Including extensive details here, which can be edited when the bill is created, can save data entry time.

For example, a bookkeeping business could create a service item called 'Bookkeeping' with the description, 'Data entry, filing, bank reconciliation, review accounts payable, review accounts receivable, payroll, stock control and training'. When the description autofills on the invoice, additional details can be added (for example, 'bank reconciliation — savings account'), or some descriptions could be deleted (for example, 'filing'). This saves you (or other users) time, and also prompts you to leave a detailed invoice.

11. **If the item will be sold, complete the next three steps; otherwise, jump to Step 17.**

12. **Leave the box beside I Sell this Item checked.**

    The sales detail fields remain.

13. **Enter the unit price of up to four decimal places in the Unit Price field.**

    This amount appears on invoices and bills. Changing the Tax Inclusive/Tax Exclusive option on the invoice/bill affects how the item is treated for consumer tax and the total for the transaction.

14. **Select the sales account from the drop-down Account field.**

    Refer to the section 'Defining inventory accounts', earlier in this chapter, when selecting an account.

15. **Select the default tax rate from the drop-down Tax Rate field.**

    This rate can be overridden when processing an invoice.

16. **Enter a detailed item description in the Sales Description field.**

    The description automatically appears on invoices and can be overridden.

17. **Click the green Save button.**

Importing and exporting item details

Inventory item details can be exported from and imported into Xero. This is a useful feature if you have existing data and are converting to Xero, or if you need to make bulk changes to item details (such as increasing selling prices). Inventory files can be exported to CSV and PDF files and can be imported from CSV files. Refer to Chapter 3 for instructions of how to export and import CSV files into Xero and how to convert CSV files into an editable spreadsheet format.

When is inventory not really inventory?

Inventory items do not need to be physical objects. They can be services. For example, I could set up *Training, Half-day training* or *One-on-one training* as items in Xero but, in fact, they are services. Setting up services as inventory items saves time populating the description area of an invoice. Inventory items don't have to be something you can hold or throw at a wall!

To export the inventory items as a PDF report, go to the Inventory Items dashboard, click on the Import/Export button and select Export to PDF from the drop-down list. The Inventory Items.pdf can be located in your downloads folder.

Managing Inventory Items

Once set up, you may need to occasionally review and update your inventory in Xero. The following sections show you how.

Making use of inventory items reports

Xero has two reports relating to inventory item information: Inventory Items Summary and Sales by Item. In both reports you have the option to show inventory in the currency it was purchased or sold.

Xero's inventory items reports detail the following:

- ✔ **Inventory Items Summary:** This report shows purchase and sales details, including net total. If a manual opening balance was entered, you can manually calculate total inventory on hand by selecting to view the report from the start of the life of the item. *Remember:* Xero only allows you to run a basic periodic inventory system, so this option isn't ideal.

- ✔ **Sales by Item:** This report details current unit price, quantity sold, total sales and the average price of the inventory item for a selected period. The last two values are exclusive of consumer tax. Below the inventory sales information is an interesting summary, splitting out sales between item sales, other sales, cash sales and credits. Drilling down on the Item Name displays details of sales during the period selected of that item.

To access the inventory reports, go to the home dashboard menu bar, click on Reports⇨All Reports and select the relevant report from the Reports dashboard.

Searching for and reviewing inventory items

To locate an item, go to the Inventory dashboard and use the search bar. As you start to enter a description, Xero automatically searches and starts making suggestions.

Editing and deleting inventory items

To edit an item, simply go to the Inventory Items dashboard, click on the relevant item and then click the Edit Item button. The Inventory Item Detail window appears (see Figure 13-2). To attach a file, click on the file storage symbol on the top right and follow the process of adding a file. *Note:* This facility is not available when creating a new inventory Item.

At the bottom is a section headed Recent Transactions, which lists transactions against the selected inventory item, including details of the quantity and unit price. If you have multi-currency, you click on the foreign currency unit in the Total column to reveal the exchange rate used. For further insights into multi-currency, see Chapter 15.

Make any changes here as required and, once satisfied, click the Save button to record the changes.

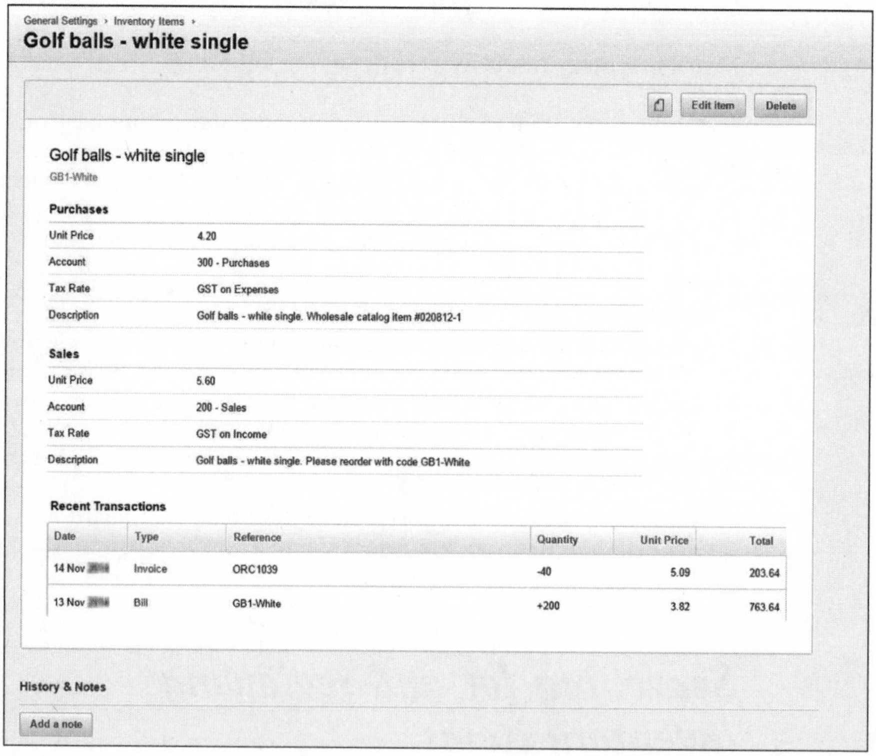

General Settings › Inventory Items ›
Golf balls - white single

☐ Edit item Delete

Golf balls - white single
GB1-White

Purchases

Unit Price	4.20
Account	300 - Purchases
Tax Rate	GST on Expenses
Description	Golf balls - white single. Wholesale catalog item #020812-1

Sales

Unit Price	5.60
Account	200 - Sales
Tax Rate	GST on Income
Description	Golf balls - white single. Please reorder with code GB1-White

Recent Transactions

Date	Type	Reference	Quantity	Unit Price	Total
14 Nov 2014	Invoice	ORC1039	-40	5.09	203.64
13 Nov 2014	Bill	GB1-White	+200	3.82	763.64

History & Notes

Add a note

Figure 13-2: The Inventory Item Detail window.

Items on repeating bills and invoices can't be deleted. The repeating bill or invoice needs to be deleted, or the item removed from the repeating template, before the item can be deleted. (Refer to Chapter 6 for information on invoices and Chapter 7 for more on bills.)

All you have to do is go to the Inventory Items dashboard, check the box to the right of the item and click the red Delete button. A confirmation window opens, and you just need to click the green OK button to confirm the items should be deleted.

Once deleted, items are no longer available to allocate to transactions and can't be viewed on the Inventory Items dashboard. Furthermore, if you edit an approved bill, invoice or credit note (adjustment note) or have transactions in Draft or Awaiting Approval status, the item does a Bermuda Triangle on your records and vanishes!

Adjusting Inventory Balances

While living in Toronto a friend of mine managed a warehouse of expensive make-up and perfumes. He'd tell me of the creative way stock was pilfered by staff. They'd carve the pages of books out to encase perfume bottles perfectly, wear overcoats during summer or bring massive lunch boxes to work! (My friend also used to invite me to awesome VIP discount days, so my make-up bag misses him big time!)

Inventory requires adjusting for a variety of reasons — recognising an opening balance, damage, theft and technological obsolescence. Adjustments to quantity and/or dollar values of inventory need to be reflected in your records.

Periodic stocktakes

Every year around the world, accountants gather clipboards, travel to distant locations, put on yellow safety vests and infiltrate storage rooms, with the purpose of counting stock. Stocktakes happen in the weirdest of places; I've donned winter coats, boarded cherry pickers and travelled through massive warehouse freezers counting frozen sausage rolls and party pies. (I much preferred the times I was counting chocolate bars or make-up sets. Fortunately, my client who distributes *guano* — the poo from cave-dwelling bats, and a highly effective fertiliser — has never called me in for a stocktake!)

A *stocktake* is a count of the business inventory on hand, typically done at the end of the financial year, though some businesses do it more regularly. A periodic inventory system (refer to the section 'Periodic and perpetual inventory', earlier in this chapter) relies on stocktakes to manually update the Asset and Direct Cost accounts in Xero.

If you're using an inventory system add-on, the update provided by the stocktake gives the business an accurate idea of stock quantity owned by the business, and so allows your accountant to reconcile physical stock to the inventory records, and calculate the difference. With accurate knowledge about stock movements and stock on hand, you can deal with theft, slow-moving items, damaged stock, technology obsolescence, warehouse processes and generally make informed decisions about your inventory.

Determine a regular date to undertake a stocktake. Typically, this date is at the end of a period — for example, the end of the financial year. Determine actual stock levels and multiply the results by the purchase value to determine actual value.

Adjusting inventory values

To adjust stock values you first need to undertake a physical stocktake to determine the actual value of inventory on hand (refer to the preceding section). You then follow these steps:

1. **Check the current stock value in Xero by reviewing Inventory Accounts on the Balance Sheet as at the stocktake date.**

2. **Compare actual value determined from the stocktake to book value of inventory and calculate the difference (if any).**

3. **Record a manual journal to adjust inventory account values.**

   Refer to Chapter 12 for details on how to enter a manual journal (an example is shown in Figure 13-3). For specific fields within the manual journal, note the following:

   • Narration field: Add a clear description, such as Adjusting Stock Value

   • Date field: Add the date of the stocktake

   • Amounts: Select Tax Exclusive

   Note: The manual journal example shown in Figure 13-3 records an increase in inventory asset value. To record a decrease in asset value the Inventory Direct Cost account would be debited and the Inventory account would be credited.

   Typically the debit entry is written above the credit entry in a journal entry.

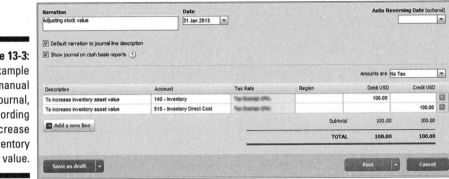

Figure 13-3:
An example
of a manual
journal,
recording
an increase
in inventory
asset value.

4. **Check Inventory Accounts on the Balance Sheet as at the stocktake date reflect the actual stocktake value.**

   If balances don't match, check and correct the journal entry.

Adjusting inventory quantities

Inventory quantities in Xero can be adjusted via a manual journal, but don't do this if you have complex inventory! This is a workaround for those with very small, simple inventory like a client who self-publishes a small number of books. The process works well, because we're only monitoring a few items.

Before adjusting stock values, check your accountant is in agreement with the changes you propose. (Yearly opening and closing stock values need to be included in your Profit and Loss report.) To adjust stock quantities first undertake a stocktake (refer to the section 'Periodic stocktakes', earlier in this chapter). Then you can follow these steps:

1. **Check current stock quantities by reviewing the Inventory Items Summary report as at the stocktake date.**

   Check current recorded stock levels by reviewing the Inventory Items Summary report for the full life of the inventory. Export it to CSV, open it in Excel and manually calculate current stock levels on hand (refer to Chapter 3 for more on exporting CSV files to Excel).

2. **Compare actual quantities determined from the stocktake to book quantity of items and calculate the difference (if any).**

3. **Record an increase in quantities via a bill.**

Include the following details on the bill:

- Contact name, Reference and Description: Stocktake

- Date and Due Date: Date of stocktake

Select the item and enter the calculated difference (the amount the quantity needs to increase by) in the quantity column.

Enter a Unit Price of '0.00' (because the value of this transaction is zero).

Note: To record a *decrease* in item quantities, create a sales invoice instead of a bill at the step and proceed in the same way.

4. **Repeat for any other items that need to be recorded.**

5. **Approve the bill.**

You approve a sales transaction if recording a decrease in item quantities.

Xero processes the transaction as a quantity adjustment. To ensure desired quantities have been achieved, check the Inventory Items Summary report. If not, review the entry recorded.

You may have realised the value adjustment (refer to the preceding section) can also be done via the bills and invoices option covered in this section. Yes, you're correct. You can enable payments to the inventory accounts, create an invoice or a bill and manipulate the unit price so the Amount equals the required value adjustment. You can then pay the bill or receive payment from the inventory account. But beware — this process is a little tricky, so only try it if you feel confident.

Accessing Add-On Solutions

If you want to manage a robust inventory management system, you need to use Xero with an add-on solution. All solutions offer comprehensive inventory management solutions, and in some cases they have extensive capabilities in other areas. See Chapter 16 for more and visit www.xero .com/add-ons for the latest list of inventory systems.

Chapter 14

Working with Fixed Assets

*O*ne of the first work projects I undertook was a fixed asset audit. I was given a list of assets, told to find them and update their status. It was like a game of hide and seek. I made my way around the various buildings, searching for the assets and checking them off the list. I searched high and low for one particularly asset and, eventually, found it in an unopened wooden box under a table. It had never been used and no-one even knew what it was for — it just arrived one day and slotted itself under the table and into the Balance Sheet, absorbing valuable cash. Perhaps not the wisest of investments!

In this chapter, I cover Xero's Fixed Asset Register and explain how you can use it to keep track of fixed assets and depreciation through the year.

Recognising Fixed Assets

A *fixed asset* is an asset that has an expected life of more than a year. It is a significant investment for any business because it utilises cash that could be used elsewhere in the business. This is why maintaining an accurate Fixed Asset Register is so important for your business. Typical small business fixed assets include cars, buildings, computers and office equipment.

When is an asset not an asset?

For some purchases, you may have flexibility about whether the purchase is classified as a fixed asset or an expense. Work with your tax accountant (who should have expert knowledge of the tax rules in your country) to determine whether business purchases are fixed assets or expenses. I've seen clients purchase what appear to be assets, and then work with their tax accountants to (legally) classify these as an expense, and vice versa.

What you may prefer in a particular case depends on the outcome of the treatment of the purchase.

If treated as a fixed asset, the purchase is allocated to your business's balance sheet and depreciation is written off against profit over the deemed life of the asset. If treated as an expense, the purchase is written off against the profit in the year incurred, thus reducing company tax in that year.

Entering a fixed asset into the register

Assets need to be assigned to the Fixed Asset Register in Xero so you can monitor them and depreciation can be applied. In this section, I outline how to create fixed assets accounts and enter a fixed asset purchase in Xero. *Note:* In the steps outlined in this section, I use the example of entering a motor vehicle on Xero's Fixed Asset Register. The motor vehicle was purchased on 1 November for $10,000 (tax exclusive).

Creating fixed asset accounts

Before entering fixed assets into Xero, you need to create your fixed asset accounts.

The financial accounts you receive from your tax accountant are likely to combine fixed assets into relevant groups, and contain the detail on the Fixed Asset Register. This means you need to create accounts for the fixed asset groupings. However, many small business owners I've worked with like to see cars listed separately in the Balance Sheet, because the purchase is a major expense of the business, and owners want to keep the investment front and centre of the Balance Sheet — so that's what I've explained in this section. However, I'm not encouraging you to create 100 (or more) individual fixed asset lines! You could easily follow the steps outlined in this section to create fixed asset accounts that collect purchases into similar groupings, and refer to Xero's Fixed Asset Register for all asset details — streamlining your accounts!

Here are the steps for creating fixed asset accounts for a simple car investment:

1. **Create a fixed asset account and select your account type and tax rate.**

   Refer to Chapter 2 for guidance on creating a new account. For the purchase of a vehicle, you could call the fixed asset account CARS. The account type would be Fixed Asset and tax rate would be Consumer Tax on Capital. Refer to your tax adviser for guidance on the tax treatment on your purchase.

   Using the licence plate in the individual asset account name helps identify the motor vehicle.

2. **Create a contra fixed asset depreciation account and select your account type and tax rate.**

   In this example, this account could be called Less Accumulated Depreciation on CARS, with the account type Fixed Asset and tax rate as Exclusive of Consumer Tax. Any transactions allocated to this account should not be reported with regular consumer tax reports submitted to your relevant tax authorities.

   Allocate the contra fixed asset depreciation account an adjacent number to the fixed asset account created in Step 1, so these accounts appear together in financial reports.

   Contra is an accounting term for accounts with a balance that's opposite to the typical nature of their account type. A fixed asset may have its own unique fixed asset and contra asset account, depending on how you want to display them in the chart of accounts. By selecting account type Fixed Asset and allocating adjacent account numbers, they appear together in the Fixed Asset block on the Balance Sheet.

3. **Create a depreciation expense account and select account type and tax rate.**

   The account could be called Depreciation Expense, with the account type Expense and tax rate as Excluded Consumer.

All depreciation can be allocated to a single depreciation expense account. Refer to Chapter 2 for more on setting up accounts.

Purchasing and recording a fixed asset

After you've created your fixed asset accounts (refer to preceding section), you can 'purchase' your asset through Xero. To do so, you just need to process and approve the purchase, allocating it to the required account. In this example, you'd allocate the purchase to the CARS account, dating it 1 November.

Technically, a fixed asset can be added to the Fixed Asset Register without recording a purchase; however, doing so means the original value isn't reflected in the Balance Sheet. Processing a purchase to a fixed asset account automatically creates it as a *pending* fixed asset. If you initially allocate a purchase to an asset account, save it, then re-allocate it to a different account, it still remains in the asset register as a pending fixed asset. Once tagged as a pending asset, you need to manually remove this asset from its limbo state in the asset register (see the section 'Deleting a draft asset', later in this chapter, for more).

Note: A standard user can record asset purchases.

To record a fixed asset already 'purchased' in Xero (refer to preceding section), follow these steps:

1. **Access the Fixed Asset Register by clicking on the menu bar Accounts⇨Fixed Assets.**

   The purchased asset is sitting in the pending items area.

2. **Double click the desired asset and the Fixed Asset detail window opens.**

   See Figure 14-1. The account name, description from invoice and purchase date will autofill.

3. **Click on the Asset Number field to understand how the Fixed Asset number was created.**

   The prefix can be defined, and the automatic numbering of fixed assets is sequential and can be overridden. Just don't confuse this with the account number found on the chart of accounts.

FA-0004 Holden UTE

Pending See original bill   ⊡ 1   Asset Options ▾

Asset Details

Item	Asset Number	Account	Purchase Date	Region	Purchase Price
Holden UTE	FA-0004 ▾	710 - Motor Vehicl ▾	13 Oct ▦▦▦ ▾	▾	10,000.00

Description

Holden UTE
6 cyl 3.6L
Manual
Royal Blue with silver trim

To add web links type the URL including http://

Depreciation

Asset Type	Depreciation Rate	Depreciation Method	Depreciation Account
Motor Vehicle	20 %	Straight Line ▾	416 - Depreciatior ▾

Save   Register ▾   Cancel

Figure 14-1: The Fixed Asset detail window in the pending items area.

Click on the paper icon to upload documents stored on your computer that relate to the fixed asset purchase.

4. **Enter a detailed description in the Description field.**

   This is an opportunity to enter serial numbers and warranty details.

5. **Enter the asset type in the Asset Type field.**

6. **Click Save to save your changes.**

Dealing with depreciation

As assets are expensive and used for an extended period of time, allocating the full cost of an asset to a single year doesn't accurately reflect business performance. And doing so minimises profit for that year. A more realistic representation is to allocate part of the cost of the asset to each year over its life. *Depreciation* is an accounting tool used to allocate the cost of a fixed asset over the life of the asset.

Xero offers two depreciation methods: Straight Line and Diminishing Value. Here's how the two options work:

- ✔ **Straight Line depreciation:** The depreciation amount in the first year is the same for all subsequent years. If $10,000 is allocated a depreciation rate of 20 per cent, for example, every year the depreciation expense allocated to the asset is $2,000, meaning the asset is written off in five years.

- ✔ **Diminishing Value depreciation:** In this method, the depreciation rate (say, 20 per cent) is applied to the diminished value of the fixed asset. The first year amount (20 per cent × $10,000 = $2,000) is identical to that used in the straight line depreciation scenario. In the second year, the depreciation rate is applied to the reduced value of the asset (in this example, 20 per cent × $8,000 = $1,600). The depreciation expense gradually gets smaller and smaller, and the fixed asset remains on the books for a significantly longer period of time than if the straight line depreciation method had been used. This process may also be known as *Reducing Balance* (UK) or *Declining Balance* (US).

Note: Allocation and processing of depreciation can only be performed by users with Adviser status in Xero.

Allocating depreciation

Here's how you allocate depreciation in Xero:

1. **Enter the depreciation rate in the Depreciation Rate field of the Fixed Asset detail window.**

   Refer to Figure 14-1. If the depreciation rate changes, the depreciation rate field can be edited during the life of the asset.

2. **Select the Depreciation Method from the drop-down list.**

3. **Select the depreciation expense from the Depreciation Account on the drop-down list.**

   Refer to the section 'Creating fixed asset accounts', earlier in this chapter, for details on creating your depreciation account.

4. **In the Accumulated Depreciation Account, select from the drop-down list.**

   The account chosen depends on the asset you're allocating depreciation for. Continuing the motor vehicle example, you would select Less Accumulated Depreciation on CARS from the drop-down list.

   Note: The option to choose the account only appears the first time you add a type of fixed asset to the register. Continuing the car example, if you add a subsequent car, Xero will assume you want to use the same Accumulated Depreciation Account. If needed, this account can be changed when you run depreciation on the Fixed Assets.

5. **To register the asset, click the green Register button.**

Processing depreciation

To process depreciation follow these steps:

1. **Access the Fixed Asset Register by clicking on the menu bar Accounts⇨Fixed Assets and check that it's correct and up to date.**

2. **Click the Depreciation button.**

   The Depreciation window opens. Depreciation can be processed monthly or any monthly combination, up to the end of the financial year end. A fixed asset start date is listed.

3. **If the fixed asset start date is incorrect, click on the Start Date button, select the correct start date and click the green OK button.**

   The start date is the date you started managing your fixed assets in Xero. If assets were procured prior to this date, the asset value (at date of purchase) and accumulated depreciation needs to be entered as at the start date.

4. **Enter the end of the financial year in the Depreciate To field.**

   If you're entitled to claim a full year's depreciation, regardless of when the asset was purchased, change the purchase date to the start of your financial year. (Check with your accountant if unsure.)

5. **To process the depreciation click the blue Update button.**

   If during processing an accumulated depreciation account wasn't allocated, you now have the option to assign the account.

6. **Click the blue Export button to export a breakdown by asset in spreadsheet or PDF format.**

7. **In the Accumulated Depreciation Account, select from the drop-down list.**

   Continuing the motor vehicle example, you would choose Less Accumulated Depreciation on CARS from the drop-down list.

8. **Approve the selection by clicking the green Approve button.**

Rolling back depreciation

If depreciation has been incorrectly recorded, it can be rolled back to the point where you started. To process a depreciation roll back, follow these steps:

1. **Access the Fixed Asset Register by clicking on the menu bar Accounts⇨Fixed Assets.**

2. **Access the depreciation window by clicking the blue Depreciation button.**

3. **Click the Rollback Depreciation button.**

4. **At the Rollback Depreciation To field, select the date depreciation needs to be rolled back to from the drop-down list.**

5. **Click the green OK button.**

   All depreciation is rolled back to the selected date. All sales or disposals applied after the date rolled back to are reversed.

Selling or removing a fixed asset from the register

Assets may be sold or disposed of — in which case, they need to be removed from the Fixed Asset Register. *Note:* Assets can only be removed from the register by users with Adviser status in Xero.

Deleting a draft asset

Pending assets haven't been recorded on the Fixed Asset Register. If you initially allocate a purchase to an asset account, save it, then decide not to treat it as a fixed asset and re-allocate it to an expense account, the purchase stays in limbo in the pending fixed asset area. To delete a pending asset follow these steps:

1. **From the menu bar, click on Accounts➪Fixed Assets and select the Pending Items tab.**

2. **Select the item to be removed and click the red Delete button.**

   This won't delete purchase bills related to the item.

Selling a fixed asset

You can only process the sale of an asset if you have Adviser status in Xero.

Processing the sale of an asset in Xero is tricky and involves allocating capital gain on the sale of the asset, so you may want to refer this process to your tax accountant.

To record the sale of a fixed asset, follow these steps:

1. **From the main menu bar, click on Accounts➪Fixed Assets and select the Registered Items tab.**

2. **Select the item to be sold.**

   The Fixed Asset detail window opens (see Figure 14-2).

3. **Click on the Asset Options button in the top right corner and select Sell from the drop-down menu.**

   The Fixed Asset Sales window opens (see Figure 14-3).

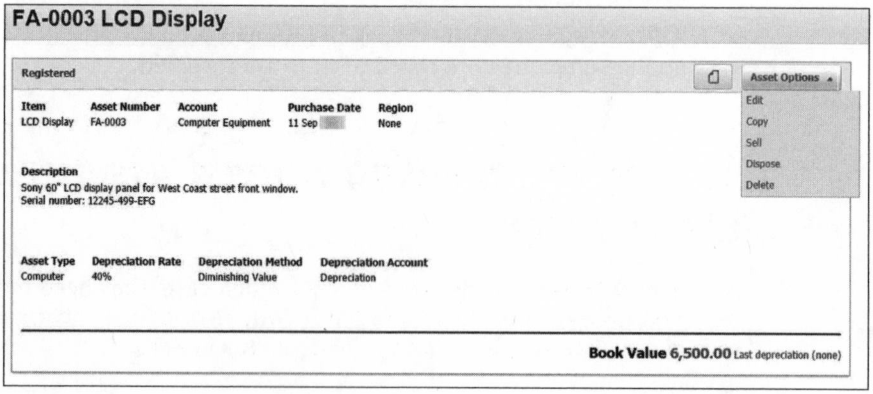

FA-0003 LCD Display

Registered						Asset Options ▲

						Edit
Item	Asset Number	Account	Purchase Date	Region		Copy
LCD Display	FA-0003	Computer Equipment	11 Sep	None		Sell
						Dispose
Description						Delete
Sony 60" LCD display panel for West Coast street front window.						
Serial number: 12245-499-EFG						

Asset Type	Depreciation Rate	Depreciation Method	Depreciation Account
Computer	40%	Diminishing Value	Depreciation

Book Value 6,500.00 Last depreciation (none)

Figure 14-2: The Fixed Asset detail window.

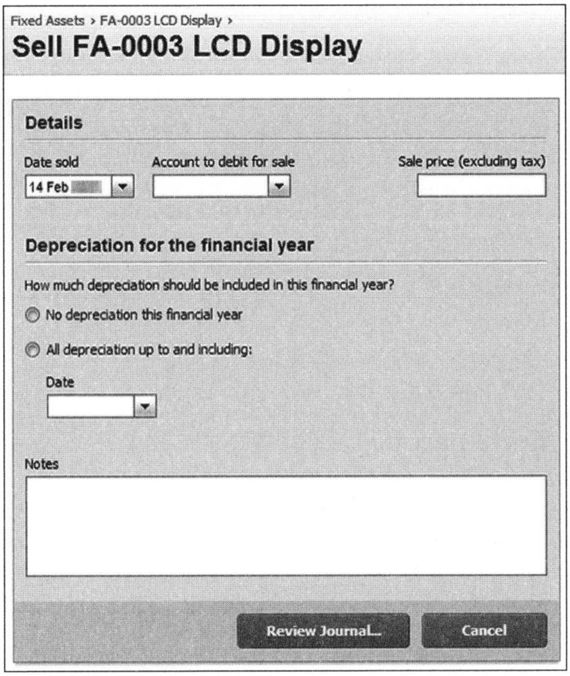

Fixed Assets > FA-0003 LCD Display >

Sell FA-0003 LCD Display

Details

Date sold
14 Feb ▓▓▓ ▼

Account to debit for sale
▼

Sale price (excluding tax)

Depreciation for the financial year

How much depreciation should be included in this financial year?

○ No depreciation this financial year

○ All depreciation up to and including:

Date
▼

Notes

Review Journal... | Cancel

Figure 14-3:
The Fixed
Asset Sales
window.

4. **Enter the date sold in the Date Sold field.**

5. **Enter the suitable general ledger account In the Account to Debit for Sale field.**

6. **Enter the sale price exclusive of consumer tax in the Sale Price (Excluding Tax) field.**

7. **Choose whether to allocate part or no depreciation.**

   Here you have the opportunity to allocate depreciation to the fixed asset up to the date of sale for the part of the financial year the fixed asset was owned by the business, or no depreciation, as follows:

   • To allocate no depreciation select No Depreciation for the Final Year.

   • To allocate depreciation for part of the financial year select All Depreciation Up To and Including and select the date in the Date field.

8. **Enter any notes about the sale or the asset in the Notes field.**

9. **To review the journal created by the sale, click the blue Review Journal button.**

   The Review Journal window appears, summarising the history and disposal of the asset.

10. **Allocate the Total Capital Gain to a suitable account.**

11. **Allocate the Loss/Gain on Disposal to a suitable account.**

    A new account may need to be created to accommodate this transaction. I'd love to advise you what a 'suitable account' may be; however, the account chosen depends on your business structure and how the fixed asset has been treated historically. If unsure, speak with your tax accountant and check with the Tax Office in your jurisdiction for advice on a suitable account for this process.

12. **Once you are satisfied, post the journal by clicking the green Post button.**

    The Fixed Asset detail window appears, highlighting the asset is now SOLD and details any Gains & Losses and Capital Gain recognised.

Disposing of a fixed asset

Assets can be deemed as disposed of for a number of reasons: Technical obsolescence, no longer working, damaged or they are given away to a charity. Recognition of the disposal needs to be recorded in Xero. *Note:* Only users with Adviser status in Xero can record the disposal of an asset.

To record the disposal of a fixed asset, follow these steps:

1. **From the main menu bar, click on Accounts⇨Fixed Assets and select the Registered Items tab.**

2. **Select the item to be disposed of.**

    The Fixed Asset detail window opens.

3. **Click on the Asset Options button and select Dispose from the drop-down menu.**

    The Fixed Asset Disposal window opens.

4. **Enter the date the asset was disposed of in the Date Disposed field.**

5. **Choose whether to allocate part or no depreciation.**

    Here you have the opportunity to allocate depreciation to the fixed asset up to the date of disposal for the part of the financial year the fixed asset was owned by the business, or no depreciation, as follows:

    • To allocate no depreciation, select No Depreciation for the Final Year.

    • To allocate depreciation for part of the financial year, select All Depreciation Up To and Including and select the date in the Date field.

6. **Enter any notes about the disposal or the asset in the Notes field.**

7. **To review the journal created by the sale, click the blue Review Journal button.**

   The Review Journal window appears, summarising the history and disposal of the asset.

8. **Allocate the Loss/Gain on Disposal to a suitable account.**

   A new account may need to be created to accommodate this transaction. Speak with your tax accountant and check with the tax office in your jurisdiction for advice if unsure.

9. **Once you are satisfied, post the journal by clicking the green Post button.**

   The Fixed Asset detail window appears, highlighting the asset is now DISPOSED and details any Gains & Losses and Capital Gain recognised.

Accessing Fixed Asset Reports

I've worked with a consulting business in the city for many years. The business engages an expensive accounting firm to prepare the company tax reports. One year, the tax accountants sent out a detailed depreciation schedule. (In the past, the accountants had only sent through a summary, which was simply accepted.) So the owners were interested and surprised when they looked at the detailed depreciation schedule. The listed fixed assets included items that the business no longer owned or no longer worked, or were part of the fit-out at a previous occupancy. Furthermore, identical assets were being depreciated at various rates. Grrrr! So I and the owners reviewed the schedule and worked out fixed assets were overstated by about $16,000. The owners asked the tax accountant to adjust the accounts, which resulted in $16,000 being allocated to the financial year's depreciation expense account, profits being reduced by the said amount and, accordingly, company tax also being reduced.

It's essential you review a detailed Fixed Asset Register and depreciation schedule for your business at least annually, to ensure depreciation is accurately allocated. By incorporating the Fixed Asset Register into your accounting system, you have the opportunity to stay closer to these accounts.

Your fixed assets tie up a significant amount of capital, and accurately maintaining the Fixed Asset Register is essential. Whenever you look at a report, ask yourself whether the numbers seem reasonable. If not, investigate further!

Xero offers several reports to view information about your fixed assets:

- ✔ **Depreciation Schedule:** The Depreciation Schedule report details actual or estimated depreciation allocated to fixed assets via the Fixed Asset Register. Depreciation that has been entered by an alternative method, such as a manual journal, isn't shown here — so avoid using manual journals for depreciation!

  To access the Depreciation Schedule report, from the menu bar, click on Reports⇨All Reports⇨Depreciation Schedule.

  To access the next generation Depreciation Schedule report and additional customisation options, from the menu bar, click on Reports⇨All Reports and then click the hyperlink Try Out the New Reports⇨Depreciation Schedule.

- ✔ **Fixed Asset Reconciliation:** The Fixed Asset Reconciliation reports on the difference between fixed assets listed on the Fixed Asset Register against the fixed assets listed on the Balance Sheet. Ideally, the difference is nil. A difference signifies an asset may not be registered or depreciation hasn't been correctly processed through the Fixed Asset Register.

  To access the Fixed Asset Reconciliation report, from the menu bar, click on Reports⇨All Reports⇨Fixed Asset Reconciliation.

- ✔ **Disposal Schedule:** The Disposal Schedule report details fixed assets that have been disposed of during the period. Using the report settings customisation options, you can view details of the Fixed Asset, like purchase and disposal date, cost and sale price, capital gain and loss figures.

  To access the next generation Disposal Schedule report, from the menu bar, click on Reports⇨All Reports and then click the hyperlink Try out the new reports⇨Disposal Schedule.

- ✔ **Balance Sheet:** The Balance Sheet reports on the fixed assets and the accumulated depreciation assigned to that fixed asset. Use the customise layout options (refer to Chapter 2) to group and subtotal the fixed assets.

  To access the Balance Sheet report, from the menu bar, click on Reports⇨Balance sheet.

- ✔ **Profit and Loss:** The Profit and Loss details the depreciation expense. To access the Profit and Loss report, from the menu bar, click on Reports⇨Profit and Loss.

Chapter 15

Working with Multi-Currency Transactions

I love freesias so I was over the moon when asked to help a client who imported this delicately perfumed flower. Due to space constraints, however, we worked next to the flower fridge (brrrr!), and I soon discovered the flowers, while still looking lovely, have minimal scent when cold. But onto the accounts. The business owner seemed to be in a good space — cash flow was positive, the bank balance was healthy and the business appeared to be booming. But those bothersome books needed updating and 'Xero hero' moi arrived on the scene and started tidying up the accounts for the business. We were both shocked by what was uncovered. The business actually only just broke even on what the lovely flowers were bought and sold for — all profits were actually generated from favourable currency movements during the year. In a different market environment where the currency fluctuated in an adverse direction, this flower business would incur significant losses.

Expanding a business overseas or selling imported products is an exciting step, but you need to fully understand and plan for exchange rate implications. Unexpected currency fluctuations can be favourable, or can critically drain your cash flow and profit. Just because you're busy and selling lots of stock, it may not mean that your business is actually profitable!

Setting Up Multi-Currency in Xero

Multi-currency features are only available in the Premium subscription Xero packages. If you're on a smaller plan, you can opt to move into a larger one. Once you upgrade, you can choose to downgrade after 30 days. (Downgrading ends the currency feeds into Xero, but the existing multi-currency transactions remain in the file.) Only the original subscriber for your Xero plan can arrange for you to move to a Premium subscription.

So to enable the multi-currency options and add currencies (covered in this section), you may first need to upgrade.

Upgrading your Xero plan

To upgrade your Xero plan, follow these steps:

1. **Log in to Xero and go to the MyXero area.**

   You can also access this area on mobile by typing my.xero.com into your browser.

2. **Click on the blue Upgrade link.**

3. **Select the Premium plan.**

4. **Confirm billing details.**

   Voila! You are upgraded and can access multi-currency features.

Adding currencies to Xero

Currency is a system of money in general use in a particular country. The official currency of many countries is the dollar unit; however, each country's dollar is valued differently. You can't go to the United States, for example, with one New Zealand dollar and purchase one US dollar's worth of goods. Furthermore, currencies aren't all in dollar units; they may be in yen, baht, pounds or euros.

Adding currency feeds

Your base or home currency in Xero is set when your file was created (refer to Chapter 2). Once selected, your base currency can't be changed — if you do need to change it, you need to start your Xero accounts all over again. If you want to transact in multiple currencies, currencies need to be individually added to the file.

To add currency feeds follow these steps:

1. **Click on Settings⇨General Settings⇨Currencies and click the Add Currency button.**

   The Add Currency window opens.

2. **Select a new currency from the drop-down menu.**

   Keep it tidy and only add the actual currencies needed. The business may trade with a variety of countries, for example, but may only ⇨transact in the American dollar. In this case, just select USD United States Dollar from the list.

3. **Add the currency by clicking the green Add Currency button.**

Setting up multi-currency contacts

The default currency contacts transact in is defined in their settings and can be overridden on individual transactions. Therefore, a single contact can transact in multiple different currencies. This can keep your contact list very neat — but keep in mind that some reports, such as the Aged reports, don't split out the different currencies owed for a single contact. If you want this information, you need to create a contact associated with each currency.

To allocate a default foreign currency to a contact card, follow these steps:

1. **Click on Contacts⇨All Contacts, locate the client and click Edit.**

2. **Select from the Default Currency drop-down menu.**

3. **Click the green Save button.**

Processing Multi-Currency Transactions in Xero

If your business has agreed to sell goods in a foreign currency, an invoice is raised in the foreign currency, which has implications for tax rates and exchange rates. I cover these implications in the following sections, as well as creating an invoice in a foreign currency, receiving part payment against this invoice and purchasing in a foreign currency. *Note:* You're unable to assign a default currency to an inventory item, only to invoices.

Understanding tax rates

To assist in processing and interpreting any tax implications, many clients I've worked with apply separate tax rates for individual currency sales and purchases. This is not necessary but may help you clearly identify what rates were applied.

For example, tax rates for US$ and NZ$ transactions could be set up with the criteria shown in Table 15-1 (the initial file created will have 0 per cent in the % column).

Table 15-1	Possible Tax Rate Display Names		
Tax Rate Display Name	*Tax Type*	*Tax Components*	*%*
$US Export	Sales	Consumer Tax	0
$US Import	Purchases	Consumer Tax	0
$NZ Export	Sales	Consumer Tax	0
$NZ Import	Purchases	Consumer Tax	0

Working with foreign currency exchange rates

Foreign currency exchange rates (or *forex* rates) represent the relationship between two different currencies. For example, if the Australian dollar is trading at 0.91 to the US dollar (AUD/USD 0.91), a single Australian dollar is worth US$0.91.

Foreign currency exchange rates feed into Xero via a currency translation service known as XE.com, updated every hour. Once connected, historical exchange rates are available. Of course, the rate from XE.com, the rate published by financial institutions and the rate actually applied to the transaction may vary, so the XE.com rate can be overridden.

Creating a foreign currency invoice

In this section, I cover creating a new invoice in a foreign currency, using the example of a sale for US$1,000.

To create an invoice in US dollars, follow these steps:

1. **Create the Sales Invoice.**

   Refer to Chapter 6 for more on creating invoices. In this example, you would enter the sales amount as $1,000.

2. **Enter the Invoice Date.**

3. **Enter the Invoice Due Date field.**

   Entering +1M in this field means the Invoice Due Date field should autofill with a date one month after the Invoice Date. Refer to Chapter 5 for guidance on setting up default due date information.

4. **Click on the Currency field and select from the drop-down menu.**

   Only currencies already set up are available in the drop-down menu; however, you can add additional currencies by clicking the + Add Currency . . . option and select the desired currency from the Select a Currency drop-down menu. Click the green Add Currency button and the currency is added to the invoice.

   For this example, you'd select USD United States Dollars. Beside the currency field the XE.com exchange rate as per the invoice date appears. For example, '1 AUD = 0.91 USD (01 Oct 2014)'. *Note:* If the invoice date changes, the exchange rate automatically updates.

   Selecting US dollars means USD is clearly stated in the Amount column and beside the total figure.

5. **Click the green OK button.**

6. **Complete the remaining invoice, and select the tax rate.**

   In this example, you'd choose $US Export (refer to Table 15-1).

7. **Click the green Save button.**

At the bottom of the invoice is information about the foreign currency transaction translated into your base currency:

- ✔ Realised
- ✔ Unrealised
- ✔ Net

Beside those numbers are tiny green (good) and red (negative) movement indicators, so you can quickly see if the exchange rate changes have had a favourable effect on the transaction. (See the following section for more.)

Currency gain or loss

When the original date of a foreign currency transaction is different to the settlement date, the movement in the exchange rate between the two dates results in a currency gain or loss. If the transaction hasn't yet been settled, it's defined as an *unrealised* currency gain or loss and fluctuates in line with the current exchange rate feed. Once the transaction has been finalised, the currency gain or loss is *realised* and no longer fluctuates. Both realised and unrealised currency gains or losses are reported in the Profit and Loss Statement as an operating expense called Foreign Currency Gains and Losses.

As long as no payment is received against this invoice, the unrealised and net amount detailed at the bottom of the invoice remain the same. If part payment is received against the invoice, the related currency gain or loss is realised, and summing the realised and unrealised amounts equals the net amount. Once full payment is received, finalising the transaction, the currency gain or loss is realised and the realised amount equals the *net* amount.

The Balance Sheet in Xero reflects the base currency dollar value of the outstanding amount in the Accounts Receivable account. This fluctuates depending on the current exchange rate. The Balance Sheet also includes a notation that details rates and the date used to convert the balance into your base currency dollar.

The Profit and Loss reflects the Unrealised Currency Gain account, split out across the periods that it occurs. A loss is reflected as a positive amount, and a gain is reflected as a negative amount.

Manually changing invoice exchange rates

Most Xero users accept the default exchange rate provided by XE.com — and this is the simplest option! However, some tax accountants I work with prefer to use the Australian Taxation Office average foreign exchange rates published monthly, so the invoice exchange rate needs to be manually changed every time. Check with your tax accountant and the regulations of your jurisdiction about the exchange rates to use in your business. It's quicker to opt for XE.com's default exchange rate; however, if you want to override the exchange rate, here's how to do it:

1. **When creating a foreign currency invoice, override the suggested exchange rate (if required) by clicking on the blue Exchange Rates link beside the Currency field.**

   The Exchange Rates window (see Figure 15-1) opens, with details of the XE.com exchange rate provided.

To override the XE.com exchange rate for this specific transaction, select the option below the XE.com rate and enter the desired exchange rate. You then also have the option to apply the edited rate to all new transactions on the applicable date.

Once payment has been applied, the currency and exchange rate can't be changed.

Receiving part payment against the sale

In some cases, you may receive a deposit, or part payment, against a foreign currency invoice. For example, and following the example in previous sections of a sale for US$1,000, say you receive a US$500 part payment against this sale.

To process a deposit, follow these steps:

1. **Record a partial payment against the invoice by entering the payment in the Amount Paid field.**

   In this example, you'd enter US$500 in this field.

   Non-base currency invoices can be paid in either the invoice currency or the base currency of your bank account, but you can't receipt in other currencies. In this example, if the Xero file was set up in NZ dollars, payment against the invoice could be received in NZ dollars or US dollars, but no other currency.

2. **Enter the invoice due date in the Date Paid field.**

3. **Select the bank the payment was deposited into from the drop-down list.**

4. **Enter the applicable exchange rate, if required.**

   You need to include the applicable exchange rate if the money is receipted into a non-USD account.

Aa an alternative to the preceding steps, you can record a part payment against a foreign currency invoice by reconciling the payment via the bank statement. Just make sure you uncheck the Show Base Currency Items Only option while reconciling. Refer to Chapter 8 for more guidance.

The Balance Sheet in Xero reflects the receipt of payment in the respective bank account and the remaining outstanding amount in the Accounts Receivable account.

The Profit and Loss now reflects three currency accounts:

- ✔ Bank Revaluations
- ✔ Realised Currency Gains
- ✔ Unrealised Currency Gains

If you don't override the day's exchange rate and compare the Profit and Loss before and after applying the payment, the net effect is the same. However, once the payment is made a partial currency gain or loss is realised in the Realised Currency Gains account.

The Bank Revaluations account reflects the effect of fluctuating exchange rates on the balance(s) of foreign currency bank account(s). Even if no transactions were recorded against the foreign currency bank account(s), if the exchange rate moved, the value of foreign currency bank account(s) is readjusted in the Balance Sheet, and the Bank Revaluations in the Profit and Loss Statement would reflect the movement every month.

Receiving the payment directly into a base currency dollar account has no effect on the Bank Revaluation account.

Once payment has been fully received against an invoice, no unrealised gains are recorded. If the transaction occurred over a period of time, any unrealised gains recorded in earlier periods are netted off to a balance of zero once the transaction is finalised.

Transferring between foreign and base currency bank accounts

To transfer money between a foreign bank account to your base currency bank account, follow these steps:

1. **From the dashboard, locate the bank account the unreconciled money transfer transaction belongs to and click on the blue Reconcile Items button.**

   Access this transaction from the dashboard (refer to Chapter 8 for more).

2. **Create a match for the money transfer by clicking on the Transfer tab on the left.**

3. **From the drop-down menu, select the other bank account.**

   If the default currencies of the accounts are different, a Currency Conversion panel opens below the transaction (see Figure 15-2).

4. **Enter the amount as it appears in the base currency statement in the Amount field.**

   The exchange rate automatically adjusts. Entering the transaction this way is so simple, because you enter the actual amounts as they appear on the statements, and leave it to Xero to do the hard exchange rate calculations. However, you should still check that the exchange rate appears correct.

   Unfortunately, when currency is converted, the banks stick their hands out and charge a fee. The associated fee of the originating bank can be entered in the Include Bank Fees panel.

5. **Enter the bank account the bank fees are being charged through in the To field.**

6. **Enter text in the description field.**

   For example, you could enter *Currency conversion charges* here.

7. **Select the required account from the drop-down Accounts list.**

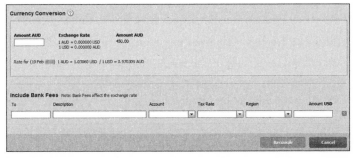

Figure 15-2:
The Currency
Conversion
panel.

8. **Select the appropriate tax rate for bank charges in the Tax Rate drop-down list.**

   To identify foreign currency transaction expense, using the $US Export tax rate makes sense.

9. **Enter the bank charges in the Amount field.**

   The bank fee of the recipient bank is added separately because this panel doesn't allow for alternative currencies in the amount field.

10. **To record the transfer, click the green Reconcile button.**

Purchasing in a foreign currency

The processes undertaken to record purchases in a foreign currency mirror the Sales processes. Just use the import tax rate to aid in identifying any purchases made. (Refer to the section 'Creating a foreign currency invoice', earlier in this chapter, for more information.)

Global custom bills can be tricky transactions to process. The invoice may be entirely for consumer tax — unlike normal transactions that have standard rates applied to them.

To process a customs bill, follow these steps:

1. **Process the bill.**

   Refer to Chapter 7 for more information on processing purchases.

2. **Don't worry about multi-currency transactions.**

   The customs bill is typically paid in the business's base currency, so multi-currency isn't an issue.

3. **Select the consumer tax account in the Account field.**

   Yes — this will be allocated directly to consumer tax.

4. **Select Consumer Tax on Imports in the Tax Rate field.**

5. **Allocate the full consumer tax amount to the transaction line.**

   Be careful not to get other small charges like admin mixed up in this transaction.

6. **Process the bill as per normal.**

The consumer tax should appear on the consumer tax report. When the actual payment for the goods purchased is processed, make sure the tax code allocated excludes this payment entirely from the consumer tax report.

Conversion Balances and Multi-Currency Bank Accounts

If you had an existing multi-currency bank account when your Xero account was created, you need to enter the account's conversion balance. However, the multi-currency bank account needs to be added to the data file before a conversion balance can be added (refer to Chapter 2 for more on setting up accounts).

After adding the multi-currency bank account, to enter a multi-currency conversion balance follow these steps:

1. **From the menu bar go to Settings⇨General settings⇨Conversion Balances.**

2. **To add the multi-currency bank account, click the Add a New Line button and select the multi-currency bank account.**

   A nil balance appears as a blue link.

3. **Click on the balance of the multi-currency account, and enter the originating currency amount and the exchange rate as at conversion date.**

   The base currency amount can't be edited. To achieve the correct base currency amount, edit the originating currency amount or the exchange rate.

4. **To accept the balance, click the green OK button.**

Viewing Reports in Foreign Currency

Foreign currency can quickly become complicated and many implications with regards to tax, currency and exchange rates are involved. As multi-currency has been built into the core engine of Xero, it calculates real-time gains and losses on the fly. Work closely with your accountant or adviser to understand the effect foreign currency has on your business reports.

From the reports available within Xero, one report specifically highlights how currency fluctuations are affecting foreign currency transactions. This is the Foreign Currency Gains and Losses report.

To access the Foreign Currency Gains and Losses report from the menu bar, go to Reports⇨All Reports⇨Foreign Currency Gains and Losses. This brings up the report (see Figure 15-3). The amounts receivable and payable are split out by currency.

Other reports affected by an unpaid foreign currency transaction, such as the Balance Sheet, include within them the foreign currency transaction translated as per the exchange rate provided by XE.com.

To access the Aged Payables report from the menu bar, click Reports⇨Aged Payables. At the bottom of the report are notation references detailing the exchange rate applied to the transaction.

When the multi-currency feature is utilised in Xero, Bank Revaluations, Realised Currency Gains and Unrealised Currency Gains accounts are automatically created. You can't post directly to these accounts, nor can you find them in your chart of accounts. They are shown in the Profit and Loss report, and grouping them together makes viewing them easier (refer to Chapter 9 for more on grouping items).

Figure 15-3: The Foreign Currency Gains and Losses report.

Foreign Currency Gains and Losses

████ ██████ (AU)

From 1 February ████ to 28 February ████

Add Summary

	Balance		Balance AUD	Realised Gain	Unrealised Gain	Realised Gain YTD	Unrealised Gain YTD	FX Exposure
Accounts Receivable								
Australian Dollar	15,806.55	AUD	15,806.55	0.00	0.00	0.00	0.00	0.00
Total Accounts Receivable			**15,806.55**	**0.00**	**0.00**	**0.00**	**0.00**	**0.00**
Accounts Payable								
Australian Dollar	8,507.78	AUD	8,507.78	0.00	0.00	0.00	0.00	0.00
Total Accounts Payable			**8,507.78**	**0.00**	**0.00**	**0.00**	**0.00**	**0.00**
Total Gain (Loss)				**0.00**	**0.00**	**0.00**	**0.00**	**0.00**
Bank Accounts								
Business Bank Account	(1,251.08)	AUD	(1,251.08)		0.00		0.00	0.00
Business Savings Account	(51.72)	AUD	(51.72)		0.00		0.00	0.00
USD	(700.50)	USD	(683.56) 🛈		16.94		16.94	16.94
Total Bank Accounts			**(1,986.36)**		**16.94**		**16.94**	**16.94**
FX Exposure								**16.94**

This report uses the most up-to-date exchange rate data available to convert foreign currencies into Australian Dollar. Enter exchange rates for 28 February ████.

Notes

1. Figures converted into Australian Dollar using the following rate:
   1.02478 USD United States Dollar per AUD. Rate provided by XE.com on 21 Feb ████.

Chapter 16

Xero Online Network

I have a friend who is a simultaneous Japanese-to-English translator. Many people can translate languages, but only a rare few can do it simultaneously. As Barack Obama speaks to the United Nations audience, for example, his English words are translated into the world's different languages by simultaneous translators. The non-English audience wear headphones and hear Obama's translated words in real-time, and the whole audience feels the emotion of the speech and reacts together.

Xero networks operate in a similar manner: Information can flow seamlessly from one solution to another. This allows you to view completed jobs from a job management solution translated into Xero sales invoices (refer to Chapter 6 for more on sales invoices), Xero financial data (Chapter 9) translated into colourful graphs in a reporting solution or integrate with a robust inventory solution, for managing stock (Chapter 13). Double handling of data doesn't occur, and crosschecking between systems isn't necessary — minimising errors and saving time. Utilising networks can transform your business's ability to manage operations, and interpret management and financial reports — in other words, it could be a game changer! Network connections can be achieved through importing data, *application programming interface* (API) technology, and general and specific connectors.

In this chapter, I explain how the Xero to Xero network works, and share what you need to know about API technology. I explore the different types of connectors and add-on solutions and highlight what to consider when deciding on a solution. To exploit and extract full value from integrated systems you need to ensure they're set up correctly and stay curious about what's possible — this chapter points you in the right direction.

The add-on solutions available to work in with Xero are constantly changing. For a current list of what's available in the specific area you require, see xero.com/add-ons.

Working with Xero to Xero Networks

Xero files can be connected with other Xero files utilising a network key. My web designer uses Xero, for example, and sent me a Xero network invite so our Xero files could connect. When he sends me an invoice, he opts to simply send it via the Xero network. I'm notified via email that I received a draft bill from my web designer and simultaneously a draft bill automatically appears in my Xero. I still need to allocate an account and consumer tax code to the bill and approve it, but utilising Xero to Xero connection minimises data entry, improves cash flow, and eliminates the excuse that the dog ate the bill! (Refer to Chapter 5 for guidance on sending a network invite, Chapter 6 for more on emailing invoices and Chapter 7 for processing and coding draft bills.)

I've seen the Xero to Xero connection work particularly well with associated businesses that do interrelated (and sometimes confusing!) transactions. For example, I work with a client who runs two businesses — one business hires out packaging containers, and the other business ships freight. The freight business frequently hires the packaging containers, so the hiring business sends draft sales invoices through the Xero to Xero network to the freight business. The freight business approves the sales invoices and payment against the invoices can be made by cash, as in a normal business relationship, or offset by intercompany loans, as is typical for interrelated businesses. Refer to Chapter 2 for guidance on enabling payments against loan accounts.

Understanding the Benefits and Risks of Add-On Solutions

Implementing business management solutions is an important decision and a major investment for a business, so make sure you pick the right solution and get it set up properly. The following sections cover some aspects you should consider before you commit to an add-on solution.

Getting under the hood: Understanding API

Application programming interface (API) is technology that acts like a key, unlocking different software solutions and allowing them to talk with other software solutions. API is a protocol that enables fields to be matched and data to flow from one system to another system, opening up real-time communication channels.

Xero has a published API — meaning other software developers can look at the API and match their software solution to it. Some add-on software solutions that link in with Xero are created to directly sync with Xero; other solutions are more generic in nature and you use a connector to help them talk, match fields and click together (a bit like building blocks). Some developers can also create customised software solutions tailored to meet specific business requirements.

Unless you're a developer, you don't need to worry about how API technology works — you simply need to understand what it is capable of. And the possibilities are endless. Implementing integrated Xero solutions unleashes the power of intelligent business systems, data mining capabilities and predictive analysis. Ultimately, this means small business can compete with the big boys!

Ascertaining implementation costs

When selecting a solution, ascertain the initial implementation and ongoing costs. Sometimes people say to me, 'I'm not investing $25 a month in this — I can do it myself.' However, as a person, your one natural resource restriction is time — you can't create more time for yourself. If you value your time at, say, $50 per hour and investing $25 a month in a solution frees up 30 minutes of your time in the month, it's a good investment. You've an extra 30 minutes to work on other areas of the business — or perhaps run sand between your toes.

When comparing costs across options, also identify the time and money saved from investing in a solution.

Looking at longevity

You need to check the longevity of both the product and its provider. For example, check whether additional users can access the product if your business grows. Likewise, check whether downsizing with the product is practical if your business downsizes.

If the business is likely to grow in size — be it employees, product offerings, transactions or locations — ascertain if the solution is able to scale up and perhaps across different branches. Identify limitations and assess if workarounds are acceptable. Keep in mind, of course, that technology is evolving so quickly that restrictions can dissipate overnight — meaning today's issue may be non-existent tomorrow.

You may be satisfied with the longevity of the product and it being able to provide for your future needs, but what about the longevity of the provider? The provider may look great today but try to get an idea of their future plans. If Xero updates are required in the add-on solution, will the provider be around to implement them? Check the version release — if the release is '1.0' (or similar), they've only released one version and, if you try it, you may be the guinea pig testing the solution in a live environment! Look for a solution that has gone through a few version releases.

Do an online search using the solution's name and read feedback about them in forums. Do they appear to be responsive to their existing customers?

Checking response times

Check out the support options the add-on solution provider offers — for example, telephone, live chat, email or an account manager. Don't confuse sales support with ongoing technical support — the sales areas may operate totally separately to the support area, once you're committed to the product. Test the provider out by sending in a technical question via the support area and see what the response is like.

Understanding intellectual property security

Determine the controls in place over entering, accessing, editing and extracting information from the solution. You want to ensure a disgruntled employee can't extract customer information, and erase business data in one fell swoop.

Making Use of Online Cloud Integration Specialists

If you don't want to undertake an add-on implementation on your own, online specialists can help your business quickly get up and running using Xero add-on integrated solutions. These experts can assist with:

- ✔ Answering questions
- ✔ Providing feasibility studies
- ✔ Defining work flow processes
- ✔ Field mapping
- ✔ Training and ongoing support
- ✔ Turnkey implementation

Many of the websites for specific add-on solutions can point you in the direction of experts on their product — such as their own in-house gurus, bookkeepers, add-on partners and advisers. Your existing Xero advisory team may be able to help you with the implementation, but using an expert in a particular product may be faster and cheaper!

Getting a Feel for Available Solutions

Xero has an approved list of add-on solution 'partners' that have demonstrated their product integrates with Xero, and they have appropriate end-user documentation. Other products are also available that can communicate with Xero — but these haven't gone through the process of being listed as add-on solution partners.

You may hear the ubergeeks using the terms *horizontal* and *vertical* when referencing add-ons. A horizontal add-on works across all industries or businesses. An example of a horizontal add-on is Debtor Daddy, which actively chases accounts receivable, Quotient, which enables businesses to generate quotes, or even Spotlight Reports, which provides insightful reporting to businesses. A vertical add-on specialises in niche industries — for example, Coreplus, which is health practice management software, or Deputy, which manages rosters and timesheets. Of course, it's not always that simple, and some solutions may be a little bit horizontal and a little vertical — but you get the general gist of how these terms are used!

In this chapter, I cover various Xero add-on solutions; however, I'm not endorsing any particular solution. The purpose is to open up your mind to the possibility of what features are available, and how you could use them in your own business to improve productivity.

The following sections look at solutions that have been listed as add-on solution partners, grouped by function.

Connectors

General and specific connectors are available. A general connector lets you connect numerous applications to Xero through one device. Data synchronises automatically across business systems, automating work flow, minimising time-consuming data entry and reducing mistakes — if you've set it up correctly!

I've found some connected systems may have the required fields, but a defined link hasn't been built into the connection — meaning the data can't flow from one solution to the other. You need to identify what information you actually want to be synchronised and check if it's possible with the solution provider.

A general connector like OneSaas or Zapier enables integration across multiple solutions — so, for example, a client can purchase products via eBay, which automatically updates Batchbooks CRM, and feeds invoicing and customer data into Xero. This automation means the business operator doesn't need to manually recreate every sale.

A specific connector links Xero to a single solution. For instance, ACT! is a popular CRM (see following section). ACT! Link by Xact Software is software linking the two solutions. Or another available option is RM Importer, a product allowing a retail store to remain with MYOB Retail Manager for their existing POS system, but change their accounting system from MYOB AccountRight to Xero.

With all connectors you typically have the option of hourly or daily syncs. The syncs depend on matching the fields of data — for instance, if you want to transfer information about inventory, item fields need to be available to link both solutions.

The capabilities of the general connectors are truly astonishing — visit their websites to see all the different solutions they work with.

CRMs

A customer resource management (CRM) system centralises customer information — essentially, it's a customer-focused knowledgebase. These systems allow the business to understand and serve clients efficiently and effectively — hopefully maximising profits!

In a business, client information can be sourced from contact history, sales tracking, marketing result, customer profiles and — ta da! — accounting software.

The business benefits of a CRM include the following:

- ✔ Assist in preparing responses to common queries.
- ✔ Avoid customers falling through the cracks.
- ✔ Ensure staff know the complete history between the business and the client.
- ✔ Manage opportunities in the pipeline.
- ✔ Measure lead to customer conversion and response time.

Xero has an inbuilt link via its Smart Lists function to the online marketing company Constant Contact. Refer to Chapter 5 for an overview how this integration works.

Debtor tracking

A debtor tracking solution reviews existing accounts receivable data and, from that insight, can produce visuals, charts, automatically follow up on receivables via emails, SMS or phone calls, or apply fees to outstanding invoices. These solutions rely on accounts being reconciled on a timely basis, and combined with online invoicing have been proven to reduce debtor days, in turn improving cash flow. Following up on outstanding invoices is never a pleasant task; automated emails are much less confronting and can be a massive time-saver.

The business benefits of a debtor tracking solution include the following:

- ✔ Eliminate repetitive administrative tasks around debt collection
- ✔ Improve cash flowing into the business
- ✔ Reduce time and cost involved in collecting debts
- ✔ Vanquish awkward conversations with customers

e-commerce

The term *e-commerce* (or electronic commerce) refers to the selling of products or services over the internet, with e-commerce generally revolving around a shop on a website.

An online shop on a website typically automatically creates invoices when orders are received, and sends the invoices to customers in real-time. Customer information can then be populated or updated in Xero from the transactions. Solutions are also available for specific industries, such as Checkfront, which offers a hosted booking system solution.

The business benefits of integrating e-commerce with Xero include

- A mobile store open and accessible 24/7
- Improved cash flow management, and updated cash flow information
- Reduced data entry because invoices, orders and payments are linked together — making reconciliations a breeze

Bills and expenses

Typically, the bills and expenses add-on solutions work like this: You send receipts in, they're scanned, and data is extracted and coded. The coding may include coding to your Chart of Accounts, or tracking codes and consumer tax. The data and codes are then imported into Xero. If you have lots of receipts, using these solutions minimises data entry and reduces paper storage!

Also, a solution like Receipt Bank puts the power of this technology into the palm of your hand. While at the local coffee house, you can upload images of business receipts to your iPhone, submit them for processing, and they're coded and ready to be published into Xero by the time you are back at your office.

Inventory

Xero only offers a limited inventory solution, so if you manage inventory, you definitely need to look at one of the available add-on solutions. Essentially an inventory management solution can offer some or all of the following features:

✔ Assist with stocktakes, including count sheets, and the ability to update stock and adjust stock

✔ Scan bar codes

✔ Maintain a bill of materials, like a recipe for combining components to create a new inventory item

✔ Maintain detailed records of inventory, including stock levels and restocking levels

✔ Manage all aspects of the purchasing functions, including suppliers, shipments, consignment stock and returns management

✔ Create multiple price tiers, allowing you to sell products at different prices to different clients

✔ Record periodic and/or perpetual inventory

✔ Sell items without reducing the balance of the item suitable for non-diminishing products

✔ Group products, allowing you to categorise products for groups

✔ Assess stock value, including average cost stock valuation and the ability to track inventory purchases against job costing

✔ Track inventory's location, from bins through to multiple locations

✔ Transfer stock between warehouses

Inventory add-ons' integration with Xero should update the Balance Sheet inventory accounts, and cost of goods sold on the Profit and Loss report. If just starting out, Trade Gecko has an innovative on-boarding training platform, which quickly outlines all the inventory basics you need to know and should expect from within an inventory solution.

In addition to some of the features mentioned in the preceding list, simPro has up-to-date catalogues and pricelists of major wholesale suppliers available through their system, which can save you time and help you minimise costs. StarShip prints shipping labels, allowing the business to track and trace shipments.

Job tracking

Job management software tracks the income and expenses related to a single job, so the job profit or loss can be accurately identified and the invoicing information can be transferred to Xero for timely billing. It includes the creation of the job, efficient dispatch to available staff and locations, management and progress updates. A clear understanding of work in progress (WIP) means your business can communicate progress with clients, and assign resources as necessary. Detailed monitoring of the financial performance of jobs also helps you develop accurate quotes for future work.

Several time-tracking, inventory and CRM solutions include robust job costing and job management features. A number of add-on job tracking solutions link with Xero.

Payments

An online payment gateway lets your business accept credit card payments against sales invoices. This facilitates receipting international currency without the need to open foreign bank accounts and enables quick and easy transaction reconciliations within Xero. Solutions like PayPal and eWAY, for example, can automate recurring transactions and connect to online shopping carts.

Payroll

A payroll solution can manage your business's full payroll function, including maintaining detailed employee records, timesheets, processing pay runs, monitoring payroll entitlements, and providing pay slips and any reporting necessary in your jurisdiction.

For most users, Xero has a limited payroll function so an add-on solution may be required. (Australian users can access an inbuilt payroll system that should be sufficient for many user's payroll requirements — see www. dummies.com/go/xerofd2e for more information. Users based in the United States may also have inbuilt payroll functionality — check with your Xero advisory team for more information.)

Payroll is a complex area governed by many rules and regulations. You need to identify a payroll management system compliant to the territory your business operates in. Payment Evolution provides a complete Canadian payroll solution, for example, while SimplePay.co.za offers a South African–specific solution.

A number of add-on payroll solutions link with Xero, specific for the country you do business in.

Point of sale

A point of sale (POS) solution streamlines the way you record sales in a retail management environment. Typically, the solution syncs customer and supplier records and sales, and payments records between the solution and Xero. It works with normal retail tools, such as barcoders, scanners, cash drawers and receipt printers, and allows for customisation of customer receipts and other documents. Additional features may include customer loyalty rewards tracking, stock management and sales reports.

Time tracking

A time-management system can tie into timesheets, calendars, rostering and appointment scheduling, and online booking capability. The system enables employees to track their time against jobs, clients and accounts, and can empower managers to monitor project workflow and allocate employees to complete tasks within the projects. A time-management system may include payroll and job costing within the solution, or lend itself to seamless integration. Contacts and transactions can by synced across systems.

A graphic design business, for example, could use a time-management system like MinuteDock to allocate tasks to graphic designers, and the designers could log or dock time spent on tasks. This helps managers budget and track expenses for the project. MinuteDock also includes the option of enabling clients to view time being billed to their project. The business is then able to easily collate and push detailed invoices across into Xero.

Reporting

Add-on reporting tools dissect, interpret and translate real-time Xero information into easily digestible formats, including graphs, charts and snapshots. These business intelligence tools aid with strategic planning and help you monitor financial metrics, key performance indicators (KPIs) and benchmarking — essentially, they allow you to maintain a general scorecard for business goals.

Visual data in the form of beautifully coloured charts helps any non-financial people involved in the business understand their own financial situation, and assists them to make informed business decisions and proactively deal with their future. As well as financial data, non-financial data and social media tracking can also be analysed.

Solutions are also available for specific areas or industries. The reporting tool Calxa, for example, enables the creation of budgets and cash flow forecasts particularly useful for not-for-profit board reporting. Fathom HQ facilitates integration with numerous Xero files, enabling analysis, alerts and benchmarking across the files — useful for a franchisor, for example, comparing the performance of different franchisees.

Looking at Custom Integration

If none of the available solutions meet your business's needs, you can also look at the custom integration option — that is, where you hire someone to design a solution for your specific requirements. But before you explore custom integration, take a step back and reflect on what the business is doing. Can your processes be simplified and adapted to an existing solution? A custom integration can be expensive and, with every upgrade of Xero, it may need to be adapted as well. Of course, after careful consideration, you may decide a custom solution perfectly suits what you require and will save you money and time!

To ensure a successful custom integration, you need to clearly detail what operational performance you want and any assumptions you may have for the solution. Invest the time to explore and define your requirements up-front. What appears to the layperson as a minor change may in fact require a major re-write by the solution provider, which bumps up costs!

Part V
The Part of Tens

the
part of
tens

Enjoy an additional (and free!) Part of Tens chapter about improving your cash flow at www.dummies.com/extras/xero.

In this part ...

- ✔ Read all about how to get the most out of Xero in the long term.
- ✔ Discover ten common mistakes that are made in Xero, and learn how to avoid them!

Chapter 17

Ten (Plus One!) Tips for Long-Term Success with Xero

*I*n this chapter, I highlight practices that you should adopt when using Xero to improve your productivity and ensure ongoing success. I'm never dictatorial in how you should or shouldn't run your business — but I do know that utilising the factors outlined in this chapter can help you free up your time so you can focus on more important aspects of your business, like business and strategy development. And incorporating the information produced can then assist you in making decisions.

Embrace the Cloud

Once you're set up on Xero, you can access it anywhere you can access the internet. So take a few moments and install the Xero app on your mobile devices. Once you've set up the Xero app, you can send out sales invoices onsite, engage a mobile work force, reconcile while travelling abroad or email contacts while catching a bus. Free yourself from your office desk and get comfortable using Xero remotely while waiting for a coffee at your local café.

Make Use of Networking Technology

Take the time to step back from Xero and from your business. Monitor your business processes and identify what's consuming time and whether it can be replaced through network technology. Utilising the Xero to Xero network and add-on solutions can dramatically increase productivity if doing so can replace manual processes. An add-on Xero solution like Receipt Bank, for example, extracts information from receipts and bills, securely stores scanned copies of the document, and seamlessly populates Accounts Payable, Spend Money and Expense modules within Xero. Refer to Chapter 16 for the different add-on possibilities available.

Export Data to Create Graphs

A lot of data in Xero can be exported into Google Docs or an Excel spreadsheet. Once you have it in Excel you can utilise the features of spreadsheets; data can be customised and graphs created. This means you can present information in a user-friendly manner — because, of course, preparing awesome, accurate and timely data is pointless if no-one's looking at it!

Many non-financial people prefer colourful graphs and charts over numbers — because they're able to interpret, say, the relationship between different colour block comparisons, more easily than the same information in numbers.

I've found people tend to have a few charts they understand and like to see on a regular basis. So explore this option and work out what you prefer. And if you're exporting to spreadsheets on a regular basis, explore some of the add-on reporting tools because they may save you time (refer to Chapter 16).

Set up Bank Feeds and Reconcile Regularly

One of the star features of Xero is bank feeds. Once you have set up and authorised bank feeds in Xero, all the transactions that have passed through the banks pass directly into Xero — massively reducing data entry. All you need to do is code the transactions and reconcile them.

I recommend you reconcile all bank accounts in Xero regularly to ensure information is up to date and any transactional issues are dealt with on a timely basis. It's far easier to recall what a transaction is about and deal with any issues if the transaction is recent — versus trying to sort out something that happened six months ago. Regular reconciliations also ensure the Money Coming In dashboard is correct, highlighting clients who need to be followed up for outstanding payments, so you can boost cash flowing into the business. (Refer to Chapter 8 for more on reconciliations.)

Setting up bank rules is also useful. Bank rules recognise incoming transactions and suggest the default treatment of those transactions. They only take a few minutes to set up, and focusing on setting up bank rules in the early days usually means, within about six weeks, all typical transactions are quickly reconciled. This again speeds up your processing time in Xero. (Refer to Chapter 4 for more on setting up bank rules.)

Use the Batch Payments Feature

Another time-saving technique you should adopt is electronic banking payments. Batch payments can be created within Xero and uploaded to online banking via electronic banking payments. You need to contact your bank to set up electronic banking with them — and then process transactions within Xero and produce a batch payments file, which you then upload to the bank. (Some New Zealand banks even allow the batch payment file to be sent directly to online banking – they certainly seem to be leading the way with online automation!) This process is another time-saver as data isn't being duplicated.

Keep Bank Accounts for Business Use

This tip is simple, yet it really makes a big difference to your accounts. Here it is: Use business bank accounts exclusively for business use. I agree — not particularly earth-shattering. But time and again I see accounts mixed up with personal spending, which is confusing and leads to expenses being overlooked or, worse, accidently being claimed. By not processing personal expenditure through business bank accounts, when you reconcile the account you're confident all the transactions are business related — even if you sometimes still struggle to work out what they are!

Embrace Change

Because of the online nature of Xero, changes can be implemented overnight. Typically, you're notified of the general nature of the changes; however, a change in one area may have an unexpected effect in another area. If things look different but seem to work okay, don't stress over it — accept it and work with it. It's a natural part of Xero's evolution and a unique feature of cloud solutions.

Overnight changes result in many benefits for you, the user. It means you don't have to wait for new software releases and then waste time with manual upgrades. I've done my fair share of desktop-based upgrades and they are just a huge waste of time! Xero's effortless evolution means new features are available for you to use right here, right now. The change may be the exact thing you wanted, or something that you never knew you needed, but now makes processing your accounts a little easier.

Use Tracking to Sharpen Reporting

The Tracking feature is super easy to set up and use, and leads to more powerful reporting. Xero has two available tracking categories, and numerous tracking options can be included for each category. All transactions can be allocated to a tracking option. Many reports can be customised to show comparative or individual tracking options. (You can delete tracking categories but you can't mark them as closed or inactive. If you still want the option of being able to access historical tracking information after you've finished using the tracking categories, you can add a Z to the front of the name so they drop to the bottom of the list.) Refer to Chapter 12 for more on setting up tracking options.

Take Advantage of Repeating Bills and Invoices

Repeating bills and invoices can be set up for regular transactions. You can define them to save as a draft and edit them every period, or, if the amount is known, default them to be approved and automatically sent out every period. Set it up — forget about it and watch the cash come in! (Refer to Chapter 6 for more on setting up repeating invoices.)

Collaborate with Your Xero Advisory Team

Empower experts to help you! The online nature of Xero enables specialists with permission to collaboratively support your business. Accountants, bookkeepers, virtual assistants, online integration gurus and others can jump online and into Xero, and assist as and when you need them to.

All of your business accounts are stored in the one place and, depending on the user permission levels, everyone is accessing identical data — reducing any confusion. The location of your Xero advisory team is no barrier — you don't have to rent extra office space to accommodate them — and if you have assistants located in different time zones, you can set them work in the evening, and it's done the next morning. Xero works hard for you while you sleep!

Effectively Tap into Online Storage Features

Traditionally if your accountant wanted to check a financial record, they'd email you, you'd then find some time to hunt down the paperwork, and then scan and send the accountant a copy. Maybe several days later the accountant would have the desired information details. Utilising the storage solution inside Xero enables users to access source documents online, eliminating the need to hunt through paperwork and filing cabinets. Multiple records can be attached to single transactions — and we're not just talking about PDFs. Images, Excel and Word files can all be uploaded and kept in Xero.

So you can attach Excel calculations to a complicated transaction, or include lease documents with a car purchase. Financial records can also be organised by creating folders within the Files inbox. Using this feature you can, for example, create folders for individual motor vehicles, or end of financial year accounting records, effectively sorting similar documents.

The biggest problem you'll have with Xero's online storage is working out what to do with all that freed up cupboard space — stationery versus shoes!

Chapter 18

Ten Common Mistakes Made in Xero and How to Avoid Them

*I*n this chapter, I highlight mistakes, myths and misconceptions about working with Xero. And I explain how you can identify and avoid them — ensuring you're working efficiently and effectively.

Not Making Use of Expert Help

The philosophy behind using Xero is, because it's in the cloud, you can invite experts to work on your data and provide ongoing advice during the year about your financial position. No longer do you need to wait till the end of the year to speak to your accountant!

So make sure you take advantage of expert help, when and where you need it. If you need help with the set-up, contact a Xero certified adviser (check out www.xero.com/advisors for options) to work with you during the process. This adviser can assist in identifying issues you need to be aware of, and work with you to set the file up to suit your specific business processes.

Engage a Xero-certified accountant for help with setting and monitoring goals, developing tax-mitigating strategies, and preparing financial year accounts.

TIP

If your existing accountant doesn't know Xero, introduce her to it and encourage her to embrace the cloud with you. I've worked with a number of accountants who've got their first taste of Xero from a client — and they've all said working with Xero was straightforward and that they picked it up quickly. (Of course, you could always get them to buy a copy of this book!)

Refer to Chapter 4 for more on inviting other users (such as your accountant) to access your accounts, and Chapter 11 for more on working with your accountant on end of financial year reporting.

Not Understanding Terminology Differences

I've been fortunate enough to work in accounts departments all over the world, and work with numerous accounting software — from ACCPAC to Xero, and lots in-between! Debits and credits are an international accounting language but, as you move through different systems, different clients and different countries, terminology changes. Income becomes Revenue and Proprietorship becomes Equity — you can have lots of terms with generally the same meaning.

In Australia, for example, the term credit note was replaced with adjustment note with the introduction of GST — but people colloquially still call it a credit note.

In the same area, *debit notes* are issued to a supplier to reduce the amount you owe. The terminology Xero uses for both adjustment notes and debit notes is simply *credit notes*.

Pay slips are referred to as *payslips* in Xero which seems to be the US rendering. You may uncover other instances; however, because of the areas the terminology is within, you should be able to easily understand what Xero is referring to. Sometimes, as with the Chart of Accounts, you can override the default terminology and replace it with what you're comfortable with. However, some of the terminology can't be changed. The important thing is to understand what is meant — and, hopefully, you won't even notice it after using Xero for a while.

Messing Up Bank Reconciliation Autosuggestions

Xero helpfully recognises regular transactions and, when you're reconciling these transactions in the future, makes autosuggestions appear beside the transactions. Where this can cause problems is if you incorrectly code a transaction, or code it in an unusual manner. Xero may remember the mistake and keep suggesting it for similar transactions. (Dammit, Janet!)

You can't delete Xero's autosuggestions, but you can overwrite them in the bank reconciliation screen. If Xero has memorised an incorrect autosuggestion you need to avoid using it — otherwise, you perpetuate the situation. The next time you see the incorrect autosuggestion while reconciling, you need to carefully correct and record over the autosuggestion and it replaces the one you don't want remembered.

Alternatively, at the bottom of the reconciliation screen, uncheck the box beside Suggest Previous Entries — this turns auto suggestions off.

Using a Communal User Account

If all users access via a communal, generic user name, such as ABC Bookkeeping, you can't tell who is actually accessing your file or what they are doing. You want anyone accessing your Xero file and financial data to be accountable and tagged in the audit trail.

So, instead, make sure everyone who accesses your Xero file uses their own user account, set up specifically for them with the access level you've allocated.

Not Deleting Old User Accounts

As soon as you have an inkling someone no longer needs access to your Xero file, you need to promptly act, and remove their access. Sometimes even the most normal of people end their time with a business in an unfavourable manner and do some terrible things out of spite. While users can't actually access any of your financial funds through Xero, and a limited trace of their user activity is maintained in Xero, it's much better to be careful than sorry.

To delete a user in Xero, follow these steps:

1. **From the home dashboard go to Settings⇨General Settings⇨Users and click on the name of the user to be deleted from the file.**

   The Users dashboard opens.

2. **Click the red Delete User button.**

   The Delete User window opens, checking if you're sure you want to delete the user. Confirm by clicking the red Delete User button again. You're returned to the Users dashboard and the deleted user has vanished!

While on the topic of User accounts, make sure everyone is accessing your Xero file, using their own name, and not a generic name like ABC Bookkeeping. If all users access via a communal user name, you never know who is actually accessing your file or what they are doing.

Thinking Your Xero Emails are Stored

The details of emails sent from Xero are not stored anywhere within Xero, although a note about the email sent is maintained in the History & Notes area. If you deal with hundreds of transactions, this is probably fine. If you're bespoke and like to personalise your messages, you may want to keep a copy of the email — in this case, when you send an email simply opt for a copy to be sent to your defined Xero email address, which is the email address you log in to Xero with, by checking the Send Me a Copy box (refer to Chapter 6 for more information).

Not Realising the Subscriber Owns and Controls the Data

If you pay your Xero subscription to a Xero partner — let's call her Katherine — due to Xero's legal framework, the subscriber (Katherine) owns and controls access to the data. Check out Xero's Terms and Conditions (www.xero.com/about/terms) to see how this is clearly spelt out.

Let's play devil's advocate — if the partner sold her business, she would sell on the subscriptions, and thus the control of your data. If the new owner did not pay the Xero bills, your Xero data file would be deactivated — even if you had paid the partner. You have no easy way to reactivate your data file because you don't own and control the data. Of course, many people subscribe through a reseller and the relationship works without a hitch, but data ownership, control and access is something I highlight to all my clients and is something to think about.

Trying to Make Xero Do what Your Old System Did

If you're moving from another accounting system or a paper-based system, adapting to a new system can be difficult. But don't get stuck in a rut of trying to make Xero do what your other system did. Work towards learning the new processes and names within the Xero system, so you're working with it rather than against it.

Try to find 15 or 30 minutes each day for learning new aspects of Xero. Pick an issue (or a section of a chapter from this book) to work on. Embrace the change.

Watching Your Bank Feeds Refresh

If you're using third party bank feeds, you may benefit from refreshing these on a regular basis. If they're taking too long to refresh, cancel the refresh and give it another go. If you know your bank feed refreshes can take a few moments, don't sit and watch the screen twiddling your thumbs. If you have a high-speed internet connection, you can open another tab on your computer and carry on working while the bank feed refreshes. If you have a slow connection, plan to have something productive you can do without touching your computer — while still staying close by (because you're still logged in to Xero). Sort out your paperwork, return a phone call or brainstorm goals on a whiteboard.

Paying Full Price If You're a NFP

If you're a charity, not-for-profit or have multiple Xero subscriptions, you're eligible for a discount on your monthly subscription charge! For more information, contact the Xero Billing Team.

Index

About the Author

Heather Smith is a Xero-certified consultant, the Global Communications Manager at *XU Magazine*, host of *Cloud Stories* podcast, a speaker and a mentor to start-ups. She's a management accountant with a bachelor of commerce degree, and is a fellow of the Association of Chartered Certified Accountants (ACCA) and Institute of Certified Bookkeepers (ICB). This is her sixth business book.

Heather provides online Xero set-up, conversion, training, integration, consultation and support to businesses across the globe. And, in her other hours, she's writing or speaking.

You're invited to connect with Heather via her:

- ✔ Newsletter — `bit.ly/SignUp4Newsletter`
- ✔ Podcast — `cloud-stories.com/`
- ✔ Blog post — `www.heathersmithsmallbusiness.com/blog/`
- ✔ Website — `www.heathersmithsmallbusiness.com`
- ✔ YouTube channel — `www.YouTube.com/ANISEConsulting`
- ✔ Twitter feed — `www.twitter.com/HeatherSmithAU`
- ✔ Facebook page — `www.facebook.com/HeatherSmithAU`
- ✔ LinkedIn page — `www.linkedin.com/in/HeatherSmithAU`

You can also book time with Heather via heathersmithau.gettimely.com/book and subscribe to *XU Magazine*, an independent magazine for Xero users, via `www.xumagazine.com/`.

Your comments, corrections and suggestions are welcome. You're also invited to sign up to the author's newsletter (details in preceding list) to download your free Content Marketing Toolkit.

Author's Acknowledgements

I was most thrilled when the CEO of Xero, Rod Drury, approached me and asked me to write a book on Xero. So, firstly — thank you to Rod Drury. I'm ever so grateful you had the faith in me to pull this off — now, here we are with the second edition of this best-selling book. Meanwhile, I'm in awe of the feature enhancements, market penetration and success you and the Xero team have achieved.

Thank you to the small-business rock stars who educate, motivate and inspire me. I'm elated to be a part of your journey. Thanks also to my mum and dad, and all my family and friends. And thanks to my patient editor, Charlotte Duff, and to Dani Karvess and Kerry Laundon. Also thanks to the rest of the team at John Wiley & Sons Australia Pty Ltd.

Many thanks to Xero, who have kindly endorsed the book. Xero staff around the world have answered queries into the wee hours of the morning, and the elite Xero training team have technically checked the book. So thanks to the extraordinary staff and partners of Xero — including Chris Ridd, Sue Pak, Tim Wright and Raewyn Baldwin. Special thanks to the Xero community who are together with me on this journey: the ORANGILICIOUS Catherine Walker; the #SmokinHotBookkeepers and Xero consultants, Gillian Rossouw, Lisa Martin, Gayle Buchanan and Melanie Morris; #Daredevil Jason Forbes; #ShoeFiend Wayne Schmidt; and to everyone who answers my queries on social media or shares with me their insight! Thanks also to my writing mentor and friend Valerie Khoo and the Australian Writers' Centre community — who challenge and believe in my writing.

Thank you to my family: Simon, Christopher and Charlotte. Christopher, you're hilarious and bring laughter and happiness into our lives — and are constantly slowing down our internet connection (*grrrr*) — thank you for being you. Charlotte, your energy and creativity light up a room — stay unpredictable and thank you for being you. Charlie, thanks for snoring at my feet for endless hours, keeping me company and pestering me to take you on walks. And thank you to my husband, Simon. None of this would be possible without you.

Thanks, finally, to you — for reading this book. Remember to sign up to my newsletter so you can download your free Content Marketing Toolkit.

Publisher's Acknowledgements

We're proud of this book; please send us your comments through our online registration form located at dummies.custhelp.com.

Some of the people who helped bring this book to market include the following:

Acquisitions, Editorial and Media Development

Project Editor: Charlotte Duff

Acquisitions Editor: Kerry Laundon

Editorial Manager: Dani Karvess

Production

Graphics: diacriTech

Technical Review: Xero

Proofreader: Jenny Scepanovic

Indexer: Don Jordan, Antipodes Indexing

The author and publisher would like to thank the following copyright holders, organisations and individuals for their permission to reproduce copyright material in this book:

- Cover image: © Xero Limited and affiliates, 2015. Xero® and the Xero logo are registered trademarks of Xero Limited.

- Screen captures from Xero used with permission. © Xero Limited and affiliates, 2015. Xero® and the Xero logo are registered trademarks of Xero Limited. Any data displayed in these images is fictitious, and any similarities with any actual data, individual, or entity is purely coincidental.

- Microsoft Excel screenshots used with permission from Microsoft.

Every effort has been made to trace the ownership of copyright material. Information that enables the publisher to rectify any error or omission in subsequent editions is welcome. In such cases, please contact the Legal Services section of John Wiley & Sons Australia, Ltd.

Business & Investing

978-1-118-22280-5
$39.95

978-0-73031-945-0
$19.95

978-0-73031-951-1
$19.95

978-0-73031-065-5
$19.95

978-0-73030-584-2
$24.95

978-1-11864-126-2
$19.95

978-0-73031-949-8
$19.95

978-0-73031-954-2
$19.95

978-0-730-31069-3
$39.95

978-0-73031-534-6
$39.95

978-1-742-16998-9
$45.00

978-1-118-64122-4
$39.95

Order today!

e Available in print and e-book formats.

FOR DUMMIES
A Wiley Brand

Business

Bookkeeping For
Dummies,
2nd Australian & New
Zealand Edition
978-0-73031-069-3

Businesst Planning
Essentials For Dummies
978-1-11864-126-2

Communication
Essentials For Dummies
978-0-7303-1951-1

Creating a Business Plan
For Dummies
978-1-118-64122-4

Bookkeeping Essentials
For Dummies, 2nd
Australian Edition
978-0-73031-065-5

Getting Started in Small
Business
For Dummies, 2nd Aus-
tralian
& New Zealand Edition
978-1-11822-284-3

HR for Small Business
For Dummies,
Australian Edition,
978-1-11864-030-2

Leadership For Dummies,
Australian & New Zealand
Edition
978-0-7314-0787-3

Making Money on eBay
For Dummies
978-1-74216-977-4

Mindfulness at Work
Essentials For Dummies
978-0-7303-1949-8

MYOB Software
For Dummies,
8th Australian Edition
978-0-73031-537-7

Project Management
Essentials For Dummies
978-0-7303-1954-2

QuickBooks For Dummies,
2nd Australian Edition
978-1-74246-896-9

Small Business For
Dummies, 4th Australian
& New Zealand Edition
978-1-118-22280-5

Success as a Real
Estate Agent For
Dummies, Australian
& New Zealand Edition
978-0-73030-911-6

Successful Job Interviews
For Dummies, Australian
& New Zealand Edition
978-0-730-30805-8

Successful Online
Start-Ups For Dummies,
Australian & New Zealand
Edition
978-1-118-30270-5

Workplace Conflict
Resolution
Essentials For Dummies
978-0-7303-1945-0

Writing Resumes & Cover
Letters For Dummies,
2nd Australian
& New Zealand Edition
978-0-730-30780-8

Xero For Dummies,
2nd Edition
978-0-7303-1937-5

Finance & Investing

Buying Property For
Dummies,
2nd Australian Edition
978-0-7303-7556-2

CFDs For Dummies,
Australian Edition
978-1-74216-939-2

Charting For Dummies,
Australian Edition
978-0-7314-0710-1

DIY Super For Dummies,
3rd Australian Edition
978-0-7303-1534-6

Exchange-Traded Funds
For Dummies, Australian &
New Zealand Edition
978-0-7303-7695-8

Getting Started in Property
Investing For Dummies,
Australian Edition
978-1-183-9674-2

Getting Started in Shares
For Dummies, 2nd
Australian Edition
978-1-74246-885-3

Investing For Dummies,
2nd Australian Edition
978-1-74216-851-7

Making the Most of
Retirement For Dummies
978-0-7314-0939-6

Managed Funds For
Dummies, Australian
Edition
978-1-74216-942-2

Online Share Investing
For Dummies, Australian
Edition
978-0-7314-0940-2

Property Investing For
Dummies, 2nd Australian
Edition
978-1-1183-9670-4

Share Investing For
Dummies, 3rd Australian
Edition
978-1-74246-889-1

Sorting Out Your Finances
For Dummies, Australian
Edition
978-0-7314-0746-0

Tax for Australians
For Dummies, 2013–14
Edition
978-0-730-30584-2

Order today!

ℯ Available in print and e-book formats.

FOR
DUMMIES
A Wiley Brand